Terrence McNally

TERRENCE MCNALLY's newest play, *A Perfect Ganesh,* has just completed an extended run at the Manhattan Theatre Club. Other recent plays are *Lips Together, Teeth Apart,* which played to packed houses for over a year at the Manhattan Theatre Club and off–Broadway's Lucille Lortel Theatre and has been produced in a record–breaking number of resident professional theatres throughout the country, and *The Lisbon Traviata,* which also had an extended run in New York and a tour in California. His earlier play, *Frankie and Johnny In The Clair De Lune,* has also enjoyed great success in New York, followed by productions throughout the United States, foreign countries, and London's West End. Mr. McNally wrote the screen adaptation starring Al Pacino and Michelle Pfeiffer. He also wrote the book for the musical adaptation of Manuel Puig's *Kiss of the Spiderwoman* (score by Kander and Ebb) which, directed by Harold Prince, is currently on Broadway, ran in London's West End and for which Mr. McNally won the 1993 Tony Award for Best Book of a Musical. His previous stage works include *It's Only a Play* (a revival of which was recently mounted at Los Angeles' Doolittle Theatre); *Bad Habits;* the book for *The Rink* (music and lyrics by Kander and Ebb); *The Ritz,* which he also adapted for the screen; *Where Has Tommy Flowers Gone?; And Things That Go Bump in the Night; Hope* in *Faith, Hope and Charity; Next; Whiskey;* and *Prelude and Leibestod.* He has written a number of scripts for television including, most recently, *Andre's Mother* for American Playhouse for which he won the 1990 Emmy Award for Best Writing in a Miniseries or Special. During his career, Mr. McNally has received two Guggenheim Fellowships, a Rockefeller Grant, a Lucille Lortel Award and a citation from the American Academy of Arts and Letters, and has won the Hull-Warriner Award for *Bad Habits* in 1974, for *Frankie and Johnny In The Clair De Lune* in 1987 and for *The Lisbon Traviata* in 1989. A member of the Dramatists Guild Council since 1970, Mr. McNally has been vice-president since 1981.

Published by Smith and Kraus, Inc.
Lyme, NH
Copyright © 1994 by Terrence McNally
All rights reserved

Manufactured in the United States of America
First Edition: June 1994
10 9 8 7 6 5 4 3 2 1

Library of Congress Cataloging-in-Publication Data
McNally, Terrence.
    Terrence McNally : 15 short plays / Terrence McNally.
       p. cm. --(Plays for actors series)
    ISBN 1-880399-34-2 : $14.95
    I. Title. II. Series: Plays for actors.
    PS3563.A323T47   1994
    812'.54--dc20
                            94-10070
                                CIP

Terrence McNally *15 Short Plays*

Contemporary Playwrights Series

SK
A Smith and Kraus Book

Preface

The plays in this collection represent some of my earliest work as well as the most recent. It is good to have them all in print together. I usually think my plays are dead, or at least comatose, unless they are being performed somewhere. But when they're not in print, it's as if they never even existed. Not a good feeling, I can assure you.

I like to write plays. As I get older, I'm getting more prolific. I like to see plays. I probably go to the theatre three or four times a week, which is my Personal Most Compelling Reason for living in New York. I like rehearsing plays. I never feel more alive than when I'm in a rehearsal room with five actors and a good director and everyone is waiting for me to come up with a re-write. I like discussing plays. Blood has been spilled on the dining room table at my place in the country over not a few new American plays.

The only thing I don't like is reading plays. Play manuscripts are like an architect's blueprints. We have to try to imagine what all the two-dimensional lines and drawings will look like when they are realized in space and time as actual buildings. With a play script, we must try to imagine what the play will sound and look and feel like with the right actors, designers and directors interpreting them. I don't know about you, but I'm not very good at that. The theatre is three–dimensional. Its very essence is space and time. Reading a play is like looking at a map. The journey is the rehearsal process. The destination is the production. I'm too impatient to get to Oz to be a good play reader. I want to be there.

But I've been very lucky. I've worked with many of the best theatre artists of my time. It's no secret that I write for specific actors and with few exceptions, these plays were originally interpreted by the actors I had in mind when I wrote them. Good actors allow me to write bravely. By that I mean I dare to take chances when I know my words are not only in their mouths but in their hearts and souls and nervous systems as well.

Good actors force me to write as honestly as I can. I say "force" because if you have fudged the truth in a script (and sometimes I want to take a short–cut to the end of a · scene or an act, a short–cut that the action of the play doesn't justify) a good actor's honesty will shine a very bright light on that moment of chicanery and you will have to fix it or go down in flames. Good actors are merciless that way. They can't help it. It's one of the reasons they're good actors. Mediocre actors allow playwrights to get away with murder.

My definition of a good actor is someone who uses the text to find the character and then makes it his or her own through a physical life and emotional commitment that make alive and whole what had only existed on paper and in my mind as a blueprint. If playwrights are the architects, actors are the decorators. We design a strong building that will support them. They give it color and movement and life.

My definition of a poor actor is someone who uses the text as a pretext to explore his or her psyche so that the play ends up about them as opposed to the character the playwright is asking them to collaborate with him or her on creating. These actors announce themselves usually by pre–fixing or ending every line with "I mean" or "You know" or a whole string of "Unhs" throughout any given speech. "I'm thinking what I'm going to say next because of what I'm feeling" is their usual explanation for their tics and stammers. As Noel Coward once said to an actor who had worn his patience out with such an explanation and in the process wreaked unendurable havoc on his text, "My characters speak before they think—just like in real life!".

A poor actor brings no physical imagination to a character. If an actor is not committed to the text, he will never find even the most basic "right" interior or physical life of his character. Poor actors ignore punctuation. Good actors work from it.

If you think that one of the things I look for in an actor (or director) is 100% fidelity to the text, you are 100% right. "Who do you think you are? Shakespeare?" one actor snarled at me when I objected to his non–verbal emmendations to my text.

"No," I replied, "I think I'm Terrence McNally and the only way you will find the characters I intended is to speak and use the text exactly as I wrote it."

Good playwrights are not God. God is a tyrant. Good playwrights are good collaborators. They work with good actors on shaping the text. They work with good directors on finding the best form and structure for the play. They work with good designers on giving strong images of the kind of physical world they imagine their characters to inhabit. A good playwright is responsible for everything about his play: text, design, performance.

A good director is his conduit to all these good and essential things that create good theatre.

As I get older, I get crankier about these things. I also get more ambitious and eager to realize my aspirations and more and more humbled by my realization and profound conviction that I cannot do it alone.

I think these are wonderful times to be working in the American theatre. Everything is so important now. Good plays really are a matter of life and death. We're an endangered species and we're fighting back. As long as there are civilized people on this planet, people are going to want to sit around a campfire and listen to us tell the stories of our tribe. That's human nature. That doesn't change. But we will have to work harder than ever before to hold their attention. We're not the only storyteller in town anymore. But they will listen at first and if our stories are compelling and truthful (and even entertaining), they will stick around until we have finished. It's hard work, harder than ever, I suspect and I invite you to join the many, many good playwrights, actors, directors and designers at work right now in the American theatre to fight the good fight.

Yes, these are the best of times, and, yes, these are the worst of times. I'm very glad I've been around for them. A life in the theatre is its own reward. I owe so much to so many of you. As Tommy Flowers realizes at the very top of the play I wrote about him, we really do get by with a little help from our friends.

To all of you I dedicate this collection.

—*Terrence McNally*
 May 1994
 New York City

Contents

Introduction

In 1964, a scandal called *And Things Go Bump In the Night* opened bold as brass on Broadway to scathing How-dare-they!-Never-in-my-life! reviews. At one performance an audience member jumped on stage and slapped its star Eileen Heckart for appearing in such an immoral play. And it was written by a 25 year old playwright, Terrence McNally. I had just got out of the Air Force. I couldn't wait to see it. The theater, packed for its final performance, reeled with booing and cheering. It was filled with the future.

The plays kept coming. Elaine May brilliantly directed *Next.* I can still feel the warmth of a room at the Manhattan Theater Club, then in a Ukrainian National Hall, roaring with laughter at a thrilling reading of *Bad Habits.*

By the '80s, Terrence had become one of the blessed writers; he had found a home in the Manhattan Theater Club who produced *It's Only a Play, Frankie and Johnny in the Clair de Lune, Lisbon Traviata, Lips Together Teeth Apart,* and his masterpiece (so far), *A Perfect Ganesh.* I say Blessed because for a playwright, belonging to a trusting theater only generates more work.

In 1993 Michael Kahn who was running the drama division at Juilliard asked us to start a playwriting program.

No, neither of us had the time.

Yes, we would.

The first group of Juilliard writers brought talent to spare. Two playwrights teaching in tandem only shows there is no one way to solve a problem. You have to find your own voice, your own way of doing things. During the course of this year, Terrence has written two full–length plays, and, with reckless generosity, let the class in on his work process and the development of *Love! Valor! Compassion!* and *Master Class.* That's how you teach.

In light of this fecund outpouring, how timely then to read these plays and see no matter how the talent has developed, it came full blown. The ink is still wet on these early plays, written in the bravado of their time. Read them and be amazed by their confidence, their daring, their lunatic humor, the casualness of their sexual candor, and their empathy. Like the Roman playwright Terence, his name sake with one less R, nothing human is alien to our Terrence and all is pleasurable. Read these plays in one swoop and know the plays and the playwright are one.

—John Guare

Bringing It All Back Home

Characters

SON
DAUGHTER
MOTHER
FATHER
JIMMY
MISS HORNE

Bringing It All Back Home

A living room. Comfortably furnished, nice proportions. Front door, door leading off to kitchen, stairs leading up.

SON: (*On the phone, smoking marijuana.*) Don't get so uptight, Margy, I just want to turn you on! Jeez, you'd think I'd asked you to do something really wild! . . . It's like . . . it's like flying! Sometimes you see all kinds of colors . . . Really! It's like a great big rainbow and you kind of just swim around in it . . . It is not habit forming . . . George Shirley's a queer. He's so freaked out on meth half the time he doesn't know where he's at . . . Come on, Margy, I wouldn't put you on anything that strong your first time. This is only grass . . . Rosemary Steber went to bed with guys before she ever *heard* of pot! . . . the whole ninth grade says! (*Catching sight of himself in a mirror.*) Hey, what's good for pimples? This keeps up I'm gonna ask mom to let me have my face sanded like Harry Butt. . . . Dena's pregnant? Oh cool! I wouldn't be surprised if Harry knocked her up, even if he is her brother. (*He's combing his hair.*) I can't come over . . . Aaaaw, I have to hang around this dump waiting for my brother . . . Mmmm, they're sending him home today . . . I'll ask her but it won't do any good. (*Yells up stairs.*) Mom! Hey, Mom! Can I go over to Margy's house? Mom!

DAUGHTER: (*Coming down stairs. Bathrobe, hair in rollers, drinking a coke.*) She's in the dryer.

SON: Who asked you? (*Calling again.*) Hunh, ma, can I? Please!

MOTHER: (*Off.*) I'm in the dryer!

DAUGHTER: I told you.

SON: Drop dead. (*Back into phone.*) She's in the dryer.

DAUGHTER: (*Sprawling in a chair.*) You talking to your . . . (*Good and loud.*) . . . little-whittle Margy with braces?

SON: Shove it, hunh? (*Into phone.*) I wasn't talking to *you*.

DAUGHTER: Junior high school brats!

SON: My sister the slut just walked in. (*To Daughter.*) Can't you do that stuff in your own room?

DAUGHTER: (*Buffing her nails.*) The living room belongs to all of us. And hurry up, I'm expecting a call.

SON: Fat Eddie. (*Into phone.*) This guy she goes with's so fat they use him for a goal post.

DAUGHTER: Eddie's first-string, all-state! That's how fat he is!

SON: He's as dumb as a goal post, too.

DAUGHTER: (*Wanting the phone.*) Come on, disaster area, get off the phone.

SON: Margy says maybe you could recommend Dena Butt a good abortionist.

DAUGHTER: (*Yelling upstairs.*) Momma! Momma! Johnny's starting about last winter again!

SON: Would you believe what I have to live with around here? (*Seeing Daughter on way to kitchen.*) That's right. Head for the kitchen. Fatten yourself up some more. (*Back to phone.*) I'll bring some stuff over with me tonight . . . Stay around? What for? . . . Jimmy? Naaw, all that jazz is tomorrow. All we got today is some television interview. And listen, Margy, it's good stuff, too. Acapulco Gold, so don't chicken out . . . From that guy at the filling station, who do you think? I wouldn't trust anybody else. Mikie's never burned me once. (*Daughter returns, eating potato chips.*)

DAUGHTER: (*Singsong.*) Johnny is a virgin.

SON: The whore just came back in.

DAUGHTER: Johnny is a virgin.

SON: You ought to go out for football. That way you could be on the team instead of *under* it.

DAUGHTER: Johnny is a virgin.

SON: She's already had the entire backfield. Now she's working her way across the line.

DAUGHTER: Johnny is a virgin.

SON: I wouldn't be surprised if she's diseased.

DAUGHTER: Johnny is a virgin.

SON: Talk about rigged elections for cheerleader.

DAUGHTER: Johnny is a virgin.

SON: It wouldn't be the first time!

DAUGHTER: Johnny is a virgin.

SON: I've gotta hang up. I'm gonna smack somebody's face open. I'll see you later. (*Bangs phone down.*) Now quit saying that.

DAUGHTER: Johnny is a —!

SON: I AM NOT!

DAUGHTER: Name one name.

SON: Why should I?

DAUGHTER: You can't

SON: I'm a gentleman.

DAUGHTER: You're a virgin

SON: Peggy Walsh.

DAUGHTER: Peggy Walsh?

SON: Peggy Walsh?

DAUGHTER: (*Leaping toward phone.*) What's her number?

SON: You gonna call her up and ask her?

DAUGHTER: What's her number?

SON: Come on, Susy, she's a nice girl.

DAUGHTER: What's her number?

SON: She'd kill me if she knew I'd—

DAUGHTER: Information?

SON: She's not there.

DAUGHTER: Do you have the number for a —?

SON: (*Cutting her off.*) No!

DAUGHTER: Johnny is a virgin!

SON: Well I almost did!

DAUGHTER: What happened?

SON: Never mind! Nothing!

DAUGHTER: That's more like it.

SON: She's only fourteen!

DAUGHTER: Name another name.

SON: What do you want from me? I'm only fifteen. Give me some time, hunh?

DAUGHTER: Is Billy Grey spending the night again this weekend?

SON: I don't know.

DAUGHTER: He's only fifteen, too.

SON: What does that crack mean?

DAUGHTER: As if you didn't know.

SON: As if I didn't know.

DAUGHTER: I hear things.

SON: Good for you.

DAUGHTER: Sounds.

SON: Big deal!

DAUGHTER: Noises.

SON: Just shut up.

DAUGHTER: Squeaks.

SON: He's my best friend.

DAUGHTER: You know there's a name for sub-human, sub-adolescent little boys like you.

SON: Billy's cooler than you'll ever be.

DAUGHTER: (*Spelling it out.*) F-A-I-R-Y.

SON: Godmother! It blows your mind out, hunh?

DAUGHTER: H-O-M-O

SON: Lots of guys my age fool around.

DAUGHTER: S-E-X

SON: Don't you watch those panel shows on TV?

DAUGHTER: U-A-L!

SON: I'm practically normal.

DAUGHTER: Fairy homosexual.

SON: What about when Patty Jackson used to spend the night with you?

DAUGHTER: That was different.

SON: I didn't hear things either, I saw.

DAUGHTER: Momma! Momma!

SON: There's a word for girls like you too!

DAUGHTER: I could just kill you.

SON: L-E-S

DAUGHTER: I was only fourteen.

SON: B-I

DAUGHTER: She started it.

SON: A-N

DAUGHTER: Lots of girls do.

SON: Dyke lesbian.

DAUGHTER: Well at least I grew out of it.

SON: You sure did. Now I've got the town pump for a sister. I'll probably grow up neurotic, thanks to you.

DAUGHTER: Grow up neurotic? You already are. A neurotic dwarf.

SON: I'm gonna grow.

DAUGHTER: When?

SON: Mom's getting me hormone shots!

DAUGHTER: Male ones, I hope! (*Doorbell rings.*) Get it.

SON: Get what?

DAUGHTER: The door.

SON: You.

DAUGHTER: I said get it.

SON: You make me sick the way you boss me around.

DAUGHTER: That's what little brothers are for.

SON: The raw end of the stick! (*Goes to door, opens it, admits two men carrying large box who bring it to center of room.*) Mom! It's Jimmy!

MOTHER: (*Off.*) I'm in the dryer.

SON: Jimmy's home!

MOTHER: (*Off.*) What?

SON: Jimmy, deafhead, he's home!

MOTHER: (*Off.*) I'll be right down.

DAUGHTER: (*Who has displayed herself attractively.*) Hello there! You want me to sign something? (*One of them has handed her a receipt.*)

SON: (*To the other man.*) Here you go. (*Flips him a coin.*)

DAUGHTER: And hi there to you!

SON: (*To both men.*) What are you standing there for? What kind of tip do you expect from a minor? (*The two men begin to leave.*)

DAUGHTER: Bye now! Bye now you two!

SON: Greedy bastards! (*After the men have gone.*) Well there's Jimmy.

DAUGHTER: There he is. (*They stand looking at the crate. They put their hands on it. It's like a foreign object to them. Pause.*)

SON: He was great.

DAUGHTER: Best big brother a sister ever had.

SON: That goes for me, too.

DAUGHTER: And now he's dead.

SON: That land mine tore his stomach right open, dad said. He never knew what hit him.

DAUGHTER: Do you remember what color his eyes were?

SON: Come *on*, I'm a guy. (*Silence, they keep their hands on the crate.*) Don't you?

DAUGHTER: (*After a long while.*) Well there's Jimmy.

SON: There he is.

DAUGHTER: He was a lot of laughs.

SON: You can say that again.

DAUGHTER: That goes for me, too.

SON: And now he's dead.

DAUGHTER: Poppa said that land mine tore his stomach right open. He never knew what hit him.

SON: So you remember what color hair he had?

DAUGHTER: *Johnny!* I'm his sister! (*Pause.*) Don't you? (*They move away from the crate.*)

SON: Susy, have you tried LSD yet?

DAUGHTER: Of course I have.

SON: Good trip?

DAUGHTER: What do you think?

SON: Bad, hunh?

DAUGHTER: Terrible.

SON: You heard what happened to Sandy Seeger on his trip?

DAUGHTER: What goes on at Lakeview Junior High is of very little interest to seniors at Hamilton.

SON: He jumped off the Goodwin Tower building. He was naked, too.

DAUGHTER: Big deal.

SON: Ugh! Imagine doing something like that without any clothes on and the police finding you nude.

DAUGHTER: (*Who has found a record and put it on the phonograph.*) Come on, show me the Slip 'N Slide, will you?

SON: You're too spastic.

DAUGHTER: Be nice for a change. Put yourself out a little.

SON: I can't do it with my own sister.

DAUGHTER: There's a big dance after the game with Taft Friday night. Everybody'll know how but me. Please?

SON: If you tell me how many guys you've done it with.

DAUGHTER: Johnny!

SON: All right, get Patty Jackson to teach you the Slip 'N Slide.

DAUGHTER: Only nine! *Now* are you satisfied?

SON: Nine's a lot.

DAUGHTER: Wait'll you get to Hamilton. (*They dance. It's sexy. Mother comes downstairs in bathrobe and portable dryer.*)

MOTHER: IS THAT JIMMY??

SON: NO, IT'S RICHARD NIXON!!

MOTHER: I'M IN THE DRYER!!! (*She goes into the kitchen.*)

SON: You've got it all wrong!

DAUGHTER: Well do it slower! (*Father enters in flashy bowling team shirt and windbreaker.*)

FATHER: Hello, peaches.

DAUGHTER: (*Running to him.*) Poppa!

FATHER: Mm, you smell good.

DAUGHTER: So do you.

SON: Boy, if I don't grow up neurotic somebody's gonna have to rewrite the history of psychoanalysis!

FATHER: What's that smell in here?

DAUGHTER: He's been smoking that stuff again.

SON: I have not.

FATHER: Now, son, I've told you. I don't mind you smoking marijuana but not at home. I know all the kids are doing it but not at home. Got that?

SON: (*Militarily crisp.*) Yes, sir!

FATHER: Thatta boy!

SON: You bet!

FATHER: And what did I tell you about dancing with your sister?

SON: (*Thrown.*) Hunh?

FATHER: Don't do it. You should be on the street with the other boys playing football, knocking around, getting your nose bloodied. What are you, some kind of sissy, hanging around girls all the time?

SON: I thought boys were supposed to like girls.

FATHER: Not at your age. When the time comes for girls I'll be the first one to let you know.

SON: I think it already has.

FATHER: Look, you fresh kid!

SON: I can't help it.

FATHER: You play with boys. Got that?

SON: Yes, sir!

FATHER: This country's raising a generation of faggots, but not in my house it's not.

SON: You bet!

FATHER: My boys are men.

SON: Your boy. Singular. (*Indicates crate.*)

FATHER: (*Going to it.*) So there's Jimmy.

SON: There he is.

FATHER: Most masculine son a father ever had.

DAUGHTER: You can say that again.

SON: Shut up, pig face!

FATHER: And now he's dead. You know, that land mine tore his stomach right open. He never knew what hit him.

SON: Do you remember how tall he was?

DAUGHTER: Stupid, daddy was his *father*!

FATHER: (*After a pause.*) Don't you? (*They move away from the crate.*)

SON: Dad, can I go to a shrinker, too?

DAUGHTER: Monkey see, monkey do!

SON: You don't need one.

DAUGHTER: With the strain I'm under?

SON: We all know what *that* is.

DAUGHTER: See, poppa, how he keeps bringing it up?

SON: Hunh, dad, can I?

FATHER: A boy your age seeing an analyst is just about the least masculine thing I can think of.

SON: Yes, sir!

FATHER: Just straighten up and fly right.

SON: You bet!

FATHER: Besides, the next person in this family to see an analyst is your mother.

SON: Roger!

FATHER: She's a deeply disturbed woman.

SON: Over and out!

FATHER: Now get upstairs and dress. They'll be here.

SON: You're wearing that?

FATHER: What's wrong with it?

SON: On television?

FATHER: Now look, you little snot . . . !

SON: Square!

FATHER: I'm proud of our bowling team. A bunch of men, real men, regular guys, drinking beer, horsing around. The cigar smoke gets so thick in there you can hardly see the pins for it. And oh brother, let me tell you our talk gets rough! Bowling's a man's sport you ought to try it some time!

SON: Jeez! (*He goes upstairs.*)

FATHER: (*Yelling up the stairs.*) I'd like to see you try lifting those balls! You know how much some of them weigh? Hunh? Do you? And you know how many cans of beer I killed last night? Thirteen! A big one-three!

DAUGHTER: (*Coming to him.*) Poppa!

FATHER: (*Still muttering.*) Rotten little . . . (*She kisses him.*) Hello, peaches.

DAUGHTER: Poppa, you're wonderful!

FATHER: I try, I try.

DAUGHTER: You *are.*

FATHER: (*Patting her rump.*) Up you go now. You know what to put on.

DAUGHTER: Could I, poppa? Oh poppa, could I?

FATHER: That's what I like to see my little girl the best in.

DAUGHTER: Oh poppa, you're fabulous! (*She gives him another kiss, then starts up the stairs.*) All right, acne, you've been in there long enough! (*She is gone. Father makes sure the coast is clear, then gets out telephone directory. He clearly picks a number at random, dials it and waits impatiently for it to answer.*)

MOTHER: (*Enters from kitchen, nibbling food, still under her portable hair dryer.*) The Smith's boy was arrested today.

FATHER: (*Startled, banging phone down.*) Turn that damn thing off. You can't hear yourself with it running.

MOTHER: Burned his draft card.

FATHER: Turn it off!

MOTHER: I'M IN THE DRYER! (*Father gives up, slumps in his chair. Mother goes right on talking.*) I told Betty letting him grow his hair so long was just the beginning. But no, she said all the boys were doing it and didn't Teddy look cute. Sure he'll look cute, I said to her, *cute behind bars.* I swear! Don't people read *Time* magazine anymore? Long hair is one of the seven danger signals.

FATHER: (*Shaking his head in despair.*) Mona, Mona, Mona.

MOTHER: Dirt and rampant liberalism are the other six!

FATHER: I'm sure they are.

MOTHER: WHAT'S A MOTHER TO DO?

FATHER: You'd better get ready. They'll be here any minute.

MOTHER: Did I see Jimmy? I'll say I saw Jimmy! I'll probably trip over it and break my neck.

FATHER: You just do that.

MOTHER: (*As she stands looking down at crate, touching it with her head.*) The most patriotic son a mother ever had. And now he's dead. They say he never knew what hit him. That dirty Communist land mine tore his stomach right open. (*Pause.*) It's such a big box. I don't remember him being so long. Maybe he grew more over there. (*Turns to Father.*) I'M IN THE DRYER! (*She goes upstairs. The moment she leaves, Father is on the telephone again.*)

FATHER: Terminal 5-1451? . . . Hello, baby . . . never mind who . . . what are you wearing? . . . just out of the shower, hunh? . . . (*The lights on him are dimming and the sound of his voice is fading.*) . . . you sound like the kind of girl who knows what a good time is . . .

JIMMY: (*Sitting up in the crate.*) Well here's Jimmy. Here he is. (*Flashes a smile.*) Dad's making one of his obscene phone calls. This might be my only chance to talk. (*He climbs out of crate, steps forward.*) I'm really dead, you understand, but I can clear the air up a little bit. At least get the facts straight. I'm six foot one . . . *was*, I *was* six foot one, sorry about that . . . weighed one fifty-nine, had blue eyes and hair the color commonly called dirty blonde. Now don't feel too badly that they didn't remember all that. I couldn't answer the same questions about any of *them*. I mean *jeez*, I'm just their son and brother! But I can't understand half the things they've said about me. Like Suzy. How can you call someone a good big brother when he took a brick and knocked your permanent front teeth out? That's a bridge she's flashing. Johnny's decided I was a load of laughs. What's an Italian pushing a baby carriage? That's the only joke I can remember, and even so I forget the punch line. And like everybody else I must have heard hundreds, thousands of jokes in my lifetime. I just never could remember them. And God only knows I never made one up. Dad's decided I was masculine all of a sudden and mom's gnawing the patriotism bone. I swear I don't know who they're talking about. And that bit about he never knew what hit him! At first I was just startled, I mean I never expected it to happen to me, but after a minute or two it hurt like hell. You have your guts hanging out and see how it feels! I'm sorry. I'm not meant to show any emotion. I'm dead. Thank you for your attention. (*He gets back into the crate.*) Is anybody wondering how it feels to be dead? I'll try to tell you. It's a . . . funny feeling. Funny because it's so hard to talk about. You see, there I was just kind of slopping around and I'd never really thought about what being alive meant and so now it's kind of hard to compare the two. But when I stepped on that mine I knew *something* had hit me, I can tell you that! Christ Almighty, it hurt! (*Flashes a smile.*) Well here goes Jimmy. Here he goes. (*He signals the peace sign and lies back down. Lights have come back up on Father on the phone.*)

FATHER: . . . Tell me more, angel puss, tell me more! (*Noises from upstairs.*) I gotta go. I'll call again. . . Meet? Us? What are you, some kind of nympho! (*Bangs down phone as Daughter rushes down the stairs, dressed in her cheerleader's outfit.*)

DAUGHTER: (*Waving pompoms.*)

Flying pig! Flying pig!

Oink! Oink! Oink!

(*Repeat several times. There is no stopping her, in fact. Father beams, egging her on. What he likes best about her outfit is the tight sweater.*)

SON: (*Banging down the stairs, dressed in mod clothes.*) The hair spray's so thick up there with those two, I'm getting cancer of the eyeballs. Wow! Are they red. (*Watches Daughter's performance.*) Boy, Jimmy cleared out of this house just in time! The neuroses around this dump are really getting to me. (*He goes to telephone.*)

MOTHER: (*Coming down stairs, suburban attire.*) Right before your very eyes and you don't even see it!

FATHER: Hunh?

MOTHER: One of the seven danger signals!

SON: (*On phone.*) Hello, Margy? It's your lover.

MOTHER: Look at his hair!

DAUGHTER: (*Trying to get phone.*) Do you have to monopolize that thing?

MOTHER: Well do something about it.

FATHER: Jimmy. I mean Johnny.

SON: They're on my back. I'll call you later. (*Hangs up phone.*)

FATHER: You heard your mother. Get a haircut.

SON: Yes, sir! (*Starts to leave.*)

MOTHER: Not now.

FATHER: Later.

SONS: You bet!

FATHER: Roger!

SON: Over and out! (*Grins.*) You'll make a man out of me yet.

MOTHER: (*Peering out window.*) I wonder what's keeping them?

DAUGHTER: Can I do a cheer for the cameras?

FATHER: Anything you want, peaches.

SON: Sure, show everybody.

DAUGHTER: See how he starts on me?

SON: All I said was—!

DAUGHTER: Momma, Johnny's making cracks about what happened last winter!

MOTHER: (*Comforting her.*) Hush there, sshh! Well don't look at me, Sam. He's your son. Do something.

FATHER: You heard your mother.

SON: All I said was—!

DAUGHTER: (*Covering her ears.*) Don't let him talk about last winter, momma. Don't let him, don't let him, don't let him, don't let him! (*She has a tantrum right on the spot.*)

MOTHER: (*When she is quiet.*) You see what you've done.

FATHER: Good Lord, Mona, all the boy said was—!

DAUGHTER: Aaaaaaaaaaaah!

MOTHER: (*With dignity.*) Lots of girls Susy's age get into trouble. They're nearly all doing it.

DAUGHTER: (*Between sniffles.*) Shelly Hines . . . Carrie Pope . . . Billie Lockwell. . .

MOTHER: Gretchen Heller.

FATHER: The little Herlihy girl.

SON: Dena Butt?

MOTHER: Dena Butt?

DAUGHTER: With Freddy Heller!

SON: Who told you?

DAUGHTER: I heard!

MOTHER: As you can see, Johnny, girls who get into trouble are no laughing matter.

DAUGHTER: Tell momma how much pot you've been smoking lately!

MOTHER: Some of the nicest girls in town have had abortions. They're no better than Susy.

DAUGHTER: And all those pills you've got hidden under your socks!

MOTHER: As far as this family is concerned, Susy never *had* an abortion. Willie Young never existed.

FATHER: You getting this all down, son?

DAUGHTER: Tell her about you and Billy Grey!

MOTHER: In fact, show me a girl Susy's age who *hasn't* been in trouble and I'll show you a girl who has something wrong with her.

FATHER: Your mother's right.

DAUGHTER: (*Drying her tears.*) Of course she is.

MOTHER: And to top it all off and bring this story to its happy ending, Susy, as we all know, has mended her ways.

SON: Hah!

DAUGHTER: (*Bawling again.*) You see? You see?

SON: All I said was hah! Everybody's so touchy in this house!

DAUGHTER: I'll kill him! I'll kill him! (*Nails bared, she's chasing him around the room.*)

SON: Whore! Slut! Strumpet!

MOTHER: (*Despairing now.*) What can we do with them?

FATHER: (*Defeated, too.*) I don't know . . . I don't know. (*Doorbell rings. Everybody freezes. Pause.*)

MOTHER: Get it.

FATHER: You.

SON: Not me again.

DAUGHTER: I can't. (*Doorbell rings.*)

FATHER: Mona!

MOTHER: It's your house.

DAUGHTER: Make Jimmy go.

SON: *There's* Jimmy!

DAUGHTER: I meant *you*, brat. (*Doorbell rings.*)

FATHER: Goddamnit, I won't go. Who's the man in this house anyway?

MOTHER: You're the one who made an issue of it. Women have pride, too, you know!

DAUGHTER: That's right.

SON: (*Who's looked out the window.*) They're leaving. (*There is a mass rush to the door. The room is empty. We hear voices off.*)

JIMMY: (*Sitting up in the crate.*) A *dope pusher*! I just remembered the punch line! "An Italian pushing a baby carriage is a dope, pusher!" (*He makes the peace sign and lies back down as family returns with Miss Horne and two television cameramen. Miss Horne is a svelte, rather young African-American television reporter.*)

MOTHER: (*So affably.*) What's your first name, honey?

MISS HORNE: Fatima Beloved of Ali X.

MOTHER: Oh dear!

MISS HORNE: And none of you honkies better use it. It's Miss Horne to you. Where's the body? We'll do the interview over there.

FATHER: Smoke?

MISS HORNE: Why not? (*She rips off filter.*)

FATHER: Drink?

MISS HORNE: You been nipping at it?

FATHER: We've had a few, actually.

MISS HORNE: What the Muslims don't know won't hurt 'em. (*He fills her glass.*) Three fingers, honky!

FATHER: Sorry.

SON: (*To TV crew.*) Any of you cats got some grass on you? Aw come on, you're in show business.

DAUGHTER: (*To television men; provocatively seated.*) Hi there! And a hello to you!

MISS HORNE: Let's get this show rolling. They yours? (*Parents nod.*) All right honky brats, over here. (*To Daughter.*) What are you smiling at?

DAUGHTER: (*Her standard answer, she loves giving it.*) I'm not smiling actually.

MOTHER: It's her eyes.

DAUGHTER: They twinkle all the time and that gives my face the appearance of a smile.

MISS HORNE: Get you! (*Son laughs.*) Cut it out.

SON: I thought *I* was a salty one!

MISS HORNE: It's not salt, sonny. Any bus I drive, you're in the back of it.

FATHER: Now just one minute—I

MISS HORNE: You're on the air. (*The family freezes, inane smiles. Miss Horne's voice assumes the cool, efficient tones of a professional broadcaster.*) Six o'clock news. Human interest feature. We're taping. (*The TV lights blaze, the camera whirs.*)

MOTHER: (*Terse whisper.*) Sit up, Susy. *Up!*

MISS HORNE: The war became a reality today for a family in exclusive Milford Haven. We spoke to them in their . . . (*With some sarcasm.*) . . . tastefully furnished living room.

MOTHER: Thank you.

MISS HORNE: Behind them . . . in a plain wooden crate . . . was the body of their oldest son.

MOTHER: That's our Jimmy.

FATHER: That's our Jimmy all right.

SON: A land mine ripped his stomach right open.

DAUGHTER: He never knew what hit him. (*From inside the crate, Jimmy raps in protest.*)

MISS HORNE: Tell us something about Jimmy. What kind of boy was he? We'll start with the youngest.

SON: He was . . . he was cool. (*Pause.*) I guess. (*Pause.*) I mean . . . no, he was cool.

DAUGHTER: Jimmy had a smile that could knock your eyes out. Girls were crazy for him.

MISS HORNE: What were some of his interests?

DAUGHTER: Oh, you know. . . usual stuff.

MISS HORNE: He was typical then?

FATHER: Very typical! Simple, good-natured, down to earth . . . (*Aside to Son who fidgets, yawns.*) Stop that, Jimmy!

SON: I'm not Jimmy.

FATHER: You know who I mean! (*Then.*) Excuse me. Where was I?

MISS HORNE: Run of the mill.

FATHER: That's Jimmy to to T! But above all . . . and this is how I'll most remember him. . . Jimmy was a real man. A man's man.

SON: Hah! That isn't what you used to say.

FATHER: He wouldn't be in that box, son, if he weren't anything but a man. The Army's gonna shape you up, too, one day. God bless it.

MOTHER: The main thing to say about Jimmy is that he was an American. A good American. I suppose the word "patriot" is old hat.

FATHER: Don't cry, mother.

MISS HORNE: Is this a moral war?

SON: Don't look at me.

DAUGHTER: I'm just in high school.

FATHER: Real men don't ask questions like that.

SON: She's not a man.

MOTHER: Neither do real Americans.

MISS HORNE: All right, then, and on a lighter note: How has Jimmy's death affected your routine of daily life?

SON: It hasn't.

DAUGHTER: It has too! We stayed out of school three whole days after we got the telegram. And we don't have to go tomorrow either because of the funeral.

SON: Really, ma?

MISS HORNE: Will you be on the field leading the student body for the Taft game Friday night?

FATHER: She certainly will.

MISS HORNE: I gather it's an important game for Hamilton?

DAUGHTER: I'll say it is. (*Directly to camera.*) Beat hell out of Taft!

FATHER: Could she . . .? (*Motioning to Daughter.*) Go ahead, peaches.

DAUGHTER: (*In a flurry of pompoms.*)
Flying pig! Flying pig!
Oink! Oink! Oink!
(*She continues cheering.*)

SON: That's right, show everybody.

MOTHER: Susy, your skirt, keep it down!

SON: It's no secret what *she* is!

FATHER: Atta girl! Do the split now.

MISS HORNE: Thank you, Susy. Susy, that will do.

DAUGHTER: (*A final outburst before sitting.*) All the way to state, team, all the way to state!

FATHER: Isn't she terrific?

MISS HORNE: It seems then your life has been relatively unaffected by Jimmy's death?

FATHER: (*Reflectively.*) Well, you know, life continues. That's the beautiful thing about death, life continues.

MOTHER: Jimmy was as American as apple pie.

FATHER: (*Consoling her.*) Mother, mother.

MISS HORNE: Can you describe your emotions when you got the news about Jimmy?

SON: I cried.

DAUGHTER: Me, too. For days and days.

SON: Ella Exaggerator!

DAUGHTER: Oh shut up!

FATHER: It hit me pretty hard at first. But the more I thought about it . . . I hate to use this word . . . well, the happier I got. Thank God my son was a man. After all, how many American fathers can say that? If you hadn't guessed it, I'm kind of a virility nut. I even worry about my little Johnny here. Thank God for the army, hunh? It really straightens these boys out.

SON: Yes, sir!

MOTHER: I was proud. Miss Horne, let me tell you. I was *proud* of Jimmy. His father says he died like a man. I say he died like an American. What more can a mother ask? You see this flag? It came with the body. I thought that was very sweet of them. Washington cares.

FATHER: We all do, Mona.

MOTHER: These are proud tears, America.

SON: It's a local show, ma.

MOTHER: I shed them with pride.

DAUGHTER: Momma, don't have an attack.

MOTHER: My son died an American! Mothers of the World, may you live to see the day your sons die American!

SON: She thinks she's on Telstar.

MISS HORNE: One final question. Why did Jimmy die? (*Pause.*)

SON: Who wouldn't die if they stepped on a land mine and had their stomach ripped open?

DAUGHTER: That's not what she means, stupid. Jimmy died defending the American way of life. Everything good, that's what he died for. You and me. So we could go to school and football games and dances in the gym just like he did. So we could have color TV and our own rooms and live in a nice house in a nice part of town. Jimmy died for you.

SON: (*Chastened.*) I didn't know that.

DAUGHTER: Don't you study civics? If people like Jimmy don't die for the American way of life there won't *be* an American way of life.

SON: Cripes!

FATHER: What your sister's trying to tell you, son, is that Jimmy died so we could say to the world: This, this was man. Dying, you see, my son, is the real test of a man's masculinity. And Jimmy passed it.

SON: And how he did! Wow.

MOTHER: And there's more to it than that, Johnny. Your brother died because he was an American.

SON: I'm an American and I'm not dead.

MOTHER: You're too young. You'll get your chance.

SON: What about dad?

MOTHER: He's too old. He's had his.

FATHER: (*Aside.*) That's a lousy crack to make on television, Mona!

SON: What about you and . . ?

DAUGHTER: We're *women*!

MOTHER: Right or wrong, Jimmy gave his life for his country and if that's not the American way of doing things, I'd like to know what is.

SON: *Who* right or wrong? Jimmy or his country?

MOTHER: Both. Both right. Jimmy *and* his country.

DAUGHTER: Boy, you're dumb.

FATHER: Live and learn, son, live and learn.

SON: Yes, sir!

MISS HORNE: Mrs. . . .

MOTHER: (*Head bowed.*) Mona, just Mona.

MISS HORNE: We can say then you're proud your son died as an American?

FATHER: As a man, too!

DAUGHTER: We all are!

MOTHER: Yes, that you can say, yes.

MISS HORNE: (*Slight change of tone.*) Did you know your son *did* know what hit him?

MOTHER: I'm sorry, I don't understand.

MISS HORNE: That it was forty-five minutes of pain and terror before he lost consciousness?

MOTHER: What do you mean?

MISS HORNE: That he sat under a tree holding his large intestine in the palm of his hand?

MOTHER: The telegram said he . . . I have it right here.

FATHER: Hey, what is this?

MISS HORNE: That your son never knew why he was over there or what he was fighting for?

MOTHER: The telegram. . . I can't find the telegram . . .!

DAUGHTER: Momma!

FATHER: Look, lady, take your left-wing politics somewhere else!

MOTHER: I had it somewhere . . .

MISS HORNE: Do any of you know *anything?* (*Short pause, they all look at her in consternation.*) Or *want* to?

MOTHER: It was right here!

MISS HORNE: Six o'clock news. Human interest feature. Cut. (*TV lights are turned off.*)

FATHER: I want you people out there to know this is a *Negro* who's saying all this!

MISS HORNE: You're off the air.

FATHER: A black troublemaker!

MISS HORNE: All right, let's get out of here. (*TV crew begins to get ready to leave.*)

FATHER: Sure, just leave now! Look what you've done to my wife. She's upset.

SON: What channel are we gonna be on?

DAUGHTER: Will we be in color?

FATHER: I can't do anything for her when she gets like this.

SON: Hey, man, you sure you ain't got any grass?

DAUGHTER: Bye now. By now, you two!

FATHER: I hope you're pleased with yourself. (*Mother sits rigid, tears streaming down her face, not listening to anyone.*)

MISS HORNE: (*As the TV crew precedes her out.*) You can see yourself at six o'clock. (*She goes.*)

FATHER: I just hope you're *pleased!* (*Consoles Mother.*)

SON: What was all that about?

DAUGHTER: Beats me. (*Phone rings. Son and Daughter race for it. Daughter wins.*) Eddie? . . . Fine, how are you? . . . you're kidding! (*To Son.*) The Taft quarterback broke his leg at practice! (*Back to phone.*) Groovy! . . . I'll wait out in front . . . aaaw, they're hysterical as usual . . . okay, but hurry up. (*She hangs up.*) Tell mom I'm getting a coke with Eddie.

SON: You tell her.

DAUGHTER: Selfish! You wouldn't put yourself out for Jesus Christ if he came back. (*Picks up purse.*) I love my poppa! (*Runs out door. Son glowers, goes to phone.*)

SON: Margy? . . . I'm coming over now with some stuff. If you chicken out, I swear I'm gonna kill you. . . Hey, guess what? The show's in color! Bye. (*Hangs up.*) I'm going to Margy's.

FATHER: Please don't, mother, don't cry like that.

SON: Dad, I'm going to Margy's.

FATHER: You'll only upset yourself.

SON: I SAID I AM GOING TO MARGY'S!

FATHER: Communist propaganda, every word of it!

SON: Boy, I'm not only getting neurotic, I'm not even getting understood! (*He leaves.*)

FATHER: Mona, I'm going to have to leave you now. It's bowling night. Will you be all right? Just remember your own words, mother. You're proud your son died as an American. And I'm just as proud he died as a man. They can't take that away from us. You got that? Say it. I'm proud of my son—(*Mother moves her lips, no sound comes out.*) Good girl. Just keep saying that to yourself over and over. Pretty soon you'll feel better. I bet you're not even awake when I get home! (*Nudges her playfully.*) Lazy bones I'm married to! (*Gets up.*) Don't stop! Over and over and over and over and over and . . . (*He is tiptoeing out the door.*) . . . over and over and over and over and . . . (*He is gone. Mother sits, reciting her soundless litany. The room is very still.*)

JIMMY: (*Sitting up in crate.*) I've figured something out while all that was going on. The main reason I wish I was alive is so I could figure out why I was dead. (*Puzzles a moment.*) Yeah, that's it. (*Lies back in crate. Pauses. He sits up again.*) Do something for her, why don't you, hunh?

MOTHER: Jimmy.

JIMMY: Tell her . . . I don't know. Tell her she's right. Tell her you're proud I died as an American.

MOTHER: Jimmy.

JIMMY: Tell her you're proud I died as a man.

MOTHER: Jimmy.

JIMMY: You could even tell her I *was* a lot of laughs.

MOTHER: JIIIMMMMYYYYY!

JIMMY: (*After a long pause.*) Then do us all a favor. Don't watch the six o'clock news. (*He starts to make the peace sign, decides not to this time and lies back slowly.*)

MOTHER: (*Emotions spent now, a little voice.*) Jimmy? (*Pause.*) Jimmy? (*Pause.*) Jimmy?

Noon

for Anthony DeSantis

MORNING, NOON AND NIGHT was first presented by Circle in the Square on Broadway: Theodore Mann, Paul Libin and Gillian Walker; on November 28, 1968, at the Henry Miller's Theatre, with the following cast:

KERRY . . . . John Heffernan
ASHER . . . . Robert Klein
ALLEGRA . . . . Jane Marla Robbins
BERYL . . . . Charlotte Rae
CECIL . . . . Sorrell Booke

Characters

ASHER
KERRY
ALLEGRA
CECIL
BERYL

Noon

While the house lights are still up, we hear a phone ringing—ringing and ringing and ringing. Endlessly. Just when the play is about to begin, the person on the other end gives up and the ringing stops.

We are in a large room, maybe a loft, no furniture, perhaps a few crates to sit on if necessary.

Kerry, in his early thirties, medium build, pleasantly outgoing, enters. He carries a flight bag. He's out of breath from climbing stairs.

KERRY: Christ! oi vey! and mamma mia! (*Catches his breath.*) Somebody ought to report this place to the Red Cross. *Whoof!* I thought there were laws about this sort of thing. I mean this beats Mexico City. Dear God! My heart! (*Calls.*) Hello! I'm here. You said after twelve and . . . (*Looks at his watch.*) well, you know what the early bird catches! (*Pause.*) Hey? Anybody home? Dale? (*BONG. BONG. Enormously loud tolling sounds as a clock, somewhere nearby begins to tell the hour. BONG. BONG. BONG.*) *Ow!* (*Covers his ears. The clock continues to toll. Asher, in his early twenties, tall, thin, and nervous, will come up the stairs and into the room during the following. He is carrying several books. It is impossible to talk over the tolling, but Kerry tries to get a word in whenever he can.*) I thought Big Ben was in London! (*BONG. BONG.*) I'll be with you in a minute! (*BONG. BONG.*) The door was open! (*BONG.*) I took the liberty! (*BONG.*) I hope you don't mind! (*BONG.*) I SAID THE DOOR WAS OPEN, AND I TOOK THE LIBERTY OF JUST WALKING IN! (*The clock has stopped tolling.*) Hey, friend, you got the time? (*He laughs.*)

ASHER: (*He looks at his wrist watch.*) It's just noon.

KERRY: No kidding! (*Shaking hands.*) Hi. I'm Kerry.

ASHER: Hello.

KERRY: Nice place you got. All you need is a ski lift and earplugs. Did you check for nose bleed?

ASHER: This isn't my place.

KERRY: You don't live here?

ASHER: No.

KERRY: Good! I can stop feeling sorry for you. And if I didn't have to worry about getting my tail back down, I could even stop feeling sorry for me.

ASHER: Oh. The stairs. Yes. They're really something.

KERRY: I don't have to ask if you do this often. You'd be up on manslaughter charges. (*Reading from an imaginary headline.*) "Large numbers have heart attacks climbing stairs. Dale is charged." (*He laughs.*)

ASHER: It's quite a climb, all right.

KERRY: Just out of curiosity, what was wrong with your place?

ASHER: Huh?

KERRY: Your place. What's wrong with there?

ASHER: Nothing.

KERRY: Got a roommate, hunh? Me too. She's a bitch about things like this. Come to think of it, she's a bitch, period.

ASHER: I don't have a roommate.

KERRY: No?

ASHER: I mean a lover.

KERRY: Oh.

ASHER: Mistress is what I'm trying to say!

KERRY: Then you're married?

ASHER: Me?

KERRY: You keep a very large dog then?

ASHER: What dog?

KERRY: You can't be that ashamed of your place . . .

ASHER: I'm not.

KERRY: You *do* have a place, don't you?

ASHER: Well, sure.

KERRY: 'Cause I'd sure as hell love to know what was wrong with it. If it's any worse than this, you ought to write your congressman. How are you fixed for time?

ASHER: Fine.

KERRY: I'm supposed to be on a business lunch. (*Sits on a crate.*) Dale what?

ASHER: Hunh?

KERRY: Not that it really matters, but anyway, Dale what?

ASHER: Dale what?

KERRY: You. Your last name.

ASHER: I'm not Dale.

KERRY: I thought you said Dale.

ASHER: No, it's Asher.

KERRY: On the phone it sounded like Dale.

ASHER: What phone?

KERRY: My phone. Your phone. Last night.

ASHER: I think you're confusing me with someone else. My name's Asher.

KERRY: (*Shaking hands.*) Hi, Asher. I'm still Kerry.

ASHER: Hello.

KERRY: Do we start all over again?

ASHER: This isn't my place.

KERRY: I think we've pretty well established that.

ASHER: I'm supposed to be meeting someone here.

KERRY: No kidding?

ASHER: Hunh?

KERRY: After all those stairs, it figures you're meeting *someone* up here. Unless you're some kind of calf-nut.

ASHER: What?

KERRY: (*Slapping his leg.*) Calf-nut. Here! Leg muscles.

ASHER: No. Not especially.

KERRY: Me either. I'm a chest-and-biceps man. You work out?

ASHER: In a gym? No.

KERRY: At home? You know, those Royal Canadian Air Force exercises really work. I took an inch off here with isometrics.

ASHER: I don't work out anywhere.

KERRY: How come?

ASHER: I . . . just . . . don't.

KERRY: You should.

ASHER: I know.

KERRY: You look like you work out.

ASHER: Thank you.

KERRY: You look like you work out a lot.

ASHER: (*Beet red by now.*) They said right after twelve.

KERRY: You're right on time. (*Loosening a few buttons.*) It's hot up here.

ASHER: I know.

KERRY: Take your jacket off.

ASHER: I know I'm right on time!

KERRY: We both are.

ASHER: It's my problem. I'm never late for anything. Everybody else always is and I'm waiting. Sometimes I think I'm the only person in the world who thinks right after twelve means right after twelve. God knows, girls never do. They're always late. I have a theory why.

KERRY: I like your trousers.

ASHER: Hunh?

KERRY: Your pants. They're nice.

ASHER: Oh.

KERRY: They're a good fit. Nice and snug on you.

ASHER: They're just off the rack.

KERRY: It's a nice fabric too.

ASHER: I guess.

KERRY: Lightweight.

ASHER: They're just summer pants.

KERRY: Clinging, though.

ASHER: What?

KERRY: Clinging. It's a good clinging fabric.

ASHER: They shrunk a little.

KERRY: (*Shaking his head.*) Then they'd just be tight. No, yours cling.

ASHER: They're just pants.

KERRY: Well, I'd sure as hell love to get my hands on a pair like yours.

ASHER: Ordinary summer pants. They sell them anywhere.

KERRY: Not with that clinging quality.

ASHER: Sears and Roebuck.

KERRY: (*Still shaking his head.*) Your usual lightweight summer trousers don't give you support like that. Not anymore.

ASHER: What?

KERRY: Support. Here. Keep the whang from waggling. It's a problem.

ASHER: (*Taking of his jacket.*) You're right.

KERRY: You hang out all over the place, too?

ASHER: It's hot up here! (*Suddenly.*) Can I ask you something?

KERRY: Sure.

ASHER: Are you—

KERRY: (*At once.*) Unh-hunh!

ASHER: . . . Are you meeting someone named Dale too?

KERRY: (*Momentarily deflated.*) Oh. I *thought* I was meeting someone named Dale. Why?

ASHER: I think we both are.

KERRY: Dale gets around.

ASHER: Do you know Dale?

KERRY: No. Do you?

ASHER: No.

KERRY: Does it matter?

ASHER: I guess not.

KERRY: 'Cause any friend of Dale's is a friend of mine.

ASHER: You just said you didn't know Dale.

KERRY: All right, screw Dale!

ASHER: That's what I had in mind.

KERRY: Ditto! (*Pause. Asher paces.*) I guess you don't even need shorts with trousers like that.

ASHER: Shorts?

KERRY: Underwear. B.V.D.'s. Skivvies.

ASHER: Sure you do.

KERRY: Well, whatever you've got on under there, they're doing a fantastic job.

ASHER: What?

KERRY: Of keeping you in place.

ASHER: Oh.

KERRY: Are they boxers?

ASHER: What?

KERRY: Are you wearing boxer-type shorts or jockies?

ASHER: Jockey. Boxer. The baggy-type ones!

KERRY: (*Solemn agreement.*) Yeah, they give you more mobility. Now your jockies are more for support. It's a real choice. I switch back and forth myself.

ASHER: (*Trying to change the subject.*) Do you know Dale the way I know Dale?

KERRY: (*Not really letting him.*) I thought we'd just agreed that neither of us had had the pleasure. Yours, of course, are as fantastic as your trousers.

ASHER: My what are fantastic!

KERRY: Your shorts. It doesn't look like you're wearing any and that's the whole secret, of course.

ASHER: I mean, did you put one of those ads in one of those papers and someone named Dale answered?

KERRY: What do you think?

ASHER: Maybe one of us ought to leave.

KERRY: I don't follow.

ASHER: Well, you were here first. I mean, it might be awkward, three of us.

KERRY: That depends on Dale, wouldn't you think?

ASHER: You see, I hadn't planned on an . . . (*Almost swallowing the word.*) an orgy.

KERRY: Do you mind if I ask what make they are?

ASHER: Make?

KERRY: Your fabulous undershorts. What brand are they?

ASHER: I couldn't tell you, I'm sure.

KERRY: Where'd you pick them up, then?

ASHER: I don't remember.

KERRY: A men's specialty store?

ASHER: I wouldn't think so.

KERRY: Because if they're from a men's specialty store, they're probably a French or German import. The French are fantastic with men's underwear. The work with nylon has been extraordinary.

ASHER: I'm sure these are just Fruit of the Loom.

KERRY: Oh.

ASHER: Or something like that!

KERRY: I bet not, though.

ASHER: I don't think I've ever been in a men's specialty store.

KERRY: You probably have and didn't know it. They're popping up all over the place lately.

ASHER: I don't even know what a men's specialty store is!

KERRY: Do you always pace in little circles?

ASHER: Only when I'm nervous.

KERRY: I'm not making you nervous, am I?

ASHER: No, this does! Even my palms are sweating.

KERRY: What?

ASHER: This. Up here. I've never done it before.

KERRY: Now you're really putting me on.

ASHER: Why? Have you?

KERRY: You couldn't tell?

ASHER: I don't mean sex. Sex doesn't make me nervous. I love sex.

KERRY: Only your palms sweat.

ASHER: Taking an ad to have sex and then some girl answering it makes my palms sweat! I may never do this again. I'm a wreck already!

KERRY: Oh! I thought you were trying to tell me you were a virgin.

ASHER: A virgin! Hah! That's a good one. A virgin! Hah!

KERRY: I wouldn't have minded.

ASHER: Well I would! A virgin! Jeez! I can't think of anything I'm more definitely not. A virgin. Ha!

KERRY: Some people have all the luck.

ASHER: Luck?

KERRY: Fruit of the Loom and a fit like that!

ASHER: I wasn't thinking about that!

KERRY: Of course you weren't. Why should you? If I could find summer pants and shorts like that, I wouldn't think about it either. I guess I'll just have to stick with these until something better comes along. Talk about hot! I don't think it's possible to have hotter pants than I do. They've actually steamed up on me! My knees are roasting. And they're tight, too! I mean, here's your real difference between lightweight summer-clinging and plain goddamn tight. I feel like I'm going to burst out of these half the time. Look at the thighs alone. Tight as two sausages in these. And support! I don't even want to go into that. Hell, it's like flying buttresses in here. I'm so supported I could split. (*He's standing right in front of Asher.*)

ASHER: Why don't you buy bigger pants?

KERRY: They're no answer. It's all in the fabric and the kind of shorts.

ASHER: Oh.

KERRY: No, I'll just bide my time with these until the right fabric and pair of shorts come winging my way. (*During the following he will take an air mattress out of his flight bag and begin to inflate it with a pump. Asher will try not to notice.*)

ASHER: What made you think I was virgin anyway? Jeez! I kissed my cherry good-bye way back in the eight grade. Whatever men call it. I lost it. After a hayride around White Rock Lake. It's in Dallas. That's where I grew up. Her name was Mary Beth Page. She was a little tubby, but still she was pretty. And she wasn't any town pump, either. It was her first time, too.

KERRY: (*Still pumping.*) Are you sure those are Fruit of the Looms?

ASHER: I told you I thought so.

KERRY: But you're not sure? The only reason I ask is I'd hate to go out and invest in a pair and then get home and find out I wasn't getting the same kind of support.

ASHER: I'm pretty sure that's what they are.

KERRY: I wish you could be more definite.

ASHER: Well, when I get home I suppose I could look and call you, if you want.

KERRY: I won't be in.

ASHER: Tomorrow then.

KERRY: I'm leaving town. I don't know how long I'll be away.

ASHER: I'm sorry. (*Kerry has finished pumping. The mattress is just lying there now.*)

KERRY: I don't suppose you'd? . . . I know it's an imposition, but I'd really appreciate getting this thing settled for once and for all.

ASHER: There's no place to . . . !

KERRY: We're just two men.

ASHER: What if Dale walked in? I'd look ridiculous.

KERRY: (*Explosive.*) Got it! (*He leaps toward Asher.*)

ASHER: Hunh?

KERRY: Turn around.

ASHER: Turn? . . .

KERRY: I can just pull the waistband up and read the label right off.

ASHER: (*Pulling his shirt out of his pants.*) Well, if it's really that important to you! . . .

KERRY: Hey, your shirt's nice, too! What is that? Cotton percale?

ASHER: Really, I don't know! Please, hurry up.

KERRY: You try reading upside down.

ASHER: Fruit of the Loom uses an insignia. A cornucopia, I think.

KERRY: A.R.S.? Arse?

ASHER: That's my laundry mark!

KERRY: You know something? You've got your shorts on backwards.

Either that or the brand name's up front.

ASHER: Backwards?

KERRY: Backwards! I can feel the fly crotch opening.

ASHER: My underwear's on backwards?

KERRY: (*Laughing.*) All these years of looking for the one underwear with the perfect support, and his trick is to wear them backwards! It's incredible!

ASHER: I've never put my underwear on backwards in my life!

KERRY: You did this morning, God bless you! And I think we've found something. This is it, baby, this is it! (*He's turning Asher around.*)

ASHER: What are you doing?

KERRY: Front or backwards, I still want to know what make they are.

ASHER: I can do it!

KERRY: Stand still.

ASHER: Really I can?

KERRY: J.C. Penny!

ASHER: That's *like* Fruit of the Loom.

KERRY: J.C. Penny cotton boxers worn backwards! A rank amateur gets his drawers on cockeyed and successfully and single-handedly dynamites every theory of male genital support going. Like I said, it's incredible! (*He's undone Asher's belt, unzipped his fly. Asher's pants drop to his knees.*) Shoes.

ASHER: Hey!

KERRY: You can't get your pants off with your shoes on. Dummy!

ASHER: I don't want my pants off!

KERRY: What are you? Some kind of faggot?

ASHER: Faggot?

KERRY: Or are you trying to call me one? For Christ's sake, I just want to see you in your shorts.

ASHER: I know, but . . .

KERRY: Guys are guys.

ASHER: Hunh?

KERRY: You're a guy, aren't you?

ASHER: Well of course I am.

KERRY: Be proud of it!

ASHER: I am!

KERRY: You'd never know it.

ASHER: (*Half trips, half stumbles out of his pants.*) All right?

KERRY: How can I tell?

ASHER: Hunh?

KERRY: Your shirt.

ASHER: My shirt?

KERRY: It's in the way. I can't see you or your shorts.

ASHER: (*Pulls his shirt up.*) Okay?

KERRY: Just take it all the way off, hunh?

ASHER: I . . .

KERRY: You're sure acting like a faggot. And a faggot virgin at that.

ASHER: Well, I'm not. Either one!

KERRY: I said you were *acting* like . . .

ASHER: All right! (*Takes off his shirt.*) There. Okay?

KERRY: Turn around. Slowly! (*While Asher's back is turned, Kerry gathers his clothes and hides them.*) Again.

ASHER: I feel like a . . . a . . .

KERRY: What do you do?

ASHER: A model!

KERRY: You're a model?

ASHER: I feel like a model. I'm a writer.

KERRY: Figures.

ASHER: Hunh?

KERRY: What else do you do?

ASHER: What else? . . .

KERRY: God, you're exasperating. In bed. What do you do in bed?

ASHER: Everything. (*He's scratching his head, puzzled, looking around for his clothes. Kerry is putting a 45 rpm record on his portable phonograph. The music is a Jackie Gleason "Music for Lovers Only"-type selection.*)

KERRY: Everything?

ASHER: You know . . . everything. I'm not inhibited, if that's what you're asking. My ad said it. "Culmination of your most sensuous desires."

KERRY: (*Sniffing an amyl nitrate capsule.*) Keep talking!

ASHER: Say, have you seen my? . . . (*Sees Kerry sniffing.*) What's that?

KERRY: "Have poppers." That's what my ad said. (*Long ecstatic moan.*) Oooooooooooh! (*He offers a sniff to Asher.*)

ASHER: No, thank you.

KERRY: I thought you did everything.

ASHER: In bed.

KERRY: That's what this is for.

ASHER: You mean? . . .

KERRY: Get those colored lights going.

ASHER: *Streetcar.*

KERRY: Hunh? Now you've got me doing it.

ASHER: *A Streetcar Named Desire.* Colored lights going. Tennessee Williams.

KERRY: Tennessee Williams uses poppers?

ASHER: I wouldn't be surprised at anything Tennessee Williams uses. Did you ever read his plays?

KERRY: (*Offering a "popper" again.*) Here. Relax. Fly with me.

ASHER: I guess they're a lot like marijuana and opium and stuff like that?

KERRY: You'll see! You'll see!

ASHER: I don't really approve of drugs . . . *any* artificial stimulus, for that matter . . . but I think a writer has to leave himself open to any new experience. Don't you?

KERRY: (*Putting the "popper" in Asher's hand.*) Wide open.

ASHER: Look at George Plimpton! (*Sniffs.*) Wow! (*Sniffs again, laughs.*) You know something? I don't see my pants. (*Sniffs again.*) You know something else? I don't care. (*Sniffs again.*) I'm getting a headache. (*Sniffs again.*) Hey, it's gone already! (*Reeling happily.*) Hoo! Do I feel wild and randy! Randy and wild!

KERRY: (*Getting Asher onto the air mattress. It's a job.*) Just lie back. It's going to be beautiful.

ASHER: (*Lying down now, eyes closed.*) Where's Dale?

KERRY: (*Quickly stripping to flowered bikini shorts.*) "Young gay man, mid-twenties"—that's me, baby—"digs groovy sex with hung horny bisexual guys over eighteen." (*A snore from Asher; Kerry bends over him.*) Asher? (*Allegra's voice offstage is heard calling brightly: "Bonjour!"*) Shit! (*He hides quickly as Allegra, early twenties, with a nice face and body, taut-nerved, bounds into the room. She seems unaffected by the stairs.*)

ALLEGRA: *Bonjour! Bonjour!* (*Her accent is execrable.*) *Je regrette d'être en retard* . . . (sorry to be late!) . . . *le trafic, ça c'est formidable* . . . (the traffic was terrible.) . . . but *me voici tout de même* . . . (I'm here all the same!) . . .*Bonjour! Bonjour!* (*Asher mumbles*

something in his daze.) *Ne parle pas anglais, mauvais garçon* . . .
(bad boy) *Il faut parler français tous les temps* . . . (all the time)
. . . *si vous vraiment voulez parler comme un native* . . . (really
want to speak like a native.). (*Asher mumbles again.*) *Non, non,
non et non!* (*Asher regards her with a glassy stare.*) *Je m'appelle
Allegra. Allegra* . . . (that's Italian for full of pep!) *J'ai lu votre
avertissement* . . . (read your ad.) . . . *et je suis allée dehors de ma
tête* . . . (went out of my head!) You want French lessons? You're
going to get French lessons! *Fou du sexe!* . . . (sex maniac!)
(*Moves away from him. His dazed eyes are never off her.*) *Premiere lecon français. Les articles des habits!* . . . (articles of clothing!). I'm double-parked, so we'd better get right to it, mon élève
. . . (you student, you!) (*Pointing out each article of clothing.*)
Voici la blouse. Voici les boutons de la blouse. J'ai un . . . (*Unbut-
toning as she counts them.*) . . . *deux* . . . *trois* . . . *quatre
boutons.* (*Her blouse is open.*) *J'enleve ma blouse.* (*Takes off her
blouse.*) *Voici la lupe. Voici le zipper de la lupe.* (*Unzips her skirt.*)
Adieu à la lupe. (*Steps out of her skirt.*) *Voici les nylons.* (*Takes off
her stockings, sings the "Marseillaise" while she does so.*) *Patrio-
tique chanson français!* (*Stands in front of Asher.*) *Maintenant je
suis presque nu* . . . (Nearly naked.) . . . *mais pas encore* . . . (Not
yet, brown-eyes.). *Je reste dans brassier et panties pour le temps*
. . . (I'm keeping these on for a while.). *Il faut savoir d'abord* . . .
(First.) . . . *les parts du corps* . . . (Parts of the body . . . yours and
mine, long lashes!) (*Comes right next to him.*) *La bouche.* (*She
kisses him.*) *Les cuisses.* (*Hand on his thighs.*) *La poitrine.* (*Other
hand on his chest.*) *Le coq.* (*Points this time.*) *Le chat.* (*Points at
herself, then laughs wildly.*) *Je ne suis pas vraiment
nymphomanique* . . . (I'm not really a nympho.) . . . *mais* . . . can
we drop the French lesson a minute? There's something I really
want to tell you. I've never done anything like this in my life.
Honest. I've wanted to, but I come from a pretty conservative
background. Dull, you'd call it. *Seducteur!* (*Gives him a playful
nudge.*) But when I read your ad in that paper, it like turned me
on. Turned me on? I'm a girl on fire! (*Moving around the room
now.*) You see, I'm stuck out in Flushing with this creep-liberal-
intellectual-lawyer husband, who likes to talk about it all the
time, and I'm going out of my mind out there with him and all

his damn books. It's his fault I'm here. His and Grove Press. He's a big liberal about all sorts of things, but especially Grove Press. Those books can warp a girl. But try telling him that. "The only obscene word in the English language is the word obscene." Him, Carlton Schapiro, and he's the Oscar Wilde of Greater Flushing! I didn't even want to read them at first. But he was always nagging at me. "They're not dirty," he'd say, "they're not dirty." Fuck him, they're not dirty! I practically had a nervous breakdown over the last one he gave me. *Moist*, it's called. Just *Moist*. It's about an American girl tourist in Spain who ends up on a breeding ranch . . . out there on the pampas, with the bulls she's doing it! . . . but Carlton says it's an allegory. I could just kill him. I mean, he's down at the Civil Liberties Union or the NAACP half the time, and I'm stuck in Flushing reading Grove Press stuff and climbing the walls. I've tried branching out with him. You know, wilder stuff, like I've been reading about. And he says, "What's the matter with you, Allegra? My mother said you dancers were all sick in the head and sex maniacs." (I'm a dancer, I guess you noticed.) I said, "Dancing has nothing to do with it, Carlton. It's what I'm reading in those books." I wish you could have heard him. "That's only in books. Real people don't do things like that. You're a sensitive, intelligent girl." I could have slugged him for that crack. I'm so sick of being a sensitive, intelligent girl after reading Grove Press, I could spit. I mean, I'm still a nice girl deep down inside, but I can't be a nice girl twenty-four hours a day. Not after what I went through last weekend with *Moist*. Your ad saved my life. You see, Carlton got me started reading those kinds of newspapers, too. I think he subscribes to every one of them. It took a lot of nerve to call you . . . thank God, you're a stranger, that makes it okay at least . . . but when I finally got my nerve up and dialed and then you sounded so . . . well, sexy, just like your ad . . . I mean like I flipped. (*Pause.*) You don't waste much time chatting a girl up, do you, Dale? It's better you don't talk. I came here to degrade myself. Treat me bad, Dale, treat me really bad. (*Asher is starting to come out of it.*) I know. Keep it in French. "Beginner in French needs female with firm, clean, shapely body to practice on. No charge for this service. Special attention given to handicapped girls." That last part is so Grove

Press! I hope these'll do for handicaps. (*She starts to remove her bra.*)

ASHER: (*Fully awake, in horror at what he sees approaching him.*) Aaaaaaaaaaaaaaaaaaaaaa! (*He runs screaming from the room.*)

ALLEGRA: Dale? *Merde!* (*Beryl, fortyish, handsome, large-boned, has come into the room.*)

BERYL: Thanks for telling us about the stairs!

ALLEGRA: The . . . ?

BERYL: My husband's having a stroke on one of the goddamn landings!

ALLEGRA: Your . . .

BERYL: I told you we'd be bringing equipment!

ALLEGRA: Equip—?

BERYL: Now get your pink little tuch down there and help him!

ALLEGRA: I . . .

BERYL: Look, you little chippy, no lip!

ALLEGRA: (*Beside herself.*) Yes! (*She runs out of the room.*)

BERYL: (*Scowling at the room.*) A two-hundred-thousand dollar home in Westchester County with special rooms for this sort of thing and we have to come here! I swear I'm going to divorce that man one day . . . divorce him so fast he won't know what hit him! (*She's seen the phone, dials a number.*) Hello, Mrs. Firth? It's me again. I forgot to tell you. Caroline has a dance class at one-thirty. Someone will be by for her, but see that she's got her leotard on this time. (*Asher has edged back into the room. She sees him.*) What are you doing, you little nit? They're on the stairs. Give them a hand!

ASHER: Who? . . .

BERYL: You heard me! (*Asher hurries off.*) And Mrs. Firth, if the man calls about the pony for Johnny's birthday tomorrow, tell him to have the little beast there at two . . . (*Kerry has come back into the room. She sees him.*)

KERRY: Hello.

BERYL: Well don't just stand there, newt! They need you.

KERRY: Who?

BERYL: Them. On the stairs. Now go to it!

KERRY: Yes, ma'am. (*He hurries out.*)

BERYL: Is the baby sleeping? . . . Well, tell the nanny she *can't* go on strike! I swear, Mrs. Firth, I swear, being a suburban mother is even harder than being a city one . . . I appreciate your solicitude. It's what we're paying you for! (*Hangs up.*) God, God, God. What's to become of us all? (*Allegra has returned. She is struggling with a large trunk.*) How is he?

ALLEGRA: Fine, I guess.

BERYL: You guess, you little tramp?

ALLEGRA: I offered to help him and he beat me off with his cane.

BERYL: And you loved it! He's a forceful man, my husband. Over there! (*Allegra drops the trunk; crashing metallic sounds.*) You'll pay for that my pet.

ALLEGRA: I'll? . . .

BERYL: Not so fast! You'll have to wait for it. Beg.

ALLEGRA: Hunh?

BERYL: I'll have my martini. Eight-to-one. With a twist.

ALLEGRA: Your martini?

BERYL: You thought that was a purse, didn't you, you silly bitch?

ALLEGRA: It looks like a purse.

BERYL: Of course it looks like a purse! It's a portable bar. They're the rage in Westchester. Now hop to it. (*While Allegra mixes.*) Pretty deplorable diggings, if you ask me.

ALLEGRA: You know something?

BERYL: I don't remember addressing you, whore.

ALLEGRA: You're pretty forceful yourself.

BERYL: Thank you.

ALLEGRA: I mean, I don't even know you and you've got me waiting on you hand and foot. That plus the insults.

BERYL: The fault, my dear Dale, is in your nature. Yours is a submissive one.

ALLEGRA: I'm not Dale. My name is Allegra.

BERYL: But you're willing to serve. Submission and discipline, that's the ticket! (*Toasting with her martini.*) Discipline and submission! (*Spits it out.*) I said eight-to-one, you jelly-slimed harlot! You left baggage, you painted tart! You bloated lymph node, you raven-trussed hussy!

ALLEGRA: Tressed. You mean raven-tressed.

BERYL: Silence, bitch, when I'm reviling you!

ALLEGRA: Oh, now really, Beryl!

BERYL: Beryl?

ALLEGRA: It's what they call you, isn't it?

BERYL: You dare use my name?

ALLEGRA: It's stenciled right on the bag. Beryl and Cecil.

BERYL: I'll blind you first! With white-hot tongs. Pluck those eyes from your head with pincers.

ALLEGRA: If you're not careful, you're going to hit someone with that riding crop.

BERYL: You! You!

ALLEGRA: I wouldn't recommend that. I know karate.

BERYL: Bravo! I love a slave with spunk.

ALLEGRA: I'm very good at it, in fact.

BERYL: Cecil should be here for this.

ALLEGRA: I'm a black belt!

BERYL: He adores black belts!

ALLEGRA: I'm warning you! (*They struggle, but it's more like shadow-boxing. No real contact is made. Beryl flailing at the air with her riding crop; Allegra warding her off with a few karate chops.*)

BERYL: (*Huffing.*) Don't *try* so hard! I'm not a teeny-bopper!

ALLEGRA: You started it!

BERYL: I'm just trying to turn you on.

ALLEGRA: With a riding crop?

BERYL: Our ad *specified.*

ALLEGRA: What ad?

BERYL: The one you answered!

ALLEGRA: I'm here for French lessons! (*Cecil has entered the room in a sedan chair borne by Kerry and Asher. He's just in time to see Beryl lunge at Allegra, only to trip and fall instead.*)

CECIL: Seize that woman! (*Asher lets his end of the chair drop, spilling Cecil onto the floor.*) Unh! (*Asher has taken Beryl's arm and is helping her up.*)

BERYL: Not me, you idiot! Not the queen. Her!

ALLEGRA: (*To Asher.*) Where have you been? I told you I was double-parked!

ASHER: Hunh?

BERYL: (*Deflated, to Allegra.*) You didn't have to take all the fun out of it!

KERRY: (*Attending to Cecil.*) Mister! Hey, mister! (*To Beryl.*) Hey, lady, is this your husband?

BERYL: Well, he's not my *lover*!

KERRY: He's blacked out.

BERYL: Of course he has! He does this to me all the time. Can't wait till he gets there, and then I'm the one with egg on her face. (*She joins Kerry and Cecil.*)

ALLEGRA: (*To Asher.*) I wish you'd told me how many people would be here.

ASHER: I wish you had.

ALLEGRA: Hunh?

ASHER: Is your name Dale?

ALLEGRA: Isn't yours?

ASHER: I'm Asher.

ALLEGRA: I'm Allegra.

ASHER: Who's Dale?

ALLEGRA: That's Beryl and he's Cecil.

ASHER: And he's Kerry.

ALLEGRA: Oh, dear. (*They are both suddenly aware of their lack of clothes, but there's not much they can do about it gracefully.*)

BERYL: Cecil, wake up, Cecil! You're causing a scene.

KERRY: He's out like a light.

BERYL: You're making a fool of yourself, Cecil, in front of *them*!

KERRY: Wait! I think he's . . .

BERYL: Nobody obeys *fainting nellies*, Cecil!

KERRY: Yes! He's coming around!

CECIL: (*Opens eyes, looks around, gets to his feet, everyone in the room is watching him. He speaks with a German accent.*) All stripped down, are we?

BERYL: That's my Cecil!

ASHER: Well, you see, I—

CECIL: All stripped down and ready to have a go at it, were we? (*He's methodically tearing his clothes off. Underneath he's wearing black leather underwear and high leather boots.*)

BERYL: They were, Cecil, they were! I caught them at it!

ALLEGRA: I only—

CECIL: All stripped down and ready to have a go at it without waiting for Cecil and Beryl, were we? Were we?

BERYL: Punish them, Cecil, punish them!

CECIL: Swine! Pigs! Dogs! (*He blacks out again.*)

ALLEGRA: What was that all about?

ASHER: Is he mad at someone?

BERYL: I'm terribly sorry. What can I say? You said right after twelve . . . we show up half an hour late . . . the traffic was unbelievable, it gets worse all the time . . .and now this. I'm sorry and that's the long and the short. Shall we get started? He'll wake up. (*She has started to undress.*) I'm delighted there's more than one of you. Of course it was naughty of you not to mention it. One of you will pay for that. By the way, I'm Beryl. Which one of you is Dale?

ALLEGRA: What unusual lingerie!

BERYL: It's lizard, you tacky trollop!

ASHER: Hey, now just a minute!

BERYL: Shut up, slime!

KERRY: Who the hell do you think you are?

BERYL: You, too, you little blob! Now which one of you is Dale?

ALLEGRA: None of us is.

BERYL: (*Thrown.*) You're joking. You must be joking.

ALLEGRA: I'm Allegra.

ASHER: I'm Asher.

KERRY: I'm Kerry.

BERYL: Oh, God.

ALLEGRA: I think you owe us all an apology.

BERYL: (*In great and sudden panic.*) Cecil! Wake up, Cecil! We're in the wrong place!

CECIL: (*Responding.*) Our subject for today is leather.

BERYL: (*Mortified.*) Cecil, please, they can hear you!

CECIL: (*Starting to rave.*) What is leather? What are its origins? Its uses?

ASHER: I know!

BERYL: Must you humor him? Can't you see he's a sick man? (*Urgent, to Cecil.*) It's the wrong place, Cecil!

CECIL: (*Shaking her off, moving about the room.*) Why is leather the symbol of intellectual genius?

ASHER: I never heard that before.

BERYL: I could just die, I'm so embarrassed. Cecil, sshh!

ASHER: (*To Allegra and Kerry.*) I'm a writer. It seems to me I would have heard about leather being a symbol of genius.

CECIL: (*Railing at them.*) All the great geniuses have belonged to the leather cult!

ASHER: I can't think of one.

CECIL: Goethe, Schiller, Beethoven, Thomas Mann!

ASHER: All Germans.

CECIL: And all leatherists! What do you think Goethe was wearing when he wrote his Faust? Cotton? Was Schiller in silk when he created his masterpieces? Would the world have Beethoven's nine symphonies had he been wearing satin? Can you mention Thomas Mann and wool in the same breath? You cannot!

ASHER: What about Mozart?

CECIL: (*Apologetic.*) Mozart! Mozart was Austrian, you *dummkopf!* All great art is German, and German art is leather!

KERRY: Leather?

CECIL: Leather! Leather, I tell you!

ALLEGRA: (*To Asher.*) I like Mozart, too.

CECIL: Beryl, Beryl, who are these people? Must they be disciplined like all the others? *Ach! Mein Herz* is heavy! (*He's getting a whip out of the trunk.*)

BERYL: If you'd just listen to me!

CECIL: Speak, *Liebchen*, speak.

BERYL: I've been trying to! We're in the wrong place.

CECIL: (*Stunned.*) What do you mean? . . . the wrong place? . . .

BERYL: They're not our kind of people.

CECIL: Not our kind? . . .

BERYL: Just look at them.

CECIL: (*As if transformed; all trace of German accent vanishing.*) Well . . . hello there . . . I guess I got a little carried away just then . . . hah, hah, hah! . . . Cecil's the name . . . you're right, it's warm up here. Kind of makes you delirious . . . well, I guess the missus and I better shove off now . . . the kids'll be wanting their supper . . . hah, hah, hah! . . . Whew! Sure is warm! . . . Hell of a day for a ballgame!

BERYL: Cecil has these little attacks, you see.

CECIL: Never know when they're gonna hit me.

BERYL: It could be anywhere.

CECIL: Let's face it, I'm a dying man.

BERYL: We certainly hope we haven't inconvenienced you . . .

interrupted anything . . . barging in like this.

CECIL: I told Beryl it didn't look like the place. Hah, hah, hah! (*Awkward silence.*)

KERRY: May I say something?

BERYL: I wish somebody would.

KERRY: I think we should all put our cards on the table.

BERYL: Stop pussyfooting?

KERRY: Exactly. Now we all came here expecting to meet someone named Dale. Right? (*Embarrassed assents, much head-hanging.*) Right after twelve, he said.

ASHER: She. It was a she.

KERRY: I don't think that matters much at this point.

ASHER: To me it does.

KERRY: The fact is, this Dale person called all of us, conveniently forgetting to mention he-or-she had spoken to the others.

CECIL: When we saw the three of you, naturally we thought . . . hah, hah, hah!

BERYL: Cecil, please!

KERRY: And now Dale doesn't show.

ASHER: (*Looking at his watch.*) It's still only . . . I mean, maybe he . . . she's still on her way.

KERRY: Not very likely.

CECIL: Do you suppose? . . . No, it couldn't possibly.

BERYL: What?

CECIL: Right after twelve meant right after midnight?

BERYL: Don't be ridiculous.

ASHER: It is the more usual time for it.

ALLEGRA: It?

ASHER: (*Gulping.*) You know!

KERRY: I think it's a pretty safe assumption someone's played a trick on us.

BERYL: No!

KERRY: I'm afraid so.

BERYL: What kind of sick mind would do a thing like that?

ASHER: It takes all kinds of people to make up a world!

BERYL: But what kind of perverted, twisted, warped, maimed, mutilated mind would play a joke like that?

CECIL: (*Shaking his head.*) I don't know, I don't know what people are coming to any more.

ALLEGRA: What a spooky weirdo this Dale must be!

ASHER: And noon's such an inconvenient time for . . . I mean, people are busy at noon! I had a deadline with my publisher. I write textbooks.

ALLEGRA: What about me, all the way in from Flushing?

BERYL: We drove in from Westchester in this heat and traffic!

KERRY: Listen, I don't know if I still have a job when I get back.

CECIL: Morning, noon or night, wild horses couldn't drag me up here again.

KERRY: All right then, let's put the rest of our cards on the table. Since we're all here . . . and at no little inconvenience . . . I suggest we try working something out.

CECIL: (*Brightening at the prospect.*) You mean? . . .

KERRY: I mean!

CECIL: What do you think, honey?

BERYL: (*Weighing it.*) Well . . .

KERRY: (*Persuasive.*) After all, we did all come here for the same thing. Hell, we even advertised, we wanted it so bad.

ALLEGRA: I beg your pardon! I answered an ad. I never took one. There's a big difference!

KERRY: Really? What?

ASHER: Are you people talking about an . . . (*Gulping on the word again.*) orgy?

BERYL: (*Becoming convinced.*) I hate to see an afternoon wasted.

CECIL: (*Agreeing.*) I had work, too. I mean I'm not exactly unemployed, you know.

KERRY: Asher?

ASHER: (*Bluff bravado.*) Sure, sure! Why the hell not?

KERRY: You, Allegra?

ALLEGRA: It's certainly worth a try. Even if you're not Dale, you're both kind of sexy. I mean we could . . . wow!

ASHER: Don't talk like that.

ALLEGRA: What's wrong with you?

ASHER: Nice girls don't say things like that.

ALLEGRA: Wait a minute! Are you that "sensitive writer, Harvard Ph.D., who's seeking a grownup girl to share wonderful conversation and Bach," who's been advertising like mad lately?

ASHER: It's a Columbia Ph.D., actually.

ALLEGRA: That's the creep!

ASHER: What's wrong with that?

ALLEGRA: Give Carlton a toot on the phone next time. You two were made for each other. (*To Kerry.*) I guess that makes it us. What do you say? *Qu'est-ce que vous dites?*

KERRY: (*Nodding toward Asher.*) I want him, actually.

ALLEGRA: Him?

KERRY: He turns me on, what can I tell you?

ALLEGRA: *Ecch!*

BERYL: Tolerance, dear, a little tolerance for God's creatures.

ASHER: *You* were the queer!

KERRY: Elementary, my dear Watson.

ASHER: You could have fooled me!

KERRY: Well? What do you say?

ASHER: You mean? . . . Of course not!

KERRY: It doesn't exactly hurt, you know.

ASHER: I said no!

KERRY: Come to think of it, you're not masculine enough.

ASHER: (*Aghast.*) Not . . . masculine enough!?

KERRY: (*Appraising Cecil, now.*) I like a man with balls in his voice, hair on his chest . . .

ASHER: (*To Allegra.*) I've got hair on my chest.

ALLEGRA: Drop dead!

KERRY: A guy with nice musky male smells.

CECIL: (*So affably.*) You see this fist, fruit?

KERRY: (*Smiling at him.*) It was worth a try, wasn't it? (*They laugh and shake hands.*)

BERYL: Cecil?

CECIL: (*For both of them.*) "Extremely attractive Westchester couple—

BERYL: (*He's left a word out.*) White!

CECIL: ". . . both of dominant nature, seek couples and singles who would enjoy serving as our slave—"

BERYL: Any combination of you would do.

CECIL: "Must be of submissive nature and be willing to serve." (*A pause.*)

BERYL: (*Still hopeful.*) Discretion assured!

ALLEGRA: I've read *The Story of O*, thank you.

BERYL: And didn't you like it?

ALLEGRA: I thought it was funny.

BERYL: Funny? Funny!

KERRY: You don't go my route, I don't go yours.

CECIL: I think we've . . . as the saying has it . . . bombed out, Beryl.

KERRY: (*His turn to be affable.*) I'm sorry, but I specifically stated no disciplinarians.

ASHER: (*Dawning on him.*) I know what that means. Oh, gosh. Oh, gosh!

BERYL: (*Trying to figure something out.*) Maybe if we . . . you and she could . . . no! Cecil and him . . . and then . . . *no.*

CECIL: (*Eagerly.*) What, Beryl?

BERYL: Nothing. Just a wild thought.

ASHER: (*To no one in particular.*) All I want is a sensitive girl I can relate to. What's so unusual about that?

ALLEGRA: (*A voice in the wilderness.*) Fucking, anyone?

KERRY: (*After a beat.*) Well, *that* . . . as the other saying has it . . . would seem to be *that.*

BERYL: And I'm getting dressed.

ALLEGRA: I think we'd all better.

ASHER: I've had it with advertising. I'm going back to hanging around the Village. NYU's down there.

KERRY: The next time I meet anyone, it's going to be at my place.

ALLEGRA: I'm so mad I could spit.

CECIL: Can we give anyone a lift?

ASHER: Do you go up the West Side?

BERYL: My dear, we stay as far away from the West Side as we possibly can. (*Ring. The telephone. Everybody freezes.*)

ASHER: Hey, the phone's ringing. (*Ring.*)

CECIL: Did you tell Mrs. Firth where we'd be? (*Ring.*)

KERRY: It's not for me. (*Ring.*)

BERYL: Don't move anybody. Just stay put. (*Ring. Ring. Ring.*)

ALLEGRA: Maybe it's Dale.

BERYL: Oh, my God! Quick! (*They race for the phone. Beryl gets it.*) Hello . . . who is this? (*To the others.*) It's Dale! It's Dale! (*They gather around her.*) Yes, this is Beryl! . . . my husband? He's right beside me. . . (*To Cecil.*) he said hello, Cecil.

CECIL: Well, you tell that practical joker he can just—

BERYL: Yes, Allegra's here, too. . . . (*To Allegra.*) He said "*bonjour.*"

ALLEGRA: Tell him *va aux enfers!* Go to hell!

BERYL: Yes, they're both here, too . . . of course they didn't hit it off!

ASHER: (*Recoiling at the thought.*) You can say that again!

KERRY: (*Trying to get the phone.*) I'll tell that bitch a thing or two!

BERYL: Let me handle it.

CECIL: She's terrific at this.

BERYL: (*Into the phone.*) Listen, you, wherever you are . . . Paramus!
. . . I *know* where Paramus is; now you just listen to me. You
have some nerve, getting us all here and then not showing up. I
suppose you think that's pretty funny. Well, let me tell you something—

CECIL: (*So proudly to the others.*) What'd I tell you?

BERYL: (*Sudden delight.*) You couldn't make it because you're all tied
up? (*Sotto voce.*) Cecil! (*Back into the phone; cooing.*) What do
you mean, you're all tied up? (*Angry again.*) Oh, you're just busy
you mean! (*Resuming her tirade.*) Well, let me tell you— (*She listens, then to the others.*) Do we want to go to Paramus?

CECIL: Out of the question.

ASHER: Paramus, that's in New Jersey.

KERRY: I'd rather cruise Hackensack.

BERYL: (*Back into the phone, with great dignity.*) We're afraid not.
Nothing could get us out there. Not after this. (*She listens.*)

CECIL: I guess that's telling him.

BERYL: (*Hushing Cecil, then into the phone.*) What? You're disciplining
someone? . . . Where? . . . a bowling alley? At this time of day?
What kind of bowling alley is that? . . . *OH!*

CECIL: (*On the alert.*) What? What?

BERYL: Sshh! (*Back into the phone.*) Who? . . . a young man . . . yes . . .

KERRY: (*Eagerly.*) Keep talking!

BERYL: And he wants a young girl to practice German lessons with?
(*Looking at Allegra.*) Will French do?

ALLEGRA: Don't split hairs! I'm very lingual.

BERYL: And he's got his sensitive sister with him? (*She's looking at
Asher.*) A poetess?

ASHER: A poetess? Oh, wow!

BERYL: (*Businesslike now, getting the facts.*) Now let me get this
straight. You're in Paramus, at a bowling alley, disciplining a

young man who wants a young girl to practice German lessons with, and he's got his sensitive poetess sister with him? (*To Cecil.*) How soon can we get there?

CECIL: Fifteen minutes.

BERYL: We can make it in ten! (*Into the phone.*) What's the address?

ALLEGRA: Ten minutes? In this traffic?

CECIL: Just watch us.

BERYL: (*Writing it down.*) 143. Got it. Now hold everything and just sit tight . . . (*Harsh.*) Ten minutes, half an hour, just wait for us! (*Listens.*) You'll answer for that, pig (*Sweetly.*) Yes, of course we'll hurry. (*Listens, looks at Kerry.*) What? . . . Don't bring the fag. You hate fags. He wouldn't fit in. Of course I understand. (*Looks away, rambling on.*) Tell me something, are they being very naughty? (*She relishes the answer.*) We're on our way! (*She hangs up.*) Don't just stand there, Cecil. Pack. (*There is a great flurry of activity now as they make ready to leave.*)

ASHER: Are you people talking about another orgy?

BERYL: (*Making haste.*) The branding irons, Cecil. Don't mix them with the tongs!

ALLEGRA: I'll be right behind you. It's a blue Plymouth.

BERYL: Cecil drives like a bat out of hell.

ALLEGRA: I'll keep up.

ASHER: (*Watching them get ready.*) Hey! Hey! Everybody! What about me? I'm willing to try it, at least. I've never been to an orgy, orgy! ORGY! before. See? I'm losing my inhibitions. To be frank, I could use the experience!

BERYL: Take the trunk.

ASHER: Wow! Thanks a lot! A poetess. Oh, wow! (*He goes down the stairs.*)

ALLEGRA: (*Following.*) Paramus, *ici je viens!* Paramus, here I come! (*They are both gone.*)

BERYL: Paramus! Whoever dreamed I'd end up in Paramus!

CECIL: (*On the stairs.*) Say, isn't that where Dot and Hugh live?

BERYL: I wouldn't put it past them. (*Cecil is gone. She sees Kerry.*) Come on, anyway.

KERRY: (*Mustering up all the dignity he can.*) I've been on my goose chase for the day, thank you.

BERYL: But a bowling alley! I'm sure we can whip something up for you.

KERRY: No, thank you.

BERYL: Well, just don't get too depressed. Promise? Something will turn up. It always does. Hope! We can't live with it and we can't live without it! (*She runs down the stairs. We hear them all laughing as their voices die away.*)

KERRY: (*Shouting down the stairs.*) Sure, go ahead, laugh! You'll get there and nothing'll happen either! I bet there's no such thing as Dale! (*Paces, yells down again.*) And thanks a lot. I was here first, just remember. Hell, I wasn't going to hurt anybody. (*Pauses, paces, yells again. He's been hurt, you see.*) I hope you get stuck in the tunnel. (*Realizes they're gone.*) I hope it caves in on you! (*He is alone in the room. Slowly, sadly, he begins to gather his things, and make ready to leave. And then—at a great distance— we hear a voice on the stairs.*)

VOICE: (*From afar.*) Dale? (*Kerry freezes.*) Dale? . . . (*Kerry goes to the stairwell, looks down.*) Dale? (*Kerry runs his fingers through his hair, generally spruces himself up. The voice is getting closer.*) Dale? (*Kerry has started to smile. The future is his.*) Dale? (*Slow fade.*)

Curtain.

Botticelli

for my brother, Peter Sean McNally

BOTTICELLI was first produced by Channel 13 in New York City on March 14 and 15, 1968, directed by Glenn Jordan with the following cast:

```
WAYNE  . . . . . . . . . . . . . . . . . . . . . . . . . . . . . . . . . . . . . . . . . Kevin O'Connor
STU  . . . . . . . . . . . . . . . . . . . . . . . . . . . . . . . . . . . . . . . . . . . . . Roy London
MAN . . . . . . . . . . . . . . . . . . . . . . . . . . . . . . . . . . . . . . . . . . Tom Matsusaka
```

Characters

WAYNE
STU
MAN

Botticelli

The scene takes place among jungle foliage. There is afternoon sun and shadows, insect noises. Two soldiers, Wayne and Stu, are seen crouching, holding their rifles.

WAYNE: No, I'm not Marcel Proust.

STU: Proust was a stylist.

WAYNE: And he died *after* World War I.

STU: You sure?

WAYNE: 1922.

STU: Yeah?

WAYNE: November 4, 19—

STU: All right! (*A pause.*) What's up?

WAYNE: (*Stiffening.*) I thought I heard something. (*Relaxes.*)

STU: Are you a . . . let's see . . . are you a Polish concert pianist who donated a large part of the proceeds from his concerts to the cause of Polish nationalism?

WAYNE: Oh, that's a real brain-crusher, that one is!

STU: Well, are you?

WAYNE: No, I'm not Paderewski.

STU: Are you sure you're dead?

WAYNE: Oh, brother!

STU: A dead European male in the arts beginning with P?

WAYNE: Why don't you write it down?

STU: Got it! You're a controversial Russian poet, novelist, dramatist and short-story writer.

WAYNE: Sorry, I'm not Pushkin.

STU: Pushkin wasn't considered controversial.

WAYNE: Who says?

STU: I do.

WAYNE: He was part Negro.

STU: What's controversial about that?

WAYNE: Dumas *père?*

STU: Don't change the subject. Controversial Russian writer. Come on. I've got you stumped, hunh? Look at you. Drew a blank. Hunh? Hunh?

WAYNE: I hope it's not Boris Pasternak you're crowing about.

STU: Drop dead, will you?

WAYNE: Then give up, hunh? (*Tenses.*) Sshh! (*Relaxes.*) Not yet.

STU: You'd think he'd starve in there by now.

WAYNE: Maybe he has. Why don't you go see?

STU: And get a grenade in the face? That tunnel could be half a mile long, for all we know. He's buried in there like a groundhog. No sir, I'm holding tight, staying right where I am, sergeant's orders. I got all the time in the world to wait for that bugger to stick his head out. (*Wayne starts making a cigarette.*) Are you a ? . . . I'm running dry. P's the hardest letter in the alphabet.

WAYNE: Wanna turn on?

STU: How much we got left?

WAYNE: If he's not out of there by tonight, we're in trouble.

STU: Do you keep a diary?

WAYNE: Sure. Every night.

STU: No, who you are! Does he keep a diary?

WAYNE: I'm not Samuel Pepys.

STU: Smart ass! (*They smoke.*) Would you say this is the best part of the whole war?

WAYNE: What is?

STU: This. Pot.

WAYNE: No. I'd say Raquel Welch was.

STU: Yeah.

WAYNE: Those goddamn white leather boots up to here . . . and that yellow miniskirt . . .

STU: Hey, are you the outstanding English baroque composer?

WAYNE: I'm not Henry Purcell. I thought Raquel Welch looked like a sexy . . . ostrich.

STU: Do the words "Rape of the Lock" mean anything to you?

WAYNE: No, and they don't mean anything to Alexander Pope either.

STU: Nuts!

WAYNE: Look, let me tell you who I am, hunh?

STU: No I said.

WAYNE: Brother, you're stubborn.

STU: And *you're* a Victorian playwright!

WAYNE: I'm not Arthur Wing Pinero.

STU: Sir.

WAYNE: Hunh?

STU: Sir Arthur Wing Pinero.

WAYNE: I know!

STU: You didn't say it.

WAYNE: I'd rather talk about Raquel Welch.

STU: Sure you would. You're getting stoned.

WAYNE: I'm not getting anything else.

STU: You still worrying about that letter from Susan?

WAYNE: Not since Raquel Welch I'm not.

STU: I bet.

WAYNE: Let her get a divorce. I don't care. Hell, the only mistake I made was thinking I had to marry her. I should've sent her to Puerto Rico. She could've had a vacation on me, too.

STU: Only you had scruples.

WAYNE: Leave me alone.

STU: Jesuit high school, Dominican college scruples.

WAYNE: God, you're insensitive. Wait'll *you* get married.

STU: Maybe I never will.

WAYNE: Yeah!

STU: I might not.

WAYNE: You'd marry the first girl looked twice at you. Yours is one wedding I wouldn't want to miss. There's always Marlene Schroll.

STU: "As You Desire Me!"

WAYNE: What the—?

STU: You wrote "As You Desire Me."

WAYNE: I'm not Luigi Pirandello.

STU: Okay, but simmer down, hunh?

WAYNE: It's a dumb game.

STU: Your idea.

WAYNE: I was trying to kill time.

STU: Well, if we had something intelligent to discuss . . .

WAYNE: What's wrong with Raquel Welch?

STU: Nothing. She's the quintessence of intelligence.

WAYNE: I'm gonna bust you in the mouth. (*A pause.*) I wish I'd burned my draft card.

STU: Are you a Russian composer?

WAYNE: I'm not Prokofiev.

STU: An Italian composer?

WAYNE: I'm not Puccini.

STU: An Italian composer?

WAYNE: I'm not Ponchielli.

STU: An Italian composer?

WAYNE: What are you, a record?

STU: An Italian composer?

WAYNE: All right, who?

STU: Pizzarella.

WAYNE: Go to hell.

STU: What's wrong with Pizzarella?

WAYNE: There's no Italian composer named Pizzarella.

STU: How do you know?

WAYNE: I know!

STU: Well, maybe there is.

WAYNE: Yeah, and you just made him up. Pizzarella. Look, if you're gonna play, play fair. Boy, you haven't changed since college. Even in charades you'd try to put something over.

STU: Like when?

WAYNE: Like when you did *The Brothers Karamazov*. Only you did it in Russian. How could anybody guess *The Brothers Karamzov* in a game of charades when you were doing it in Russian?

STU: It would've been too easy in English.

WAYNE: No wonder you never made the chess and bridge teams. Those are precise games. You don't muck with the rules in *them*. (*A pause.*) Typical. Sulk now.

STU: I'm thinking.

WAYNE: (*Rolls over on his back, looks up at the sky.*) You know what I can't get over?

STU: Mmmmmm.

WAYNE: Poor Father Reilly.

STU: Yeah.

WAYNE: I mean, just dropping dead like that. God, we were lucky having him for a teacher. And of all places to drop dead. He loved Rome the same way some men love women. I think he lived for his summer vacations. As much as he gave his students, his heart was always in Rome on the Spanish Steps or the Pincio. And I guess it was all those steps and hills that finally killed him. A great man.

STU: Wayne?

WAYNE: Yeah?

STU: An Italian composer?

WAYNE: You see this fist?

STU: I just thought of two more.

WAYNE: Real ones?

STU: Give up, you'll see.

WAYNE: If they're not, buddy! . . .

STU: (*Looking at his watch.*) You've got fifteen seconds.

WAYNE: Unh . . . unh. . . unh. . . quit making me nervous . . . unh . . .

STU: Ten!

WAYNE: Palestrina!

STU: Who else?

WAYNE: Palestrina and . . . unh . . .

STU: Pizzarella?

WAYNE: Can it! Palestrina and . . .

STU: Five seconds.

WAYNE: Pergolesi. Giovanni Pergolesi! (*A burst of machine-gun fire, they both flatten out.*) That dirty little . . . (*Aims, ready to fire.*)

STU: (*Terse whisper.*) Homosexual Greek philosopher.

WAYNE: Brother, are you warped. I mean, that's disgusting.

STU: Come on.

WAYNE: Plato wasn't homosexual.

STU: You were right there, climbing the Acropolis with him.

WAYNE: Your mind is really sick. A remark like that turns my stomach.

STU: Who made any remarks?

WAYNE: It's not even funny. (*The firing stops.*) Where the hell is he? Come on, buster, stick your neck out. He's shooting to see if anybody's out here. We'll just have to sit tight.

STU: Apropos the Parthenon, did you by any chance supervise the rebuilding of it?

WAYNE: I'm not Phidias. What are we on now? Your Greek kick?

STU: You're a fine one to talk about *that.*

WAYNE: There's something crawling on you.

STU: Hey! What the hell is it? This country. Bugs in your shoes, bugs

in your hair, bugs in your food. Look at him go. Eight legs . . .
no, ten! . . . I guess those are wings . . . nice antennae . . . I used
to be scared of bugs.

WAYNE: Do you have to have a conversation with him?

STU: *Bon soir,* bug. (*Crushes the bug.*)

WAYNE: I could never do that.

STU: Bugs have souls now, too?

WAYNE: Shut up about all that, will you?

STU: I don't suppose you're an Italian poet?

WAYNE: I'm not Petrarch, Einstein.

STU: It was just a wild guess.

WAYNE: You're never going to get me.

STU: I'm not going to give up, either.

WAYNE: Stubborn, stubborn, stubborn!

STU: I'd lose all self-respect if I weren't.

WAYNE: Sshh.

STU: I mean, the only reason to begin a game is to win it.

WAYNE: I said shut up! (*The Man has come out of the tunnel. He's
young, emaciated. He pauses at the entrance, quivering like a
frightened rabbit. Spot light on him.*) Look at the little bugger.

STU: Not so little through these sights.

WAYNE: Not yet! He has to come this way. Wait'll he's closer.

STU: You're not a French painter? A great master of the classical
school?

WAYNE: I'm not Poussin.

STU: I've got another one. Impressionist.

WAYNE: French?

STU: Yeah.

WAYNE: I'm not Pissarro.

STU: I can't think of any more P's

WAYNE: All right, *you* gave up, I'm—

STU: No! (*The Man has begun to move cautiously away from the tunnel opening.*)

WAYNE: Here he comes. Quiet now.

STU: Were you an Italian sculptor working with Giotto on the cam-
panile in Florence?

WAYNE: I'm not Pisano. Get ready.

STU: Okay, and this is it, Wayne. Did you write a famous "Lives?"

WAYNE: I'm not Plutarch. Let's go. (*The Man's face contorts with pain as he is cut down by a seemingly endless volley of gunfire. He falls, twitches, finally lies still. Wayne and Stu approach.*)

STU: Is he dead? I just asked!

WAYNE: Let's get back to camp.

STU: Okay, I give up. Who are you?

WAYNE: Pollaiuolo.

STU: Who?

WAYNE: Pollaiuolo, Antonio Pollaiuolo.

STU: That's like Pizzarella. (*They start moving off. The spot stays on the Man's face.*)

WAYNE: Italian painter, sculptor and goldsmith. 1432 to 1498.

STU: Well, I never heard of him.

WAYNE: Famous for his landscapes and the movement he put into the human body.

STU: Never heard of him.

WAYNE: He influenced Dürer, Signorelli and Verrocchio. (*They are off stage, just voices now.*)

STU: Them I've heard of.

WAYNE: "Portrait of a Man"? "The Labors of Hercules"? "David"? "The Martyrdom of St. Sebastian"? "Tobias and the Angel"?

STU: Never heard of him.

WAYNE: The tomb of Sixtus IV?

STU: Never heard of him.

WAYNE: Good God, he was a contemporary of Botticelli!

STU: Never heard of him.

WAYNE: Christ, you're dumb.

STU: I NEVER HEARD OF HIM. (*The spot stays on the Man's face. There is a slow fade.*)

Next

for James Coco

NEXT was first presented by Lucille Lortel on August 13, 1967, at the White Barn Theatre, Westport, Connecticut, directed by E. Frederick Davies, with the following cast:

MARION CHEEVER .... James Coco
SGT. THECH .... Elaine Shore

Subsequent productions were seen on Channel 13 in New York City and at the Berkshire Theatre Festival in Stockbridge, Massachusetts.

The revised script of NEXT which follows was first presented by the Theatre-In-Progress Workshop of the Berkshire Theatre Festival on August 29, 1968, at The Barn, Stockbridge, Massachusetts, directed by Elaine May, with the following cast:

MARION CHEEVER .... James Coco
SGT. THECH .... Elaine Shore

This version was then presented by Lyn Austin on February 10, 1969, at the Greenwich News Playhouse, New York City, directed by Elaine May, with the following cast:

MARION CHEEVER .... James Coco
SGT. THECH .... Elaine Shore

Characters

MARION CHEEVER
SGT. THECH

Next

The scene opens in an examination room decorated in neutral colors; anonymous-looking. Stage left there is an examination table, a scale and a cabinet filled with medical equipment. Stage right there is a desk and two chairs. The only bright color in the room is the American Flag, center stage. As the curtain rises, the room is empty.

SGT. THECH: (*Off stage.*) Next! (*Marion Cheever enters. He is a fat man in his late forties and he is nattily dressed. He carries a brief case.*)

MARION: Hello? I'm next! (*He looks around, puts down his brief case, takes out a cigarette case, lights one up, sits in front of the desk and waits somewhat impatiently.*)

SGT. THECH: (*Entering.*) No smoking.

MARION: (*Rising.*) Good morning. Good morning! (*Briskly.*) Well! I think we can get this over with rather quickly.

SGT. THECH: No smoking.

MARION: (*Snuffing out his cigarette.*) I'm sorry. Filthy habit. (*He's put his hat on her desk. Sgt. Thech hands it back to him.*) Oh my hat! I'm sorry! (*He looks for a place to put it. There is none, so he puts it on the floor.*)

SGT. THECH: (*Already busy at her desk with papers and forms.*) Your card and bottle, please.

MARION: (*Rummaging in his brief case.*) As I was starting to say, I think we can get this over with rather quickly. There's obviously been a mistake. (*He laughs.*) I mean I—

SGT. THECH: The government does not make mistakes. If your country has called you it has its reasons. May I have your card and bottle, please?

MARION: (*Still going through his brief case.*) I thought to myself, "My God! They can't mean me."

SGT. THECH: That's it.

MARION: Is that it? (*Hands her the card. She begins to type.*) I thought to myself there must be someone else in my building with the same name because why else would I get a card to come down here?

SGT. THECH: Is your name Marion Cheever?

MARION: Yes, it is. But you know I just had a fortieth birthday and I thought to myself nobody sends a card like this to a man like me.

SGT. THECH: They're taking older men.

MARION: How old exactly?

SGT. THECH: It's inching up all the time. May I have your bottle please?

MARION: (*Looking in brief case.*) Inching up all the time, is it? The bottle, yes, here it is! (*He hands her his urine specimen.*)

SGT. THECH: Strip.

MARION: I didn't know that . . . the inching up all the time.

SGT. THECH: Remove all articles of clothing including your shoes and socks.

MARION: Who are you?

SGT. THECH: Your examining officer, Sgt. Thech. And by the authority vested in me by this government, I order you to strip.

MARION: A lady examining officer! Oh that's funny! They must be pretty hard up these days.

SGT. THECH: And if you have not begun to strip in the next ten seconds I will complete these forms without further examination and report you to the board of examiners as fit for duty.

MARION: (*As if coming out of a trance.*) Oh my God, I'm sorry. I didn't hear one word you said. I don't know what I was thinking of. What did you say? That if I hadn't—

SGT. THECH: Begun to strip in the next ten seconds . . .

MARION: You will complete those forms . . .

SGT. THECH: Without further examination. . .

MARION: And report me to the board of examiners? . . .

SGT. THECH: As fit for duty.

MARION: (*Biting his lip.*) Do you think that's fair?

SGT. THECH: Would you prefer not to strip?

MARION: Indeed I would!

SGT. THECH: Very well, then I will stamp these forms—

MARION: No, don't do that!

SGT. THECH: Then you have ten seconds. (*Timing him.*) One one-thousand, two one-thousand . . .

MARION: I'm going to strip! (*While Sgt. Thech counts.*) I'm going to let you do it because not only am I over forty, I am not a healthy over forty and—

SGT. THECH: Seven one-thousand.

MARION: (*To make her stop.*) Where do I go?

SGT. THECH: (*Points to the center of the room.*) Right over there.

MARION: Right over there. Well! Everybody else is doing it, why not?

SGT. THECH: (*Filling out a questionnaire.*) Your name.

MARION: Do you have a little hanger?

SGT. THECH: Use the stool. Your name.

MARION: Cheever. Marion Cheever.

SGT. THECH: Do you spell Marion with an o?

MARION: I do, yes.

SGT. THECH: Age.

MARION: Forty . . . eight! Forty-eight.

SGT. THECH: Sex.

MARION: Did you put that down? I'm forty-eight years old.

SGT. THECH: Sex.

MARION: Well what do you think I am?

SGT. THECH: Color of hair.

MARION: Brown, Black. Blackish brown.

SGT. THECH: Eyes.

MARION: Two.

SGT. THECH: Color of eyes . . .

MARION: I'm sorry! Blue. Blue-green. Aqua.

SGT. THECH: Occupation.

MARION: (*Still apologizing for the eyes.*) You rattled me.

SGT. THECH: Occupation.

MARION: I don't know what's the matter with me.

SGT. THECH: Your occupation, Mr. Cheever.

MARION: I'm a dancer.

SGT. THECH: Toe or tap.

MARION: Oh really! Toe or tap! I'm the assistant manager of the Fine Arts Theatre, 58th Street and Park Avenue. You've probably heard of us. Toe or tap! I was funning!

SGT. THECH: How long.

MARION: Is what?

SGT. THECH: How long have you been the assistant manager of the

Fine Arts Theatre?

MARION: I'm sorry. How long have I been assistant manager for the Fine Arts Theatre? About twelve years. (*He has removed his shirt by now. His undershirt is torn and dirty. He's trying to find something to hide behind.*)

SGT. THECH: Marital status.

MARION: (*Eyeing the American flag.*) Single. Single now. Divorced I guess is what I'm supposed to say. (*He will use the flag to cover himself as he continues to strip. Sgt. Thech doesn't see all this, as he is behind her and she is busy typing in the questionnaire.*)

SGT. THECH: How many times.

MARION: Twice.

SGT. THECH: Number of dependents.

MARION: Three girls.

SGT. THECH: Sex.

MARION: I said three girls!

SGT. THECH: Ages.

MARION: Fourteen, twelve, and two. Two with my first wife and one with my second.

SGT. THECH: Did you finish grammar school?

MARION: I certainly did.

SGT. THECH: High school.

MARION: You bet.

SGT. THECH: College.

MARION: No, I never got to college. I meant to but I never—

SGT. THECH: Do you belong to a church?

MARION: I just never got there. You know what I mean?

SGT. THECH: Do you belong to a church?

MARION: Oh yes!

SGT. THECH: Which denomination.

MARION: The Sacred Heart of Jesus.

SGT. THECH: Which denomination.

MARION: Roman Catholic. What do you think with a name like that? It's a temple?

SGT. THECH: Do you attend church?

MARION: You bet.

SGT. THECH: Regularly or occasionally.

MARION: Yes, unh-hunh, unh-hunh!

SGT. THECH: Regularly or occasionally.

MARION: Yes, regularly on occasion.

SGT. THECH: Is your father living or deceased.

MARION: Living.

SGT. THECH: His age.

MARION: Seventy-two.

SGT. THECH: Is your mother living or deceased.

MARION: Deceased.

SGT. THECH: Age at death.

MARION: Thirty-one.

SGT. THECH: Cause of death.

MARION: Natural causes.

SGT. THECH: Be specific.

MARION: Heart.

SGT. THECH: Any brothers.

MARION: Yes.

SGT. THECH: How many.

MARION: One. He's alive.

SGT. THECH: Sisters.

MARION: Two. They're both alive. Both living.

SGT. THECH: Do you live alone?

MARION: At the present time I do. I get a lot of company, of course, but unh, officially, for the record, I live alone.

SGT. THECH: Do you own your own home?

MARION: No. It's a . . . you know . . . residential hotel for . . . unh . . . me. Single men. (*Marion has undressed now and is sitting on a low stool. The flag is draped across him.*)

SGT. THECH: (*Turning to a new page.*) Measles.

MARION: What?

SGT. THECH: Have you ever had the measles?

MARION: Oh measles! No, no I haven't.

SGT. THECH: Chicken pox.

MARION: No, I never had chicken pox.

SGT. THECH: Whooping cough.

MARION: I think it *might* have been. I was coughing an awful lot and I was very sick.

SGT. THECH: Yes or no.

MARION: No. It wasn't *exactly* whooping cough but—

SGT. THECH: Rheumatic fever.

MARION: (*Thinking hard.*) Unh! Did I have rheumatic fever? Is that what it was? No, no I don't think so.

SGT. THECH: Mumps.

MARION: (*Jumping at this.*) Yes! Yes, yes, yes! Now just a minute on the mumps.

SGT. THECH: Tuberculosis.

MARION: They weren't your ordinary mumps.

SGT. THECH: Jaundice.

MARION: Will you please let me tell you about my mumps. I was in bed for months. I practically had last rites!

SGT. THECH: Venereal disease.

MARION: I don't think you realize how serious my mumps were.

SGT. THECH: Venereal disease.

MARION: Not yet! I just wish you'd let me tell you about my mumps!

SGT. THECH: Allergies.

MARION: What about allergies?

SGT. THECH: Are you allergic to anything?

MARION: Yes, yes, as a matter of fact I am.

SGT. THECH: Go on, explain.

MARION: I know this sounds silly but I'm allergic to peach fuzz. I swell up like a balloon.

SGT. THECH: Anything else.

MARION: No, but I can't even go near a fruit stand. All I have to do is look at a peach and—

SGT. THECH: Any history of epilepsy.

MARION: Me and peach fuzz is no joke!

SGT. THECH: Have you a family history of diabetes?

MARION: Diabetes? Well why not. Somebody must have had it.

SGT. THECH: Heart attacks.

MARION: I told you about that.

SGT. THECH: Cancer.

MARION: Bite your tongue!

SGT. THECH: Nervous or mental disorders.

MARION: I'm a nervous wreck!

SGT. THECH: Do you smoke?

MARION: You saw me. Remember? When you came in here, the first thing you said—

SGT. THECH: How much.

MARION: Three packs a day. Twenty cigarettes to a pack, that's sixty cigarettes. That's a lot of smoking.

SGT. THECH: Do you drink.

MARION: That, too, oh yes!

SGT. THECH: How much.

MARION: Whenever I smoke. Smoking makes me want to drink and drinking makes me want to smoke. It's a vicious circle.

SGT. THECH: Do you take any drugs?

MARION: Anything! Give it to me and I'll take it.

SGT. THECH: Name the drugs.

MARION: Aspirins and bromo seltzers for the hangovers, Nikoban for the smoking. And Miltown! I take lots of Miltown.

SGT. THECH: For what purpose.

MARION: Because I am a nervous wreck. For what purpose!

SGT. THECH: All right, Mr. Cheever, on the scale now, please. (*She turns and sees him draped in the American flag.*) Drop that flag.

MARION: I was just admiring it! I have one just like it at home. (*Sgt. Thech returns the flag to its proper place. Marion all the while walks along with it, unwilling to give up its protection.*) The same colors, the same shape. It's amazing how similar they are! (*Sgt. Thech is pulling the flag away from him.*) Then could I have a little robe or something? I mean I don't know if it's of any interest to you but I'm right on the verge of another bad cold. (*Sgt. Thech hands him a sheet.*) Thank you. Thank you. (*Sgt. Thech salutes the flag, then makes ready to examine Marion.*) I'm going to write somebody a letter about this.

SGT. THECH: On the scale.

MARION: (*Wrapping the sheet around himself.*) I'll refuse to go, you know. You're just wasting you're time, I hope you understand.

SGT. THECH: On the scale, Mr. Cheever. (*Marion gets on the scale and plays with the weights.*)

MARION: You know something? It's wrong. At least ten pounds off. Easily that.

SGT. THECH: Don't tamper. (*She is washing her hands.*)

MARION: What are you going to do? Operate? (*Sgt. Thech comes to the scale and weighs him. Next, she makes ready to measure him. When she raises up the measuring pole, Marion starts and backs off the scale.*) Would you warn someone before you do that? You know you could put someone's eye out with that thing.

SGT. THECH: Step back onto the scale. (*Marion gets back onto scale while Sgt. Thech measures him. When she swings the pole back into place Marion jumps off again.*)

MARION: You missed me by that much!

SGT. THECH: (*At the examining table.*) Sit on the edge of the table.

MARION: (*Under his breath.*) I hate this whole day! It's goddamn humiliating, that's what it is. Calling a man in here and—

SGT. THECH: On the table, Mr. Cheever.

MARION: (*Trying a new approach.*) I'm sorry I'm not cooperating. You have your job to do and I'll try to help in every way I can.

SGT. THECH: (*At his back, listening with a stethoscope.*) Breath. In, out. In, out.

MARION: In, out. See when you ask me how simple it is? (*Sgt. Thech's stethoscope is at his chest now. Marion is very ticklish.*) Don't do that! (*He laughs while Sgt. Thech listens to his heart.*)

SGT. THECH: Unh-hunh!

MARION: What did that mean? "Unh-hunh?" You heard something you didn't like?

SGT. THECH: Open. (*She has a tongue depressor down his throat.*)

MARION: Just ask me and I'll open! You don't have to lunge at me like that! (*Sgt. Thech checks his eyes with a light.*) It's on! (*Sgt. Thech looks into his ears with a light.*) I hate this. I hate it a lot. (*While Sgt. Thech checks his ears.*) When you were examining my heart, did you hear something I should know about? It wasn't very subtle, going "unh-hunh" like that. It's my ticker, so if there's anything wrong I'd like to know about it. (*Sgt. Thech has crossed the room. She turns to face him and speaks very softly. We just see her lips moving.*) What? What did you say?

SGT. THECH: Your hearing is perfect.

MARION: Now just a minute. I will not be railroaded.

SGT. THECH: (*Holding up an aye chart.*) Read this chart.

MARION: All of it?

SGT. THECH: The third line.

MARION: (*Running all the letters together.*) TOZDY!

SGT. THECH: The second line.

MARION: The second line's a little fuzzy.

SGT. THECH: Try the top line. Mr. Cheever.

MARION: (*With much squinting.*) The top line's a real problem. Let's see . . . it's a . . . no . . .Z!

SGT. THECH: Excellent.

MARION: Now just a minute. It's an E. I said it was a Z. Now I failed that test. You give me credit for failing.

SGT. THECH: Failure is relative in any case, private.

MARION: Private?

SGT. THECH: (*Back at the examining table.*) Lie down.

MARION: You called me private.

SGT. THECH: Lie down.

MARION: You've got me inducted already when I haven't even been given a full opportunity to fail yet.

SGT. THECH: This is your opportunity, Mr. Cheever, don't pass it up. (*Timing him until he obeys.*) One one-thousand, two one-thousand . . .

MARION: (*Getting onto the table.*) All right, I'm lying! Jut stop all that counting. (*Sgt. Thech begins to take his blood pressure.*) I've heard of shanghaiing but this little episode is really a lulu. It's white slavery if you think I'm passing this test. Out and out kidnapping. I simply won't go. You can't just take a man out of civilian life and plop him into the army. So there's a war on, I didn't start it. (*Lifts his head up a moment.*) I think you'll find I have a labile blood pressure. It can rocket at a moment's notice.

SGT. THECH: Keep your head down.

MARION: What do they want with me anyway? I'm on the verge of my big break. Do you know what that means to a civilian? I've stood in the back of that lousy theatre for eleven years and they are going to promote me next winter. I am going to be the manager at quite a substantial raise in salary, thank you. Unh-hunh, sergeant, I'm not going into any army, war or peace!

SGT. THECH: (*While she makes ready to take a blood sample.*) I want you to close your eyes and count to ten slowly and then touch the tip of your nose with your left index finger.

MARION: Oh, all right, that sounds easy. I don't mind this part at all. One, two, three, four . . . this is very restful . . . five, six— (*Suddenly sitting up.*) Wait! Wait, wait, wait, wait, wait! I saw it. (*Sgt. Thech is holding a syringe.*) I hate needles. I'm not afraid of them,

I just don't like them.

SGT. THECH: Shall I complete the forms, Mr. Cheever, or will you let me continue with the examination?

MARION: I know you must do your job, but please be very careful. I have very small veins. Don't be nervous.

SGT. THECH: Lie down.

MARION: You have all the time in the world. And no air bubbles! (*Sgt. Thech is drawing blood.*) Oh my God! I'm going to have a heart attack right on this table. (*Sgt. Thech finishes, empties his blood from the syringe into a test tube.*) I'm bleeding. Look at this, I'm bleeding. (*Sgt. Thech's hands go under the sheet as she checks his spleen, liver, kidney, etc.*) Just tell me what it is you're looking for and I'll tell you where it's at!

SGT. THECH: In.

MARION: In!

SGT. THECH: Out.

MARION: It's out!

SGT. THECH: In.

MARION: In! In! Oh my God, oh!

SGT. THECH: On your feet.

MARION: On my feet! Bleed someone to death and tell him on his feet. Sure, why not? Here I go, sergeant, on my feet!

SGT. THECH: Drop your shorts.

MARION: What?

SGT. THECH: You hear me. (*Timing him.*) One one-thousand, two one-thousand . . .

MARION: Drop my shorts? Oh no, sergeant, that I flatly refuse.

SGT. THECH: You're a candidate for national service. I am your examining officer and I am ordering you to drop your shorts.

MARION: (*While Sgt. Thech counts.*) Now wait just a minute. Let me explain something. I'm not wearing shorts. I have this . . . well, *problem.* . . and I have to wear this . . . well sort of a *girdle* and—

SGT. THECH: Drop your girdle.

MARION: (*As Sgt. Thech is nearing the count of ten.*) Yes! Yes, of course, I'll drop it. I just thought I should explain about my back problem and the abdominal muscles. I thought you'd want to know about them. (*Marion has worked off the girdle. It drops to the floor. Sgt. Thech is approaching him.*) It's off! I swear to God it's off! (*Sgt. Thech has her hand under sheet and at his groin.*)

SGT. THECH: Turn your head and cough.

MARION: Oh really!

SGT. THECH: Cough.

MARION: Cough!

SGT. THECH: Again.

MARION: Cough!

SGT. THECH: Again.

MARION: How many hernias are you checking for? Two's about average, you know. Cough!

SGT. THECH: Well done, Cheever. Now sit.

MARION: (*Sits on the edge of the examining table while Sgt. Thech checks him for reflexes.*) You're terrific you are! You and Pegeen ought to team up. She was my first wife. Talk about your lady wrestlers and roller-derby queens! But next to you, she was Snow White. But I foxed her. Just when she thought she had me where she wanted me, I sprang the divorce on her. On what grounds, may I ask? she growled . . . fat hands on her fat hips. . . Dutch Cleanser I used to call her. On exactly what grounds? (*Sgt. Thech is busy completing some forms.*) Mental cruelty, I smiled, and boy did that answer ever throw her for a loop! She begged me to change it to adultery but I held firm. You should have seen the look on that judge's face in Juarez when I dropped that little bombshell. Mental cruelty!

SGT. THECH: All right, Mr. Cheever, you can get dressed now. Your physical examination is over.

MARION: (*Caught in midair.*) Oh. It's over. Well that wasn't so bad. How did I do? Am I 4-F?

SGT. THECH: You have nothing to worry about. I found no evidence of physical abnormality.

MARION: (*Aghast.*) You found no evidence of physical abnormality? Now wait a minute. What about my labile blood pressure? On no. sergeant, I'm not done in here. Not yet. I want more testing. You're not convinced. I'm not leaving until I get a better verdict. What about my sinus condition? Did you know I had one? Of course not, you didn't look up my nose. What kind of examination is it without looking up a person's nose? A lot of things could be wrong up there. I can't breathe seven months out of the year. Would you write that down, please? And what about my eye test? I know I failed my eye test!

SGT. THECH: (*Busy at her desk tabulating the examination results.*) If you won't cooperate, I have to judge you on the basis of objective evidence. You do not squint, you're not wearing glasses and you saw my lips moving at a distance of over fifteen feet away. We have ways of evaluating the condition of a subject whether the subject cooperates or not. You'd have to be a lot smarter and better rehearsed than you are to fool an examining officer.

MARION: (*Triumphant.*) All right, then what about my feet? You didn't even make me take my socks off. That's all right. I'll do it myself. Here. Now look at this. They're flat. I'm not ashamed. See how flat they are? Do you see any arch? Of course you don't. You call that normal? And see, see all those corns? My feet are covered with corns. And I'll tell you something, something highly abnormal: I was born with all these corns. That's right, sergeant, I was born with corns. They are hereditary. Ask yourself, is that normal? (*Sgt. Thech continues working at desk.*) And look! (*He shakes his arms in front of her.*) No muscle tone. All flab! See how the skin just hangs there? And it's not a question of diet. I've dieted all my life. I simply don't burn fat! (*Now showing her his teeth.*) And teeth! My teeth. They're full of decay. If I have a candy bar I have to have an inlay. I swear to God I do. My gums are very spongy. I mean I'll probably have a coronary in five years . . . if I live very carefully. (*Desperately trying to attract Sgt. Thech's attention.*) And sergeant, here, watch this, look now, sergeant, over here, see this? . . . (*He removes is toupee.*) You didn't know that, did you? It fools lots of people but there it is. I lost all my hair in a period of thirteen months after my last divorce. It just went! Right out by the roots it came. Is that normal to lose so much hair in thirteen months? And that's not hereditary, sergeant. My father still has every hair in his head. You know what my kind of hair loss is? Nerves, sergeant, plain old-fashioned nerves! It's highly irregular he should have all his and I don't have mine! And what about my mind? You haven't asked me one single question about my mind. For all you know I could be a raving lunatic. I could be a—

SGT. THECH: (*She's into the psychological and intelligence tests.*) I have twelve apples.

MARION: (*Thrown.*) You have what?

SGT. THECH: You have twelve apples. Together we have. . .

MARION: (*Involuntarily.*) Twenty-four apples. (*He realizes what he's done and groans.*)

SGT. THECH: I have a pie which I wish to divide as follows: one-fourth of the pie to Fred, one-fourth of the pie to Phyllis, one-fourth of the pie to you. How much pie will I have left for myself?

MARION: (*Thinks a moment.*) Who are Fred and Phyllis? I mean maybe Phyllis didn't finish all her piece and then there'd be more for you. A quarter and a half!

SGT. THECH: You are on a train going sixty miles an hour. Your destination is a hundred and twenty away. How many hours will it take you to get to your destination?

MARION: I would say three days. But then I don't take trains. I really wouldn't swear to that answer.

SGT. THECH: Who was the first President of the United States?

MARION: George Washington. Was that right?

SGT. THECH: Who were the allies of the United States in the Second World War?

MARION: The good people.

SGT. THECH: Who were its enemies?

MARION: No one. We had no enemies.

SGT. THECH: Who are the allies of the United States now?

MARION: Just about everyone.

SGT. THECH: Who are its enemies?

MARION: Who can tell?

SGT. THECH: Name three of the twelve Apostles.

MARION: Joseph . . . and his brother . . . and his sister!

SGT. THECH: In what year did Columbus discover America?

MARION: 1776. No, wait, it was 1775!

SGT. THECH: What is the great pox and how does it differ from the small pox?

MARION: The great pox is greater than the small pox. However, both are poxes.

SGT. THECH: If you found an unopened letter lying on the sidewalk, fully addressed and stamped, what would you do?

MARION: I would probably step on it. I mean who wouldn't? You're walking along, you'd be surprised what you step on.

SGT. THECH: If you were seated in a theatre and you saw a fire break out nearby before the rest of the audience noticed it—what would you do?

MARION: This one's right up my alley. As a theatre manager I know about this. The main thing is I wouldn't want to start a panic. So I'd very quietly leave and go home.

SGT. THECH: If you found a wallet lying on the sidewalk—what would you do?

MARION: I'd be delighted. I never find anything.

SGT. THECH: What is the similarity between a chair and a couch?

MARION: A chair and a couch? You can sit on them.

SGT. THECH: A rabbit and a squirrel.

MARION: (*Reasonably.*) You could sit on a rabbit and a squirrel. The rabbit might even like it.

SGT. THECH: What is the difference between a giant and a dwarf?

MARION: The difference? I see the similarity all right but the difference is tricky.

SGT. THECH: A profit and a loss.

MARION: A profit is when the loss is greater than the sum. It's exactly like giants and dwarfs.

SGT. THECH: A man and a gorilla.

MARION: Hair. Lots of hair.

SGT. THECH: Complete the following sentences. People obey the law because . . .

MARION: Because! Because they have to obey it.

SGT. THECH: I am happiest when my family is . . .

MARION: Yes! I think we all are. Well aren't you?

SGT. THECH: What is the meaning of the following proverbs. He who laughs last laughs best.

MARION: Yes . . . well . . . that means that *he* who laughs *last* laughs *best.*

SGT. THECH: A rolling stone gathers no moss.

MARION: That's one of my favorites. It means that a rolling *stone* . . . gathers no *moss!*

SGT. THECH: I am going to say a word.

MARION: Did I get that one right?

SGT. THECH: After I say it I want you to say the first word that comes to your mind without thinking.

MARION: Are you sure?

SGT. THECH: You have one second. Tree. Tree!

MARION: I'm sorry. I was thinking. I couldn't help myself.

SGT. THECH: House.

MARION: House. The first word that comes to mind when you say house is house.

SGT. THECH: Father.

MARION: (*Drawing a blank.*) Father . . . father . . .

SGT. THECH: Grass.

MARION: Green. There, I got one!

SGT. THECH: Shower.

MARION: Tree. When it showers you stand under a tree with your father.

SGT. THECH: Snake.

MARION: Juicy. Juicy snake.

SGT. THECH: House.

MARION: Whores. No, no! that's not right.

SGT. THECH: Mother.

MARION: None. I mean—

SGT. THECH: Green.

MARION: Colors. Green colors.

SGT. THECH: Floor.

MARION: Me. Really! I'm on my feet all day.

SGT. THECH: Purse.

MARION: Snatch. Purse snatcher.

SGT. THECH: Have you ever suffered from night terrors?

MARION: Terribly.

SGT. THECH: Insomnia.

MARION: Of course insomnia! Because of the night terrors.

SGT. THECH: Sleepwalking.

MARION: Absolutely! In the morning my ankles are so swollen!

SGT. THECH: Anxiety states.

MARION: This is so good in here this part! Keep on.

SGT. THECH: Hallucinations.

MARION: Of grandeur. Of course terrible grandeur!

SGT. THECH: Delusions.

MARION: They're not the same thing? Listen, can't we go back to the anxiety states?

SGT. THECH: Compulsive eating.

MARION: No, I've never been bothered by that. About my anxiety states—

SGT. THECH: Have you ever indulged in homosexual activities.

MARION: They have been very good to me.

SGT. THECH: When did you stop?

MARION: Who said anything about stopping? They're a small but vital minority. The Fine Arts Theatre welcomes them.

SGT. THECH: Did you have a normal relationship with your mother?

MARION: I'm sure she thought so.

SGT. THECH: Did you have a normal relationship with your father?

MARION: After we stopped dating the same girl, everything was fine.

SGT. THECH: Do you have any history of bedwetting?

MARION: Even my top sheet is rubber.

SGT. THECH: Have you ever attempted suicide?

MARION: No, but I've thought of murder.

SGT. THECH: Are you now or have you ever been a member of the Communist party?

MARION: I wouldn't be surprised. I mean you join anything nowadays and next thing you know it's pinko.

SGT. THECH: What is your responsibility to your community.

MARION: Unh . . . to shovel the snow.

SGT. THECH: What is your responsibility to your family.

MARION: To be there.

SGT. THECH: What is your responsibility to your country.

MARION: To be there.

SGT. THECH: (*Abruptly.*) All right, Mr. Cheever, you may go now. The examination is over.

MARION: The whole thing?

SGT. THECH: That's right.

MARION: Well? How did I do? Am I 4-F yet?

SGT. THECH: I don't think you have anything to worry about. I doubt if they would find someone like you acceptable.

MARION: (*Stung but hiding it.*) Oh well good. Good. Based on what? The last two answers?

SGT. THECH: The entire psychological examination.

MARION: I see. Well then I *am* 4-F?

SGT. THECH: You'll get your classification in the mail.

MARION: I can hardly wait.

SGT. THECH: You may go now. I'm through with you. (*Sgt. Thech turns her back to him and begins typing up his test results.*)

MARION: (*Beginning to dress.*) Oh don't worry, I'm going. Nothing in the world could make me stay here. Granted, I've enjoyed all this. I mean you've been just wonderful. It must be difficult examining someone while they're still alive and breathing! And your attention has been so flattering. I'm not used to so much fuss. You're great, just great. The way you concentrated on me. I never distracted you from me once. I'm sure you have a big future ahead of you. (*Sgt. Thech types.*) Now you're through with me and would like me to go. You have taken my time, you have taken my blood, you have taken my urine, you have taken my secrets and now you would like me out of here so you can digest them in private. Isn't that right? Well I'm not going. If I go I take *all* of me with me. I'd like my blood and my urine back! I mean I'm 4-F, you can't have any use for them. (*Sgt. Thech types.*) You know I am not simply the sum total of my parts. I am someone. I am a citizen. I have my rights. I pay my taxes, I serve my jury duty, I buy American. I don't make trouble. I support the administration. I keep my mouth shut. I believe everything I read. I do all that and that gives me rights! I want my blood and urine back and I . . . I demand an apology! I have given everything to everyone and now I want something back! Don't tell me about responsibilities. I visit my kids, I bring them presents; I visit my father, I bring him presents; I visit my sisters, their kids get presents, too. I pay my rent; I pay my alimony; I meet my car payments—a hot red Mustang I can hardly fit behind the wheel of, but I'm meeting those payments! I do everything I'm supposed to do . . . I'm never late for work . . . and now I demand a reward! I want a reward. You owe me something. My country owes me something. Somebody owes me something. Because I have nothing! My big break? A lousy twenty-bucks raise. Big deal, crap! My children don't give a damn. What do I get on Father's Day? A lot of crap from Woolworth's their mothers picked out. My father doesn't recognize my voice on the telephone. My mother is dead. I've been married twice. You think it's fun, a man my age going home alone at night? Who looks at men like me after a while? I know what I look like! I'm no fool! (*Sgt. Thech continues typing.*) You know what the ushers at the theatre call me behind my back? Fatso. Yeah! that hurts. But when I become *the* manager I am going to fire those ushers and hire new ushers and *they* will call me Fatso behind my back. Because that is exactly what I am. A fatso. I am nothing but what I eat. But I feed myself. Nobody feeds me. And I eat everything I want. When I want candy, I eat candy. When I want a pizza at two a.m., I call up and order pizza. I'm going to get older and fatter and someday I'm going to die from overweight and smoking. But when I go, I'm paying for my own funeral and I'm going to give myself the best funeral that money can buy. Because dead or alive I pay my own way! Those niggers on relief, can they say that? They cannot! And they get to do everything. They get to riot, they get to loot, they get to yell, they get to hate, they get to kill! They get in the papers, they get on television and everybody pays attention. Everybody cares. And what do I get? There's nothing on television about me. My name's not in the Sunday papers. And I'm the one who does everything he should. I'm the one who never makes trouble. I'm the good citizen. But everybody else gets to do everything! You see those teen-age girls with their skirts up to here strutting around with their hair all piled up and driving a man crazy. And those men all like fags with that hair and those pants. They do anything they want. They have anything they want. And I get shit! (*He bangs on Sgt. Thech's desk with his fist. Sgt. Thech goes on typing.*) How dare you call me in here, examine me, ignore me, dismiss me and tell me I'm not acceptable. You are not acceptable! I want my orange juice. You took my blood and I want my orange juice. I know my rights. I want my radiator fixed. I want those people next door to turn their radio down when I bang on the wall. I want quiet. I want my sleep. I want them to stop all those parties upstairs. I want people to listen to me when I call up and make complaints. Not just sit there and type. Stop it! And listen to me! (*Sgt. Thech has finished typing up her report.*) I said stop! (*He puts his hands over the typewriter keys.*) Good. Very good! (*Now Marion will describe everything Sgt. Thech does while she is doing it—as if he were giving her the orders to do it.*) That's right. Fold the paper. Open the drawer. Put it away. Close it. Now you're doing exactly what you're told. Get up. Fold the sheet. Check the instruments. Make sure you've got everything. One final check now. Excellent. Now out you go. Close the door. There! (*Sgt. Thech has left the room, closing the door behind her.*) All right, on the scale now. Cheever! Do I have to? Why not? There's nothing to be afraid of. (*Marion gets on the scale.*) You're the perfect weight, just right for your height. You're an excellent physical specimen, Cheever. Am I? You're in very good shape. You're very acceptable. (*Marion steps off the scale.*) On the table now. (*Marion crosses to the examination table.*) Lie down. (*Marion obeys.*) Give me your arm. Will it hurt? Not you, Cheever. You're very brave. (*Marion moves his lips silently: "Can you hear what I'm saying?"*) Yes, you said, "Can you hear what I'm saying?" Your hearing is perfect. I know. Now read the chart. The last line, the smallest letters. "A-W-G-H-L." Excellent, you have perfect vision. Rest now. Thank you. (*Marion lets his head drop on the table.*) Tell me about it. I was thirteen years old. Yes, go on. I came home and she wasn't there. Yes. It was so sudden. None of us knew. We all thought she would always be there and then when she wasn't . . . (*His voice trails off in tears.*) You must have been very sad. I was, I was. I felt so cold. Didn't you tell anyone how you felt? Nobody asked me. I'm asking you. I never got to say good-bye. I understand. (*Short pause.*) On your feet now. I don't think I can. Yes, Cheever, you can do it. You're very strong now and very brave and very acceptable. (*Marion gets up off the table.*) Up now, shoulders back, walk tall. That's it. You're doing fine. (*Marion goes to Sgt. Thech's desk, puts on her white examination coat which she has left over her chair, sits, types a moment, then looks up.*) You have ten seconds to strip. By the power vested in me by the United States government I order you to remove all articles of clothing. One one-thousand, two one-thousand, three one-thousand, four one-thousand. Sorry. You are not acceptable. (*His head spins around as he looks straight ahead into the audience.*) NEXT! (*The lights snap-off.*)

Curtain.

¡Cuba Si!

for Melina Mercouri

¡CUBA SI! was first presented by the Act IV Theatre on July 16, 1968, at the Gifford House, Provincetown, Massachusetts, directed by Harris Yulin, with the following cast:

CUBA	Viveca Lindfors
FIRST FALSE MARIA	Lauren Simon
SECOND FALSE MARIA	Karen Mitchell
MARIA	Adele Mailer
REPORTER	Martin J. Cassidy
THIRD FALSE MARIA	Lauren Simon

Subsequently, ¡CUBA SI! was presented by Lucille Lortel at the ANTA Matinee Series on December 9 and 10, 1968, at the Theatre De Lys, New York City, directed by Harris Yulin, with the following cast:

CUBA	Viveca Lindfors
THE FALSE MARIAS	Susan Sharkey
MARIA	Lois Markle
REPORTER	James Catusi

Characters

CUBA
FIRST FALSE MARIA
SECOND FALSE MARIA
MARIA
REPORTER
THIRD FALSE MARIA

¡Cuba Si!

Explosions and sounds of gun fire are heard. Cuba runs on, dressed in khaki fatigues, swathed in cartridge belts, carrying a machine gun. The setting is Central Park.

CUBA: Bastard! Hooligan bastard! (*Volley of shots; Cuba flattens out on ground.*) You never get Cuba! Cuba get you first! (*She returns the fire.*) How you like those apples, Mr. CIA? (*Pause; then a single shot is returned.*) Okay, buster! You ask for it! (*Cuba lobs a grenade; explosion.*) Right in the kisser!

VOICE: (*Offstage.*) I'm dying, Cuba!

CUBA: Good.

VOICE: (*Offstage.*) What?

CUBA: GOOD! (*Cuba sits up, brushes off dirt.*) Bastard. Dirty hooligan bastard. (*Takes out a cigar, looks at the audience.*) Havana Corona. I smoke after battle fatigue. *Muy bueno.* You like? You can't have. Cuba *verboten* you. Anything Cuban *verboten* you. Cuba like China. Only Cuba is closer. Cuba is here. (*Bites off the cigar end, spits it out.*) I am Cuba. Cuba is my country and Cuba is my name. (*Lights the cigar, puffs.*) Why you say Cube-a? Is pronounced Cuba. Say it right or I kill you. (*She laughs hugely.*) How I get here? I hijack plane. Is cheap way to travel. Why I come? To make the revolution. Fidel call me in his office. He say, "Cuba, *vaya a los Estados Unidos* and make the revolution. I smell a rat brewing." And Fidel have a very good nose for rats. "*They* make the Bay of Pigs; *we* make the Bay of Pigs. I make you the vanguard of the revolution. *Hasta la vista. Ciao.*" For one year I am the vanguard of the revolution! I'm getting itchy. This is the tiny beachhead I have established in Central Park. Is pretty nice, too. I am waiting my reinforcements. Soon they come. Today I think. I wake up with a hunch. Your sky will buzz with friends of Cuba. Then we strike. Cuba very restless for ta-ta-ta-ta-ta! (*Pause.*) And Cuba very tired. (*Calls off.*) Maria, *chocolate caliente!* (*Then.*)

Everyone try to kill Cuba. They chase her up and down, under and over. Cuba running night and day from the assassins. Like a go-go girl they make her. Is awful life for her in *los Estados Unidos*. Cuba take a vacation when this thing blow over. Cuba go to Miami Beach. (*First False Maria enters with steaming choco-late.*)

FIRST FALSE MARIA: (*Blowing brightly.*) *Chocolate!* (*Cuba plugs her with revolver; First False Maria falls down dead.*)

CUBA: That not Maria. That was spy bitch with poison chocolate. You see how they all try to kill me? (*Another woman enters with chocolate.*) This is maybe Maria.

SECOND FALSE MARIA: *Chocolate!* (*Cuba plugs her with revolver; Second False Maria falls down dead.*)

CUBA: I had another hunch. (*Maria enters with chocolate.*) This looks like Maria. This looks very much like Maria. But I stay on tiptoe. I cross-examine her. (*Addressing her.*) Maria?

MARIA: Nnnnnnnnnnnn.

CUBA: *Come esta?*

MARIA: (*An expressive shrug.*) Mmmmmmmmmmmmm.

CUBA: (*Big smile.*) That's a clincher! (*She takes the chocolate. There is a terrific explosion right behind her.*) I fix you buster! (*She lobs a grenade; explosion, then silence.*) Are you dead?

VOICE: (*Offstage.*) Yes!

CUBA: Then go to hell! (*Sits with the chocolate.*) Son of a bitch, those buzzards get my goat. Like ten go-go girls they make me! (*To Maria.*) Maria, *despachalos!* (*Maria will remove the bodies of the two false Marias.*) That is Maria. She is my friend. You know what I mean? The only one who stick with me. Thick or thin, the rain and the snow, one year waiting, the days when no one comes: I have Maria. The bastards take her husband and her sons and kill them. They put them against a wall and pull a trigger. Maria saw this thing happen. They held open her eyes. They take every-thing she love and pull a trigger. Ever since that day, Maria talk very little. But she hate. When we make the revolution I make Maria a queen. Be good with this woman or I kill you three times. (*Looks at her watch.*) Soon they come, my friends. The hunch is growing all the time. (*Gets up, paces.*) I hate this Central Park! The ground has lumps and it's cold and it's damp. And I hate eating pigeons. I miss my country. I miss the sea. I miss Antonio. Ah! Antonio is my lover. My husband knows this, his wife knows this, Fidel knows this. But they don't dare to make the brouhaha. Is right? the brouhaha? Why? Because they are this big and Antonio is this big! Like a colossus he is! They peep at his legs like chickens they are so tiny. It is a love affair like two giants. When he holds me I am as big as that cloud. Bigger! Next to him you are shit. (*Pause.*) I said next to him you are all shit. (*Pause; she laughs hugely.*) Why you bite your nails? (*Reporter enters.*) Hands up, buster, or I plug you!

REPORTER: *Yo soy jornalista.*

CUBA: No interviews.

REPORTER: I'm from the *New York Times*.

CUBA: That's good?

REPORTER: It's not the *Village Voice*.

CUBA: I like the *Village Voice!* That's a hippie paper.

REPORTER: I'm sure the *Village Voice* likes you.

CUBA: I don't know about the *New York Times*.

REPORTER: (*Ready to write this down.*) So you like hippies?

CUBA: I said no interviews.

REPORTER: This piece will be for the Sunday edition.

CUBA: Sweetheart, *niño,* I'm an atheist.

REPORTER: I'm talking about circulation. Everybody buys the *Times* on Sunday. Even hippies.

CUBA: I'm too tired. Later, *chico.*

REPORTER: Quite frankly, and I'm being perfectly blunt, I think you and your revolution could stand a little plug.

CUBA: I plug you between the *ojos* you don't clear off my beachhead.

REPORTER: Then could you tell me where I might find Cuba Dos? Maybe she's willing to talk. What's the matter?

CUBA: I spit at that name.

REPORTER: But she's your ally.

CUBA: Cuba Dos is no ally. Cuba Dos is my archenemy and rival. I hate the bitch.

REPORTER: I really would like to see her.

CUBA: They call her Cuba Dos because she is the number two revolutionary woman in the world and I am the number one. She hates my guts. Cuba Dos is more dangerous for me than any spy bitch.

I fix her wagon good one day. Any questions, you talk to me!

REPORTER: But you—

CUBA: You make the interview, buster, or this time I really plug you. (*Calls off.*) Maria, *chocolate caliente para dos!* (*Big smile for Reporter.*) Okay!

REPORTER: (*Flustered.*) Give me a second!

CUBA: I give you two.

REPORTER: Unh . . . when did you first become involved with revolutionary politics? (*After a pause.*) Well?

CUBA: That's a ball breaker.

REPORTER: I mean when did you . . . how long have you been involved with subversive activities?

CUBA: (*Brightly.*) Why you bite your nails?

REPORTER: I'm sorry . . . was I? . . . it's a nervous habit. I—

CUBA: *Americanos* have too many nervous habits. They are tight, squeezed up, like fists. What you write?

REPORTER: What you just said.

CUBA: Why?

REPORTER: It's interesting.

CUBA: (*Laughs hugely.*) Bull shit! (*Third False Maria enters with chocolate.*)

THIRD FALSE MARIA: *Chocolate!* (*Cuba plugs her with revolver; Third False Maria falls down dead.*)

CUBA: They are so boring, these spy bitches. Are you a spy bitch, buster?

REPORTER: (*Horrified.*) Oh my God. (*Maria has entered with chocolate.*)

CUBA: *Despachala!* (*Maria takes out Third False Maria.*) You don't like chocolate?

REPORTER: You killed her.

CUBA: That's revolutionary politics, sweetheart. You think because I laugh I play games?

REPORTER: Just shot her dead.

CUBA: I kill them before they kill me. One day that change.

REPORTER: How many others have you . . . ?

CUBA: I'm not an adding machine.

REPORTER: Oh!

CUBA: You gonna make sick on yourself?

REPORTER: I'm not used to violence. I usually interview theatre personalities.

CUBA: You know Greta Garbo?

REPORTER: No!

CUBA: I adore Greta Garbo.

REPORTER: I'm just not used to the sight of blood.

CUBA: Garbo drinks it for breakfast! (*Huge laugh.*) You don't write
that down? *That* is interesting.

REPORTER: (*Composing himself.*) Now where were we?

CUBA: In Central Park. I am always in Central Park.

REPORTER: About your politics?

CUBA: It is because of my politics that I am always in Central Park!
You're a young man, so be a bright young man. Use your noo-
dle. You think I like it here? After Cuba? Have you ever been to
Cuba?

REPORTER: No.

CUBA: The air is that thick there! With the sea, with flowers . . . with
the scent of them . . . with music and people laughing.

REPORTER: People laughing? In Cuba?

CUBA: Yes!

REPORTER: (*Skeptical.*) I'll take your word for it.

CUBA: You better, buster! At night when the sea winds come I am a
very happy person.

REPORTER: You mean the little river breezes off our Hudson?

CUBA: I mean the sea winds in my Cuba. Here I can't breathe. Here
you have smog.

REPORTER: Smog's in Los Angeles.

CUBA: That's in California!

REPORTER: New York is sooty.

CUBA: Well I don't like it. I don't like this city.

REPORTER: Well of course you haven't seen very much of it.

CUBA: That's what you think, toots. At night I go around. I infiltrate.
The subways, the other parks, the Staten Island Ferry. I see
what's cooking and I don't like it. The rich people look sad, the
poor people look sadder.

REPORTER: Then you *are* a Communist?

CUBA: That's okay with me, sweetheart.

REPORTER: I mean you carry a card?

CUBA: My first husband carried a card. He's dead. I carry a gun.

REPORTER: (*Nervous; the gun is pointed at him.*) Unh . . . what else have you seen on your little nocturnal forays?

CUBA: Don't big word me, *chico*. What's a foray?

REPORTER: A trip.

CUBA: That's LSD.

REPORTER: A walk, a stroll.

CUBA: What's nocturnal?

REPORTER: Something that happens at night. (*Cuba laughs hugely.*)

CUBA: When something happens at night for me, it's not a walk!

REPORTER: I wish you'd put that gun away.

CUBA: (*Having thought it out, now proceeding with it carefully.*) Okay, how's this? On her nocturnal forays out of Central Park, Cuba has seen many things. Is right?

REPORTER: *Muy bueno.*

CUBA: *Habla espanol?*

REPORTER: *Muy poquito.*

CUBA: That's not so hot.

REPORTER: You started to say . . . ?

CUBA: Ah! This language barrier. I make a speech, I talk to the hippies in the Meadow of the Sheep and my heart is in my throat I get so scared I say the wrong words.

REPORTER: . . . what you've seen in the city?

CUBA: You give me a bum steer what means nocturnal foray?

REPORTER: Of course not.

CUBA: Give me one bum steer in my English and I kill you.

REPORTER: Please! You don't need that.

CUBA: I make you nervous?

REPORTER: Your gun goes.

CUBA: I put it away.

REPORTER: Thank you!

CUBA: You're still pretty nervous.

REPORTER: You've made me tense. Political writing isn't my thing. I told you I usually interview theatrical personalities.

CUBA: I'M NOT A THEATRICAL PERSONALITY?

REPORTER: No. Yes. I don't know.

CUBA: Why you don't know Greta Garbo?

REPORTER: I JUST DON'T. I'M SORRY, OKAY?

CUBA: Okay.

REPORTER: (*Still letting off steam.*) YOU KNOW NOT EVERYBODY IN THE WORLD CARES ABOUT YOU AND YOUR STINKING REVOLUTION. THERE ARE OTHER THINGS. LIKE REALITY, LADY. (*Pause.*) I'm sorry I . . . You were saying?

CUBA: (*Like recitation.*) On her nocturnal forays out of the park, Cuba has seen your city: it stinks. Your politicians: they stink. Your social programs: they stink. Your newspapers: they stink. Your public transportation: it stinks. Your architecture: it stinks. Your theatre: it stinks. Your cinema: it stinks. Your leader: he stinks. Your leader's lady: she stinks. A reporter: you stink. Only one thing does not stink: your young people. (*Pause.*) Why you say not everyone in the world care about the revolution?

REPORTER: I lost my temper. I said I was sorry.

CUBA: Why you say that?

REPORTER: It's not important. One man's opinion. Look, I'm here to interview you.

CUBA: If everyone in the world doesn't care about the revolution, then there will never be one.

REPORTER: No kidding.

CUBA: And there will be one.

REPORTER: Sure there will! Any minute now.

CUBA: You don't believe me.

REPORTER: My grasp on reality is fairly sound, thank you!

CUBA: *De nada.*

REPORTER: Take a look around you. One year you've been here. Where are your allies? What have you accomplished?

CUBA: My *friends* are coming.

REPORTER: Where are they?

CUBA: In the air maybe. Any minute now!

REPORTER: Do you think if anyone big took you or your revolution very seriously you'd be allowed to stay here smack in the middle of a public park?

CUBA: No one allows me. This is a beachhead. I establish it, I defend it!

REPORTER: With what?

CUBA: My life.

REPORTER: Two policemen with Mace could clear you out of here in five minutes.

CUBA: Let them dare! (*Then.*) What's Mace?

REPORTER: A chemical they use for controlling civil disorders.

CUBA: It hurts, this Mace?

REPORTER: (*Nodding.*) And it causes temporary blindness.

CUBA: The bastards!

REPORTER: You're scared of pain?

CUBA: Of course I am.

REPORTER: I thought people like you thrived on it.

CUBA: That's because people like you don't know nothing.

REPORTER: Actually, I don't think you have much to worry about. They'll probably let you stay here indefinitely. At least through spring.

CUBA: No one *let's* me stay here. This is a guerrilla camp.

REPORTER: It's a tourist attraction.

CUBA: You're the only tourist in it, buster.

REPORTER: And not a very well attended one from the look of things.

CUBA: I don't listen to you no more.

REPORTER: With winter coming on, the skating rink is bound to out-draw you.

CUBA: What skating rink?

REPORTER: All you're getting now is overflow from the zoo.

CUBA: Fuck *The New York Times* and fuck you, too.

REPORTER: Even your hippies are deserting you.

CUBA: *The Village Voice* adores me.

REPORTER: Sure! That's why they're all over at the Mall digging the Airplane or turning on. Free rock's a tough act to compete with. So's pot.

CUBA: Cuba's airplanes drop pot bombs on all of you.

REPORTER: People get bored, Cuba. They want novelty.

CUBA: I show them novelty.

REPORTER: Just look how sparse your crowd is. Six months ago you had twice that number on a good day like this.

CUBA: What you mean, my crowd?

REPORTER: (*Pointing.*) There. Those people behind the police barriers looking over here through binoculars. (*While Cuba scans the distant crowd through her own pair of binoculars.*) It's kind of sweet how the police look out for you people. Mayor's orders, of course. It gives the city a nice liberal reputation. The binoculars were some smart little Jew's idea. He rents them out for twenty-five cents an hour.

CUBA: I never saw these people before. *Ça, c'est formidable!* (*Calling.*) Maria, *mira! Venga aquí y mira!* (*Maria joins her.*) And they say Cuba has no friends!

REPORTER: Friends? Those are gawkers, freak collectors!

CUBA: My hunch was true!

REPORTER: You know what they call you? The Madwoman of Central Park.

CUBA: *Venceremos*, Maria!

REPORTER: The snotty ones with college degrees make that La Folle de Central Park.

CUBA: (*Putting down her binoculars.*) *Merde* on you, *chico*, this is the day I have been waiting for! (*Waving to the people.*) Friends! *Amigos!* You have come and Cuba welcomes you! Fidel promised you would be here when I needed you! Fidel has not lied. Come! Join me! Together we make the revolution. Today is the day. The moment is now. We are the moment.

REPORTER: Not a mouse stirring.

CUBA: They can't hear me.

REPORTER: (*Shaking his head.*) Trouble is, they have!

CUBA: (*Using a bull horn.*) Friends! *Amigos* of the revolution! I am Cuba. I have waited for you a very long time. You have come this far, now come all the way! Together we shall join hands and overcome. The revolution is ours. Make it yours and come. Join me, *amigos!* (*Getting a chant started.*) *Ven-ce-re-mos! Ven-ce-re-mos! Ven-ce-re-mos!* (*An egg is thrown.*)

REPORTER: Say, that kid's got a terrific arm on him!

CUBA: Wait! Listen to me! The time has come to step forward. Do not go back. (*More eggs are thrown.*) Among you are friends of Cuba. Her lovers!

REPORTER: They're drifting off.

CUBA: (*Singling out individuals.*) You! Are you a man who looks about him and says this will not do? Yes? Then you are Cuba's lover!

REPORTER: That guy's looking for a john.

CUBA: And you! Mister! A man who is not indifferent when there is hunger and despair. *Si? Si!* I call you my lover!

REPORTER: You're losing him to the Good Humor man.

CUBA: Amigo! Wait! I know you! A man who says politics belong to the people and not the fools and crooks! Come back then! You too are Cuba's lover!

REPORTER: Sounds like Cuba's a whore.

CUBA: Cuba embraces you! Her arms are large!

VOICE: (*Offstage.*) And so's her mouth! All men are her lovers! And they are always among you!

REPORTER: They've all gone, lady. (*To Maria.*) Tell her, hunh? It's all over.

CUBA: (*Still using the bull horn, but her voice growing less and less loud so that at the end of the speech she is almost talking to herself.*) You who walk the shoreline and feel the sun on their backs, the wind on their face and smell the sea smells and their hearts burst for being alive . . . those men are Cuba's lovers. Your poets are her lovers . . . your students and young people, *todos amantes!* . . . An old woman whose eyes are still bright, she is my lover, too. . . Any man or woman whose heart beats quicker, they are my lover and my friend . . . Come join hands with Cuba and together we will make the revolution. (*Pause.*)

REPORTER: Are you up to a little friendly advice after all that? Look, call it a day, why don't you? Pack up your tents and ponchos and go back where you came from. There must be a hundred flights a day to Miami. You've got a pistol. I don't imagine a little non-scheduled stop-over in Havana would phase anyone. Not any more.

MARIA: (*With terrifying force and suddenness.*) VENCEREMOS!

CUBA: (*Softly.*) Venceremos, Maria. (*Maria withdraws.*)

REPORTER: You're staying? (*Cuba nods her head.*) But there's not going to be a revolution. (*Cuba is still nodding her head.*) You saw what just happened. Americans are happy, that's what you people don't understand about us. (*During this he prepares to photograph Cuba.*) Well maybe "happy" is the wrong word but at least we're content. We're a country that's pretty well satisfied with itself. And with good reason. Sure we've got problems, but we're big enough to absorb them and we're big enough to settle them. Peacefully. We're so big about it we can even absorb you. We'll let you speak your piece . . . a little smile now! . . . only don't be too surprised when no one's willing to listen to you. (*Cuba gives him that "little smile"; Pow! the flashbulb goes off.*) Now I can understand revolutions where you come from. I think the heat causes most of them. Everyone gets itchy in the summertime. Only you've got it all year long. Some people think air-conditioning Harlem would settle our racial problems. They're being facetious, of course . . . okay, another smile now. . . but still, when did you last hear of trouble in a place like Maine? (*Cuba is smiling; Pow! of the flashbulb.*) Revolutions are for humid little countries with dictators. America's a big air-conditioned democracy. Oh all right, so there was France and Russia, even this country once . . . chin up now, look determined . . . but there was a need for those revolutions. An historical need. But this is *now.* (*Cuba's chin is up; Pow! of the flashbulb.*) Sure there's talk of trouble flaring up here. I'm sure you've read the papers. It's probably why you're here. Well, you're too late. Or you're sure as hell too early. Look this way now. Nothing's going to happen. Not in the ol' U.S.A. (*Pow.*) You can talk all you want about disorder and violence but planting bombs in subways never solved anything. Sure you can frighten people but . . . hell, *I'd* be frightened if I thought it would ever come to arson and snipers . . . is there some kind of victory sign you could give me? Terrific! . . . but the day this country comes to anarchy is the day I ship out. (*Cuba gives him a victory sign; Pow!*) You people are barking up the wrong tree. Sure there's things wrong with this country, but we'll work it out. We're a democracy, remember. And a minority of radicals isn't going to intimidate us . . . let me get a shot of you eating that pigeon . . . I know what you people want and how you want it—on a silver platter. Sorry, Cuba, in this country you get what you deserve, not what you *think* you deserve when in truth you don't deserve anything. Hold it! (*Pow!*) That stuff you preach, it won't make any headway here. Cuba is for Cubans and you're a hell of a long way off base as far as anyone in the big leagues is concerned. (*Pow!*) Take a tip. Go on back home. You don't scare anyone. (*Starts to pack up; Cuba still hasn't moved from her pose.*) You know something? and I like you, you sit there much longer waiting for God-knows-what to happen and you *will* be the Madwoman of Central Park. (*Cuba is motionless.*) Suit yourself lady. But it's going to be long cold winter. And a longer, colder one after that.

CUBA: (*Turning to him.*) You got your story, buster?

REPORTER: No, but I got my interview. There is no *story.* Stories have beginnings, middles and ends.

CUBA: I give you a beginning.

REPORTER: Well at least that's a start.

CUBA: Maybe I give you a middle.

REPORTER: I'm listening.

CUBA: I might even give you an end. (*There is an ominous rolling sound from the heavens. It sounds very much like the rumble of approaching airplanes. The Reporter looks up startled. Cuba begins to laugh. but it is only thunder and the first drops of rain have begun to fall. The Reporter forces a nervous smile and hurries off. The thunder grows louder and the rain is falling harder. And there is Cuba, sitting on her rock, getting drenched, smiling now . . . waiting. A terrific flash of lightening, a very loud clap of thunder and blackout.*)

Curtain.

Sweet Eros

for Robert Drivas

SWEET EROS was produced by Michael Ellis on November 21, 1968, at the Gramercy Arts Theatre, New York City, directed by Larry Arrick with the following cast:

YOUNG MAN . . . . Robert Drivas
GIRL . . . . Sally Kirkland

SWEET EROS was first presented by the Theatre-In-Progress Workshop of the Berkshire Theatre Festival on July 22, 1968, at the Lavender Door, Stockbridge, Massachusetts, directed by Gordon Rogoff with the following cast:

YOUNG MAN . . . . Spencer Trova
GIRL . . . . Joan Pape

Subsequently, SWEET EROS was presented by the Act IV Theatre on July 30, 1968, at the Gifford House, Provincetown, Massachusetts, directed by Ann McIntosh, with the following cast:

YOUNG MAN . . . . Andrew Winner
GIRL . . . . Lisa Richards

This production was then invited to the 1st International Experimental Theatre Festival at Brandeis University, Waltham, Massachusetts, on August 20, 1968.

Characters

YOUNG MAN
GIRL

Sweet Eros

Scene 1

The stage is dark. Then a large hanging lamp comes slowly on. In the narrow pool of light it sheds we see a chair with its back to us. Seated in the chair, her hands tied behind her, is the Girl. She has long auburn hair.

Sitting near her on a low stool is the Young Man. He is in his middle twenties, good-looking, trim. He watches her closely.

YOUNG MAN: Hello. (*The Girl struggles to free herself.*) Don't. (*He continues to stare at her. Slow blackout.*)

Scene 2

The scene is the same as before. In the pool of light we see the Girl, still tied in the chair. The Young Man is watching.

YOUNG MAN: So there's really no reason it was you. Once I'd made my mind up, it could have been anyone. You just happened to cross my path before the next person. (*He lowers his eyes.*) I said there'd be no lies. (*He looks up at her.*) It couldn't have been just anyone. I wouldn't have taken a child or an older person. Someone in a religious order. A handicapped person, I wouldn't have taken a young man my age. A lot of people I wouldn't have taken. I wanted a girl. (*The Girl struggles.*) Don't. (*The Girl doesn't stop.*) Please. (*The Young Man sits watching her. Slow blackout.*)

Scene 3

The scene is the same as before.

YOUNG MAN: So I suppose it was inevitable. I mean when you want to do something that bad that long, sooner or later you do it. The morality of it doesn't even enter the question. Not after a while. There comes a day when what's right is what you want to do and what's bad is what you want to do and don't. And I wanted this for a long time. It was preying on me, getting me down. There were nights I couldn't sleep, thinking about it. It started off just being an idea . . . one of those cool, safe abstractions that never got anybody into trouble . . . and then damnit if it didn't go erotic on me. I mean I really couldn't sleep. That's when I knew I was really in a bind. But the whole plan just seemed so damned risky! Not unreasonable, mind you, but risky. You can imagine: the police, the one chance in a million of hurting you, morning-after remorse on my part. The same things that cross a murderer's mind probably. And then yesterday morning, overnight, just like that, I woke up thinking. "What the hell?" I'm young, reasonable–looking, clean—certainly I wouldn't terrify her and maybe she'll like me by the time it's over. I'm rich enough—so there's money when it's done if she's got hard feelings. I'm in the country—no chance of neighbors hearing if I took the gag off too soon. And I'm a good person. Mmm. I like myself. That's important. Well, all that's what I was thinking when I woke up yesterday. So I took the car, drove into the city, saw you walking your dog (I assume it was yours), and here you are. Easy. (*He lowers his eyes, then raises them.*) I had to kill the dog. (*The Girl struggles.*) He barked. (*The Girl continues to struggle.*) HE BARKED! (*The Girl stops struggling.*) He was a nice dog. I'm sorry he barked. (*He smiles at the Girl; sits watching her. Slow blackout.*)

Scene 4

The scene is the same as before.

YOUNG MAN: If you really look at another person, you'll find they're rather strange. Oh, I recognize the physical resemblance, but after hair, nose, eyes, mouth, teeth, neck, arms, legs and all, it stops. The resemblance, I mean. Once you're done with externals, people are pretty strange propositions. Know what I mean? (*He smiles.*) I think insects are less strange to one another than people are. Take ants. An ant either really accepts another ant or he doesn't even think about it. The point is, they cooperate. There's no friction with ants. They make do. Then take people: they don't accept each other, which is fact number one about them, and fact number two, that's *all* they think about. So there's non-cooperation, friction. Let's face it: humans are tense together. (*He takes off her shoes.*) My first woman . . . notice I don't say wife . . . was so fraught she couldn't cope at all. They carted her off eventually. And yet you'd have thought she had everything going for her: good background, I mean she was bred within an inch of her life; a big fat inheritance after a touching reunion with her daddy on his deathbed; a spiffy career (though I didn't care much for her work after the first few collages, somebody up there liked those monumental oils she'd knock off over the weekend); and me. I include myself in this girl's cornucopia because I loved her. I mean she was lucky. Somebody *cared* and, sister, there aren't words enough to tell how much I loved this person. (*He is taking off her stockings now.*) Sounds ideal, no? For her, I mean. Well, there was a fly in this girl's ointment, and he had two arms, two legs, and his name was me. She couldn't stand me. No, I'm confusing you. She could stand *me*; it was my love for her she couldn't stand. This was a girl who could not bear to be loved and believe me when I tell you this person worshiped her. Oh, she was holy to me! I was just out of college when we met, she was a few years older; so maybe the flaw, I mean the fly, was already there. That's what her friends said. Only I didn't believe that. I still don't. I loved her. It should have been enough. At least it should have mattered. (*He starts to unbutton her blouse.*)

So there we were. Me loving her; her . . . liking me, enjoying the company but hating how much closer I wanted us to be, even the thought of it. Nevertheless, I loved here more every day and every day the worse it got. She took to drinking, ridiculing my work (I was teaching the new math at the time), neglecting the housework (we'd set up welter-weight housekeeping), sleeping around (with *my* friends—otherwise I wouldn't have minded—I would have cared but I wouldn't have minded) and generally making a pig of herself. (*He has worked her blouse down over her bound arms.*) Pig whore, I started calling her. Pig whore. She'd smile at that and show her rotten teeth (I never figured out how she could have made a Palm Beach debut with a mouth like that) and just call me something worse. Her names for me would change, but not mine for her. It was perfect. Pig whore! Pig whore! Oh, did we ever scrap! (*He takes off her bra.*) Real knock-down-drag-outs. Name calling, doors slamming, fisticuffs, the works. Only trouble with that was I'd feel just rotten every time I landed her a good rap on the mouth. When she got me with an ashtray she'd laugh and shriek and jump up and down, show all her teeth. Always aimed for the groin, too. God, she was cunning! But when I'd land her a fistful (I didn't think men should throw things) I'd instantly feel the most incredible remorse. I'd help her up, walk her to the bathroom, clean the blood up. It used to ruin my evenings. God, it was frustrating. (*He is working her skirt down over her ankles.*) Anyway, years passed like this. Three, to be exact. And then there was this one morning. Like yesterday. I woke up, sensed her in the bed beside me (her breath reeked in the A.M.; Bat Breath, I called her), and thought to myself, "I've had it." So I dressed, left her a note and never saw the silly bitch again. (*He pulls down her half-slip.*) They say she woke up about four that afternoon (a little late, even by her standards), scrounged around for her instant coffee, found the note and promptly went berserk. She went into a deep and swift decline, buoyed herself briefly with her gallery owner (he'd lusted for her since the first pale collage), found out he was queer to boot, declined some more, made a public ass of herself at three consecutive *vernissages* and one museum opening, and was eventually committed to an asylum somewhere upstate. Now her decline and fall, mind you, except that last part, could all be hearsay. Like I said, I never saw the silly bitch again. (*Short pause.*) But she'd taught me a lesson. People . . . and I didn't include myself . . . people don't like to be loved. (*He removes her panties.*) My second woman . . . well, she taught me something, too. When we met, soon after my famous note, she was young (younger than myself, she insisted, though I was never convinced of it), successful (she modeled; pick up any issue of one of those magazines and there she was), and beautiful. It hurt to look at her. I mean she dazzled the eyes and I'm not one for overworked clichés. And the cherry on the icing was this: this Venus, this Juno, this Cybele loved me! (*Pause.*) So now I had everything going for *me*. I was adored! I mean this girl was put on earth for no other purpose than to love. She did things for me you couldn't get a concubine to do. Alcohol rubs! The most intricate, thirteen-herbs-and-twelve-saucepans recipe prepared any hour of the day at my convenience. She hand–laundered my shirts and I mean she was up to here in suds. And then she ironed them and put them on hangers. She shined shoes, this girl! Personal services you can't *buy* any more. But she was more than a domestic, you understand. I'd given up teaching and started writing by then. She helped me! She wouldn't just read the poems and smile and nod her head. No, she'd take a pencil and make *x*'s, change words, edit, everything! When the work was good she made me feel like a king. When it wasn't she'd tell me why and I'd still feel like the best poet who ever lived. A divine amanuensis, yes! but Euterpe too! She inspired poetry! In bed we started out a house afire and then proceeded to total conflagration. I mean there was nothing she wouldn't do to satisfy me. Me. Nothing. You understand what those two words mean in bed? Love-making so violent I couldn't stop until I'd made her cry out. And another night I'd be so tired I'd just lay back and let her please me. I say "let her." She wanted to. And dark sex: the kind you dream about in your deepest self. I could tell her and she'd understand. She accepted those desires. Things done on an ottoman, in chairs, over chairs. A touch of leather, a taste of violence, the merest suggestion of costume. All the ways of making love, even when it's not. (*Pause.*) Our nights were nearly perfect then, our sleep like two cubs cuddled, our mornings a time for the dearest laughter, our days productive and meaningful (we were each a beaver about our work), and our evenings so quiet and gentle alone together that she lost all desire to see other people. I remember when the television broke and she never even bothered to have it fixed. And she'd liked her TV in the beginning. (*Short pause.*) A different girl, a different ointment, but the same fly, alas. I couldn't stand her loving me. Here I had everything I wanted . . . well, everything I thought I wanted . . . and I didn't want it at all. This time I didn't leave a note. I told her to her face. When she came in that day, I went straight to the point. "I don't love you." She just looked at me. I didn't have to explain; she understood. "I don't love you." Let's say I thought she understood. We slept together that night . . .we even tried making love, only you can imagine it wasn't like before . . . and the next morning she helped me pack my things. She kissed me when I left . . . smelling like flowers (she always did in the mornings after her bath; I remember that), I waited until about six that evening before calling her to see how she was getting on. I was glad when she didn't answer. It meant she was out meeting people. I had a date, why shouldn't she? She was getting over it. Good! I thought. After all, feelings change. Mine had, so were hers. The next night, again no answer. I didn't even feel guilty any more. In fact, I was a little miffed—maybe she'd turned wanton on me. About the sixth day I began to get worried. There weren't mutual friends to call simply because there weren't any. She'd cut them all off, remember. And yet I didn't want to use the key (naturally, she'd let me keep it). What if she were with someone? Or worse, what if she weren't? I couldn't humiliate her like that. But by the tenth day I forgot all about the pros and cons of it and just went over there. I had this terribly strong desire to make sure she was all right. Know what I mean? I suspected the worst but it was more terrible than that. She was lying on the bed, the bottle of pills on the floor beside her. She was nude. The cat (oh yes, we'd kept one . . . an orange tabby she insisted on calling Melville) looked up startled when I entered the bedroom and scurried away. He'd eaten away a good deal of her face, you see, naturally there'd been no one to feed him, and I guess he knew he was in for a spanking. I called the police. There was an autopsy, cause of death listed as probably suicide and a rather shabbily, I thought, attended funeral. But then she hadn't wanted friends after me. There was no note, of course. (*Short pause.*) Since then I've lived alone out here in envy of the ants. I think I understand them. People just . . . seem strange to me. People . . . and since her too I've had to include myself . . . people don't like to be loved. (*He undoes a ribbon. Her hair tumbles over her shoulders.*) What I want from you is simpler. (*He removes the gag, rests his hand on her shoulder. The Girl struggles. Soundlessly, he moves his mouth: "Don't." Slow blackout.*)

Scene 5

Pow! Pow! Pow! The sounds of a battery of exploding flashbulbs are heard. Only the silhouettes of the two characters are seen.

YOUNG MAN: Violence. Don't talk to me about violence. Eight million kikes. (*Pow!*) They *think* eight million kikes. (*Pow!*) Niggers nobody keeps statistics on. (*Pow!*) Napalm can make a chin slide down to a chest and stick there. Melt fingers till they're webbed. (*Pow!*) Heads cracking open on dashboards. Steering columns crunching through chests. An eye speared out on a door handle. (*Pow!*) My mother died of uterine cancer. (*Pow!*) Old Mrs. Groner, the fruit stand down the road, eighty-one and arthritic, found with her throat slit. Her purse was missing. It had $1.42 in it. (*Pow!*) The dog barked, you understand. He barked. (*Pow!*) Violence. Don't talk to me about violence. (*Pow! Pow! Pow! Pow! Blackout.*)

Scene 6

Gentle music is heard. The Young Man is sitting on the stool holding a bowl of soup and feeding the Girl with a spoon.

YOUNG MAN: The happiest day of my life? There've been so many. I might choose a year, though. (*He dabs her lips with a napkin.*) Careful. (*He goes on feeding her.*) The eighth grade. That was the year everything happened to me. I got to kiss girls on the mouth; I had my own identity tag for the city pool; when my mother drove me places she stopped coming in; I started liking my little brothers; I had to pay full price admission to the movies. Oh, that was a very good year for me! (*Spoon in hand.*) Wider. (*Then he takes some for himself.*) We organized a club, some boys and I. We called it the Smut Club . . . "smut" was a very big word then . . . and we met in a storage room over Mel Porter's garage. We'd go there after school . . . it was parochial and very strict . . . to smoke cigarettes, play poker, look over our infinitesimal collection of soft-core pornography for the God-knows-what-hundredth time. All the good parts in the books were carefully marked, so you didn't have to waste time reading the clean parts. The magazines were mainly *National Geographics* but there were a couple with white girls with no tops on. Mel's brother gave us a picture he bought in Paris that had two people in it, but it was blurry and they were Chinese or something. One of the guys, Jim I think his name was, taught us to masturbate up there. His brother had taught him and he was crazy to show us. Well, we were appalled. A couple of us actually were sick. But of course we all raced the hell home to try it out for ourselves. It was like an epidemic, the way it caught on. Father Flynn had so many confessions of it over one weekend that he kept us all in after school and made a little speech about how bad it was for you. It didn't faze anyone; we just stopped telling him about it. (*The Girl is resisting the soup.*) You'll need your strength. (*The Girl takes the soup.*) And that was the year I did something cruel. Oh, it was boyish, to be expected perhaps, but nevertheless it was cruel. We had a lay art teacher in the eighth grade. I mean she wasn't a nun. I guess this lady was the fattest woman who ever lived.

Three hundred pounds and I don't exaggerate. Somehow she managed to play tennis. To keep her figure, we used to snicker. One day, filing in from recess, we saw her tennis shorts on the back seat of her car. We put them on, four of us, two in each leg, and marched into class like that. She was at the blackboard; the class went into an uproar. She pretended she was angry, of course, and told the sister to keep us after school. But she was hurt and we never saw that woman again. (*Short pause.*) It just came to me! There was one night I'd call the happiest of my life. It was a hayride. The whole class went. There was a full May moon. We laughed a lot, pushed one another off the wagon and spiked our Cokes with rum. I kissed the girl I wanted to kiss and came home covered with hay. That's all I can remember and yet I'd swear it was the happiest time of my life. I don't know why. I was just happy then. That was the eighth grade, too. (*The Girl shakes her head, resisting more soup.*) It's homemade. (*The Girl shakes her head again, stops, accepts the soup.*) That's better. (*He takes a spoonful. Slow blackout.*)

Scene 7

The Young Man is reading from a hand-written letter.

YOUNG MAN: And I was thinking of mailing this for you! (*Finds his place.*) " . . . I'd better go now. So, don't be too surprised if I just up and quit the job and head out there. I'm not pushing marriage, understand, I like our arrangements fine, only so much sleeping alone is bad for my complexion. Ha ha ha!" (*To the Girl.*) Close your legs, hunh? (*Back to the letter.*) "Oh, remember your slipper Spud liked to gnaw on? The sides are all gone and he's working on the sole. That dog! I swear! Well, that's it for now, lover. Nothing else is new. If anyone ever tells you working in a bank is fun, tell them from me they're crazy. And don't let your hair get any longer; you'll spend half your nights like me— in curlers. You artistic types! And then there's little me, the slave of convention, but can I help it if I'm the stable kind? But I guess you've had your fill of Boho's. (Bohemians, female species. Ha ha ha!)" (*To the Girl.*) Your thighs. I asked you to close them. Together. Tight. Like this. (*Back to letter.*) "I'm signing off now, *hombre mio.* The late show is coming on and it's a good one tonight. Terry Moore and Robert Wagner. I think I saw it when it was new, but I'm not positive. I've got the new *Life*, just in case. So. And this time I mean it. But honey, meeting you is the only thing that ever happened to me worth shaking a stick at. Oh, Charlie, I miss you and want you and need you and love you and want you so bad! I never felt like this about anyone anytime anywhere. I swear to God I never did. Write me you love me, even a little bit. Ooooooooo! the movie just came on and I haven't seen it! I love you. Xxxxxxxxxxx. Pam." (*To the Girl.*) YOUR THIGHS. I WANT THEM CLOSED, YOU SPRAWLING PIECE OF BAGGAGE. COVER YOURSELF. (*Pause.*) Silly bitch. (*He rips up the letter. Slow blackout.*)

Scene 8

The sounds of a running shower are heard offstage. The Girl has a knife in her hands and is trying to cut herself free.

YOUNG MAN: (*From the shower.*) Of course they would! People don't understand arrangements like ours. Remember how *you* resisted when—Ow! Is that a bitch when the water runs cold or isn't it? . . . Hey, you stopped!

GIRL: (*Singing, at once.*)
Plaisir d'amour ne dure qu'un moment
Chagrin d'amour dure toute la vie.

YOUNG MAN: (*While she sings.*) But now we're getting along beautifully, don't you think? I mean you must be pretty used to me by now. Again!

GIRL: (*Singing, at once.*)
Plaisir d'amour ne dure qu'un moment

Chagrin d'amour dure toute la vie.

YOUNG MAN: I feel like writing tonight. You can amuse yourself, can't you? . . . Hoo! that soap's slippery!

GIRL: *Plaisir d'amour . . .* (*The knife falls; her hands are still bound, her wrists bloodied. The Girl stops singing; the water is turned off. A short silence. The Young Man appears at the edge of the light, fully dressed. He comes to her, frees her wrists, wipes away the blood.*)

YOUNG MAN: (*Gently.*) Silly bitch. (*Slow blackout.*)

Scene 9

The Girl is in the chair. The Young Man is kneeling before her. He has a clipboard on which he will make notes.

YOUNG MAN: (*Scrutinizing the Girl's face under a large magnifying glass.*) Unless you're willing to go over someone with a fine-tooth comb (that's a scratchy metaphor!), you miss so many details about them, I should think. (*With a tape measure.*) Right shoulder . . . (*Measures it, writes it down.*) Left . . . one-eighth of an inch longer. I've got one that's higher than the other. It's not uncommon. (*Using the magnifying glass.*) Oh oh! There's a blackhead ripe for squeezing if I ever saw one. (*Notes it down.*) I wouldn't touch that mole on your neck for a thousand dollars. (*Pauses a moment to rub his eyes.*) Close work is tiring, you can't imagine. (*Examines her eyes.*) Aha! They're gold-flecked, your eyes. You see, and all along I was thinking there was nothing interesting about them. That's something else that's new about you. People are eternally interesting, the closer you look. Still, they're so strange! Don't move. (*He removes something from her eye with tweezers.*) A bit of lash. Almost microscopic. (*Makes a note of it.*) Very good. Working with you I find a steady, decisive hand absolutely essential. (*He leans toward her.*) Say when. (*Slow blackout.*)

Scene 10

The stage is in darkness; the chair is empty.

YOUNG MAN: There! Get your knees up higher. That's it. (*Short pause.*)
An East-West alliance is our only solution. Unfortunately, we're
years from one. I'm afraid it's chaos staring us in the face for another two decades at the very least. (*Short pause.*) I come fast.
(*Short pause.*) I had an active interest in world affairs for a long
time. I mean I was fiercely political. A lot of us were. Only . . .
(*He moans; then silence. He lights a cigarette, regards her by the
light of the match.*) I was saying something. (*He blows out match.
Blackout.*)

Scene 11

*The Girl is in the chair. The sound of a typewriter is heard off-
stage.*

YOUNG MAN: (*Offstage.*) "The end." (*After a moment, the Young Man
enters with a manuscript.*)
YOUNG MAN: It's good, it's very good. I'm going to be famous. (*Reading over what he has written.*) "The girl is sitting in the chair. For
days now there has been no rope. She accepts the life we share."
(*He frowns; then crosses out with a pencil.*) Goddamnit, I don't
know if you accept! (*Reads again.*) "The girl is sitting in the chair.
For days now there has been no rope." Period. (*He smiles.*) That's
more like it. (*He puts the page away.*) I guess you'd like your little
late-night newscast. Let's see. It was cold out. Oh, there was sun
all right, but not enough for shadows. There's a new number one
on the Hit Parade and calm in Washington. Skirts will be longer
and they've made a cancer breakthrough. Someone prominent
died. You might say the world just ambled today. You're better
off here with me. Oh! This is of interest. The newspapers have
forgotten all about you. There wasn't even a mention this

evening. That little upstart in Idaho's still trapped in her well. Crowded you right off the front page, she did!

GIRL: (*At once.*) *Plaisir d'amour ne dure qu'un moment*
Chagrin d'amour dure toute la vie.

YOUNG MAN: It's very comforting when you do that. I mean it. Oh God, I am so deliriously happy! (*The Girl finishes the song.*) After all, this is how I always imagined it. I have everything I want now. Give me your hand. (*She does so.*) It will be years before I'm done with you (maybe a lifetime) but you can't imagine how much less strange your body already is to me. Sometimes I look across the room at you and feel I almost know you. (*Releases her hand.*) And then there's your soul. With luck we might someday even get to it. Would you like that? (*He looks up at her.*) Of course she would. How much better words unspoken are! Forked creatures, a poet called us. There's so much more to know about a man than that! (*She looks up at him.*) You're happy here, I can tell. Why, your eyes are glowing, you're almost purring. You belong to someone and that's a good feeling. There's no strain left, we're coexisting, that's better than love. Besides, people don't like to be loved. Just go on breathing, staying at 98.6 and you'll have everything you want. (*The Girl stirs.*) What is it? (*He sees something on the floor.*) Come on, sweetheart, up you go! (*He has let an ant crawl onto his hand.*) Look. My friend, the ant. He's a beauty. Once you understand them, all ants are beautiful, but this one's especially fine. Look at him struggling, thrashing about, trying to find his way! You're in a little frenzy, aren't you there? I see the little legs going, the antennae twitching a mile a minute. (*Moving his hand all the time to keep the ant from crawling up his arm.*) Go ahead, exhaust yourself. It's hopeless, but how long before you realize that and settle down in the palm of my hand? It's not worth struggling. Soon you'll come to rest. Look, he can't stop! His death throes and he doesn't know it. I know what you're thinking, ant: "I'm lost, but I'll find my way. I won't give up the fight. It's worth my effort. And when it's done I'm going to find another ant who loves me and I'm going to love her back. There's work to be done in the nest, the other ants need me and I've got to make them proud. The community of ants must not disintegrate and I am its member. Ant things are worth caring about. There are so many ant poems to be written. I was happy for a time and I'll be happy again. It doesn't have to end this way. Keep struggling, keep the legs going, the heart beating, and I'll find my way to something better. Don't give up, that's the main thing, don't give up!" Isn't that what you're thinking, ant? There *are* poems to be written, there *is* membership in communities, it *does* matter the dog barked, you can't give up too soon. What, ant? I hear you. "Oh, it's so easy to get tired. To stop struggling. I'll call it quits, throw in the towel. It's bigger than me, I'm going round and round, not getting anywhere. I'm so small and frail, who'll care if I get crushed? There's no requiem for ants. Surrender. But no! Something tells me not to stop trying. Maybe there's a chance I'll pull through. I've got to keep the legs going. A little longer, no matter how tired, if only for the chance of finding something better, finding my way out, my way back to love and lyricism and gentleness and accepting that it's strange, this life, and that's the point of it. I'M NOT GOING TO DIE. NOT YET. NOT ME." (*He lets the ant escape.*)

GIRL: Silly bitch.

YOUNG MAN: Yes, wasn't he? (*He looks at her, smiles, then goes to her and kisses her gently.*) Another long day tomorrow. Come to bed now. (*He begins to undress. The Girl goes to the bed, gets in, lies down.*)

GIRL: *Plaisir d'amour ne dure qu'un moment*
Chagrin d'amour dure toute la vie. (*The Young Man kneels beside her. She hums the song.*)

YOUNG MAN: It's time I thought of a name for you. Laura. Would you like Laura? You don't have to answer now. We're not ready for talking to each other yet. It will come . . . in time . . . everything does. (*He gets into bed beside her.*) I like it best when you hum to me. (*Pause.*) Lower the light. Laura. (*She does so.*) I have everything I want now. Everything! (*He sleeps. Slow blackout.*)

Curtain.

Witness

for Jeb Carter

WITNESS was first presented by Albee-Barr Wilder on June 4, 1968, at the Playwrights Unit, New York City, directed by Keven O'Connor, with the following cast:

MAN . . . . Richard Marr
WINDOW WASHER . . . . James Coco
YOUNG MAN . . . . Robert Drivas
MISS PRESSON . . . . Marion Paone

WITNESS was produced by Michael Ellis on November 21, 1968, at the Gramercy Arts Theatre, New York City, directed by Larry Arrick, with the following cast:

MAN . . . . Richard Marr
WINDOW WASHER . . . . James Coco
YOUNG MAN . . . . Joe Ponazecki
MISS PRESSON . . . . Sally Kirkland

Characters

MAN
WINDOW WASHER
YOUNG MAN
MISS PRESSON

Witness

The scene is a room with several windows and two doors leading offstage. As the curtain rises we see a Man tied in a chair and gagged. Outside the window, a Window Washer is just finishing up one of the windows. The Man is trying to attract his attention. The Window Washer sees him but doesn't do anything about it. He just keeps washing.

   There is very loud music coming from a phonograph in the room. Perhaps the "Immolation Scene" or the "Dies Irae" from the Verdi Requiem. *Anyway, something classical that's good and noisy. The telephone is ringing, too. A Young Man enters.*

YOUNG MAN: (*To the Man.*) Don't move. I'll be right off. (*Waving to the Window Washer.*) Beautiful! (*The Young Man answers the phone.*) Just a minute. (*Covers the phone, speaks to the Man.*) It always rings during the part you've been waiting for. (*He listens for the music to reach a certain phrase, hears it, smiles.*) Is that a vibrato? (*To the Man.*) Is that a vibrato? (*Back into the phone.*) Yes . . . who's calling please? . . . This is he . . . and a good morning to you, Miss Person . . . *Presson,* Miss *Presson,* that's a relief. (*The Window Washer goes away.*) It depends on what you want to talk about . . . a survey! Good for you! . . . I like surveys and I like girls who take surveys . . . I don't know why. Maybe somebody should take a survey why people like me like surveys and girls who take them. Unless, of course, that's what this particular call is all about? . . . I see. Well maybe next time. Good-bye. (*He hangs up the phone, talks to the Man.*) She'll call back. How do you feel? A little dizzy, hunh? You know that damn karate really works? Don't ask me what I would've done if it hadn't. Run! But you rang the bell, I opened the door, you said . . . well STARTED to say "Good morn—!" and kee! haa! koo! Like whammo! Of course you weren't looking. I mean that *was* your classic surprise attack. Anyway, I'm sorry. It's a hell of a way to treat *Encyclope-*

dia Britannica salesmen. Friends? (*Takes the Man's arm, pumps it.*) Sure! (*The phone is ringing.*) There she is. (*To the Man.*) Do you mind opera? Lots of people hate it. Like my parents. You can nap if you want. I'll try to make this quick. (*Answers the phone.*) Hello, Miss Presson . . . I didn't hang up on you, I thought we were through . . . no, you've caught me at a dandy time. I'm just lying here naked playing with myself . . . Hey! now you're the one who asked. Sock it to me! . . . the question! I thought you were taking a survey . . . Should you tip a window washer? What the hell kind of a survey question is that? . . . Oh, YOUR window washer! You must be new in the city . . . I thought so. The answer is No, you don't. Just thank him . . . then open the window and thank him . . . then rap on the glass and SMILE at him! God, you're dumb! . . . forget I said it. I'm Arab. We're rough on our women . . . forget I said that, too. Now ask your question. Shee-it! . . . I said shit. I've never been asked that over the telephone. Usually all you survey people want to know is who I'm going to vote for or how much I'm getting lately but this one's a block-buster! The President of the United States wants to know how happy I am? . . . You know you could upset someone just calling him up out of the blue like this and throwing a question like that in his face . . . I'm not upset. I said *someone* . . . and I'm not someone. As a matter of fact, I'm not anyone . . . nothing, I was just ruminating . . . ruminating! . . . thinking, pondering . . . I LIKE big words but ruminating isn't one of them. You ARE dumb. (*To the Man.*) I know about knots. You're wasting your time. (*Back into the phone.*) You know I don't think you're emotionally stable for this line of work. You can't go around asking people how happy they are and then you fly off the handle . . . I know there's tension in the air . . . absolutely! I feel the same hostility emanations myself . . . of course you're deep in therapy, where else would you be? . . . as a matter of fact, I'm not . . . oh I hang on, I cope . . . that's my secret . . . you bet, it's a big one! (*Winks at the Man.*) I have a friend here with me. I'll ask him too, why don't I? (*To the Man.*) There's a Miss Presson representing the President's Commission on Our National Purpose on the line here and she wants to know how happy you are. (*Back into the phone.*) Would you repeat those multiple choices? He didn't hear them. (*To the Man, while listening to the phone.*) (a) Extremely (b) moderately (c) just plain (d) not too, or (e) not at all? (*The Man struggles violently.*) He said e. (*To the Man.*) You're going to hurt yourself. (*Back into the phone.*) What about my window washer? He was just outside . . . I see . . . a white-collar survey . . . only certain socio-economic strata. I understand perfectly. That nips that in the bud, doesn't it now? (*To the Man.*) I told you not to move. (*Back into the phone.*) I'm not evading your question . . . all right, the PRESIDENT's question! You're not only dumb, you're garrulous! (*To the Man.*) She's raving. (*Back into the phone.*) Could I see you sometime, Miss Presson? We could finish this in person . . . screw the regulations! . . . the last of the smooth talkers, I know, but could we? . . . I'm in my twenties . . . I'm not being coy but I am in my twenties . .. I don't do anything. I'm a prince . . . when you get here, *then* I'll pull your leg. I may even pull both your legs . . . am I really what? . . .yes, I'm naked . . . Miss Presson, you are a genuine lulu! As a matter of fact, I was and finished . . . then don't ask questions like that! (*To the Man.*) You're going to hurt yourself. (*Back into the phone.*) Anyway, and I've really got to cut this short, you can tell the Commission I'm very happy . . . I've got a friend here with me. I've got another friend on the line . . . sure, we're friends! The President is in town today and his motorcade will be passing directly beneath my windows . . . You know? What do you mean you know? . . . Yes, that's my address . . . you're putting me on . . . What apartment number? . . . I'm 6-J . . . (*Sound of stamping above.*) That's you stamping? You mean we really are in the same building? . . . I'll say it's a coincidence! You're right above me, right smack on top of me, right up over me. That's a groovy place to be . . . My word of honor, Miss P. I'm not talking dirty . . . I accept your apology, now do it some more . . . Stamp! It turns me on. (*Stamping from above.*) Do you believe it? You can almost see her up there . . . nice firm legs pumping away. I *hope* nice firm legs. (*Back into the phone.*) Miss Presson . . . Yoo hoo, Miss Presson! (*Stamping stops.*) There you are. Good girl. Catch your breath now . . . hmmm? . . . To tell you the truth, I'd rather not. You see I just had this place painted and—all *right!* But first I'll have to find something to pound back on the ceiling *with* . . . I

don't keep a broom . . . No, no! Don't come down here now . . .
After the motorcade, as soon as it happens . . . as soon as the
President passes! . . . Oh, Miss Presson . . . Miss Presson! When
they ask you, just say, : "He sounded calm enough. I even made
a date with him" . . . It means what it sounds like it means . . .
Never mind who . . . All right! "He even made a date with *me!*"
But, "He sounded calm enough." Have you got all that? . . . Of
course I'll explain . . . and as soon as I find something I promise
to pound . . . Oh, and Miss Presson! Now that you've mentioned
it, how happy are you? (*Puts the phone down slowly.*) That's de-
pressing. (*Sighs, gets up, goes to the Man.*) Sorry I took so long,
you were right on time for our appointment, too; but it's turning
out even better than I'd planned it. I'd counted on you being
here, but another one upstairs! I can't believe my luck. (*Stamping
from above.*) We better humor her. That's good parquet she's
scratching up. Takes wax beautifully. You should have seen my
floors before the painters made their mess. May I? (*Takes the
Man's umbrella.*) I stopped buying these things. I was always losing them. Only now my hair gets wet and frizzles. I look like
Simon and Garfunkel. The frizzy one. And wearing hats just
makes you bald sooner. (*Raps on the ceiling with the umbrella.*)
Up yours, Miss P.! I'm knocking her up! (*While he continues his
"conversation" with Miss Presson, the Window Washer comes into
the room through the window.*)

WINDOW WASHER: (*To the Man.*) You got a can, buddy?
YOUNG MAN: Through there, the second door. The light's on your left.
(*The Window Washer exits. The Man is struggling frantically.*)
Aaaw. Look at the marks it made. I like a nice clean ceiling, too.
WINDOW WASHER: (*Offstage.*) Light's on my what?
YOUNG MAN: Left! By the towels! (*To the Man.*) I have a brother who
was a golf nut . . . he still is, for all I know . . . and when we
were younger and sharing a room back home, he'd practice his
drives inside the house at night. Our bedroom ceiling was all torn
up. I couldn't sleep nights thinking about those marks. (*Calling
offstage.*) Would you mind terribly closing the door? Thanks! (*To
the Man.*) It's probably the only thing in the world I'm obsessive
about—good clean ceilings. All righty-y, Miss Presson, over and
out! (*He waits, listens.*) Not a mouse stirring. She must be cooling

off. (*Calling offstage.*) We'd appreciate it if you'd flush! (*Sounds of a toilet.*) Thank you! (*To the Man.*) Are you sure the thought of her stomping around up there doesn't excite you? (*Calling offstage.*) There's beer in the refrigerator. Help yourself.

WINDOW WASHER: (*Offstage.*) I was!

YOUNG MAN: (*To the Man.*) Native New Yorker. (*Calling offstage.*) Then would you mind bringing me one?

WINDOW WASHER: (*Offstage.*) What do you think I am? Room Service?

YOUNG MAN: The American proletariat, God bless it! (*Then, to the Man.*) Look, I'm not going to hurt you. I swear I won't lay a hand on you. I need a witness, it's that simple. All you have to do is sit there and . . . WITNESS, I suppose. As it's turning out . . . Miss Presson upstairs and now him . . . I'll have several. You see, the other guys who did this . . . everybody thought they were crazy.

WINDOW WASHER: (*Enters with a bottle of whiskey and a glass.*) I found the good stuff.

YOUNG MAN: Make yourself at home. (*Exits.*)

WINDOW WASHER: (*He already has. Settled comfortably, whiskey in front of him, he addresses himself to the Man, who struggles frantically.*) I'm gonna write a book someday. I swear to God, I'm really gonna do it. Just sit down and spill it all out. Know what I mean? Hunh? You know? Get it all out of my system. I already got the title. *Things I Seen Washing Windows.* You like it? 'Cause, buddy, after what I seen looking in people's windows, you and anybody else ain't seen nothing. Take just now. I'm on the floor above, doing my job, and there's this broad . . . no blinds, no shades, nothing . .. and she's all got up in this what-do-you-call-'em? . . . wrapper-type thing! that's hanging open here, hanging open there, hanging open everywhere. I mean I could see what this broad had and she knew it. And she's talking on the phone, see? And she knows I'm right out there giving her the eye and all the time she's . . . (*He demonstrates.*) . . . know what I mean? . . . kind of ROCKING . . . like she was making it with the guy she had on the other end. Okay, so maybe it WASN'T a guy she was talking to. Maybe SHE was the guy. Like I said, I seen a lot. Nothing fazes me. Not in this country. You show me the situation a window washer isn't at home in, and I'll show you the planet Mars. Boy, I love conversing with people like this! Getting it all of my chest. (*Pours himself another whiskey.*) You see something like that . . . and mister, you wouldn't believe what's going on up on the roof of this building: two Secret Service men watching a couple of teenagers make out when they're meant to be guarding the President, but I won't even go into that . . . no, you see something like that broad up there twitching with all her blinds up . . . (and she IS the real thing. I was only making a point about sexual ambivalence when I said maybe she wasn't.) . . . and you say to yourself, "What's wrong with people? What's this country coming to?" That's what my book's about: philosophy. (*Reflectively.*) You know I seen guys who couldn't make it with their wife unless they had her in a chair like that. (*The Man strikes out with his feet.*) Do that again, buddy, and I'll break 'em for you. (*Smiles, looks at his clenched fist.*) There's this terrific bar over on Tenth Avenue I go Friday nights after I leave the old lady home watching the tube. You know how everybody and his brother's out LOOKING for a fight Friday nights? My place you GET one. Smash some guy's face open for him, knock some teeth out . . . gets the rest of the week out of your system. Know what I mean? (*Pours himself another whiskey.*) One thing I could stand right now is a little loving. Go back up there, kick her window in. She wouldn't know what hit her. (*Confidentially.*) See, my old lady don't put out no more. Makes a man desperate. Too tired, she says. Just as well. Who wants her? Naaaaw, I don't mean that. Ethel, here's mud in your eye! (*Toasts her.*) Jeez, I really appreciate your taking the time off and talking to the man in the street like this. All right, so I work forty stories up—I'm still the man in the street, proud of it, and I appreciate your time. Even if you are some kind of a nut. But like I said, nothing fazes me. I seen all kinds, all colors, all shapes. Ain't nothing people do . . . alone or with one another . . . that surprises this one any more. And you want to know if I got a philosophy of life? Yeah, I got a philosophy of life all right. Live and let live. Keep your nose clean. People stink. (*The Young Man has returned, carrying a rifle.*) I think your roommate's nuts, too. (*Staggers to his feet.*) Through there, second door, the light's on my left. Keep an eye on him. (*Exits.*)

YOUNG MAN: (*Examining the rifle.*) I don't suppose you know anything about guns? I bought it at Abercrombie's and they wouldn't let me try it out first. You know how stuffy Abercrombie's is. They said I could bring it back though. At least they have a sense of humor at Abercrombie's. Nice ski shop, too.

WINDOW WASHER: (*Offstage.*) I'm leaving the door open so we can talk!

YOUNG MAN: (*Looking out the window now.*) Oh, that's nice. There's a big crowd down there already, waiting to see the President. Can you hear the band? (*Opens the window.*) It's the . . . (*Squinting.*) . . . Nag-a-nuttick . . . Naganuttick! must be Long Island . . . Junior High School Marching Band and Drum Corps.

WINDOW WASHER: (*Offstage.*) I won't even flush.

YOUNG MAN: Twirl it, baby, twirl it! There's this terrific blonde . . . she's thirteen if she's a day . . . that's right! Catch it between those legs. UNH! That's America for you.

WINDOW WASHER: (*Offstage.*) Hey! No fair in there! I can't hear!

YOUNG MAN: It's perfect motorcade weather. Just crisp enough. Blue skies like that make you think of Texas.

WINDOW WASHER: (*Entering.*) Texas! That's the state. What'd I miss?

YOUNG MAN: We're talking about the President.

WINDOW WASHER: That's right up my alley.

YOUNG MAN: Shoot.

WINDOW WASHER: That mother-hugging egg-sucker!

YOUNG MAN: I plan to.

WINDOW WASHER: Don't get me started. People can make me see all shades of red but that buzzard gives me a real Friday night–er. What's that thing that rises in your throat?

YOUNG MAN: (*Turning on the television.*) The gorge maybe?

WINDOW WASHER: Well, mine's what's rising. You're talking to the man in the street buddy, and you're scratching him where it hurts. All right, so I work forty stories up—I'm still the man in the street, proud of it, and you just waved a red flag in my face. (*Swigs whiskey.*) What are we watching?

YOUNG MAN: The President's arrival at the airport. He's making a speech before his motorcade. They're carrying it live. The whole thing, in fact.

WINDOW WASHER: Jesus Christ, you'll get me going!

YOUNG MAN: He's just the President.

WINDOW WASHER: Not mine he ain't.

YOUNG MAN: It was a landslide.

WINDOW WASHER: Should've landed ON him.

YOUNG MAN: (*Getting the set into focus; sounds of people cheering, music, etc., can be heard.*) He seems drawn.

WINDOW WASHER: (*Hunching close to the television; he can't take his eyes off it, in fact.*) Look at that mug.

YOUNG MAN: Look at hers.

WINDOW WASHER: What I wouldn't give to tell that buzzard off.

YOUNG MAN: You'd like that, hunh?

WINDOW WASHER: He wouldn't know what hit him.

YOUNG MAN: Why don't you?

WINDOW WASHER: Are you kidding? I couldn't get through the front gate.

YOUNG MAN: You don't have to.

WINDOW WASHER: What do you mean?

YOUNG MAN: There he is. (*Indicates the television.*) I do it all the time. It's a fantastic experience.

WINDOW WASHER: Yeah?

YOUNG MAN: It's saved my life.

WINDOW WASHER: No kidding?

YOUNG MAN: It gets all the bile out. Go ahead, try it. I'd like to hear what you have to say.

WINDOW WASHER: Naaw, you don't.

YOUNG MAN: Sure I do!

WINDOW WASHER: 'Cause once I let rip with that . . .

YOUNG MAN: Go ahead, rip.

WINDOW WASHER: You don't know how long I've had this in me.

YOUNG MAN: Spit it out, then.

WINDOW WASHER: He's had this coming to him.

YOUNG MAN: Sure he has.

WINDOW WASHER: I mean he's just been asking for it.

YOUNG MAN: So give it to him!

WINDOW WASHER: Know something? I'm gonna do it.

YOUNG MAN: You're in the office with him.

WINDOW WASHER: Not yet I ain't. First I gotta push my way thorough all them guards. You know, elbow my way in. He's sitting there, see, goosing his secretary probably, and I come charging in at him and he looks up, startled like.

YOUNG MAN: So does she.

WINDOW WASHER: Get her out of here! We're going to talk, buddy. You're gonna listen to me.

YOUNG MAN: Now we're cooking!

WINDOW WASHER: She out of the room yet?

YOUNG MAN: Hours ago. Screaming.

WINDOW WASHER: Next I pour myself a drink, drop some ashes on his rug, use his can, maybe.

YOUNG MAN: You're putting me on.

WINDOW WASHER: You know, show him I'm not scared of him. That's when I start, when I got him shaking.

YOUNG MAN: You're on!

WINDOW WASHER: (*After a beat, then exploding with it.*) Mr. President, you're a pain in the ass! So . . . (*He flounders.*) so shape up or ship out! (*To the Young Man.*) I guess that's telling him.

YOUNG MAN: It's a beginning. (*The Window Washer sighs, smiles, swigs his whiskey; the Young Man waits for him to continue.*) You're finished?

WINDOW WASHER: I hit on the main points. 'Course I'd also like to . . .(*Grabs the Man, is about to punch him.*)

YOUNG MAN: Hey, now simmer down.

WINDOW WASHER: I didn't know I had so many raw nerves aching.

YOUNG MAN: I've got pills.

WINDOW WASHER: Naw, I'll be okay once I . . . (*Suddenly, violently, he flings some books onto the floor.*) There, that's better.

YOUNG MAN: (*Popping pills into his mouth.*) Your face is flushed.

WINDOW WASHER: (*Laughing hugely.*) So are you!

YOUNG MAN: (*Raising the volume on the television and settling back to watch.*) He's starting his speech.

WINDOW WASHER: So are you!

YOUNG MAN: Sshh! Now it's his turn.

ANNOUNCER'S VOICE: The President of the United States. (*The cheering fades to silence, then the voice of the President is heard.*)

PRESIDENT'S VOICE: (*Very solemn.*) My fellow Americans.

YOUNG MAN: Oh oh! It sounds bad.

PRESIDENT'S VOICE: It is with a heavy heart I come before you. I am sad, I am sick, I am disgusted.

WINDOW WASHER: You're full of shit.

PRESIDENT'S VOICE: WAKE UP, AMERICA, I CRY! AMERICA, CRY I, WAKE UP! (*Applause.*)

WINDOW WASHER: (*Musing.*) Boy, somebody could pick him off right now.

YOUNG MAN: Maybe they will.

PRESIDENT'S VOICE: The moral deterioration in the West will destroy us by the year 2000 A.D.

WINDOW WASHER: Fat chance.

YOUNG MAN: It's happened before.

PRESIDENT'S VOICE: Our beloved America in moral shambles IN OUR TIME.

WINDOW WASHER: You see me crying?

YOUNG MAN: You saw that rifle.

WINDOW WASHER: One shot, right in the balls!

PRESIDENT'S VOICE: Need I continue? Death on the highways, cheating from the top to bottom, a pack a day . . .

WINDOW WASHER; Don't tell me that's not a toupee he's wearing.

PRESIDENT'S VOICE: An all-consuming attitude of get-rich-quick . . .

YOUNG MAN: That's Dad.

PRESIDENT'S VOICE: Break-up of our most holy shrine, the family.

YOUNG MAN: That *was* Dad.

PRESIDENT'S VOICE: Reckless debt. Faltering in foreign policy.

WINDOW WASHER: You telling me, Pinky?

PRESIDENT'S VOICE: Drug-addiction, alcoholism, and sexual perversion run rampant!

WINDOW WASHER: You should know! (*Confidentially to the Young Man.*) I heard about his girlfriends and all those White House orgies.

YOUNG MAN: You know someone in D.C.?

WINDOW WASHER: Naaw, but word like that, it gets around. (*Expansively.*) Still, you can't blame the buzzard. Take a look at her. Wha'd want to sleep with *that?*

PRESIDENT'S VOICE: These, and is it any wonder, have robbed America and her cities of peace and tranquillity.

WINDOW WASHER: You have! Letting all those niggers riot!

PRESIDENT'S VOICE: Fear has reared its ugly head in every part of the country.

WINDOW WASHER: And you've reared yours!

PRESIDENT'S VOICE: Are we to save ourselves? Then we must not, my fellow Americans, fail to heed the immortal words of General Douglas MacArthur!

WINDOW WASHER: Now he was true blue.

PRESIDENT'S VOICE: Let us remember his immortal V-J Day address in Tokyo Bay. "Fellow Japanese," and I quote, "we have had our last chance. If we do not now devise some greater and more equitable system, Armageddon will be at our door!" (*Sustained applause.*)

WINDOW WASHER: I seen him once.

YOUNG MAN: Who?

WINDOW WASHER: MacArthur.

YOUNG MAN: No kidding.

WINDOW WASHER: Sure. He was this close.

PRESIDENT'S VOICE: "Our problem basically is spiritual and involves a spiritual recrudescence . . . recrudescence? . . ."

YOUNG MAN: (*Shaking his head.*) Beats me, too.

PRESIDENT'S VOICE: *Anyway*, that was General Douglas MacArthur.

WINDOW WASHER: I really am drunk.

PRESIDENT'S VOICE: I say unto you, "It must be of the spirit if we are to save the flesh."

YOUNG MAN: Here it comes, the peroration. Funny how I know some big words, and others I don't.

PRESIDENT'S VOICE: People may live in beautiful modern houses where the dishes may not break, but hearts still can break.

WINDOW WASHER: That's the first thing he's said the whole damn speech.

PRESIDENT'S VOICE: THANK GOD, THERE IS A WAY OUT OF OUR DILEMMA! (*Long silence.*)

ANNOUNCER'S VOICE: You have just heard the President of the United States. (*Tumultuous ovation.*)

YOUNG MAN: Fantastic!

WINDOW WASHER: What'd he say just then?

YOUNG MAN: A mouthful, what else?

WINDOW WASHER: (*Shaking his head.*) Something about there being a way out of something? . . .

YOUNG MAN: Our dilemma.

WINDOW WASHER: Yeah!

YOUNG MAN: Listen to them roar! What a tumult!

WINDOW WASHER: (*In his cups.*) That part about the heart breaking when the dishes don't . . .

YOUNG MAN: You liked that, hunh?

WINDOW WASHER: (*With solemn nods.*) Gives you something to think about. You got any Kate Smith?

YOUNG MAN: Sorry.

WINDOW WASHER: I like Kate Smith.

YOUNG MAN: She's fat.

WINDOW WASHER: (*Sad smile.*) Yeah. (*Toasting.*) Ethel, mud!

ANNOUNCER'S VOICE: Stay tuned for the exclusive live coverage of the Presidential motorcade. (*The Young Man moves to the TV controls.*)

WINDOW WASHER: Leave it on!

YOUNG MAN: It's just the parade now. You're going to see him right outside in a while.

WINDOW WASHER: TV's better.

YOUNG MAN: I'll just lower it.

WINDOW WASHER: You're that close to 'em when something happens. (*To the Man.*) Pow! Pow! Pow! (*Laughs.*) You're all right.

YOUNG MAN: Hey, it's another Lincoln Continental.

WINDOW WASHER: And I wouldn't wanna miss it this time.

YOUNG MAN: I'm sorry, miss what?

WINDOW WASHER: Somebody knocking that buzzard off.

YOUNG MAN: You won't.

WINDOW WASHER: One shot, right in the balls!

YOUNG MAN: As I said, maybe they will.

WINDOW WASHER: Like I said, see me crying? (*His concentration on the image on the television screen is something fierce. The Young Man has crossed to the Man.*)

YOUNG MAN; How are we doing? I'm sorry I've been ignoring you but he . . . (*Thumb toward the Window Washer.*) . . . well, like he's fantastic. I just hope you're soaking it all in. Notice I haven't asked anybody's name. Don't want to. You know, involvement, it's tricky. Besides, reading the papers, witnesses are usually anonymous. Or at least they prefer to remain so. If you need anything, just holler. (*Muffled yells from the Man. The Young Man crosses to the window and looks out.*) I thought I smelled something! They're burning him in effigy. A group of nuns from the convent of the . . . (*Whips on his glasses.*) . . . Silver Veil, Laramie, Wyoming. That's a hell of a long way to come. There must be fifty of them milling around down there. Hey, there's a real looker! Go to it, sisters! (*Turns back into the room.*) God, it's a theatrical religion. I wanted to be a priest when I was a kid, and serving Mass. Those robes they got to wear with the big cross front and back and that little room they have to get dressed in and then holding the chalice up with everybody looking and us altar boys ringing those bells and beating our breasts. From that point of view it must be terrific being a priest.

WINDOW WASHER: (*Irritated.*) Hey, come on, I'm watching this!

YOUNG MAN: (*To the Man now.*) And the incense! That was the best part of all. I'd stoke the . . . I don't remember what they call it . . . the thing you put the incense in . . . I'd put in twice the amount we were meant to and I'd start waving that thing, the smoke puffing out. It was a big church but I could stink the whole place up. There'd be two thousand people at high Mass on Sundays and I'd have them all coughing. I was a terror! Brazier? No, it was something like "chasuble" only that's something you wear. I'll think of it. (*Pause, then a smile; the smile broadens to a laugh.*) We used to nip wine in the sacristy, too. That's the best-kept secret in the Catholic Church. All those little towheads skipping around the altar are potted. They'll probably try to make a big psychological thing out of all this. Don't let them. (*He comes over to the Window Washer.*) How's it going?

WINDOW WASHER: You'd think he was Lindbergh. Look at the ticker tape.

YOUNG MAN: Any action?

WINDOW WASHER: Yeah, but it was a false alarm. Somebody broke through the police lines but it was only a kid with a bunch of flowers for his old lady.

YOUNG MAN: Whose old lady?

WINDOW WASHER: Muckhead's, who else?

YOUNG MAN: Did she take them?

WINDOW WASHER: Her? What do you think? She practically jumped over the trunk grabbing 'em out of the kid's hands.

YOUNG MAN: What kind were they?

WINDOW WASHER: Roses.

YOUNG MAN: How many?

WINDOW WASHER: A dozen.

YOUNG MAN: What color?

WINDOW WASHER: (*Getting annoyed.*) How should I know? It's in black and white. Don't ask so many questions.

YOUNG MAN: Who's that in the car with them?

WINDOW WASHER: The mayor and his wife. (*Pause.*) They stink, too.

YOUNG MAN: Look at those crowds! You certainly can't say our town doesn't love you, Mr. President!

WINDOW WASHER: People turn out for anything nowadays.

YOUNG MAN: But especially the President. He's having a triumph, it looks like to me.

WINDOW WASHER: (*Glowering.*) There's still time.

YOUNG MAN: What do you mean?

WINDOW WASHER: What do you mean?

WINDOW WASHER: One shot, right in the ass.

YOUNG MAN: You said the balls.

WINDOW WASHER: I changed my mind.

YOUNG MAN: See you crying? (*Suddenly clapping his hands together with a sharp sound, almost like a rifle shot.*) Censer!

WINDOW WASHER: Drop dead, will you!

YOUNG MAN: (*Fairly bounding over to the Man.*) The thing you put the incense in, it's called a censer!

WINDOW WASHER: You're making me nervous now!

YOUNG MAN: It's fantastic how words bounce back like that—boing!

WINDOW WASHER: Can it, will you! I'm trying to concentrate.

YOUNG MAN: (*Much lower now, speaking to the Man.*) A word about motivation, and I'll leave you alone. It'll just be witnessing then, right up to the end. (*Sits on the floor.*) It was Sunday night when I had my nervous breakdown. Well, sort of a nervous breakdown. Call it a mini-breakdown. I was sitting here, glum as ever, the weight of the world on my shoulders . . . well, that's not true exactly—it was the weight of Southeast Asia and the deep Deep South . . . when all of a sudden it hit me. I think it must have been the books that triggered me. How many hundreds of them are there, would you guess? Five, maybe six? And I'd made the mistake of reading every one of them. I'm not bulling you. Look, my eyes are permanently bloodshot from it. And they're the big books, too. The . . . er . . . ugh . . . (I hate this word!) . . . the classics. Aristotle . . . Kierkegaard . . . Lorna Doone. But it seemed so important to know, what was in them . . . life and death practically. It's hard to explain why. Knowledge was something I just had the hots for. Look at all the records! I thought knowing about music . . . you know, the good stuff . . . was another life and death–er. Between the books and the music I was a frigging machine. My eyes would be . . . CALLUSED practically from another reading and I'd make myself sit down and listen to music for another six hours. And see all the newspapers and magazines? I had subscriptions pouring in here like Santa's Christmas mail. They had me brooding about a cabinet crisis in Lebanon. There's a boll weevil plague in Ghana. I got angry about Greece. EVERYTHING seemed important last week. I guess that goes to show you how young I was before last Sunday. Oh, my whole life stared me in the face that night! It was stormy weather around this place, believe you me. I was ready to chuck that entire library for one good piece of Turkish pornography. And then it hit me—my problem was this: I'd never DONE anything about this country. I'd just absorbed it. I was a cultural, political, philosophical sponge. A blotter. A blob. Like I was up to here with this country, but like I'd never done anything about it. Well, sir, I not only got off my ass, I SHOT off it! First thing I did, naturally, was pace. I asked myself, What could I do for my country? Not only that but what could I do that would mean something? I wasn't happy, this country isn't happy . . . well, are you? . . . we're all in one big winter of our discontent. God knows we're ripe for some kind of cataclysm . . . almost anything. And then I saw his face staring at me from the front page of the *Times*. (*He takes out a letter.*) Listen to this. (*He reads.*) The President of the United Sates, 1600 Pennsylvania Avenue, Washington, D.C. 20032. Dear Mr. President, You will undoubtedly be curious why I have "assassinated" you. Actually I am sick and tired of all the assassinations and I don't want another one to happen again. That's why I have had to "assassinate" you. People have got to learn that killing people doesn't change anything. I hate you, Mr. President, for all the bullshit and lies when there are so many *real* things to be done for real *people* that *you* could be doing and you're not. I guess you could say I'm disillusioned. My ambition in life has always been to do something really good and constructive (it should have been yours) and after a lot of reflection it seems the best and most constructive thing I can do is "kill" you. Maybe you'll know then how fucked up this country of yours is. I am not a Communist. I am not a hippie. And I am not a John Bircher. I feel shitty about this. I really do. Yours truly, (*He smiles.*) Holden Caulfield. (*Putting the letter away.*) Pow! Pow! Pow! (*He turns on the radio. A good loud, rock beat is blasting out.*)

WINDOW WASHER: (*Rudely awakened; he's been dozing.*) Are we watching this thing together or ain't we?

YOUNG MAN: You'll hear the sirens.

WINDOW WASHER: What sirens?

YOUNG MAN: When he's right outside you hear sirens.

WINDOW WASHER: (*Snapping off TV.*) I'm sick of looking at him.

YOUNG MAN: Have another drink.

WINDOW WASHER: (*Already helping himself.*) I'm sick of you, too.

YOUNG MAN: Come on, let's dance!

WINDOW WASHER: Dry up, will you.

YOUNG MAN: I bet you cut a mean rug.

WINDOW WASHER: What are you? Some kind of . . . ?

YOUNG MAN: Dancing fool. Let's go, shake a leg.

WINDOW WASHER: (*Watching the Young Man dance.*) Sure, go ahead, dance. That's all you punks are good for, anyway. Dancing. That's not dancing, punk, that's flitting. Say, how come you ain't in the army?

YOUNG MAN: I'm 4-F.

WINDOW WASHER: I bet you are.

YOUNG MAN: It's easy.

WINDOW WASHER: 4-F?

YOUNG MAN: Dancing.

WINDOW WASHER: My boy ain't dancing. He's over there now. Sure, they took my Joey! "Dear Dad," he writes me . . . he never called me Dad before in all his life . . . it was always Pa before. "Dear Dad, my nuts ache I'm so scared. But I'm defending the American way of life. Tell Mom I miss her and I'm coming home."

YOUNG MAN: (*Stops dancing.*) I'm sorry.

WINDOW WASHER: Then why the hell ain't you over there with him, 'stead of flitting around here like you was in some diskeytek?

YOUNG MAN: Was I flitting?

WINDOW WASHER: You look pretty goddamn healthy to me.

YOUNG MAN: (*Tapping, his head.*) Up here? There's the rub.

WINDOW WASHER: I know the type. Got his college deferment and then some shrinker to write he was too sensitive to serve.

YOUNG MAN: You're close.

WINDOW WASHER: I saw all the books. Looks like a goddamn warehouse in here.

YOUNG MAN: Or depository.

WINDOW WASHER: Don't start with your big words. I don't know what they mean and I'm proud of it. What I'm SAYING is this whole system ain't fair to a kid like Joey.

YOUNG MAN: Or his dad?

WINDOW WASHER: Him, too! I got blood inside this carcass and this system's sucking me dry.

YOUNG MAN: It's a democracy.

WINDOW WASHER: Not for me it ain't.

YOUNG MAN: Do something.

WINDOW WASHER: (*Waving the whiskey bottle.*) I am.

YOUNG MAN: Protest.

WINDOW WASHER: Fuck off.

YOUNG MAN: Dance with me.

WINDOW WASHER: I got three and a quarter ounces of shrapnel in me from defending this system. And you know something? I didn't mind then because once upon a time I thought this country was gonna mean something, and maybe was gonna make it. You know what I'm saying? I thought this country was gonna make it. My leg still gimps, but how come this system's started to sink?

YOUNG MAN: That's a good question.

WINDOW WASHER: Shit! I don't even remember what they said I was fighting for.

YOUNG MAN: I do.

WINDOW WASHER: Sure you do, punk. You read all those books. They got a chapter on this? (*He slaps his leg.*)

YOUNG MAN: Yours? No.

WINDOW WASHER: So keep your mouth shut and dance.

YOUNG MAN: Oh Miss Presson, you don't know what you started with that question of yours! Happy? We're all getting liberated down here!

WINDOW WASHER: You know damn well who's getting all the liberation in this country!

YOUNG MAN: Black people.

WINDOW WASHER: That's no secret any more!

YOUNG MAN: The colored races.

WINDOW WASHER: Only nobody wants to talk about it.

YOUNG MAN: You do.

WINDOW WASHER: Hell, they're handing 'em this country on a silver platter. The little bit *I* had they're giving THEM now and goddamn it, they'll turn on all of us someday and from my grave I'll be laughing.

YOUNG MAN: My Mrs. Jackson . . . she comes to me on Thursdays . . . she doesn't even like me calling her Ruth.

WINDOW WASHER: Only she ain't the kind I'm talking about.

YOUNG MAN: I know.

WINDOW WASHER: Then can it, wise guy! I'm talking about Lionel. All-glass buildings we share the same rig. Sure he wants freedom, little Lionel does. Freedom to take my job, stink up my building, cut my throat. I'm worse off than he is, which was okay by me until they had to TELL him I was. In my face he's grinning now! No, you take a poll, mister, you take a poll and see how much nigger love there is in this country!

YOUNG MAN: There's not much President love either.

WINDOW WASHER: We got too much freedom! All of us . . . black and white . . . got too much freedom. That's what's wrong with this country. They're always telling us how free we are, but then nothing happens, nothing changes. I never made over a hundred bucks a week in my life.

YOUNG MAN: And you never will.

WINDOW WASHER: So they give me color TV on a charge-a-plate.

YOUNG MAN: And your wife's happy.

WINDOW WASHER: I'm just waiting for sixty-five, good old pension time, and maybe a couple of years more and they can put me in a box.

YOUNG MAN: And then YOU'RE happy.

WINDOW WASHER: They promise people moons, only they ain't coughing up!

YOUNG MAN: (*Dancing wildly.*) But you're free, you're free!

WINDOW WASHER: Free to do what? I got so much fucking freedom I don't know what to THINK any more.

YOUNG MAN: No opinions, hunh?

WINDOW WASHER: I got OPINIONS. They're a dime a dozen. What I mean is don't I have a right to KNOW what right is. Give me that one and you can keep all the rest.

YOUNG MAN: (*For example.*) Take his lousy war.

WINDOW WASHER: Yeah! We're in there or we're not. He can't have it both ways.

YOUNG MAN: Just tell you where to stand.

WINDOW WASHER: Right! When this war's over I want to know who won. My boy's over there up to HERE in muck and his cousin goes off to Chicago to get his skull split open. They're both nice kids, only which one of them is right? That's not freedom, Johnny, that's confusion. He's the President, then why don't he TELL us what to think?

YOUNG MAN: He's been trying to.

WINDOW WASHER: My Uncle Fred, God rest him, bought himself a car. He was too old to be driving. They said he was doing eight-five when he had that blowout. The law says don't go over sixty. Then why does the law let them make cars that can do eighty-five? No, we all got freedom! so a stupid old man can kill himself on the New York thruway and a family of six in the other lane.

YOUNG MAN: (*Momentarily stops dancing.*) That's a rotten story.

WINDOW WASHER: I'm free, I'm free! so sure I smoke three packs a day. They write on the package I'm killing myself. Words ain't enough. Somebody MAKE me stop. Don't leave everything up to me. I can't do it. Give me some rules that you can make STICK for a change. Draw some kind of line and watch me toe it. Anything you say, mister, 'cause I'm sick of you letting me smoke myself to death, sick of getting so drunk Friday nights the whole Canarsie line could run over me and I wouldn't know it, sick of knocking my wife around when I can't stand her most nights since number one I can't stand me! Only don't tell me I'm free again.

YOUNG MAN: (*Goading him, dancing more wildly than ever.*) You're free! You're free!

WINDOW WASHER: YOU be free and see how you like it! (*And with one enormous blow of his fist he has sent the Young Man sprawling. There is a pause. The Window Washer standing, the anger and frustration flowing out of him; the Young Man on the floor. The music will seem very loud. Finally the Young Man gets to his feet, goes to the radio and turns if off. And now the room will seem very still.*) I'm sorry.

YOUNG MAN: That's okay. (*Short pause. He smiles.*) It's not really. But I know what you want now. (*There are sounds of sirens approaching at a distance from outside the windows; band music, cheering too . . . all getting closer and louder to the end of the play.*) It won't be long now.

WINDOW WASHER: I didn't mean to . . .

YOUNG MAN: Sure you did.

WINDOW WASHER: You kept riding me.

YOUNG MAN: Forget it.

WINDOW WASHER: I thought we was having a party.

YOUNG MAN: We are! You can hear the sirens. He must be getting close. (*He's at the window, looking out.*)

WINDOW WASHER: You know something?

YOUNG MAN: Yes?

WINDOW WASHER: You're free, too.

YOUNG MAN: Hot shit!

WINDOW WASHER: (*To the MAN.*) These kids . . .! (*There is a knock at the door.*)

YOUNG MAN: Who the . . . ? (*To the Man.*) You weren't expecting anyone? (*Figures it out.*) Of course!

WINDOW WASHER: These kids . . . they don't understand.

YOUNG MAN: (*Throwing open the door.*) There she is! You're just in time. (*Miss Presson edges into the room.*)

MISS PRESSON: (*Somewhat over brightly.*) Hi! I decided not to wait.

YOUNG MAN: It's that bad, hunh?

MISS PRESSON: I thought we could watch together.

YOUNG MAN: Wash together? You mean bathe? Shee-it! Hey, that's wild.

MISS PRESSON: *Watch* together. The President. I'm Miss Presson. 7-J. (*She stomps on the floor.*)

YOUNG MAN: The lady with the survey! Come on in. (*He pulls her into the room, and slams the door behind them.*)

MISS PRESSON: You're sure it's all right? I'm not disturbing you? You're not in the middle of anything important?

YOUNG MAN: An attempted assassination. Other than that I'm pretty clear.

MISS PRESSON: (*A peal of giggles.*) What a terrible thing to say!

YOUNG MAN: I know.

MISS PRESSON: You're just like you were on the telephone.

YOUNG MAN: Don't you want to know *who?*

MISS PRESSON: (*Squealing, covering her ears.*) No! (*Looking around.*) I love your apartment.

YOUNG MAN: It's not mine.

MISS PRESSON: Will you *stop!*

YOUNG MAN: Drink?

MISS PRESSON: It's awful early.

YOUNG MAN: Grass?

MISS PRESSON: What?!

YOUNG MAN: Anything?

MISS PRESSON: I'm fine just as I am.

YOUNG MAN: You can take your dress off.

MISS PRESSON: I said I was fine.

YOUNG MAN: Suit yourself. (*He goes out, leaving her alone with the Window Washer and Man.*)

MISS PRESSON: I didn't know you had so much company!

YOUNG MAN: (*Offstage.*) Old friends. Don't mind them. Make yourself at home. I've got to get set up for this.

MISS PRESSON: (*Sees the letter on the desk.*) Oh, you've been typing. Are you a writer?

WINDOW WASHER: Hello, pussycat.

MISS PRESSON: He's familiar.

YOUNG MAN: (*Offstage.*) Yeah. Very.

WINDOW WASHER: Hello, pussycat.

MISS PRESSON: He's drunk too.

WINDOW WASHER: I'm drunk, too.

MISS PRESSON: Now I remember! He's the . . . he was . . . *oh!* (*To the*

Man.) What's wrong with you?

WINDOW WASHER: He's nuts. Everybody's nuts around here. (*The Man struggles; muffled yells.*)

MISS PRESSON: Well, I'm certainly not going to miss the President for some man tied up in a chair. (*Going to the window.*) I love a parade, don't you? There's something so . . . I don't know . . . so American about them! They just make me feel good.

YOUNG MAN: (*Enters, dressed in a North African robe, picks up his rifle and crosses to the window where he joins Miss Presson.*) You know what's going through my head right now? A stupid song I must have heard when I was eight years old. "I'm LOOKing Over a Four-Leaf Clover." Was that by the Andrews Sisters? Whatever happened to all those nice musical ladies? Evelyn and Her Magic Violin. Is she dead, too? They're almost all dead . . . the best people.

MISS PRESSON: I brought confetti to throw at him. Four Sunday *Times* and a *Daily News* worth. A parade just isn't a parade for me without confetti. Tons and tons of it.

YOUNG MAN: I'm going to shoot him, Miss Presson. I'm going to kill the President.

MISS PRESSON: I've never seen such crowds! I was at a movie premiere once and I thought those were crowds. But this!

YOUNG MAN: He's such an old fart. They're all such old farts, even the young ones. Maybe I'll just puncture him and all the air will run out like a big huge balloon.

MISS PRESSON: Look at the sun shining on those trumpets and drums. Everything's so sparkling and glittery and golden down there. And the tubas! They shine brightest of all. They're the biggest, that's why.

YOUNG MAN: What are you supposed to do when you see an old man passed out drunk in the street and it's cold and it's raining and he's lying there in his own puke maybe dying? What are you supposed to do about a thing like that? Help him up? Where do you take him? Home? Do you give him money? How much? Do you hold him? How long, how tight? What do you do about people like him, Miss P.?

MISS PRESSON: (*At once.*) They're from Amagansett! I've been there. It's the most beautiful beach I've ever seen and you meet a very nice class of people. Hello there, Amagansett!

YOUNG MAN: I want him to look up here just before I pull the trigger. You know, his eyes meet mine and that barrel starring straight at him. I'd love it if it scared him so much he shit himself.

MISS PRESSON: I've got goose bumps, I'm so excited. I'm a Fourth of July baby and there were always fireworks, but never anything as exciting as this! Ooooooooo! I nearly fell that time.

YOUNG MAN: If I weren't standing at this window, if this were an ordinary day, you know what I'd want to do, Miss Presson? I'd want to fuck you. That's all, just fuck you.

MISS PRESSON: (*Never looking at him.*) I know, I know! (*Pointing.*) Look, look! He's turning the corner. He's so handsome for a President. He looks like a prince or a king or a Holy Roman Emperor, he's so handsome.

YOUNG MAN: I'm going to feel better when I do this.

MISS PRESSON: She's wearing pink! And they've got all the children with them. Oh, I could cry they're all so beautiful together. This could only be in America.

WINDOW WASHER: Sure I drink too much. Sure I like to punch people in the nose. And sure I'm going back up there and try and get me a little loving.

MISS PRESSON: (*Hurling confetti.*) Mr. President! We love you Mr. President!

WINDOW WASHER: (*At the window now, too.*) I hope to hell he blows somebody's head off with that gun, even if it's yours. One of us got to know he's still alive. Well don't he, Mr. President?

MISS PRESSON: (*Overlapping.*) He sees us! He's looking right at us!

YOUNG MAN: (*Overlapping.*) Mr. President! Here's looking at you, Mr. P.! (*The Young Man is just about to put the rifle to his cheek to fire when from outside we hear a terrific barrage of gunfire. It should sound like a rifle is being fired from every window for blocks and blocks.*)

MISS PRESSON: They're shooting him. Oh my God, they're shooting the President. Out of all those windows . . . they're pointing rifles and shooting the President! (*She turns from the window in horror and sees the Young Man with the rifle. He looks at her. She screams.*) You! . . . you! . . . oh my God! . . . no! . . . no!! . . . (*She runs from the apartment. The Window Washer has turned at her cries. The Young Man, looking right at him, is approaching him as if to offer him the rifle.)*

WINDOW WASHER: Jesus Christ, you are crazy! Put that gun down! *(He suddenly lunges forward and grabs the rifle from the Young Man, who backs away a few steps and opens his arms, as if to invite the Window Washer to shoot him. POW! POW! POW! as the Window Washer fires. But the rifle is loaded with blanks. The Young Man has started to laugh—hysterically, uncontrollably. The Window Washer has dropped the rifle in fear, anger and frustration. The Young Man keeps laughing.)* You crazy bastard! You crazy bastard! *(He runs from the apartment. The Young Man stands center stage for a beat, looks desperately at the Man, who in his terror has worked his gag loose and started to scream, and then very slowly crosses to the desk. The lights are starting to fade. At the desk, he picks up his letter to the President, looks at it a moment, then crumples it. The Man is silent now, watching him. Next the Young Man takes a small American flag from the desk and goes to the window. He stands there, looking down. He waves the flag very slowly with one hand as his other hand comes up slowly in the V-for-Victory sign. Pin spot on the Young Man and another one on the Man. The light on the Man fades. The Young Man is alone at the window, waving the flag. He is breaking down. There is a distant sound of wailing sirens. The light on him fades. Blackout.)*

Curtain.

Whiskey

for Leonard Melfi
Like the song says, a good man is hard to find.

WHISKEY was first performed on April 19, 1973, at Theatre at Saint Clement's in New York City. It was directed by Kevin O'Connor. Sets by Kert Lundell. Lighting by Charles Cosler. Costumes by Lorie Watson. Sound by Lewis Rosen. Production assistants were Suzanne Gedance and Hall Powell. The production stage manager was Jimmy Cuomo. The cast was as follows:

ANNOUNCER . . . . Kelly Fitzpatrick
I.W. HARPER . . . . Tom Rosqui
TIA MARIA . . . . Charlotte Rae
JOHNNY WALKER . . . . Beeson Carroll
SOUTHERN COMFORT . . . . Susan Browning
JACK DANIELS . . . . Michael Sacks

Characters

THE LUSH THRUSHES:

I.W. HARPER: Middle-aged, slightly balding and a little plump. His is an extremely affable nature, but when sufficiently aroused he can crack a mean bullwhip. Certainly at first glance he is extremely likable.

TIA MARIA: Middle-aged and a little plump herself. She's basically a warm and sentimental dame but occasionally the facade of brassiness obscures that fact. She is either extremely down or extremely up: laughing too hard . . . or crying. Above all, there is something very nice and maternal about her.

JOHNNY WALKER: Middle thirties, dark eyes and hair. *He* thinks he's handsome. He also thinks of himself as a mean bastard which means that he *acts* like a mean bastard. Well, most of the time.

SOUTHERN COMFORT: Early twenties, red hair and built. She's wild and sexy and arrogant and flaunts her sexuality and drinks a lot and gets like a cat in heat and just generally behaves like a bundle of dynamite.

JACK DANIELS: Early twenties, blue eyes and blonde. He has an engaging grin which isn't engaging enough to conceal the fact that he is a very dumb bunny indeed. If you told him this to his face, he wouldn't be too upset. In fact, he'd probably grin and bear it. You see, he rather enjoys playing the buffoon.

WHISKEY: A mean-tempered, extremely musical horse who occupies that very special place in the heart of America left empty when the first and original Lassie retired from the screen. Whiskey's millions of fans, of course, have no idea how mean he is. Believe me, this horse is a killer.

ALSO APPEARING IN THE PLAY (BUT NEVER SEEN) ARE:

ANNOUNCER'S VOICE: Smooth, unctuous and Texas as all git out.

URGENT VOICE: A total hysteric.

Setting

The Houston Astrodome and then a large suite in a very swanky hotel in downtown Houston. The time is now.

Whiskey

Darkness. We hear the expectant, excited murmuring of a huge crowd. Then there is a long drum roll followed by a crash of cymbals.

Announcer's Voice: Mr. President, honored astronauts, ladies and gentlemen, and all you other y'alls, Houston's unique, one-of-a-kind, internationally world-famous and fully air conditioned Astrodome brings you live and in the flesh for the first time anywhere outside of your home color TV screen, the stars of America's longest running TV series . . . ! (*He's said all this in one breath. Now he pauses, takes one, before trumpeting the name.*) THE LUSH THRUSHES AND WHISKEY ! ! ! (*A neon light across the top of the proscenium is illuminated to read: "The Lush Thrushes and Whiskey." While the orchestra vamps under each introduction.*) He's made you laugh an' he's made you cry. A quick man with the bullwhip but even quicker to right social injustice and grievances. Like the song says, a good man is hard to find. Who am I talking about? (*Pause.*) WHY I.W. HARPER, THAT'S WHO ! ! ! (*A light comes up revealing I.W. Harper standing inside a cut-out of a huge bottle of I.W. Harper's. I.W. is wearing a fawn-colored Stetson, a buckskin fringed shirt, expensive cowboy pants and black boots with rattlesnakes on the sides. The crowd roars its approval. I.W. looks terrified.*)

I.W.HARPER: (*When the crowd will let him speak.*) Howdy. After all those years you've been watching us on your TV screens, it sure is nice to see you for a change. And I'll tell you something. I've done a lot of living, a lot of loving and a lot of elbow-bending. And drunk or sober, I never met a man I didn't like. Yahoo! (*He tries, rather unsuccessfully, to crack his bullwhip. The Announcer's Voice and the orchestra come quickly to his rescue.*)

Announcer's Voice: Behind every great man there's a little woman an' I.W. Harper's no exception. What Sophia Loren is to Italy, what

Joan of Arc was to France, is this little lady to our great and golden Southwest. That bowl of peaches and cream with just a wee dab bit of vinegar to make the sweet part taste even sweeter . . . ! (*Pause.*) TIA MARIA ! ! ! (*A light comes up revealing Tia Maria standing inside a cut-out of a huge bottle of Tia Maria. She is wearing a white Stetson but it is hanging down her back from the drawstring around her throat. She wears a blouse, a suede vest, a cowskin skirt and high red boots. Again the crowd roars its approval. Tia Maria looks terrified, too.*)

TIA MARIA: *I* never met a man I didn't like. (*She pauses, and this is her legendary comic timing. You can almost feel the crowd counting the beats with her.*) Until I married I.W.! (*The crowd laughs. Tia Maria is in! She visibly relaxes and improvises a yodeled roundelay around the orchestra's vamping.*)

ANNOUNCER'S VOICE: He's mean, he's tough, he packs a big swift side iron. He don't say much but when he does you better listen. He'd as soon shoot you as spit on you. Your favorite badman and mine . . . (*Pause.*) JOHNNY WALKER ! ! ! (*A light comes up revealing Johnny Walker standing inside a cut-out of a huge bottle of Johnny Walker Black Label Scotch. Johnny is wearing a cowboy outfit entirely of black leather: hat, shirt, pants, boots, everything. Since he's squinting and trying to look real mean at the same time, he looks less nervous than I.W. Harper and Tia Maria. But he isn't.*)

JOHNNY WALKER: (*After waiting for the entire Astrodome to get as quiet as a mouse; it's a long wait, too.*) I'll tell you something, cowpoke. (*You could drive a Mack truck through his drawl.*) I'd as soon shoot you as shit on you. Spit on you! I mean spit on you! (*General consternation. Johnny Walker draws both pistols and fires, the orchestra plays loudly, anything to cover up. Johnny Walker's facade has visibly wilted.*)

ANNOUNCER'S VOICE: Now all right, you young lads, and some of you not so young ones, too! This next little gal's a real little lady and I wouldn't want her leaving Houston thinking the men here were just a pack o' prairie wolves. (*Appropriate and appreciative yells and whistles from the men in the audience.*) Aw shucks! She was born and raised in Houston, so she already *knows*! (*There is a burst of flame and a shrill scream from the shadows.*) Why she's just burning to get out there and entertain y'all . . . SOUTHERN COMFORT! ! ! (*A light comes up revealing Southern Comfort standing inside a cut-out of a huge bottle of Southern Comfort. She is wearing what could only be described as a very mini and a very mod version of a cowgirl's outfit. Lots of thigh and breast but her accessories are pretty groovy, too. At the moment, she isn't at all ready. Someone put too much kerosene on her baton ends and they are flaming dangerously. She holds them at arms length, clearly terrified and not at all ready to do anything with them but holding them as far away from her as she possibly can. Realizing she must do* something, *she turns and faces the audience, a flaming baton in each hand and forces a kind of frozen smile.*)

SOUTHERN COMFORT: Tableau, ladies and gentlemen! I call this my flaming tableau!

ANNOUNCER'S VOICE: (*To the rescue.*) And a might pretty one it is, honey. Ain't that a pretty sight, folks? Hunh? Ain't it? Well, let's show the little lady how pretty we think it is! (*He leads the audience in reluctant applause.*) Hey, now just a second y'all, settle down and see if you can help an ol' cowpoke out. I know there's *five* Thrush Lushes and Whiskey but I'll be dollgarned if I can only think of *four* o'them! Who's the one I'm missing? (*An inaudible voice from the crowd.*) Who? (*More voices calling out the name.*) You'll have to speak up a whole plumb lot louder than that. (*More and more voices.*) How do you 'spect me to hear you when you're all talking at once? Now I want to hear that name loud and I want to hear it clear. One! two! three! (*We hear the audience loud and clear.*)

AUDIENCE: JACK DANIELS! ! !

ANNOUNCER'S VOICE: Who? Captain Samuels?

AUDIENCE: JACK DANIELS! ! !

ANNOUNCER'S VOICE: Dan Janiels?

AUDIENCE: JACK DANIELS! ! !

ANNOUNCER'S VOICE: Oh! You mean that one and only rib-tickler, that court jester to the great and golden Southwest, that cowboy with a bale of hay where his head should be . . . (*Pause.*) JACK DANIELS! ! ! (*A light comes up revealing Jack Daniels standing inside a cut-out of a huge bottle of Jack Daniels. He is hatless and wearing a gingham shirt under denim coveralls. He is barefoot, too. He grins foolishly and the audience goes wild. He tries the simplest of rope tricks, makes a botch of it and his pants fall down. Clearly an audience favorite, Jack Daniels is.)*

JACK DANIELS: You know what the Texan said after he opened a bottle of Lone Star Beer with his front teeth? "Do I swallow this here little dohickey or chew?" And you know what the Yankee said who tried the same thing? "Phphphphphphph." *(He lisps through imaginary broken front teeth. The crowd laughs. The orchestra has broken into a rousing cowboy song. The five Lush Thrushes, each standing inside the appropriately marked cut-out bottle, are singing along and urging the audience to join them, especially for the hand claps. While the Lush Thrushes sing, each of them does his or her own thing: I.W. Harper cracking his bullwhip; Tia Maria improvising yodels; Johnny Walker shooting his gun; Southern Comfort trying to twirl her massively flaming batons; and Jack Daniels attempting rope tricks. All in all, it is a very colorful stage picture. One panel of the Lush Thrushes and Whiskey tableau, however, is still dark.)*

ANNOUNCER'S VOICE: *(Over music.)* And now, with all respects to this glittering array of multimillion dollar talent and very pretty feminine pulchritude. . . the word's in Webster and it's *not* dirty! . . . the star of our show. The Paderewzski on the hoof, that equine Frank Sinatra, America's favorite horse and I'm tempted to say person! . . . the one, the only, the what-other-word-but-inimitable! . . . *(Pause.)* . . . WHISKEY! ! ! *(A light comes up on the cut-out silhouette of a horse. The only trouble is there's no real horse inside it when there very clearly should be. The Lush Thrushes sing another chorus of their song and wait at the end of each line for Whiskey to tap a response with his hoof or appear . . . or anything. Consternation among the Lush Thrushes. The song continues. Tia Maria goes behind the show curtain, the other four continue singing. But even above the music we can hear Whiskey's loud whinnying and crashing hooves and Tia Maria's even louder yells. Tia Maria reappears looking disheveled, angry and holding her arm. I.W. Harper goes behind the show curtain and again we hear Whiskey whinnying and crashing his hooves. We even catch a glimpse of I.W. Harper struggling unsuccessfully with a rope that is clearly attached to Whiskey's bridle. The crowd has recovered itself suffi-*

ciently and begun to react. First there were just a few catcalls but now the general laughter is unmistakable and growing.)

I.W. HARPER: Whiskey'll be right out, ladies and gentlemen. He's just feeling a little . . . well, frisky this evening!

JACK DANIELS: You show me a horse who won't take center stage spotlight when it's offered him and I'll show you a Mexican burro who's trying to pass for a horse!

ANNOUNCER'S VOICE: Ladies and gentlemen, please. Whiskey'll be right out here to entertain you. Just a simple case of stable fright! Opening night nerves! In the meantime, I suggest we all join the Thrush Lushes in a good old-fashioned Texas sing out! (*Pandemonium reigns. The Lush Thrushes valiantly struggle to keep the song going but they have clearly lost their audience. Whiskey must be completely out of control by now from the look of I.W. Harper's struggles with the rope. Several times he has been thrown to the ground. And no matter how loud the crowd's laughter and the music, Whiskey's whinnying is louder than all. Suddenly, an excited hush falls over the crowd. From the looks on the Lush Thrushes' faces we can clearly see that something dreadful has happened. They barely continue to sing, just kind of mouthing the song as they watch this dreadful thing happening. Hardly anyone in the orchestra is bothering to play anymore. Above this ominous almost–silence, Whiskey's whinnying will seem every loud indeed.*)

I.W. HARPER: He's leaving!

TIA MARIA: The President's leaving.

JOHNNY WALKER: He's walking out!

JACK DANIELS: He's not coming back! (*What has happened and what the Lush Thrushes have seen and followed with their very own and astonished-and-humiliated eyes is this: the President of the United States has walked out on them! I.W. Harper, Tia Maria, Johnny Walker and Jack Daniels are studies in abject humiliation. Southern Comfort, however, is seething with anger. She's not about to be humiliated like this, not in her old hometown, even if he is the President.*)

SOUTHERN COMFORT: (*Running to the footlights and nailing him with her voice, it's a strong one.*) Mr. President! Hey, jowly boy, that's right, I'm talking to you! (*This time you could hear a pin drop in the Astrodome. The President has clearly turned and is listening to*

Southern Comfort.) You ought to try slipping into one o' these for size! (*And with that she flips her skirt up over her head, does a neat backbend and stays there. And now total consternation. The crowd roars, the band plays loudly, the other Lush Thrushes hustle Southern Comfort offstage and the Announcer is reduced to babbling in his microphone. Above the pandemonium . . . louder than it, in fact . . . we hear Whiskey whinnying and crashing his hooves: a sound that will continue while the light and sound of this scene fade and during the short blackout which follows while the following legend is flashed on the curtain MUCH LATER THAT NIGHT. THE NEXT MORNING, IN FACT. Whiskey's whinnying subsides to a peaceful and occasional snortle. His crashing hooves become an occasioned shift of his weight. A silence. And in the darkness we hear Jack Daniels singing "The Streets of Laredo" in a very sweet and very true voice. We are in a hotel suite. There are no lights on but enough is spilling in from the window to give us some idea of where we are. By the window, on a window seat, in fact, is where Jack Daniels is sitting and singing his song. It looks like there's been a very big party in the room not too long ago. Empty glasses and liquor bottles, overflowing ashtrays, several rolling tables sent up by room service, etc. We hear assorted snores, grunts and other sleeping noises from somewhere in the room but it is too dark to tell who is making them or from where. All this while Jack Daniels sings "The Streets of Laredo," which is a very beautiful and very sad song. Oh yes, from his singing it should be quite clear that Jack Daniels is totally, thoroughly, blissfully and roaringly drunk. Stinking. Blotto. Wiped out. Suddenly there is a loud and urgent knocking on the door outside the suite and we hear an urgent voice.*)

URGENT VOICE: Fire! Fire! The hotel's on fire! Everybody out and into the street! (*The voice by now is a shriek of hysteria.*) The main thing is stay calm! Don't anybody lose their head! (*Jack Daniels continues his song, clearly not hearing or comprehending this message of impending disaster from outside the suite. Next we hear the sound of many people in the corridor as they flee their rooms and head for the elevator and stairs. From the occasional yells, shouts and screams it should sound like a stampede is going on right outside the suite. Jack Daniels continues his song. The sounds of the stampede have faded away. Silence and Jack Daniels singing. A small bedside lamp is switched on and in the tiny shaft of light it spills we see I.W. Harper. He is wearing pajamas but they have been custom-made to look very much like the cowboy outfit he was wearing at the Astrodome: the buckskin fringed shirt, for example, is really only a stenciled pattern on a simple cotton pajama shirt but it looks pretty convincing for a moment. I.W. rolls out of bed and heads for the bathroom. From his somnambulistic movements we can tell that he is not really awake and from his swaying walk we can see that he, too, is stinking drunk. There is just enough light spilling into the bathroom to see I.W. enter and seat himself on the toilet. Jack Daniels continues his song, as unaware of I.W. Harper as I.W. Harper is unaware of him. Another bedside lamp on the other side of the same bed, in fact is switched on and we see Tia Maria. She is wearing a lady's nightgown version of I.W. Harper's cowboy pajamas. When she rolls out of bed and heads for the same bathroom, we can see that she, too, is only half awake and stinking drunk. With the two bedside lamps burning, the bathroom is even brighter and this is what we see: I.W. Harper sitting on the toilet and Tia Maria heading toward him. They are clearly on a collision course. I.W.'s jaw hangs open, he looks like he's seeing a ghost. He cannot move, he dares not speak. Tia Maria is almost on top of him when she turns and sits directly on his lap. What Tia Maria then does is this: produce the loudest, longest and most bloodcurdling scream in the history of the theatre.)*

TIA MARIA: AAAAAAEEEEEIIIIIIIOOOOOOUUUUUUU!!!!

I.W. HARPER: Honey?

TIA MARIA: AAAAAAEEEEEEEEIIIIIIIIIOOOOOOUUUUUUUU!!!

I.W. HARPER: Is that you honey?

TIA MARIA: AAAAAEEEEEEEEOOOOOOOUUUUUU!!!!

I.W. HARPER: You scared me.

TIA MARIA: OH! OH! OH!

I.W. HARPER: That's not funny. (*Tia Maria has fainted dead away. I.W. is still sitting on the toilet.*) Wow! Wow, my heart is pounding. Listen to that ol' ticker o' mine pump! First I didn't see you. Then I wasn't sure if it *was* you. And then I got afraid that if I said something I'd scare whoever it was more than they was scaring *me*. I mean I could *see* what was gonna happen but at the same time I just couldn't believe it really *would*. People don't sit on other people when they go to the toilet. I mean they just don't do that. Same goes for the people already on the toilet. Other people just plain don't sit on *them*. I sat in a lady's lap once but that was in a movie theatre and it was a real bright day out, my eyes hadn't adjusted yet, and I just didn't see her. Scared the bejeezes out o' me. Sure *felt* funny, too. (*Pause.*) Come on now, honey, get up. You know I can't go with you in here.

TIA MARIA: (*Stirring.*) What happened?

I.W. HARPER: You passed out.

TIA MARIA: Feel like I fainted.

I.W. HARPER: You been hitting that stuff pretty hard tonight.

TIA MARIA: I know what passing out feels like and this is different. It's . . . it's . . . headier.

I.W. HARPER: Headier?

TIA MARIA: More in the head. Passing out's more in the gut. I need a pill. (*She struggles to her feet.*) I'm turning on the light.

I.W. HARPER: I don't have my shades on.

TIA MARIA: Close your eyes then.

I.W. HARPER: It'll hurt, honey.

TIA MARIA: It's gonna hurt like hell. (*She turns on the bathroom lights, they both wince at the brightness.*) Oh! Wow! Oh wow!

I.W. HARPER: You okay?

TIA MARIA: I had the worst nightmare, I.W.

I.W. HARPER: Baby! Why didn't you wake me?

TIA MARIA: It was a major one.

I.W. HARPER: Those damn stingers. They'll do it every time.

TIA MARIA: I was walking along, you know? . . . just walking, nothing chasing me or anything like that . . . I was in a woods! . . . and I heard this stream . . . no, it was more like a waterfall . . . and I got real tired and I just had to rest. So far everything was real peaceful and I was feeling real good. But when I went to sit down . . . and this is the horrible part . . . I felt— (*Tia Maria has sat on the edge of the bathtub. From behind the drawn shower curtains there is a terrific whinnying and crashing of hooves. Tia Maria leaps to her feet, the shower curtains sway menacingly.*) AAAAAEEEIIIIIII OOOOOUUUUUUU!!!

terectomy.

I.W. HARPER: That was two years ago.

TIA MARIA: My liver 'n lungs are now. Bones don't heal at my age. Remember Aunt Edna? She started out breaking her little finger. Then it was her hand, then it was her wrist, then it was her arm, then it was her hip and next thing you know she was dead.

I.W. HARPER: (*Giving her a pill and a glass of water.*) Take this.

TIA MARIA: (*Not even looking at it.*) It's called the "Brittle Bones Syndrome." I know all about it. *Time Magazine* had a whole long piece on it.

I.W. HARPER: Aunt Edna was in her eighties.

TIA MARIA: So! (*She gulps the pill down.*)

I.W. HARPER: Your bones aren't brittle. They're soft and warm and cuddly and plump.

TIA MARIA: (*A new form of misery.*) That's my outsides you're talking about!

I.W. HARPER: Well I love 'em! Inside or out, honey, I love you all over.

TIA MARIA: I hate the way I look. I'm going on a diet.

I.W. HARPER: I like you just the way you are.

TIA MARIA: What do you know? While they were cutting out my ovaries I should have had 'em cut all the fat off while they was at it. I bet they could do it, too.

I.W. HARPER: Honey!

TIA MARIA: Well why not? They can cut everything else out o' you, so why not fat? If they can have heart transplant operations, they sure as shooting must have fat ones, too! Hunh, I.W. don't you think?

I.W. HARPER: Sure thing, honey.

TIA MARIA: I bet that doctor right here in Houston does 'em!

I.W. HARPER: If anyone does, honey, I reckon it's him.

TIA MARIA: Will you call him?

I.W. HARPER: First thing in the morning.

TIA MARIA: Can I have one?

I.W. HARPER: You bet.

TIA MARIA: You won't mind?

I.W. HARPER: Not if you don't

TIA MARIA: Thank you, I.W. You're a good man. Like the song says.

I.W. HARPER: All better now?

I.W. HARPER: Whiskey!

TIA MARIA: AAAAEEEEIIIIIUUUU!!!!

I.W. HARPER: Now hush up in there, you hear me? Now hush!

TIA MARIA: He's trying to kill me, don't tell me he's not!

I.W. HARPER: Thattaboy, Whiskey, steady now there. Momma didn't mean to frighten you.

TIA MARIA: Frighten *him!*

I.W.HARPER: You know he doesn't like it when you do that, Tia.

TIA MARIA: I'm sorry, but I keep forgetting that he's in there!

I.W. HARPER: Thattaboy, back to sleep now, momma's sorry . . .

TIA MARIA: Like hell she is!

I.W.HARPER: Sshh!

TIA MARIA: Goddamn that horse anyway!

I.W. HARPER: Tia!

TIA MARIA: I mean doggurn, only it comes out goddamn!

I.W. HARPER: Look at you, you're all het up. (*Whiskey is quiet now and the shower curtain stops swaying.*)

TIA MARIA: I'll say I'm het up! He tried to kill me again. That's grounds for hetting! (*She sobs.*) What did I ever do to him? That's what I'd like to know. Why does it have to be *me* he wants to get at?

I.W. HARPER: (*Getting her onto the toilet seat.*) Honey!

TIA MARIA: Well it hurts! (*And now for the first time perhaps we can see very clearly that her left arm is in a cast.*)

I.W. HARPER: Now don't wave it around like that.

TIA MARIA: Wave it? Thanks to that blasted horse tonight I may never even be able to move it again!

I.W. HARPER: It's a simple fracture, honey.

TIA MARIA: I'd like to know what's so simple about it.

I.W. HARPER: You heard the doctor.

TIA MARIA: A doggurn horse rears up and kicks my arms with his doggurn hard hooves and breaks my goddamn *tibia majore—*

I.W. HARPER: *Tibia menore.*

TIA MARIA: I don't call that simple.

I.W. HARPER: Doctors do.

TIA MARIA: That little quack.

I.W. HARPER: It happens all the time.

TIA MARIA: To little kids falling out o' apple trees! Not to 48-year-old women with lung and liver conditions still recovering from a hys-

TIA MARIA: (*Dissolving again.*) No!!!

I.W. HARPER: You want another drink?

TIA MARIA: I hate this hotel room. I hate Houston. I hate Texas. I hate Texans. My arm hurts. I'm fat. I miss Beverly Hills. Yes, I want another drink!

I.W. HARPER: Don't cry.

TIA MARIA: We made fools of ourselves.

I.W. HARPER: I hate it when you cry.

TIA MARIA: It was bad enough them laughing, but then *him* walking out right in the middle and *her* pulling that stunt . . . !

I.W. HARPER: Honey, I told you, first thing in the morning I'm gonna fire that agent.

TIA MARIA: You said you was gonna call that doctor!

I.W. HARPER: I'll call 'em both.

TIA MARIA: Can't we fire him now?

I.W. HARPER: It's after three.

TIA MARIA: Well, let's wake him, that little ten-percent runt. We're sure not getting any sleep tonight.

I.W. HARPER: Honey, let's just hope he hasn't fired *us*.

TIA MARIA: I'd like to see him try! It's all his fault.

I.W. HARPER: Of course it is.

TIA MARIA: Well isn't it?

I.W. HARPER: Sure it is, honey. He never should've booked us. We're not a live act.

TIA MARIA: Even if we were, that Astrodome's too big for people. Barbara Streisand wouldn't work in that place if she tried to. And the acoustics! Just what about them? I couldn't even hear my cues they were . . . (*She bursts into new tears.*) . . . laughing so loud!

I.W. HARPER: (*It's hopeless.*) Now you just sit right there. I'm going in there and fix us two o' the stiffest drinks anybody ever tasted. Something that'll put a little hair on your chest.

TIA MARIA: (*New wails.*) I got hair on my chest! Two black ones. I do! I do! It's those goddamn hormone shots. That goddamn doctor, I'm gonna sue that little quack. He's turning me into goddamn gorilla! (*I.W. Harper leaves Tia Maria sitting on the toilet alone in the bathroom. He comes into the main room where Jack Daniels is still sitting staring out the window and kind of humming and strumming his song.*)

I.W. HARPER: Who's that?

JACK DANIELS: It's jes' lil' ol' Jack Daniels, I.W.

I.W. HARPER: What are you doing in here?

JACK DANIELS: Nothing.

I.W. HARPER: Well go in your own room and do it.

JACK DANIELS: I can't, I lost my key.

I.W. HARPER: How'd you get in here?

JACK DANIELS: I never left.

I.W. HARPER: That's chutzpa for you.

JACK DANIELS: What is, I.W.?

I.W. HARPER: You! Most people would have the decency and common sense to go to their own room after the other people had gone to bed, especially other people whose free liquor and room service they'd been sponging on all night!

JACK DANIELS: Boy, that chutzpa sure means a heck of a whole lot for such a tiny little word. I reckon it must be one o' them Jewish show business words.

I.W. HARPER: I reckon it is!

JACK DANIELS: Southern Comfort's been teaching 'em to me. She says Tia Maria's a yenta, you and Johnny Walker are . . . let's see . . . schmucks? . . . and I'm a mensch! I'm just trying to figure out what *she* is after what she done tonight!

I.W. HARPER: Are you figuring on sitting there all night watching me and my wife sleep?

JACK DANIELS: I ain't been watching y'all sleep. I jes' been sitting here looking out the window, strumming my Gibson and sipping rye. Hell, I.W., what do you take me for? I ain't one of your perverts, like Johnny Walker. Leas' that's what Southern Comfort says he is, only she must be pretty perverted herself, doing a thing like that in front o' the President of the United States and those astronaut fellows. Some o' them are real fine men, I read. And some of them had their wives there, too. Boy, she sure set me to thinking 'bout what this country's coming to. My pa had a word for girls like Southern Comfort. He called 'em confused. And I reckon that's what Southern Comfort is. Just plain confused. Anyway, after I undressed y'all and put y'all to bed—

I.W. HARPER: You undressed us?

JACK DANIELS: I sure did! Stripped them costumes plumb off o' you and put you in your p.j.'s. Hell, I.W. I had to. You were both passed out dead drunk on the floor.

I.W. HARPER: You undressed my wife?

JACK DANIELS: Yep.

I.W. HARPER: Cut that cowboy crap! I'm trying to get a straight answer.

JACK DANIELS: Yep's 'bout as straight an answer as I can think o'.

I.W. HARPER: You actually undressed her?

JACK DANIELS: Both of you, I.W.

I.W. HARPER: That ain't chutzpa, brother, those are good old-fashioned American balls.

JACK DANIELS: What are, I.W.?

I.W. HARPER: Never mind! Just sit there and shut up. I don't even remember what I came in here for.

JACK DANIELS: You know why?

I.W. HARPER: 'Cause I'm drunk!

JACK DANIELS: That's why. Now you jes' sit there real still, I.W., and it'll come back to you. Or you'll pass out dead drunk again.

I.W. HARPER: Jesus, what a stomach!

JACK DANIELS: You ever try a raw turkey egg with kaopectate for one of those?

I.W. HARPER: No!

JACK DANIELS: Me neither. My pa swore by 'em. 'Nother time my big brother came home so drunk on moonshine and rot-gut he was like to die. Pa fixed him up real quick with a cod liver oil enema.

I.W. HARPER: I said knock it off!

JACK DANIELS: Sorry, I.W. (*Pause.*) You fixin' to throw up?

I.W. HARPER: What does it look like?

JACK DANIELS: I'll be real still then. (*Pause.*) Can I play my gittar? (*I.W. Harper nods his head.*) Can I sing?

I.W. HARPER: Anything, just don't talk. (*Jack Daniels plays and sings "The Streets of Laredo" again.*)

JACK DANIELS: I'm sure crazy 'bout this song. Sorry, I.W. (He *plays and sings a while.*) I.W.?

I.W. HARPER: What?

JACK DANIELS: Can I say jes' one thing?

I.W. HARPER: What?

JACK DANIELS: You know something?

I.W. HARPER: *What!?*

JACK DANIELS: Your wife's got hair on her titties. (*Before I.W. HARPER can explode, Tia Maria does it for him from the bathroom with another of her bloodcurdling screams. What has happened is this: the toilet on which she has been sitting holding her head and commiserating with herself has suddenly noisily and of its own accord flushed!*)

TIA MARIA: (*Bolting from the toilet seat.*) AAAEEEEEEIIIIIIOOOOOUU-UUUUU!!!! (*Her yell has roused Whiskey, who responds with another deafening series of whinnies and a beating of hooves. Again the shower curtains sway violently. All this, of course, causes Tia Maria to scream again.*) AAAEEEEEEIIIIIIIOOOOOUUUUUU!!!! (*She runs to the door, yanks at the door handle and it comes off in her hand. I.W. Harper in the meantime has run to one of the windows, leaned his head out and is busily being sick.*)

JACK DANIELS: She's screaming again, I.W. (*But I.W. HARPER is in no condition or position to reply.*)

TIA MARIA: AAAEEEEEEIIIIIIIOOOOOUUUUUU!!!! (*Jack Daniels goes to the bathroom door and from his side politely knocks.*)

JACK DANIELS: Ma'am?

TIA MARIA: Get me out of here!

JACK DANIELS: Anything wrong, ma'am?

TIA MARIA: I'm locked in the goddamn bathroom with a goddamn horse who's trying to kill me!

JACK DANIELS: What happened?

TIA MARIA: The goddamn toilet flushed! Now get me out of here! (*Jack Daniels pulls on the door handle. It comes off in his hand.*)

JACK DANIELS: Ma'am?

TIA MARIA: What? Help! Help!

JACK DANIELS: You better try from your side.

TIA MARIA: I can't. The handle's come off.

JACK DANIELS: Well, ma'am, then I guess you're up shit creek 'cause mine has, too. (*This announcement proves too much for Tia Maria, who promptly faints again.*) I 'spose I could call room service. (*Jack Daniels crosses to a light switch and turns on the overhead lights. For the first time we get a clear look at the room and it is even messier than we had imagined. Clearly a tornado has passed through the premises. But the most startling sight of all is the figure of Johnny Walker. He is passed out dead drunk over a card table. In front of him is a deck of cards laid out in a solitaire pattern. He is wearing his gun and holster, his undershorts and his boots. Clearly he has been sitting there all along, passed out over the cards like this, only we couldn't see him in the dark. He raises his head groggily when Jack Daniels turns on the lights. Johnny Walker is in a very, very, surly mood.)*

JOHNNY WALKER: What did you call me? (*Jack Daniels is having difficulty locating the telephone because of the mess in the room, so he is having to follow along the wire from the socket in the wall.)*

JACK DANIELS: You sho' was on a losing streak 'foe you passed out there, Johnny Walker.

JOHNNY WALKER: What did you call me?

JACK DANIELS: I heard o' strip poker, I played me some, too, but that strip solitaire's a new one on me.

JOHNNY WALKER: What did you call me, cowboy?

JACK DANIELS: Don't look too easy; don't look like much fun neither.

JOHNNY WALKER: Hey, hayseed; I'm talking to you! (*He takes clumsy aim with his pistol, fires, misses.)*

JACK DANIELS: (*On the telephone now.)* Hush up there now, will you? I'm trying to get room service.

JOHNNY WALKER: (*Turning his attention elsewhere.)* Hey you, fat ass, the one with his can in the air! (*He aims, fires, misses. I.W. Harper has turned back into the room. He slumps weakly on the window seat.)*

I.W. HARPER: Not tonight, Johnny, I'm too sick.

JOHNNY WALKER: What did you call me, cowpoke?

I.W. HARPER: Go in your room if you're gonna do that.

JOHNNY WALKER: Somebody called me a goddamn lousy, no 'count, shit-eating faggot! (*He fires the pistol several times.)*

I.W. HARPER: Over there, Johnny, they're over there.

JOHNNY WALKER: (*Turning.)* Where?

I.W. HARPER: You see 'em, Johnny. They're the ones, they're the ones who called you.

JOHNNY WALKER: (*Squinting, grinning.)* I see 'em, I see 'em all right. I see you red-necked, fat-assed, no-pricked bastards. I jes' hope you can see me all right 'cause you is looking at one mean drunk, pissed-off cowboy. Now which one o' you bastards said that? I want to know which one o' you called me that name.

Goddamnit, I'm gonna blow somebody's goddamn lousy, no count, shit-eating head off 'fore I get through! (*Again he fires the pistol several times. A thoroughly nonplussed Jack Daniels waits patiently for room service to answer the telephone while a relieved I.W. Harper sits quietly trying to get his head and his stomach into some kind of shape.*) Je' 'cause I wear a little pancake makeup and eye shadow don't make me no faggot. Goddamn it, I'm in show business and I have to! So I dye my hair! So do a lot o' other TV show business personalities. You calling Ed Sullivan a fruit? And yeah, I've been in a beauty parlor or two and had me a wash and a set. Show business ain't easy. Hell, I got a goddamn fully professional hair dryer . . . the kind with its own chair attached you can sit under and read magazines . . . right in *your* bedroom. That don't prove nothing. All right, so I look at myself in the mirror a lot. Women look in the mirror a lot and no one calls them faggots. And when I look in the mirror, cowboy, I got something to see. Those are arms, those are shoulders, that's a stomach, those are thighs, that's a cock. Goddamnit, someone calls me a faggot again and I'm gonna shoot this whole fucking town up!

JACK DANIELS; Boy, room service sure takes a long time to answer in this hotel!

I.W. HARPER: Jesus, have I got a head on me!

JOHNNY WALKER: What did you say? What did you say just then? The fucking CIA's bugging me, man, so don't start crowding me. This country's turning into a goddamn police state and they're hot after my ass. I can't go to Mexico without 'em searching me all over and taking off my hubcaps. They're bugging my phone, they got people at every fucking airport in this whole goddamn country watching and double watching me. Don't you call me no faggot, you goddamn CIA Jew!

JACK DANIELS: It's done rung forty-five rings so far!

I.W. HARPER: No one called you nothing, Johnny Walker.

JOHNNY WALKER: Goddamnit, I'm gonna pull this trigger if I hear that word again. Faggot? Faggot? I grew up in Waco and I was punching girls 'fore my daddy let me have my learner's permit to drive our pickup. I had their panties off and I was *in* there, and I don't mean with my finger, 'fore most guys' balls had even dropped!

Shit, the only faggots in Waco was punched-up, beat-up and stomped-on faggots. And me and my boys did the punching and the beating and the stomping. Goddamnit, I went to Texas A&M! That's a military school. Did you ever hear of a faggot from Texas A&M? From *any* military school for that matter? Hell, a place like that's so goddamned screened you can't get near the place if your big toe looks a little queer to 'em. Boy, my blood is boiling. Boy, you're getting my goat. I know the CIA is listening to every goddamn word I'm saying. Jesus H. Christ, I was a goddamn football star. We beat Texas three years running when I was on varsity. We was conference champs. I was quarterback. Did you ever hear of a gay quarterback? A cheerleader maybe, but I'll give you $500 for every gay quarterback you can name. All right, I know gay's one of them "in" words. I know it don't mean happy. But goddamn it to hell anyway! I'm in show business. I meet people. I hear how they talk. I admit it. There are certain people of the homosexual persuasion in my profession.

JACK DANIELS; Sixty-nine!

JOHNNY WALKER: What? What did I hear?

I.W. HARPER: Johnny, please, my head.

JOHNNY WALKER: Goddamn it, I am sick of those filthy words. All right, I'll admit this, too, only it's the first and last time I'm ever gonna say it clear out. There was a pansy at Texas A&M. Just one. But he wasn't in the corps. He was in animal husbandry. Now I didn't know him personally but I heard he was a damn nice guy from Tyler. 'Course when we found out he was a pansy we stomped the shit out o' him. My four years at Texas A&M were the happiest and proudest of my life. And if you don't think I fucked every weekend, then you're way off base. Hell, those College Townies drop their drawers and flop over backwards at the first sight o' field boots. A&M cadets could get laid in a goddamn convent, that's the kind of studs they are. And me being voted the Most Valuable Player of the Southwest Conference three years in a row didn't exactly hurt none either. I got laid so much at A&M I landed up in the infirmary every spring semester with sexual hyperthesia.

JACK DANIELS: Should I keep trying, I.W.?

I.W. HARPER: I'm going to be sick again.

JOHNNY WALKER: What's that about Rick?

I.W. HARPER: Not Rick, Johnny. *Sick!*

JOHNNY WALKER: Now goddamnit, leave im out o' this! Rick's my buddy. A word agin' him is a word agin' me. That boy is the finest, most pure and masculine roommate a guy ever had. I know the talk agin' him, I know the CIA's behind it all, and my finger jes' gets mighty itchy when I hear that kind o' talk. So what we got a Yak rug in the living room and some o' them Gobelin tapestries on the walls? Rick likes nice things. He can't help it he's sensitive. The hours we spend lifting weights in our private gym are some o' the most intellectually stimulating o' my life. Rick-boy don't just work out. Hell no, he talks about philosophy and music and modern art and how much he gets laid. You didn't know that, cowpoke, did you? No, the papers are all full o' Yak rugs and yellow curtains but you don't read one thing 'bout how much we get laid. Well you ask any starlet in Hollywood . . . any starlet with big titties . . . and she'd tell you what it's like round Rick's and my's place every weekend. We fuck on the beds, we fuck in the pool, hell, we even fuck on that Yak rug. I know what you're thinking, mister, so take that grin off o' your face. Rick weren't doing nothing at that pajama party. He swore to me on a stack o' Bibles he didn't know what it was gonna turn into and his word's good enough for me. Let me tell you he was one plumb mad cowboy after he found out he was consortin' with fruits. Why when the police came and took all those pictures . . . spread all o'er tarnation thanks to the CIA and the *National Enquirer* . . . Ricky was so depressed and heartsick he took to his bed for a long, long time. And then when they had that goddamn trial, CIA again, that's when he got really sick and had to withdraw from his TV series. It ain't true he was fired. He was too sick, too sad and plain too disgusted to work. And you saw what happened: "Mr. George" went clear off the air six weeks after Rick-boy left it. Shit, I told him, a situation comedy 'bout a goddamn hairdresser ain't no good for a cowpoke's image anyhow. Anybody calling Ricky Rivers a goddamn faggot is calling Johnny Walker one, too!

JACK DANIELS: I'd hang up, I.W., only it says right here "24-hour room service."

I.W. HARPER: Beer. That's what I need.

JOHNNY WALKER: What did you call me?

I.W. HARPER: Beer. I said I could use a beer.

JOHNNY WALKER: I warned you cowboy! (*Johnny Walker draws his pistols and fires wildly all around the room. It is a noisy and serious barrage of gun fire. I.W. Harper and Jack Daniels dive for cover. When it is over, the room will seem very quiet, except for Whiskey raising a new fuss in the bathroom. Johnny Walker stands, pistols smoking and a mean grin on his face.*) Now what did you call me?

I.W. HARPER: Nothing, Johnny Walker.

JACK DANIELS: Not one durn thing, Johnny.

JOHNNY WALKER: That's better. (*One of Johnny Walker's bullets has hit the bathroom door, which is slowly and creakily swinging open. Whiskey is still whinnying and beating his hooves. What they see, however, is Tia Maria passed out on the floor.*)

I.W. HARPER: Honey!

JOHNNY WALKER: Oh my God!

JACK DANIELS: You do that, Johnny Walker? (*I.W. Harper and Johnny Walker rush to the bathroom and bend over Tia Maria. Jack Daniels looks in from the door.*)

I.W. HARPER: Tia? Tia honey?

JOHNNY WALKER: I was jes' fooling.

JACK DANIELS: Sure don't look like you was, Johnny.

I.W. HARPER: She's still breathing.

JOHNNY WALKER: I swear to God, I.W., I didn't know she was in there.

JACK DANIELS: Somebody ought to call a doctor.

I.W. HARPER: We'll get her on the bed.

JOHNNY WALKER: I wouldn't hurt a fly, you know that.

I.W. HARPER: Take her feet. (*I.W. Harper and Johnny Walker carry Tia Maria into the main room and put her on the bed.*)

JACK DANIELS: Hush up now, Whiskey. We got a real sick lady on our hands. (*Jack Daniels closes the bathroom door. In a little while Whiskey will be quiet again.*)

JOHNNY WALKER: How bad is she?

I.W. HARPER: I can't tell.

JOHNNY WALKER: Where'd I get her?

I.W. HARPER: I can't tell that neither. I don't see any blood.

JACK DANIELS: That poor lady. We got booed in the Astrodome, the President of the United States got showed Southern Comfort's thing, we all got passed-out drunk and now Johnny Walker's shot her.

I.W. HARPER: (*Over his shoulder to Jack Daniels.*) Don't just stand there. Call a doctor.

JACK DANIELS: That's what I was saying, I.W. Somebody ought to call a doctor.

I.W. HARPER: You!

JACK DANIELS: Okay, I.W., if I can ever raise that operator. I think she must've gone to sleep. (*Jack Daniels goes to phone again, lifts receiver, waits patiently.*)

I.W. HARPER: Honey? Can you hear me, honey?

JOHNNY WALKER: It's me, Tia. Johnny. It's your old friend, Johnny.

I.W. HARPER: You're going to be all right, honey, everything's going to be all right now. Just tell me where it hurts. (*Tia Maria is beginning to come around.*) Don't try to talk. You'll tire yourself. Just lie back real still and wait for the doctor.

JOHNNY WALKER: Open the other eye, Tia. See if you can open the other one, too.

I.W. HARPER: Don't crowd her like that! Give her some air!

JOHNNY WALKER: Just stay calm, we're all here, nothin's going to happen.

I.W. HARPER: Can I get you something, honey?

JOHNNY WALKER: The main thing is to rest.

I.W. HARPER: How 'bout a shot?

JOHNNY WALKER: You're not running any fever.

I.W. HARPER: More pillows, honey?

JOHNNY WALKER: (*Offering his cigarette.*) Drag on this, it'll soothe you.

I.W. HARPER: I said quit crowding her!

JOHNNY WALKER: Who's crowding?

I.W. HARPER: You are!

JOHNNY WALKER: You're right on top o' her yourself!

I.W. HARPER: She's my wife!

JOHNNY WALKER: I shot her!

JACK DANIELS: Try spitting on her. Pa always used to spit on us and we all healed. He claimed spit was a natural healer. He made a fine honey-and-cobweb poultice, too.

I.W. HARPER: Are you getting that doctor?

JACK DANIELS: I'm trying to, I.W.

TIA MARIA: (*Sitting up.*) What happened?

I.W. HARPER: How do you feel, honey?

TIA MARIA: I'm not sure.

JOHNNY WALKER: Don't try to talk.

I.W. HARPER: Will you stop crowding my wife? Give her some room to breathe in!

TIA MARIA: What happened?

I.W. HARPER: Just lie back, honey, save your strength.

JOHNNY WALKER: I'm trying to see where she's wounded!

I.W. HARPER: What do you think I'm doing?

TIA MARIA: I remember this terrible nightmare . . . it must have been the stingers, I've never had one this bad before . . . I remember sittin in something . . . ! (*She shudders at the memory.*)

I.W. HARPER: Me.

TIA MARIA: Hunh?

I.W. HARPER: That was me you sat in.

TIA MARIA: That's not funny, I.W., I'm trying to get my thoughts straight.

JOHNNY WALKER: I don't see anything!

TIA MARIA: And then I came to in this antiseptic tile room . . . like a hospital only it was more like a restroom and you were there, I.W., and I said I was thirsty and you said you were going to fix me something with hair in it . . .

JACK DANIELS: That's called a hair o' the dog, ma'am.

TIA MARIA: No, you said a gorilla. You were going to fix me a gorilla. Next thing I was sitting, waiting for you to come back . . . it seems I was on a . . . you know, a sanitary convenience. . .

JACK DANIELS: You mean a toilet, ma'am?

TIA MARIA: And all of a sudden it flushed! I was just sitting there and it flushed!

JACK DANIELS: Boy, I bet that scared the shit out o' you! (*Jack Daniels has a yuk! yuk! yuk! kind of laugh when he tells and laughs at his own jokes.*)

JOHNNY WALKER: It's a new hotel, Tia. They don't have all the bugs ironed out yet. That's all it was.

TIA MARIA: And then . . . oh, my head is spinning! . . . and then . . .

I.W. Harper: It's not important.

Tia Maria: Don't I get a drink?

I.W. Harper: Sure you do, honey. Johnny!

Johnny Walker: She's your wife.

I.W. Harper: You shot her.

Tia Maria: Now I remember! He tried to kill me, I.W.!

Johnny Walker: I didn't mean to Tia, honest I didn't!

Tia Maria: That damn horse tried to kill me again! It was horrible!

I.W. Harper: (*Comforting her in his arms.*) Honey!

Tia Maria: He hates me, I.W. Whiskey hates me.

I.W. Harper: You're just imagining things. Like you said, you had a little nightmare.

Tia Maria: It sure seemed real.

Johnny Walker: You don't remember any shooting?

Tia Maria: No!

Johnny Walker: You're sure?

Tia Maria: What's wrong with you? I sat in something terrible, the toilet flushed on me, a horse tried to kill me and now you want somebody shooting at me, too! Give me that! (*Tia Maria takes the drink from Johnny Walker and downs it in one gulp.*)

Johnny Walker: I knew it! Hell, I don't think I even grazed her. She passed out dead drunk, that's all. She can sleep it off. And thanks for scaring me half to death.

Tia Maria: What's he talking about?

Jack Daniels: If'n I ever get that operator, I.W., should I tell her we don't need no doctor now? Or should I hang up? It's done rung fifty-four rings this time.

Tia Maria: What's going on here?

I.W. Harper: Now don't upset yourself, honey.

Tia Maria: And what's all this fussing over me for? All o' them doing in our room?

Jack Daniels: Lost my key, ma'am. Fifty-*seven*, I.W.

I.W. Harper: Yes, hang up!

Tia Maria: What's he calling a doctor for anyway?

I.W. Harper: It's nothing, Tia. Never mind.

Tia Maria: Not for me I hope.

Jack Daniels: Yes, ma'am. I.W. was afraid you were a real sick little lady. We all were, 'specially Johnny Walker.

TIA MARIA: Why I feel fit as a fiddle and rarin' to go!

JOHNNY WALKER: Sure you do!

TIA MARIA: Why thank you, Johnny.

JOHNNY WALKER: You're stinking drunk.

TIA MARIA: What did you say?

JOHNNY WALKER: But hell, that's nothing unusual.

TIA MARIA: Who's calling who drunk?

JOHNNY WALKER: Oh, come off it, Tia, you're potted.

TIA MARIA: From the look o' you three, I'd say you were pretty stinko yourselves.

JACK DANIELS: That's right, ma'am, we are.

I.W. HARPER: Now don't move around too much, honey.

TIA MARIA: I can drink you three skunks under any table.

JOHNNY WALKER: We've seen you.

TIA MARIA: Any night o' any week.

I.W. HARPER: Don't rile her, Johnny, she'll start that damn screaming.

TIA MARIA: Who's getting riled? Look, look how steady I am. You see that hand shaking? Don't tell me I got the D.T.'s, you pickled fruit. And what are you grinning at, you little wino?

JACK DANIELS Nothing, ma'am.

I.W. HARPER: Tia, honey, please.

TIA MARIA: Leave go o'me, you old rummy.

I.W. HARPER: (*To Johnny Walker.*) See what you started?

TIA MARIA: If there's one thing I can't stand it's being treated like a drunk.

I.W. HARPER: Nobody's treating you like anything, Tia.

TIA MARIA: Can you do that?

JOHNNY WALKER: What?

TIA MARIA: You're so drunk you can't even see straight.

JACK DANIELS: What'd she do, I.W.?

TIA MARIA: I crossed my eyes.

I.W. HARPER: You're not drunk, Tia.

TIA MARIA: 'Course I'm not.

I.W. HARPER: Nobody said you were.

JACK DANIELS: My pa could cross his eyes. All the time. My pa was cross-eyed. (*He laughs his yuk! yuk! yuk! laugh.*)

TIA MARIA: I had a nightmare and passed out. All this carrying on and calling up doctors, you'd think somebody *had* shot me. (*Tia*

Maria starts to laugh. It gets bigger and bigger. I.W. Harper and Johnny Walker start laughing, too.) I wouldn't put it past you!

I.W. HARPER: Honey!

TIA MARIA: Or that one!

JOHNNY WALKER: Tia!

TIA MARIA: 'Course it sounds like something Southern Comfort would do!

I.W. HARPER: *Anything* sounds like something Southern Comfort would do!

JOHNNY WALKER: She'd flaming baton you to death, if she could ever get one lit!

TIA MARIA: Where is that little pill-popping, dope-smoking, alcoholic floozy anyway?

I.W. HARPER: God only knows, Tia!

JOHNNY WALKER: She's off entertaining the troops!

TIA MARIA: The war's over!

JOHNNY WALKER: Not hers!

TIA MARIA: Southern! Southern Comfort!

I.W. HARPER: Honey, ain't we got enough people in here?

TIA MARIA: Hell, no, this is a party. A shooting party. Gimme that gun, Johnny.

I.W. HARPER: Tia!

TIA MARIA: I'm goin in there and shoot that goddamn horse.

JOHNNY WALKER: You shoot that horse, Tia, and I'll help you bury him!

TIA MARIA: That's one way to break up an act!

I.W. HARPER: Or cancel a too-goddamn-long running TV series!

JOHNNY WALKER: Get a few close-ups of us for a change!

TIA MARIA: Don't think I haven't thought of it! You have, too. And you!

I.W. HARPER: Who'd shoot Whiskey?

TIA MARIA: Who'd shoot anybody?

JOHNNY WALKER: Who'd shoot you?

TIA MARIA: Hoo hoo hoo!

I.W. HARPER: Ha ha ha!

JOHNNY WALKER: Hee hee hee! (*The laughter fades to silence.*)

JACK DANIELS: Johnny Walker shot you, ma'am. He thought somebody called him that name again, shot a whole round off to prove it and you ended up on the bathroom floor. (*Now Jack Daniels*

Starts to laugh. It too gets bigger and bigger.)

TIA MARIA: What'd he say?

I.W. HARPER: Nothing.

JOHNNY WALKER: Shut up, you durn fool.

JACK DANIELS: (*Still laughing.*) I cannot tell a lie.

TIA MARIA: He said *something*, I.W.

I.W. HARPER: Drunk talk, crazy stuff.

JOHNNY WALKER: Now keep your trap closed.

JACK DANIELS: (*Laughing.*) My pa said any man who tells a lie is a liar.

JOHNNY WALKER: Your pa also said any man who rocks the boat when the boat don't need rocking is gonna get a fist in his face.

I.W. HARPER: Two fists.

JACK DANIELS: (*Stops laughing.*) He did?

JOHNNY WALKER: You're goddamn right he did!

JACK DANIELS: You two knew my pa?

I.W. HARPER: A terrific old bastard.

JOHNNY WALKER: I loved that old fart.

JACK DANIELS: Boy, it sure is a small world.

I.W. HARPER: See, honey, nobody shot nobody.

JACK DANIELS: Anyway, Johnny Walker shot you, ma'am. (*Jack Daniels explodes in a new fit of laughter.*)

TIA MARIA: You what?

JOHNNY WALKER: I was jes' fooling around, Tia, honest, I didn't mean to.

TIA MARIA: Oh my God, I've been shot, I.W.!

I.W. HARPER: We just thought you'd been shot.

TIA MARIA: AAAAEEEEEIIIIIOOOOOUUUUUUU!!!

I.W. HARPER: But you weren't. See, there's no blood.

TIA MARIA: AAAAEEEEEEIIIIIIIOOOOOOOOUUUUUU!!!!

I.W. HARPER: Come on now, honey, they'll think we're murdering someone up here.

TIA MARIA: AAAAAEEEEEEEIIIIIIIOOOOOOOOUUUUUU!!!! (*And she faints again.*)

I.W. HARPER: I give up.

JOHNNY WALKER: How does she do it?

JACK DANIELS: She sure yells a lot, I.W. Hurts my ears.

JOHNNY WALKER: You didn't have to tell her what happened! We had her all calmed down.

JACK DANIELS: I'm sorry, Johnny, I wasn't thinking.

I.W. HARPER: Tia? Tia honey?

JOHNNY WALKER: Leave her alone. Out cold's the best thing for her.

JACK DANIELS: You want another doctor for her, I.W.?

I.W. HARPER: No!

JACK DANIELS: I jes' asked.

I.W. HARPER: My poor honey, my poor drunk honey. I was drunk when I met you, you was drunk when we married and we've been drunk together ever since. I'm going to make it up to you, honey, I swear to God I am.

JOHNNY WALKER: Hey, now come on, I.W.!

I.W. HARPER: This gal was an angel when I met her, a goddamn angel. She was so thin I could get my hands around her waist. Her hair was so gold in the sun it made you squint to look at her. And skin so cool and smooth and white it made you think of cream. A goddamn angel. She had nice titties, too.

JACK DANIELS: I don't think we should be hearing this, Johnny.

JOHNNY WALKER: It's okay, I.W., everything's gonna be okay.

I.W. HARPER: And now look at her. I did that to her. I did! I did!

JOHNNY WALKER: Don't, I.W., you're only tormenting yourself.

I.W. HARPER: I know.

JOHNNY WALKER: Well don't.

I.W. HARPER: I want to. Look what I did to her. I did! I did!

JOHNNY WALKER: No, you didn't

I.W. HARPER: Yes I did.

JOHNNY WALKER: No, you didn't

I.W. HARPER: Yes I did.

JOHNNY WALKER: No you didn't.

I.W. HARPER: Yes I did!

JACK DANIELS: Seems he ought to know what he did to his own wife, Johnny.

I.W. HARPER: Just look at her and tell me I didn't do that. Go on, tell me! (*Tia Maria belches loudly in her sleep.*)

JACK DANIELS: What *did* he do to her, Johnny?

I.W. HARPER: (*Throwing himself on Tia Maria.*) My honey, my poor drunk honey. I'm going to make it up to you, honey, I swear to God I am.

JACK DANIELS: Don't cry, I.W.

JOHNNY WALKER: Leave him be. It's good for him.

I.W. HARPER: Did I ever tell you the story about the first time I met Tia Maria?

JACK DANIELS: Lots o' times.

I.W. HARPER: It was at Cotton's, this little beer 'n bar-b-q joint outside o' Robstown.

JACK DANIELS: You told us, I.W.

I.W. HARPER: She was in the ladies' room being sick and I was so drunk I walked in there thinking it was the men's.

JACK DANIELS: That's how it happened.

I.W. HARPER: Did I tell you about our wedding night when we rolled off that balcony?

JACK DANIELS: Down in Mexico. That's a real good one!

I.W. HARPER: Our first real break in show business?

JACK DANIELS: You was on the radio, coast to coast, and that time somebody else got sick.

I.W. HARPER: How we broke into TV?

JACK DANIELS: Yep, that one, too.

I.W. HARPER: About our series and why it's been running so long?

JACK DANIELS: I'm on the series with you, I.W.!

I.W. HARPER: Don't anybody want to know what I did to my poor drunk honey? Don't anybody care?

JOHNNY WALKER: We all *care*, I.W. Trouble is, we all *know*.

I.W. HARPER: Nobody knows! Nobody cares! I'm going to make it up to you, honey, I swear to God I am. (*He throws himself onto her for a final time.*)

JOHNNY WALKER: It's okay now, I.W. everything's okay.

JACK DANIELS: Boy, he sure loves that little lady.

JOHNNY WALKER: Jes' let it all out now.

JACK DANIELS: I wonder if my pa loved my ma like that. I wish I hadn't been half an orphan all my life. And now I'm a whole one. (*And now Jack Daniels cries a little, too. Johnny Walker gets up and pours himself another drink.*)

I.W. HARPER: (*Sitting up.*) Why don't you clear out now? I know! You lost your key. Sleep in his room, sleep in the hall, I don't care.

JOHNNY WALKER: Les' have a nightcap, I.W. Jes' one.

I.W. HARPER: It's late.

JOHNNY WALKER: It's early.

I.W. HARPER: It's late!

JOHNNY WALKER: Speaking frankly, I.W., I don't think you're in any shape to be left alone right now.

I.W. HARPER: Sure I am.

JOHNNY WALKER: I don't think so, I.W.

I.W. HARPER: I am, too!

JOHNNY WALKER: No, you're not.

I.W. HARPER: I am, too!

JACK DANIELS: There y'all go again.

I.W. HARPER: Suit yourself, only don't tell me what kind o' shape I'm in. (*He pours himself a drink.*)

JOHNNY WALKER: Thanks, I.W. You see, I don't think I'm in much shape for loning it tonight, neither. That's one damn solitary hotel room I got waiting for me over there. Nothing but me and four walls. I jes' feel like being with someone tonight.

JACK DANIELS: Can I stay, too, I.W.?

I.W. HARPER: If you keep that dumb mouth closed.

JACK DANIELS: Like before?

I.W. HARPER: That's right.

JACK DANIELS: You fixing to be sick again?

I.W. HARPER: No!

JACK DANIELS: That's good. (*Jack Daniels pours himself a drink, sits on the windowseat and strums "The Streets of Laredo" on his guitar. I.W. Harper is leaning against the headboard of the bed with Tia Maria sleeping it off by his side. Johnny Walker is sitting on the floor.*)

JOHNNY WALKER: You really thinking o' canceling the tour, I.W.?

I.W. HARPER: I sure as hell ain't thinking o' extending it!

JOHNNY WALKER: It's a lot o' money.

I.W. HARPER: That was a lot o' booing tonight, too.

JOHNNY WALKER: Damn that horse anyway. He's gonna come out on cue tomorrow night if I have to kill him.

I.W. HARPER: If there *is* a tomorrow night.

JOHNNY WALKER: They were pretty mad, the management, I guess, hunh?

I.W. HARPER: Hell no! Why they just loved refunding all that money!

JOHNNY WALKER: That damn agent promised us Whiskey wouldn't act up like that.

I.W. Harper: That same damn agent promised me you'd be able to get your first line out.

Johnny Walker: I'm sorry, I.W.

I.W. Harper: I know you are, Johnny, and I'm sorry I said it.

Johnny Walker: I'd as soon shoot you as spit on you. I'd as soon shoot you as spit on you. See? Now I can do it.

I.W. Harper: Only right here and now ain't out there and then.

Johnny Walker: Now I know why they call it stage fright.

I.W. Harper: Now you know why they call it show business.

Johnny Walker: Well Southern Comfort didn't exactly help things none either!

I.W. Harper: And now I know what they call a show *stopper!*

Johnny Walker: Well I blame her *and* the horse.

I.W. Harper: We *all* stank, if you want to know the truth.

Johnny Walker: Tonight was our first time live. We'll get better.

I.W. Harper: Like hell we will. There's not enough talent in this room to piss on.

Johnny Walker: I resent that, I.W.

I.W. Harper: So resent it. You're young, you're dumb, you'll find out. Either that or you'll make it big like we did.

Johnny Walker: I couldn't stand it if I felt like you.

I.W. Harper: You heard that crowd tonight.

Johnny Walker: A live audience is different.

I.W. Harper: I know. They can get at you.

Johnny Walker: You're forgetting one thing, I.W. People like us.

I.W. Harper: They tolerate us.

Johnny Walker: Our show's the longest running series on television.

I.W. Harper: Drunk cowboys are still a novelty. Next year, ten years, it'll be drunk Indians.

Johnny Walker: We're gonna last, I.W. Hell, everybody loves a drunk!

I.W. Harper: Everybody loves Whiskey.

Johnny Walker: That's what I'm saying.

I.W. Harper: Everybody loves that horse! He's the whole show. The last ten episodes we haven't been on the screen more'n five minutes. He's bigger than Lassie. He's bigger than Flipper. He's bigger than Black Beauty. And you can just thank your lucky stars we're all a part of one big fat William Morris Agency package. Without him, Tia and I'd be back on Dust Bowl radio shows plugging Geritol and calling square dances, you'd be back driving that truck, that one would be back where we found him, standing out on the same farm road selling the same mangy vegetables off o' the same mangy truck bed, and Southern Comfort'd be off somewhere undergoing psychiatric treatment.

JOHNNY WALKER: I wasn't driving a truck when you met me. I was a football star.

I.W. HARPER: You was a former and faded football star, Johnny Walker, and you was driving something.

JOHNNY WALKER: It was only a temporary position. I was between things.

I.W. HARPER: Temporary positions like that have a funny way of turning into full-time ones. What you was between was sixty-five dollars and being flat on your ass.

JOHNNY WALKER: I had offers. Sports announcing, public relations, lots o' things.

I.W. HARPER: If you say so.

JOHNNY WALKER: It's true. You just never knew me in my prime.

I.W. HARPER: Well you sure caught me and Tia in ours! (*There is a pause. I.W. stretches out on the bed, ready to sleep.*)

JOHNNY WALKER: I.W.? It's been my prime, too. All o' ours prime. Don't cancel.

I.W. HARPER: It may not be up to me, Johnny.

JOHNNY WALKER: Just don't you do it. The Lush Thrushes and Whiskey is all I got.

I.W. HARPER: Us, too, Johnny.

JACK DANIELS: I.W.?

I.W. HARPER: What?

JACK DANIELS: You and Johnny Walker are talking.

I.W. HARPER: I know!

JACK DANIELS: Well that don't seem rightly fair. I'm one of the Lush Thrushes, too.

I.W. HARPER: I said shut up.

JACK DANIELS: Okay, I.W.

I.W. HARPER: Now everybody shut up. Just sit there and drink. Nobody say nothing.

JOHNNY WALKER: I'll drink to that. (*At this point we begin to hear, though very faintly at first, a girl's voice singing "Hare Krishna"*) *and the delicate ting! ting! of finger cymbals. Tia Maria belches loudly in her sleep. Jack Daniels stops strumming.)*

JACK DANIELS: I.W.?

I.W. HARPER: What?

JACK DANIELS: Can I say jes' one last thing?

I.W. HARPER: Yes.

JACK DANIELS: I hear music.

I.W. HARPER: Good.

JACK DANIELS: Somebody singing and little bells tinkling.

I.W. HARPER: That's nice.

JACK DANIELS: You hear something, Johnny Walker?

JOHNNY WALKER: Somebody singing.

JACK DANIELS: Me, too.

JOHNNY WALKER: More like chanting though. And a ringing sound, like little bells.

JACK DANIELS: I.W.?

I.W. HARPER: What?

JACK DANIELS: Johnny Walker hears somebody singing and little bells tinkling, too.

I.W. HARPER: He's right.

JACK DANIELS: Just thought I'd mention it. (*Jack Daniels strums his guitar again. Smoke is starting to billow out of one of the closet doors. Jack Daniels sniffs something, stops strumming again.*) I.W.?

I.W. HARPER: What?

JACK DANIELS: Now I smell smoke.

I.W. HARPER: That's nice.

JACK DANIELS: You smell anything, Johnny Walker?

JOHNNY WALKER: Smoke.

JACK DANIELS: That's what I said.

JOHNNY WALKER: But it's a sweet smoke.

JACK DANIELS: I thought there was something funny about it.

JOHNNY WALKER: More like incense.

JACK DANIELS: I.W.?

I.W. HARPER: What?

JACK DANIELS: Johnny Walker smells smoke, too.

I.W. HARPER: Good for Johnny Walker.

JACK DANIELS: But it's a sweet smoke.

I.W. HARPER: I'm glad.

JACK DANIELS: More like incense.

I.W. HARPER: If you keep this up, Jack Daniels, I am going to have a nervous breakdown.

JACK DANIELS: You are?

I.W. HARPER: Yes. I am very calm and very relaxed and very drunk but you are still giving me a nervous breakdown.

JACK DANIELS: I'm sorry, I.W. I'll try and be real still then. (*There is a long pause while Jack Daniels strums his guitar and Johnny Walker and I.W. Harper drift further and further away. Tia Maria stirs in the bed and finally sits up.*)

TIA MARIA: Oh!

JACK DANIELS: (*Whispered.*) How you feeling, ma'am?

TIA MARIA: What happened?

JACK DANIELS: You screamed and passed out dead drunk again.

TIA MARIA: Oooo, my poor head is ringing. I hear music.

JACK DANIELS: We all do.

TIA MARIA: Somebody singing and little chimes tingling.

JACK DANIELS: It's nice, ain't it, ma'am? (*Tia Maria pours herself another drink, leans back on the headboard next to I.W. Harper.*)

TIA MARIA: Something's burning.

JACK DANIELS: We know.

TIA MARIA: Where's it coming from?

JACK DANIELS; The closet.

TIA MARIA: It's pretty.

JACK DANIELS: The closet, ma'am?

TIA MARIA: The smoke. (*Tia Maria closes her eyes and enjoys the smoke. Jack Daniels strums his guitar.*)

JACK DANIELS: My pa always said where there's smoke there's fire.

TIA MARIA: (*Trying to focus.*) Fire?

JACK DANIELS: Yes, ma'am, that's what he said.

TIA MARIA: Fire?

JACK DANIELS: Where there's smoke there must be fire.

TIA MARIA: AAAEEEEEIIIIIIOOOOOOUUUUUU!!!!

I.W. HARPER: (*Stirring.*) Aw come on, honey, knock it off!

TIA MARIA: AAAAAAEEEEEEIIIIIIOOOOOOOUUUUUUU!!!!

JOHNNY WALKER: Dammit, Tia, we're trying to sleep!

TIA MARIA: AAAAAAEEEEEIIIIIIIIOOOOOOOUUUUUUU! (*She faints again.*)

JACK DANIELS: Boy, she sure does that a lot! And loudly, too! (*Jack Daniels sits and strums his guitar. Tia Maria is out cold. I.W. Harper and Johnny Walker have rolled back over and are trying to sleep. At the same time the closet door is opened from inside to reveal Southern Comfort. She is sitting on the floor in a lotus position. Several sticks of incense are burning in front of her. She's wearing a headband and finger cymbals and bra and panties.*)

SOUTHERN COMFORT: Goddamnit, anyway, will you make her stop!? I'm trying to meditate in here. And if I can't concentrate how the hell am I ever gonna levitate? Get my goddamn ass in the air? It ain't all that goddamn easy! So tell her to cool it, hunh? What's her goddamn problem anyway? (*Southern Comfort slams the closet door shut just as abruptly as she opened it. Jack Daniels has stopped strumming, of course, and from the doubletake he does you'd think he's never seen a half-naked girl before . . . which, quite possibly, he hasn't. Now he gets up, goes over to the closet door and politely knocks.*)

JACK DANIELS: Southern Comfort?

SOUTHERN COMFORT: Leave me alone.

JACK DANIELS: What are you doing in there?

SOUTHERN COMFORT: What the fuck does it look like I'm doing?

JACK DANIELS: I'm not rightly sure. Maybe if I could have one more look at you I could tell you that more clearly.

SOUTHERN COMFORT: I can't talk now.

JACK DANIELS: You don't have to talk, ma'am. Jes' come out here and kind o' stand around some.

SOUTHERN COMFORT: I said buzz off. I can't levitate with you yakking at me. (*Southern Comfort resumes singing "Hare Krishna" and playing the finger cymbals. Jack Daniels runs over to I.W. Harper stretched out on the bed.*)

JACK DANIELS: (*Trying to rouse him.*) I.W.! Hey, I.W., wake up now, quick! (*I.W. mumbles incoherently in his drunken sleep.*) Southern Comfort's sitting in the closet, and she say's she fixing to levitate! (*I.W. Harper mumbles some more and rolls over onto his stomach. Jack Daniels now tries to rouse Johnny Walker.*) Johnny, wake up, Johnny! (*Johnny Walker mumbles incoherently.*) Southern Comfort's going to levitate!

JOHNNY WALKER: That's nice.

JACK DANIELS: Don't you want to see?

JOHNNY WALKER: Wake me when it's time. (*Johnny Walker rolls over and snores happily. Jack Daniels goes back over to the closet again.*)

JACK DANIELS: Southern Comfort?

SOUTHERN COMFORT: What?

JACK DANIELS: I've been wondering. 'Spose I came in there and levitated with you?

SOUTHERN COMFORT: Hah! I knew you'd ask me that!

JACK DANIELS: Hunh?

SOUTHERN COMFORT: I said I can't talk now. (*Southern Comfort resumes singing "Hare Krishna."*)

JACK DANIELS: Now how am I gonna get her out o' there or me in? (*He stands there thinking until he gets his one and only idea of this entire play. First he turns off the overhead lights so that the room is just light enough to see in. Next he picks up his guitar and starts strumming and singing "Hare Krishna" in his true and clear voice along with Southern Comfort in the closet. Their duet grows and grows, both more loudly and more exuberantly.*)

SOUTHERN COMFORT: Is that you, Jack Daniels?

JACK DANIELS: Yes, ma'am, that's who it is.

SOUTHERN COMFORT: You're sure grooving with that mantra.

JACK DANIELS: I know, ma'am. That's what I'm doing with it.

SOUTHERN COMFORT: Are you cool, man?

JACK DANIELS: Ma'am?

SOUTHERN COMFORT: Are you cool, man?

JACK DANIELS: Oh yes, ma'am, I'm real cool.

SOUTHERN COMFORT: Don't call me ma'am, man.

JACK DANIELS: I was jes' fixing to ask you the very same thing!

SOUTHERN COMFORT: Now keep grooving with that mantra. I'm coming out dancing.

JACK DANIELS: You bet, Southern Comfort! (*Jack Daniels attacks the song with fresh enthusiasm. The closet door slowly opens and Southern Comfort comes out dancing and working her finger cymbals. At the first sight of her, Jack Daniels's fingers fall right off his guitar. But he recovers.*)

SOUTHERN COMFORT: Hey, man.

JACK DANIELS: (*Dazzled.*) Hey!

SOUTHERN COMFORT: I didn't know you were hip.

JACK DANIELS: You didn't?

SOUTHERN COMFORT: I thought you were as straight as they come.

JACK DANIELS: Me?

SOUTHERN COMFORT: It's nice to know we're soul brothers.

JACK DANIELS: It sure is.

SOUTHERN COMFORT: I like you, Jack Daniels.

JACK DANIELS: I like you, Southern Comfort.

SOUTHERN COMFORT: I can talk to you.

JACK DANIELS: Go ahead, shoot.

SOUTHERN COMFORT: How stoned are you?

JACK DANIELS: (*Uncertainly, he doesn't know this expression.*) Not too stoned. Maybe fair to middling.

SOUTHERN COMFORT: Oh, that's too bad. I thought maybe you was way up where I was.

JACK DANIELS: I'm pretty stoned, though. For me. But I could get stonier.

SOUTHERN COMFORT: Stonier! I like that word, stonier. It was groovy of you to use it.

JACK DANIELS: And if I get much stonier, I'll be a rock! No, a boulder! (*Jack Daniels laughs his yuk! yuk! yuk! laugh.*)

SOUTHERN COMFORT: Don't be a drag, man. Like this dance is starting to be a drag. (*She stops.*) Like your guitar is starting to be a drag. (*He stops playing.*) Things get to be a drag for me. I freak out. That concert tonight was a drag.

JACK DANIELS: And you sure as shooting freaked out, Southern.

SOUTHERN COMFORT: I guess I showed him.

JACK DANIELS: You sure did. You showed eighty-one thousand other people, too.

SOUTHERN COMFORT: If he don't know now how I feel about sexist racism in this country, I don't guess he ever will.

JACK DANIELS: How *do* you feel?

SOUTHERN COMFORT: Like I'm getting ready to flip out again. (*She sits.*) That trying to levitate gets to be a drag, too.

JACK DANIELS: Did it work?

SOUTHERN COMFORT: Only about yay high.

JACK DANIELS: Is that all?

SOUTHERN COMFORT: Well hell, I was only in there five or six hours.

That swami said it could take all the way up to twelve. But who the hell's got that kind of time?

JACK DANIELS: What swami?

SOUTHERN COMFORT: (*Pouring herself a drink.*) Some creep who was trying to make me in the dressing room before we went on. At least he said he was a swami. He looked like a Mexican with a beard and turban. Swami Sanchez he called himself. He couldn't keep his hands off me.

JACK DANIELS: Well I'm real glad you came out o' that closet, Southern Comfort. Ain't no fit place for a pretty girl like you.

SOUTHERN COMFORT: You say that like every other hung up, strung out, uptight cat I meet.

JACK DANIELS: How's that?

SOUTHERN COMFORT: Like the only reason you're glad I'm out there is cause I'm not wearing any clothes.

JACK DANIELS: I'm not glad, Southern. I mean, I *am!* You know what I'm trying to say.

SOUTHERN COMFORT: Clothes are symbols, that's all they are.

JACK DANIELS: Damn right they are.

SOUTHERN COMFORT: Symbls of repression and I want to be free!

JACK DANIELS: I don't blame you, Southern.

SOUTHERN COMFORT: I'm never gonna wear any again.

JACK DANIELS: That's a damn good idea, Southern Comfort.

SOUTHERN COMFORT: It'll blow their minds.

JACK DANIELS: Yeeeeeeeoooooooooow!

SOUTHERN COMFORT: That's exactly what I mean.

JACK DANIELS: (*Realizing he's gone too far.*) I was jes' agreeing how good an idea it was for you not to wear anymore clothes ever again.

SOUTHERN COMFORT: Nobody's making me ashamed of my body. Are you?

JACK DANIELS: No, ma'am. I think you got a real fine one.

SOUTHERN COMFORT: Not my body, who cares about that? Yours.

JACK DANIELS: (*Looks down at his body, he's never thought about this before, then.*) How could I be ashamed of it? It's the only one I got.

SOUTHERN COMFORT: Beautiful.

JACK DANIELS: I would't exactly call it that.

SOUTHERN COMFORT: Your mind's beautiful, your head. "How can I be ashamed of it? It's the only one I got." Can I write that in my journal if I can remember it?

JACK DANIELS: Sure.

SOUTHERN COMFORT: Everything in life is beautiful. What is, is. And what is, is beautiful. That's my philosophy.

JACK DANIELS: It's a damn pretty one, too.

SOUTHERN COMFORT: I know.

JACK DANIELS: It's just about the prettiest philosophy I ever heard. Boy, am I glad I got you out o' that closet so we could set and talk like this.

SOUTHERN COMFORT: There it is again.

JACK DANIELS: (*Startled, looking over his shoulder.*) What?

SOUTHERN COMFORT: That tone in your voice.

JACK DANIELS: Ain't no tone, Southern.

SOUTHERN COMFORT: Sexual hangups.

JACK DANIELS: I swear to God, Southern Comfort, the tone of sexual hangups is the last thing in the world you hear in my voice.

SOUTHERN COMFORT: You don't want me that way?

JACK DANIELS: No, ma'am, I most emphatically do not!

SOUTHERN COMFORT: That's okay, too, Jack Daniels. Love between two cats can be a beautiful and groovy thing.

JACK DANIELS: It's sure noisier'n hell.

SOUTHERN COMFORT: Or two chicks. It doesn't matter.

JACK DANIELS: (*While visions of chickens copulating dance in his head.*) It don't?

SOUTHERN COMFORT: But it's best between a cat and a chick.

JACK DANIELS: (*Choking on this one.*) It is?!

SOUTHERN COMFORT: (*Getting ready to sneeze.*) Sure . . . ah! ah! ah! . . . what do you think? . . . ah! ah! ah! . . . you never tried it? . . . atchoo!

JACK DANIELS: You're catching cold.

SOUTHERN COMFORT: (*Shaking her head.*) It's my allergy.

JACK DANIELS: Can I get you anything?

SOUTHERN COMFORT: (*Lighting up a joint.*) This is the only thing that helps. (*Jack Daniels watches her smoke, his eyes widening in astonishment.*)

JACK DANIELS: Boy, you sure take deep drags. That's smoking like it's going out o' style. I guess it *must* help your allergy. (*Jack Daniels's eyes have been feasting all over Southern Comfort's body.*)

SOUTHERN COMFORT: What are you staring at?

JACK DANIELS: I thought I saw something on you. A bug.

SOUTHERN COMFORT: It's a mole.

JACK DANIELS: From here it looked jes' like a little bug.

SOUTHERN COMFORT: The mole's here. You were looking there.

JACK DANIELS: Maybe it moved. (*He hangs his head.*)

SOUTHERN COMFORT: Don't apologize, you don't ever have to apologize for anything. I'm turning you on, Jack. That's good, that's groovy. Go with it.

JACK DANIELS: I will, ma'am, I promise I will.

SOUTHERN COMFORT: If it had been a bug, Jack Daniels, just supposing it had been, what would you have done?

JACK DANIELS: Well, ma'am first I would have plucked it off you and then I would have squashed it to death.

SOUTHERN COMFORT: That turns me off, Jack, that turns me off a whole lot, that answer does.

JACK DANIELS: I'm sorry, Southern Comfort.

SOUTHERN COMFORT: I'm beginning to think you were just pretending to be hip. Anybody who kills bugs, who doesn't respect all life, is no soul brother of mine. You're a plastic hippie, Jack Daniels. I'm going back in the closet.

JACK DANIELS: Don't do that! There's a reason I said I'd kill the bug.

SOUTHERN COMFORT: It would have to be an awfully good one to keep me out here. Boy, that answer turned me right off you, man.

JACK DANIELS: (*Stalling for time.*) It is, it is a good one.

SOUTHERN COMFORT: I'm listening.

JACK DANIELS: I saw a bug that looked jes' like your mole on my ma's shoulder once. I didn't kill it. And you know what happened? It killed her.

SOUTHERN COMFORT: Oh man, what a bad scene that must have been for you!

JACK DANIELS: Real bad, only worse for my ma. Ever since, whenever I see a bug like that I kill it. Ordinarily I wouldn't hurt a fly. Hell, I even love black widow spiders and scorpions. It's jes' that one bug I'm down on.

SOUTHERN COMFORT: What month were you born? November!

JACK DANIELS: (*Her change of subject are too fast for him.*) What month?

SOURTHERN COMFORT: You must be a Scorpio. I groove with Scorpions.

JACK DANIELS: Are we still talking about bugs?

SOUTHERN COMFORT: I groove on astrology. I'm Cancer.

JACK DANIELS: I was born in February.

SOUTHERN COMFORT: That's okay, too. My first spade lover was a Pisces.

JACK DANIELS: You had a spayed lover?

SOUTHERN COMFORT: Who hasn't nowadays?

JACK DANIELS: How'd he get spayed?

SOUTHERN COMFORT: He was born spade, silly.

JACK DANIELS: How'd you ever meet someone like *that?*

SOUTHERN COMFORT: I picked him up. I just walked right up to him on Sheridan Square in that Greenwich Village . . . I was visiting in New York when all this happened . . . and said to him "Hey, man, you dig white chicks?"

JACK DANIELS: What'd he say?

SOUTHERN COMFORT: Nothing. He just grabbed my arm and dragged me down in that subway stop they got there and raped the hell out of me.

JACK DANIELS: That black bastard.

SOUTHERN COMFORT: Don't say that, I deserved it.

JACK DANIELS: I don't follow.

SOUTHERN COMFORT: (*Getting ready to sneeze again.*) Well wouldn't you . . . ah! ah! ah! . . . rape me . . . ah! ah! ah! if you were a spade? . . . ah! ah! ah! . . . and everything I'd done to you? . . . atchoo!

JACK DANIELS: What exactly is it you're allergic to, Southern?

SOUTHERN COMFORT: (*Another sneeze coming on.*) Hair.

JACK DANIELS: You mean like fur rugs and things?

SOUTHERN COMFORT: My own hair. Atchoo!

JACK DANIELS: That must be hard.

SOUTHERN COMFORT: It's a goddamn drag! Atchoo! (*Southern Comfort lights another joint.*)

JACK DANIELS: You're lucky you got a good supply o' them cigarettes. What do you do when you run out? (*Southern Comfort shakes her head indicating she can't talk.*) Sorry, Southern. You keep that smoke in. My pa was allergic to yellow onions. He had to rub Crisco oil all o'er himself when he broke out.

SOUTHERN COMFORT: Oh wow!

JACK DANIELS: It's good, hunh? You're lucky. Most people hate anything that's good for 'em. (*Southern Comfort passes the joint to him.*) No, thank you.

SOUTHERN COMFORT: It's good stuff.

JACK DANIELS: In the first place, I don't have no allergies and in the second, I don't smoke.

SOUTHERN COMFORT: It'll loosen you up.

JACK DANIELS: I am loose. Hell, I'm so loose I jangle.

SOUTHERN COMFORT: I mean sexually.

JACK DANIELS: Oh. Well I guess I better try me some. Give me that butt, woman. (*Jack Daniels takes the deepest drag he can and holds it.*)

SOUTHERN COMFORT: I'm more than a vagina, Jack Daniels. (*Jack Daniels chokes on the joint.*) I am a human being.

JACK DANIELS: Yes, ma'am, I know that. That's jes' what I was thinking.

SOUTHERN COMFORT: That's what they all say. You don't know the real me. The real me's right here, staring you in the face, only nobody ever sees her.

JACK DANIELS: I see you, Southern.

SOUTHERN COMFORT: I know what you see when you look at me.

JACK DANIELS: Well, seeing's how you're not wearing any clothes . . .! (*Jack Daniels laughs his yuk! yuk! yuk! laugh but this time it's to conceal his embarrassment.*)

SOUTHERN COMFORT: You're that terrified of any real commitment? I feel sorry for you, Johnny.

JACK DANIELS: I'm Jack. Sorry for me?

SOUTHERN COMFORT: Do you want to make love to me or not?

JACK DANIELS: Yes, ma'am, I surely do, but why sorry for me?

SOUTHERN COMFORT: Make love to me, Johnny. Here and now and hard and beautiful.

JACK DANIELS:. (*Indicating with his head that they are not alone.*) Don't you think maybe we ought to go in another room?

SOUTHERN COMFORT: I wouldn't give them that satisfaction.

JACK DANIELS: I'm talking 'bout our satisfaction.

SOUTHERN COMFORT: You want me, Johnny, don't you?

JACK DANIELS: Yes, I want you, I want you a whole lot but . . .! 'N my name's Jack.

SOUTHERN COMFORT: It's that important to you?

JACK DANIELS: No, but . . .

SOUTHERN COMFORT: I'm freaking out, Johnny, I'm really freaking out. I feel bad vibrations coming from that ledge out there and I don't want to have to do that again.

JACK DANIELS: Do what?

SOUTHERN COMFORT: Jump. Do I turn you on, Johnny? Tell me that I turn you on.

JACK DANIELS: Yes, you turn me on.

SOUTHERN COMFORT: Oh God! Oh wow! Oh groovy!

JACK DANIELS: And you'd turn me on even more if you'd jes' call me Jack.

SOUTHERN COMFORT: I hate Jack, I can't call you Jack. Jack was a bass player with the Grateful Dead before they made it big and it was a really bad scene with him. Don't ask me to call you Jack, Johnny, please don't make me do that!

JACK DANIELS; Okay, Southern, okay!

SOUTHERN COMFORT: I'm freaking out, Johnny, I'm really freaking out tonight.

JACK DANIELS: I think I can see that, ma'am.

SOUTHERN COMFORT: You have nice fingernails.

JACK DANIELS: What?

SOUTHERN COMFORT: You have nice fingernails. Tommy Tyler has terrible fingernails. All bitten and ugly.

JACK DANIELS: Who's Tommy Tyler?

SOUTHERN COMFORT: A drummer I lived with for six months in Hollywood. He gave me the clap. Let's not talk about him. It was another bad scene. Hurry up, Johnny, please! (*Southern Comfort rips open his shirt.*)

JACK DANIELS: Hey!

SOUTHERN COMFORT: Oh God, freedom!

JACK DANIELS: This is my good shirt. (*Then.*) What's the matter?

SOUTHERN COMFORT: You don't have hair on your chest.

JACK DANIELS: I know.

SOUTHERN COMFORT: You said you had hair on you chest. No! I'm confusing you with Stevie Menchek. It doesn't matter.

JACK DANIELS: Who's Stevie Menchen?

SOUTHERN COMFORT: Some sideman I met in Tiajuana. He's not important. He beat the shit out of me. I don't want to talk about him.
You just reminded me of him for a minute. Only he had hair on
his chest. Make love to me, Johnny, what's the matter, don't I
turn you on?

JACK DANIELS: How many times do I have to say yes?

SOUTHERN COMFORT: Prove it then, Johnny, prove it. Don't be afraid of
me. I'll be good with you. I won't laugh. I promise not to laugh.

JACK DANIELS: If you'd jes' set still for a minute maybe I could! (*Jack
Daniels manages to kiss her. A good long kiss which gets more and
more serious. Finally Southern Comfort breaks loose and holds
him off.*)

SOUTHERN COMFORT: No!

JACK DANIELS: What's the matter?

SOUTHERN COMFORT: It's not fair to you like this.

JACK DANIELS: What ain't?

SOUTHERN COMFORT: There's something about me you don't know.

JACK DANIELS: Can't it wait?

SOUTHERN COMFORT: It's too important.

JACK DANIELS: Go ahead then.

SOUTHERN COMFORT: I'm frigid, Johnny.

JACK DANIELS: I don't mind.

SOUTHERN COMFORT: I can't have a climax. I can lie there and go
through the motions but I can't have a climax.

JACK DANIELS: That's okay, too.

SOUTHERN COMFORT: It's not a very pretty story. I grew up right here in
Houston. I was pretty, I was the national champion baton twirler
and I only dated football players. Sound familiar? The typical
American girl. The first boy I went all the way with was Bobby
Barton. Bobby was the state champion high school quarterback
and since I was a champion, too, only a national one, it was
pretty natural that we should get together. It was in the back seat
of his daddy's Ford Fairlane on our eleventh date. Remember
them? They were two-toned with a chrome trim that made kind
of a dip along the door. Anyway, I really enjoyed it and Bobby
did, too. I started going all the way with him on every date we

had. Gee, it was swell. Then one day after school during football practice somebody tackled Bobby and he just didn't get up. I mean he was dead. So then I started dating Bobby's best friend, Terry Walsh, who played right guard and who'd been the one who'd accidentally killed Bobby when he tackled him during practice that time. I went all the way with him on the fourth date. He had a sports car, a reptile-green MG, so we had to spread blankets on the ground first. Terry got killed during the game with Lubbock for the state quarter finals down in Austin. Spontaneous concussion. My senior year at Sunset I started dating and going all the way with Tiny Walker, who played left end and who used to be Terry and Bobby's real good friend. He drove a blood-red, chopped down Plymouth Fury with dual carburetors and two front seats that you could make go flat down like a dentist's chair. Tiny was small but powerful and he'd been tackled lots of times by bruisers a whole lot bigger than that linebacker from Sweetwater. But when Tiny died like that I stopped dating football players. I felt like a jinx on 'em, you know what I mean? And I knew people were starting to say things about me behind my back. I stopped twirling, started drinking, got to hate Houston so much I couldn't stand it here any longer, ran away from home and got into show business. Now I sleep around a lot, but only with musicians; they don't die on you like football players. (*A pause.*) I told you it wasn't a very pretty story.

JACK DANIELS: Dog sad's what I'd call it.

SOUTHERN COMFORT: Dog what?

JACK DANIELS: Dog sad, ma'am. Sad like a dog.

SOUTHERN COMFORT: I see what you mean. I guess it is. I never really thought about it like that. Dog sad.

JACK DANIELS: My pa thought it up. Never ever heard anybody say it but him.

SOUTHERN COMFORT: You still want me, Johnny?

JACK DANIELS: Yes, ma'am, I think so.

SOUTHERN COMFORT: You're worried I'll be bad for you.

JACK DANIELS: Hell no, I never played football in my life.

SOUTHERN COMFORT: What then?

JACK DANIELS: There's something maybe you ought to know about me. I'm kind o' drunk, Southern. I may not be able to . . . you know.

SOUTHERN COMFORT: That's okay.

JACK DANIELS: It ain't like I don't want to, you understand. I want to real bad.

SOUTHERN COMFORT: Sometimes it's nice just holding someone real still and nobody talking even.

JACK DANIELS: Maybe so, but that don't mean I ain't gonna try first. (*Tia Maria is starting to stir on the bed.*) Jes' not in here, Southern, okay?

SOUTHERN COMFORT: Where's your room?

JACK DANIELS: We can't in there. I lost my key.

SOUTHERN COMFORT: Mine's out too. Hansel and the Toad People are crashing in there.

JACK DANIELS: Hansel and the Toad People?

SOUTHERN COMFORT: This rock trio I picked up at the Continental Trailways bus terminal. They're so freaked out and sex mad they'd be all over us. Orgies aren't my scene. Those creeps from the Brass Pussycat had me all over the place. Please, Johnny, I don't want to talk about them.

JACK DANIELS: What were you doing at a bus terminal?

SOUTHERN COMFORT: Meeting people, what else? Come on, and bring a bottle.

JACK DANIELS: Where we going?

SOUTHERN COMFORT: The closet, and bring your guitar, too.

JACK DANIELS: Ain't it awful small in there?

SOUTHERN COMFORT: What are you figuring on? A rodeo?

JACK DANIELS: I 'spose we could always levitate. (*Jack Daniels laughs his yuk! yuk! yuk! laugh as he follows Southern Comfort into the closet and closes the door behind them. Tia Maria sits up in bed.*)

TIA MARIA: I.W.? I.W.? The two kids went into the closet together and I don't think it was to hang up any clothes. (*I.W. Harper mutters in his sleep and snuggles up closer to Tia Maria, who fumbles for a cigarette and match, lights up and pours herself a drink.*) Boy, am I gonna have a head on me tomorrow morning. I don't want to think about it. I don't even want to wake up. I feel like that time we got drunk in Denver during that Windstorm and I woke up in the middle of the night and told you I was gonna be sick only the toilet didn't work and you yelled "Over here" and when I ran to the window the damn thing blew open and my head went right through it. Eighteen stitches they took in my scalp. Boy, I was mad at you the next day. It wasn't your fault but I had to be mad at someone. You're a good sport, I.W. (*Tia Maria laughs and strokes I.W. Harper's head while he just snuggles closer.*) I know I'm just a fat 'n foolish, middle-aged lady drunk who screams a lot and eats too much candy and I don't know why you put up with me half the time but I do love you, I.W., and ain't that the main thing, loving somebody? And I guess you love me a little bit, too. Hell, honey, you'd have to! Look at poor Johnny Walker asleep on the floor there. He ain't got no one. Hey, Johnny! Johnny Walker! You want to get up here into bed with I.W. and me? We'll let you. (*Johnny Walker groans drunkenly in his sleep.*) He don't want to come, I.W. That's okay, too. I still love you, Johnny. Even sleeping it off on the floor like some drunk dog who ain't got no dignity, I still love you. And if those kids would quit a-hugging 'n a-kissing in that closet and come out here I'd tell them I loved them, too. I love all those kids like they was my own. I know I ain't their ma but I feel like their ma and I like that feeling. There ain't no harm in that. Is there, anybody? Me and I.W. wanted kids, didn't we, honey? We just couldn't have any and some nights that gets me really down and blue. But not tonight. Tonight we're just one big happy family. I like that feeling a whole lot, too. (*Whiskey whinnies softly from the bathroom.*) Sometimes I think that horse is trying to tell us something, warn us even like maybe he knows something we don't know. 'Course most of the time I think he just hates us and is trying to kill me and I wish he was dead and stuffed and put on rollers. That would be a good kind of horse to have, I.W.! (*I.W. snores and snuggles closer.*) If they cancel the tour, I.W., we're gonna go right back to Santa Monica and work up a better act. I already got two new good ideas. One is you cracking a cigar out of Southern Comfort's mouth with your bullwhip while she's twirling her flaming batons. A cigarette would be too dangerous. Maybe it ain't so hot. The other is for me to dress a whole lot more ladylike, like Barbara Stanwyck, and sashay more. I don't think I'm doing nearly enough sashaying now. I'd look real nice in white, I.W., I think you'd be proud of me in the kind of white dress I'm envisioning. (*I.W. HARPER snores and snuggles* closer.) But you know something, I.W.? Even if we don't ever appear in public again, even if they canceled our series after what happened tonight, I'd still be the happiest, luckiest lady I know. I got you, I.W. I think having you next to me, hearing you snore is the nicest sound I know, even if you are drunker than a coot. Sleep now, baby, sleep away and dream of big blue skies and red earth and all them happy things. (*Tia Maria begins to hum very softly and very lovingly to I.W. Harper, who is nestled in her arms. With one hand she strokes his head, with the other she holds her cigarette and drink. Whiskey will be heard from time to time whinnying more and more restlessly in the bathroom.*) Yes sir, I think you'd be real proud of me in the kind of white dress I'm envisioning! (*While Tia Maria hums now, she will be slowly drifting off to sleep. The lights in the room are coming down. We hear a gentle thud as the glass falls from her hand onto the carpet. She still holds the cigarette, however, and we see it spiraling smoke above Tia Maria and I.W. Harper asleep on the bed. Whiskey is whinnying more and he has started beating his hooves again. The lights in the room are nearly gone now but one stays a moment longer on that burning cigarette in Tia Maria's hand. Whiskey is making quite a bit of noise now and in the blackout that follows the sound will grow louder and louder and more terrifying, too. What we also hear are the terrible sounds and noises of a hotel fire! There are fire engines, their sirens wailing, the yells and screams of people calling for help, the hiss of high pressure hoses quenching flames and making steam. The terrible sounds build until they reach an ear-shattering, terrifying crescendo only to be abruptly cut off. What we then hear and at once is the mournful sound of a Hammond organ. When the lights come back up we are in the Houston Astrodome once again. What we see is the Lush Thrushes and Whiskey show curtain. All the cutouts where I.W. Harper, Tia Maria, Johnny Walker, Southern Comfort and Jack Daniels once stood are empty now, of course. Someone has draped them in black crepe. Whiskey's cutout is filled, however, by none other than Whiskey himself. He is an old, spindly, rather repulsive critter. As horses go, Whiskey is way down low on the totem pole. Right now he is contentedly standing in his very own spotlight noisily chewing his oats. He's been decorated with some kind of*

Red Cross badge but its difficult to tell whether such awards mean very much to him. Certainly he's oblivious to the lugubrious accents of the Announcers Voice as he drones the eulogy.)

ANNOUNCER'S VOICE: (*Over the organ music.*) . . . indeed, the entire nation will not soon recover from this stunning and tragic loss to the entertainment industry. How Whiskey alone escaped the raging holocaust that turned their multimillion dollar, fully air-conditioned hostelry into a raging inferno is Whiskey's secret and his alone. There is one happy note, fans, if happy is not too inappropriate a word to utter on this sad occasion. I have just spoken on the telephone long distance to Whiskey's agent, a certain Howard Rosenstone of the William Morris Agency in New York City, who assured me only moments ago that Whiskey will return next season as the star of his own series. I believe package was the word he used, folks, some kind of William Morris package. And now, may I ask that we all rise and stand for a moment of silent tribute to the memory of these five so-well-loved, intimately unique and already sorely missed artistes? (*The Hammond organ continues to mourn but over it we hear the sound of Jack Daniels singing and playing "The Streets of Laredo." When he does appear he is dressed exactly like he was before—overalls, shirt, barefoot, etc.—only this time everything is a beautiful, gleaming white. Also, he has sprouted the biggest pair of snow-white angel wings anybody ever saw.)*

JACK DANIELS: I'm in heaven, Whiskey. I'm one o' God's little angels now. Ain't that nice? 'Cause judging from the crowds I seen, it looks like everybody comes to heaven and gets to be one o' God's little angels. Ain't hardly no distinction at all. It's jes' like earth, too. Some people singing, some people drinking, some people fighting. Sure are a lot o' black 'n brown 'n yellow people, though! I never seen so many skin tones. It's pretty. And God's jes' like I. W. I was telling Him 'bout the time my little brother got his big right toe caught in an International Harvester tractor tread and pa had to use bear grease to get him out and He told me to keep my dumb mouth shut. He said I could play my guitar and sing though. You miss us, Whiskey? You sure don't look like it. (*Johnny Walker appears. He, too, is dressed like before only now everything is a shiny white leather. And the new pair of wings he sports are just as white, if not quite as large, as Jack Daniels's. He's carrying a newspaper and he's fit to be tied.)*

JOHNNY WALKER: What did they call me?!

JACK DANIELS: Uh oh, Whiskey, Johnny Walker and he's all het up.

JOHNNY WALKER: Just guess what they called me?!

JACK DANIELS: I wouldn't rightly know, Johnny.

JOHNNY WALKER: Well, guess!

JACK DANIELS: A fruit?

JOHNNY WALKER: What did you call me?

JACK DANIELS: I knew I shouldn't have answered when you're all worked up like this.

JOHNNY WALKER: Shut up, you dumb hick. I'll say I'm worked up. Listen to this! (*Johnny Walker is so angry he can hardly find the place he's looking for in the newspaper.*)

JACK DANIELS: Johnny Walker's gonna read us what they called him, Whiskey.

JOHNNY WALKER: "The entire cast of television's longest running series was killed last night when a fire swept through their hotel in downtown Houston."

JACK DANIELS: Is that what happened? Last thing I remember I was in the closet with Southern Comfort and next thing I knew I was here.

JOHNNY WALKER: "Miraculously, their horse and co-star escaped the flames."

JACK DANIELS: Good for you, Whiskey.

JOHNNY WALKER: "The 1,876 other guests in the hotel were evacuated without incident."

JACK DANIELS: Boy, for such a big hotel it sure had mighty poor room service.

JOHNNY WALKER: "Why only the five actors failed to leave their rooms has not yet been determined."

JACK DANIELS: Shoot, that's easy. We was drunk.

JOHNNY WALKER: Here it is, this is the part! "Authorities have ventured that one possible cause of the fire were the Lady Schick portable hair dryer and Carmecita hair curler set found in the room of the series' so-called he-man, Johnny Walker."

JACK DANIELS: They called you a so-called he-man, Johnny.

JOHNNY WALKER: Not between the lines, they didn't! I know what they meant! I know! CIA stuff, you hear me, CIA!!! (*Johnny Walker fires his pistol wildly in a violent rage. From offstage we hear a very loud OOOOOOOWW!*)

JACK DANIELS: This time you really hit someone.

JOHNNY WALKER: Oh no! (*Southern Comfort storms in. She is wearing an enormous pair of white wings and a white bikini.*)

SOUTHERN COMFORT: You grazed my butt!

JOHNNY WALKER: I'm sorry, Southern!.

SOUTHERN COMFORT: You grazed my butt, you dumb fairy!

JOHNNY WALKER: I didn't see you, honest I didn't.

SOUTHERN COMFORT: That big pouff gazed my pink touchas!

JACK DANIELS: It's only a crease, Southern.

SOUTHERN COMFORT: Well it hurt!

JOHNNY WALKER: I said I was sorry. I read something like this and I just go crazy.

SOUTHERN COMFORT: Do it again and I'll have a real cowboy work you over. (*Calling off.*) It's okay Billy! He said he was sorry!

JACK DANIELS: Who you talking to Southern?

SOUTHERN COMFORT: Billy the Kid.

JOHNNY WALKER: He's up here?

SOUTHERN COMFORT: This place is crawling with cowboys.

JACK DANIELS: I don't see him. Where?

SOUTHERN COMFORT: Over there, see? Talking to Calamity Jane.

JOHNNY WALKER: That's him all right.

SOUTHERN COMFORT: Who'd you think it was? Fat Gene Autry?

JOHNNY WALKER: Gene Autry ain't dead.

SOUTHERN COMFORT: Well you are, Johnny Walker.

JOHNNY WALKER: I know. (*Johnny Walker moves apart from Southern Comfort and Jack Daniels.*)

SOUTHERN COMFORT: What are you doing?

JACK DANIELS: Winking at that Calamity Jane. She winked at me so I thought I'd better wink right back at her.

SOUTHERN COMFORT: (*Greeting another new friend.*) Hi, Jesse, how y'all making it!

JACK DANIELS: Look, Johnny, Jesse James! It sure is crawling with 'em.

SOUTHERN COMFORT: Oh man, this place is a complete turn on!

JACK DANIELS: Have you seen Him yet?

SOUTHERN COMFORT: He flipped me out. Groovy as they come. I blew

His mind, too. I walked right up to Him and said since I wasn't gonna wear any clothes down there I sure as hell wasn't gonna wear any up here either? He freaked right out.

JOHNNY WALKER: Look who's there.

JACK DANIELS: Who is it, Johnny?

JOHNNY WALKER: The President of the United States standing with his head bowed. He came back for the memorial service.

JACK DANIELS: Boy, he really must have liked us.

SOUTHERN COMFORT: (*Confronting an old adversary.*) Hey, Mr. President!

JACK DANIELS: He can't hear you, Southern. You're one o' God's little angels now.

SOUTHERN COMFORT: I know. Oh gee! Oh wow! We all are. (*Johnny Walker, Jack Daniels and Southern Comfort stand quietly looking down as they listen to their own memorial service. I.W. Harper and Tia Maria appear now. I. W. is wearing a very handsome white rancher's suit with boots. Tia is wearing her white Barbara Stanwyck-type dress, and she really looks quite lovely in it. Both are sporting a handsome pair of white wings. They enter arm in arm, almost gliding, like a very smooth promenade.*)

I.W. HARPER: Why look at you strut, honey.

TIA MARIA: This ain't no strut, I.W., this is a real North Texas sashay.

I.W. HARPER: You're sure swinging them hips, ma'am.

TIA MARIA: Them that has, does. Them that don't, can't help it.

I.W. HARPER: What does that mean?

TIA MARIA: I don't know. It was just fun saying it!

I.W. HARPER: Why I got a regular little filly prancing 'longside me here.

TIA MARIA: That ain't no filly, I.W., that's your wife.

I.W. HARPER: You sure look mighty pretty in that dress, Tia.

TIA MARIA: I told you I would.

I.W. HARPER: Mighty pretty!

TIA MARIA: And you're just about the handsomest-looking man I ever saw. Now come on, I.W., sashay!

I.W. HARPER: You're happy up here?

TI MARIA: Happy? Why I'm jes' gonna yodel 'round God's heaven all day, I.W.! (*Tia Maria obliges with a dazzling cadenza of improvised yodels. They have come up next to Whiskey now.*) Look at that horse. He sure looks like he knows something we don't know.

I.W. HARPER: Hello, Whiskey. Just basking away in that spotlight, aren't you, feller?

TIA MARIA: Got it all to himself now.

I.W. HARPER: Tia!

TIA MARIA: I'm not saying he started that fire but he sure didn't break any legs trying to save anybody's life. I'd just like to know how he got out o' there. You gonna tell us, Whiskey?

I.W. HARPER: Leave be, honey, that's something ain't none of us ever gonna know. (*I.W. Harper and Tia Maria join Johnny Walker, Southern Comfort and Jack Daniels.*)

JOHNNY WALKER: We sure got a big crowd down there tonight.

I.W. HARPER: See that, Tia? Folks really did love us.

TIA MARIA: I kind o' always loved them, too, I.W.

SOUTHERN COMFORT: I guess I've twirled my last flaming baton.

JACK DANIELS: And I done twirled my last lariat.

JOHNNY WALKER: Goodbye, world.

TIA MARIA: Amen. (*A moment of silence and they break and begin to move apart.*)

JOHNNY WALKER: Anybody seen Wyatt Earp? I've always wanted to shake his hand.

I.W. HARPER: Wyatt's over yonder, having a shootout with Annie Oakley.

JOHNNY WALKER: Annie Oakley? She must be older than God! No wonder they call this place Heaven! (*Johnny Walker strides off.*)

SOUTHERN COMFORT: Jes' keep away from the James Boys, you latent faggot! I'm meeting them at the corral!

TIA MARIA: You look kind o' rumpled, Southern.

SOUTHERN COMFORT: You think I look rumpled? You ought to see the James Boys. Oh man, they flipped me right out! (*Southern Comfort runs off.*)

TIA MARIA: You mean she can still . . . you know . . . up here?

I.W. HARPER: Would you want her *not* to, Tia?

TIA MARIA: No, I guess not, I.W.

JACK DANIELS: I saw my pa, ma'am.

TIA MARIA: What'd he say?

JACK DANIELS: Nothing. He jes' cuffed me one real hard and said that's what I got for hanging around drunks. I'm gonna see if I can find my ma now. Then I won't be an orphan at all anymore. (*Jack Daniels goes off, playing his guitar and singing his song.*)

I.W. HARPER: He didn't mean that like it sounded, Tia.

TIA MARIA: Is that all we were, I.W.? Drunks?

I.W. HARPER: We liked our liquor, honey, there's no getting around that.

TIA MARIA: But drunks. I hate that word. Hell, it was cigarettes that killed us.

I.W. HARPER: (*Consoling her.*) We weren't just drunks, Tia. We were cowboys first off. Just poor ol' lonesome cowboys. Why, even Southern Comfort's got cowboy stamped all over her, only she don't know it yet. They could book us in the Astrodome, they could package us on TV, they could've moved us to New York City but they ain't never could've changed us. We knew who we were, Tia, and not many people do.

TIA MARIA: What were we, I.W.?

I.W. HARPER: *Cowboy* drunks.

TIA MARIA: (*Drying her eyes.*) Well, that's good enough for me. I jes' couldn't have stood being a drunk drunk, I.W.

I.W. HARPER: That's my girl.

TIA MARIA: Look at Whiskey now. He's grinning at us, I.W.

I.W. HARPER: That is kind of a smile, Tia.

TIA MARIA: You know, just looking at him being there like that, breathing and eating and grinning, and I wouldn't mind being alive again.

I.W. HARPER: You got me, Tia.

TIA MARIA: I know, I.W.

I.W. HARPER: And we got this. (*He produces a bottle of whiskey.*)

TIA MARIA: Like the song says, a good sour mash is hard to find.

I.W. HARPER: Like the song says. (*Tia Maria and I.W. Harper kiss very tenderly.*) Come on, let's get started on this. (*They start moving off, arm in arm, promenading again.*) So long there, Whiskey, don't let 'em stuff you like Trigger!

TIA MARIA: Look, I.W., look! Belle Starr driving a rig 'n surrey!

I.W. HARPER: Well I'll be goddamned! (*Tia Maria and I.W. Harper are gone. The organ music fades up.*)

ANNOUNCER'S VOICE: (*Reciting the words dolorously.*) The eyes of Texas were upon them . . . all the livelong day. The eyes of Texas were upon them . . . they could not get away. Do not think you can escape them . . . rise up so early in the morn. The eyes of Texas are upon you, too, my friends, till Gabriel blows his horn. Goodnight, Whiskey. Goodnight, folks. (*The lights begin to fade. The organ tremolos a finale. Whiskey stands chewing his oats, he whinnies, he seems to smile. Blackout.*)

Bad Habits

for Elaine May

BAD HABITS opened February 4, 1974, at the Astor Place Theatre, and May 5, 1974, at the Booth Theatre in New York City. It was produced by Adela Holzer. It was directed by Robert Drivas. Scenery and costumes designed by Michael H. Yeargan and Lawrence King. Lighting designed by Ken Billington. The production stage manager was Robert Vandergriff. The assistant to the director and assistant stage manager was Tony DeSantis. The casts (in order of appearance):

For RAVENSWOOD

OTTO	Henry Sutton
APRIL PITT	Cynthia Harris
ROY PITT	F. Murray Abraham
JASON PEPPER, M.D.	Paul Benedict
DOLLY SCUPP	Doris Roberts
HIRAM SPANE	Emory Bass
FRANCIS TEAR	J. Frank Lucas
HARRY SCUPP	Michael Lombard

For DUNELAWN

RUTH BENSON, R.N.	Cynthia Harris
BECKY HEDGES, R.N.	Doris Roberts
BRUNO	Henry Sutton
MR. PONCE	Emory Bass
DR. TOYNBEE	J. Frank Lucas
MR. BLUM	F. Murray Abraham
MR. YAMADORO	Michael Lombard
HUGH GUMBS	Paul Benedict

Characters

RAVENSWOOD
OTTO
APRIL PITT
ROY PITT
JASON PEPPER, M.D.
DOLLY SCUPP
HIRAM SPANE
FRANCIS TEAR
HARRY SCUPP

DUNELAWN
RUTH BENSON, R.N
BECKY HEDGES, R.N.
BRUNO
MR. PONCE
DR. TOYNBEE
MR. BLUM
MR. YAMADORO
HUGH GUMBS

Bad Habits

RAVENSWOOD

Bright sunlight. Lush green foliage forms a background wall. Heaven on earth. There is a table with Dom Perignon champagne, coffee service, orange juice, etc. Three chairs are at the table. A small rolling cart holds towels and suntan cream. There are two chairs and a small table, shaded by a beach umbrella.

    We hear lively baroque music. When the house lights are out, and before the stage lights come up, the music changes. Now it is "Wein, Du Stadt Meiner Traume" ("Vienna, City of my Dreams"). When the lights come up we see that the music is coming from the cassette recorder that Otto carries from a shoulder strap.

    He enters down the aisle through the audience carrying a bouquet of flowers. As he carefully arranges them on the table, we hear the voices of April and Roy Pitt.

APRIL: (*Offstage.*) We're here!

ROY: (*Offstage.*) Hey, where is everybody? Does somebody wanna give us a hand with these things? (*Otto exits behind the foliage wall, and returns carrying three large expensive pieces of luggage. April Pitt, carrying a makeup kit, and Roy Pitt, with a tennis bag, follow him in.*)

APRIL: So this is Ravenswood! Nice. Very nice.

ROY: What do you mean nice? It's terrific! Look at that clay court, honey. Real clay. Can you stand it? (*Otto starts off down the aisle with the luggage.*)

APRIL: That's Vuitton, Buddy.

OTTO: *Ja, Fraulein.*

APRIL: Just thought I'd mention it.

OTTO: *Ja, Fraulein.* (*He is gone.*)

APRIL: Jesus, Roy, it's the Gestapo. I just hope this Pepper fellow's all he's cracked up to be.

ROY: I told you: he's just gonna have us talk to each other.

APRIL: We talk to each other all the time. What's he gonna do?

ROY: Listen.

APRIL: Just listen? A hundred and forty-five clams a day and he just listens? I knew I should have checked this guy out first.

ROY: Look what he did for Sandy and Reg.

APRIL: Sandy and Reg are lesbians and they're not in show business. They run a pet shop in Montauk for Christ's sake!

ROY: But they're happy.

APRIL: Sure, they're in dyke heaven, those two. I'm talking about us, Roy.

ROY: So am I, April. You told the answering service where I'd be? I don't want to miss that call from the Coast. (*He starts off down the aisle. The lively baroque music is heard again very softly.*)

APRIL: I'm beginning not to like the smell of this whole setup. When's our first session? This Pepper character doesn't deliver, we're gonna blow this nickel joint and head straight for L.A. Right, Roy? (*But Roy is following Otto and the luggage.*) I said easy with the Vuitton, schmuck! (*She follows them off. The stage is empty a beat. The music has gotten louder. Jason Pepper, M.D., enters with Dolly Scupp. He is in an electric wheelchair with a blanket on his lap. The music is coming from a cassette recorder built into the chair. Also, the chair has an ashtray, a small shelf on the side for holding a book later, a holder for a martini glass, and a ship's bell for calling Otto. Dolly Scupp is carrying a shoulder-strap-type handbag and a book. Her right foot is in an orthopedic foot covering. Dr. Pepper is drinking a martini and smoking a cigarette. He and Dolly listen to the end of the music, then he turns off the cassette.*)

DR. PEPPER: Over there's our lake. A pond you might call it, but I like to think of it as a lake. After all, it's the only body of water for miles and miles. In the winter it's frozen over and quite covered with snow. And now look at it. Ah, the seasons, the seasons! I do love the seasons! What would we do without them? (*Thunder. Dr. Pepper puts both hands to his head and gingerly fingers his skull.*) Don't tell me that's not the music of the spheres. It's a day like this that makes you think the world is coming to an end. Only the real joke is, it's not going to rain. Oh don't get me wrong, I don't enjoy playing God *or* the weatherman, but I don't have this porous platinum plate in my head for nothing, either.

DOLLY: You look different on your book jacket.

DR. PEPPER: I know. Taller. May I? (*Dolly gives him the book she has been carrying under her arm.*) *Marriage for the Fun of It!* Oh God, are people still reading this old thing?

DOLLY: Everybody who's still married.

DR. PEPPER: I thought I knew something in those days.

DOLLY: You're being modest.

DR. PEPPER: It's my only virtue.

DOLLY: That's more than me.

DR. PEPPER: Harry didn't tell me you were coming.

DOLLY: He didn't know. I woke up this morning and said to myself, "I'm driving up to Ravenswood today." Don't ask me why. I just had this sudden urge to see you.

DR. PEPPER: It's a delightful surprise.

DOLLY: I hope so.

DR. PEPPER: You absence has made Harry's rehabilitation somewhat more difficult, you understand. I prefer to treat couples who are having difficulties *as* couples.

DOLLY: There's nothing wrong with me, if that's what you're driving at.

DR. PEPPER: Should I be?

DOLLY: Is my husband getting any better, Dr. Pepper?

DR. PEPPER: It's Jason, Mrs. Scupp. Please, I insist on it. Until we're over that little hurdle we're nowhere. And you're right, it's high time we had a little chat. Coffee?

DOLLY: Thank you. (*She crosses to the table and helps herself.*)

DR. PEPPER: Cigarette?

DOLLY: No, thanks.

DR. PEPPER: It's a special tobacco, imported from Panama, that's been fertilized with hen feces. I don't think you'll find them at your A&P in Scarsdale.

DOLLY: I wouldn't think so.

DR. PEPPER: They have an extraordinarily . . . *pungent* taste.

DOLLY: I don't smoke.

DR. PEPPER: You're joking.

DOLLY: I gave them up years ago.

DR. PEPPER: During the big scare, huh? So many of you poor bastards did. Will it bother you if I . . . ? (*He is lighting his cigarette.*)

DOLLY: Not at all. My doctor insisted.

DR. PEPPER: And who might that be?

DOLLY: Dr. Fernald.

DR. PEPPER: Helmut Fernald up at Grassyview? I might've known he'd jump on the bandwagon.

DOLLY: No, George Fernald in White Plains, the County Medical Center.

DR. PEPPER: He wouldn't drive a white Buick station wagon, usually there's a couple of Dalmatians yapping around in the back, and be married to one of the McIntyre sisters, would he?

DOLLY: I don't think so. Our Dr. Fernald's married to a Korean girl and I'm pretty sure they have a dachshund. I don't know what he drives. He's just our family doctor.

DR. PEPPER: Well that explains it. The curse of modern medicine, that lot.

DOLLY: Dr. Fernald?

DR. PEPPER: Your friendly, neighborhood, family G.P. Now don't get me started on *that*, Mrs. Scupp.

DOLLY: I thought the majority of doctors had stopped smoking, too.

DR. PEPPER: (*Exhaling.*) And doesn't that just sound like something the majority of doctors would do? Fortunately, there remains a few of us who refuse to be stampeded along with the common herd. I'm referring to men like Peabody Fowler of the Heltzel Foundation and Otis Strunk of the Merton Institute, of course. (*Dolly shakes her head.*) Rand Baskerville out at Las Palmetas? Claude Kittredge up at Nag's Head?

DOLLY: I'm sorry, but I'm not familiar with them.

DR. PEPPER: Who is? I can't discuss colors with a blind person, Mrs. Scupp.

DOLLY: But surely, Doctor, you're not suggesting that smoking is good for you?

DR. PEPPER: Of course not.

DOLLY: I didn't think so.

DR. PEPPER: What I *am* suggesting is that *not* smoking is conceivably worse.

DOLLY: I don't follow.

DR. PEPPER: Do you want to talk turkey or not, Mrs. Scupp?

DOLLY: Of course I do! And please, call me Dolly.

DR. PEPPER: Hello, Dolly.

DOLLY: Hello.

DR. PEPPER: Well, hello, Dolly.

DOLLY: It's my curse.

DR. PEPPER: You think Dr. Pepper is easy? Now let's start at the beginning and I'll try to keep it in layman's terms.

DOLLY: Thank you.

DR. PEPPER: Everything in life is bad for you. The air, the sun, the force of gravity, butter, eggs, this cigarette . . .

DOLLY: That drink.

DR. PEPPER: That coffee! Canned tuna fish.

DOLLY: No.

DR. PEPPER: It's true! It's loaded with dolphin meat. There's an article on canned tuna fish in this month's *Food Facts* that will stand your hair on end.

DOLLY: I love tuna fish.

DR. PEPPER: Don't we all?

DOLLY: I don't care what they put in it.

DR. PEPPER: Neither do I. Right now, this very moment, as I speak these words, you're ten seconds closer to death than when I started. Eleven seconds, twelve seconds, thirteen. Have I made my point? Now, how would an ice-cold, extra-dry, straight-up Gordon's gin martini grab you? (*He rings the service bell.*)

DOLLY: I'm afraid it wouldn't.

DR. PEPPER: Ah, vodka is the lovely lady from Scarsdale's poison. (*He rings again.*)

DOLLY: I'm on the wagon.

DR. PEPPER: You don't smoke, you don't drink . . .

DOLLY: And it's Larchmont. And I would like to talk about my husband. (*Otto appears from the aisle.*)

OTTO: Ze newlyweds have arrived.

DR. PEPPER: Ze newlyweds Pitt?

OTTO: *Ja, Herr Doktor.* I put zem in ze little honeymoon cabin.

DR. PEPPER: Good, Otto, good. Tell them we'll have our first session after lunch. Show them the lake, the stables, the tennis courts. The grand tour, Otto.

OTTO: I could give Mrs. Pitt a rubdown, maybe?

DR. PEPPER: No, Otto.

OTTO: Whirlpool?

DR. PEPPER: Nothing, Otto. Just the tour.

OTTO: (*Seeing that Dr. Pepper's glass is empty.*) Ze usual?

DR. PEPPER: Last call, Mrs. Scupp.

DOLLY: I'll have a Tab, maybe.

OTTO: *Nein* Tab.

DOLLY: A Fresca?

OTTO: *Nein* Fresca.

DOLLY: Anything dietetic.

OTTO: *Nichts* dietetic, *nichts!*

DOLLY: Water, then

OTTO: *Wasser?*

DR. PEPPER: *Wasser für das frau!*

OTTO: *Jawohl, Herr Doktor.*

DR. PEPPER: (*Otto has turned to go.*) *Und Otto! Dry-lich! Dry-lich! Dry-lich für ze martini!* (*Otto exits.*) It's an extraordinary race. Is Scupp German?

DOLLY: We don't know what it is.

DR. PEPPER: Then I can say it: I can't stand them. It was a German who incapacitated me.

DOLLY: The war?

DR. PEPPER: My wife. She pushed me down a short but lethal flight of stairs backstage at the Academy of Music in Philadelphia.

DOLLY: How horrible!

DR. PEPPER: It was the single most electrifying experience of my life.

DOLLY: But why would anyone do such a thing?

DR. PEPPER: In my wife's case it was self-defense.

DOLLY: You mean you tried to kill her?

DR. PEPPER: Symbolically. It's funny how no one ever asks why it was flight of stairs backstage at the Academy of Music; you must admit, it's not your usual place for an attempted homicide. My wife was a lieder singer. She'd just given an all-Hugo Wolf recital. She asked me how I thought it went and I said, "Maybe the only thing in the world more boring than an all-Hugo Wolf recital is your singing of an all-Hugo recital." The remark just kind of popped out of me. And when it popped, she pushed and down I went. Four short steps and here I am. Don't look so tragic, Mrs.

Scupp. No Anita Wertmuller and her all-Hugo Wolf recital and no Ravenswood. We divorced, of course, and she remarried some California grape-grower. Otto used to accompany her. Now Otto accompanies me. Having been unhappy in marriage, hopefully I can help others to solve their martial difficulties. Look for the silver lining, yes?

DOLLY: You never remarried?

DR. PEPPER: What on earth for? The third and fourth toes of your left foot, wasn't it?

DOLLY: The second and third of the right.

DR. PEPPER: Accidents will happen.

DOLLY: Not with a remote-control power lawnmower, Doctor.

DR. PEPPER: Those things are devils.

DOLLY: Harry was sitting on the porch controlling it. I was sunbathing.

DR. PEPPER: He didn't go into the details.

DOLLY: Of course he didn't. That's why he's here.

DR. PEPPER: He said there'd been an accident and that was why you hadn't come here with him.

DOLLY: I wouldn't have come with him even if it hadn't happened. I'm sorry, but I can't afford to take any more chances with a man like that.

DR. PEPPER: That's what marriage is, Mrs. Scupp.

DOLLY: Not with a husband who tried to kill you, it isn't! Two toes, Doctor.

DR. PEPPER: Two legs, Dolly. (*Thunder. Dr. Pepper feels his head again.*)

DOLLY: Is my husband getting any better yet, Doctor?

DR. PEPPER: I think Harry's about ready to leave Ravenswood. (*Hiram Spane enters. He is in a long bathrobe, beach sandals, and wearing sunglasses. He goes to the table and pours champagne and orange juice into the same glass.*)

DOLLY: I hope you're right.

DR. PEPPER: He'll be along shortly. You can see for yourself. Good morning, Hiram!

HIRAM: Morning? I was hoping it was late afternoon. I haven't been up this early since I saw Mother off on the Graf Zeppelin.

DR. PEPPER: I'm sure you never saw anyone off on the Graf Zeppelin, Hiram.

HIRAM: Well it was something that moved and I was there to see her off! Now I remember. Of course! It was the *Andrea Doria*.

DOLLY: Did she go down with it?

HIRAM: Cornelia Margaret Spane, my mother, never went down with or on anything. I don't believe we've been introduced. Bitch.

DR. PEPPER: This is Mrs. Scupp, Hiram.

HIRAM: I don't care who she is.

DR. PEPPER: Harry's wife.

HIRAM: Well why didn't you say so? How do you do, Mrs. Scupp? I'm sorry, you're not a bitch. And I'm only a bitch when I've got a head on me like this one. I thought *I* mixed a wicked vodka stinger! What did your husband do? Study alchemy?

DOLLY: Harry? Drinking? My Harry? Harry Scupp?

HIRAM: I understand the A.A. has a warrant out for his arrest.

DOLLY: I don't think we're talking about the same man.

HIRAM: The way I feel this morning we're probably not.

DR. PEPPER: Why don't you take that dip now, Hiram?

HIRAM: Good idea, Jason. With my luck, maybe I'll drown. You like to swim, Mrs. Scup?

DOLLY: I love to, but . . . (*She indicates her injured foot.*)

HIRAM: Come on, I believe in the buddy system: you start to drown, I'll save you. I start to drown, forget it.

DOLLY: I didn't bring a suit.

HIRAM: That never stopped anyone around this place. What do you think I've got on under here?

DOLLY: I blush to think.

HIRAM: You blush to think? I've got to live with it! If that goddamn snapping turtle doesn't attack me again. Doctor, you can tell Otto I'll be joining you here shortly for my Bullshot. (*He goes down the aisle.*)

DR. PEPPER: Hiram Spane of the Newport Spanes. They own everything. (*Francis Tear enters. He is wearing a bathing cap, a bathrobe and rubber bathing shoes. He pours himself a glass of orange juice.*)

DOLLY: (*Still staring down the aisle.*) Is he a patient here?

DR. PEPPER: Hiram's been a patient here since I founded Ravenswood.

DOLLY: What's his problem?

DR. PEPPER: You're looking at him.

DOLLY: (*Finally seeing Francis.*) Oh my God!

DR. PEPPER: Francis Tear of the Baltimore Tears. They made their fortune in plumbing. Good morning, Francis! You just missed each other.

FRANCIS: We're not speaking today.

DR. PEPPER: You and I?

FRANCIS: Hiram and me. He said something very cutting to me last night. Hurt me to the quick, he did. I don't think I'm ready to forgive him yet.

DR. PEPPER: Fine, fine, there's no point in rushing it.

FRANCIS: (*To Dolly.*) Do you think I look like an embryo, madam?

DOLLY: Not at all.

FRANCIS: Thank you.

DR. PEPPER: This is Mrs. Scupp, Francis.

FRANCIS: Hello.

DR. PEPPER: Harry Scupp's wife.

FRANCIS: Well I didn't think it was his mother. I'm Francis Tear of the Baltimore Tears. We made our fortune in plumbing!

DOLLY: Yes, I know.

FRANCIS: Somebody had to do it.

DOLLY: I suppose so.

FRANCIS: What are you in?

DOLLY: I'm just a housewife.

FRANCIS: So's Hiram! He's also in distress. Psychic distress, Doctor!

DR. PEPPER: Not now, Francis, please. I like your new bathing slippers.

FRANCIS: Do you? Hiram's mother had them sent. Hiram's mother has everything sent.

DOLLY: How nice for you.

FRANCIS: You never met Hiram's mother. You don't think I look silly in these, Jason?

DR. PEPPER: Not at all. There may be fairies at the bottom of somebody's garden but there are very sharp rocks at the bottom of my lake.

FRANCIS: Do you, Mrs. Scupp?

DOLLY: They go with the cap.

FRANCIS: That's what I was hoping. I think it's important to look your best at all times. You never know. It must be Jewish, Scupp.

DOLLY: I was telling Jason, we don't know what it is.

FRANCIS: It's Jewish. It was a pleasure, Mrs. Scupp. (*He turns to go.*)

DOLLY: Likewise, Mr. Tear.

FRANCIS: Call me Francis. Everyone else does. Except Hiram. You should hear some of the things he calls me. (*Exiting down the aisle.*) Oh, no, Hiram! I get the raft today! You had it yesterday! And this doesn't mean I'm speaking to you yet! (*He's gone.*)

DR. PEPPER: Eighteen years they've been together.

DOLLY: Are they . . . ?

DR. PEPPER: I don't think so, but if they are, I'd like to be a fly on that wall. No, I think they're just old, old friends.

DOLLY: I didn't know you treated male couples at Ravenswood.

DR. PEPPER: A male couple is better than no couple at all. Love is where you find it.

DOLLY: That's true.

DR. PEPPER: Don't be blind, it's all around you, everywhere. (*Otto returns with the martini and glass of water.*)

DOLLY: Thank you.

DR. PEPPER: *Danke*, Otto.

OTTO: Ze Fraulein would like a rubdown, maybe?

DOLLY: I don't think so.

OTTO: (*Shrugging.*) Okay. (*He takes an* Opera News *off of the towel cart, opens it, sits and reads.*)

DR. PEPPER: Cheers! You were saying?

DOLLY: Doctor . . . (*She fidgets.*)

DR. PEPPER: Don't mind Otto. It would take a lot more than your lawn-mower to get his nose out of that magazine.

DOLLY: Why did Harry try to kill me?

DR. PEPPER: Do you still want to talk turkey, Mrs. Scupp?

DOLLY: About Harry? Of course I do.

DR. PEPPER: About you.

DOLLY: What is that supposed to mean?

DR. PEPPER: Does Labor Day weekend, 1963, the parking lot outside Benny's Clam Box in Rockport, Maine, do anything for you?

DOLLY: I don't know. Should it?

DR. PEPPER: Think hard.

DOLLY: Benny's Clam Box.

DR. PEPPER: Harry was packing up the trunk of the car and you put the car into reverse.

DOLLY: Oh, that! How did you know?

DR. PEPPER: We have very complete files on our guests here, Mrs. Scupp. Ravenwood is a far cry from the Westchester County Medical Center and your quack G.P. with his Korean war bride and poodle!

DOLLY: Dachshund!

DR. PEPPER: Sorry!

DOLLY: Leave it to Harry to tell you about a silly accident like that.

DR. PEPPER: He was in traction for two months.

DOLLY: I didn't see him back there. What are you driving at, Doctor?

DR. PEPPER: Eight months later you tried to run him over with a golf cart at the Westchester Country Club.

DOLLY: It was an accident. My foot got stuck on the accelerator.

DR. PEPPER: Nobody drives a golf cart on the putting green.

DOLLY: I do! I did. I still do.

DR. PEPPER: That time he was in traction for three months.

DOLLY: You're making mountains out of mole hills, Doctor. My foot got stuck. I had new golf shoes. What's your point?

DR. PEPPER: A year later he asked you if there was water in the swimming pool before diving in.

DOLLY: I thought he asked me should he wash our Puli.

DR. PEPPER: Your Puli didn't end up in White Plains Hospital with a broken leg. Let's talk about the incident at the archery tournament.

DOLLY: Let's not.

DR. PEPPER: It's quite a story.

DOLLY: *His* version.

DR. PEPPER: I'd love to hear yours.

DOLLY: I didn't tell him to change the target when he did.

DR. PEPPER: How about his forced high dive in Acapulco?

DOLLY: He *fell.*

DR. PEPPER: Nearly six hundred feet.

DOLLY: I didn't push him.

DR. PEPPER: And what about your safari to East Africa last winter?

DOLLY: He didn't tell you about that, too?

DR. PEPPER: Harry's just lucky he's not the one who's stuffed and mounted over your fireplace, Mrs. Scupp.

DOLLY: I was delirious. A touch of malaria, I remember. I mistook him for something else.

DR. PEPPER: An albino orangutan? No, you didn't.

DOLLY: I don't want to hear these things!

DR. PEPPER: You said you wanted to talk turkey, Mrs. Scupp. All right, here's the real turkey: you and your husband have been trying to kill one another since Labor Day weekend, 1963. Why? (*A pause.*)

DOLLY: Has he been neat, Doctor?

DR. PEPPER: Neat?

DOLLY: Neat.

DR. PEPPER: Oh, neat! A little over fastidious when he got here, perhaps . . .

DOLLY: I'm talking about coasters, Doctor.

DR. PEPPER: Coasters?

DOLLY: Those things you put under glasses so they don't leave a ring.

DR. PEPPER: I can't stand them.

DOLLY: Neither can I.

DR. PEPPER: Always sticking to the bottom of your glass and then dropping off.

DOLLY: I loathe coasters.

DR. PEPPER: I loathe people who shove them at you

DOLLY: Then you loathe Harry.

DR. PEPPER: I don't follow.

DOLLY: Harry is the king of coasters. He adores coasters. He lives coasters. He *is* coasters. He's even tried to crochet coasters. Doctor, he can be upstairs sound asleep and I can be downstairs in the den watching television late at night and he'll come in with a coaster for my glass. He wakes up at three a.m. worrying I'm making rings.

DR. PEPPER: I don't know how you put up with it.

DOLLY: I haven't! Doctor, he goes into my closet and straightens my shoes.

DR. PEPPER: Usually they wear them.

DOLLY: I wish he would. I wish he *would* put them on. Maybe he'd break a leg. But no, he just straightens them. I bet you put your toilet paper on wrong, too.

DR. PEPPER: I beg your pardon?

DOLLY: Did you know you could put a roll of toilet paper on the dispenser wrong? I didn't 'till I married Harry. "Dolly! How many times do I have to tell you? The paper should roll *under* from the inside out, not *over* from the outside down."

DR. PEPPER: Over from the? . . .

DOLLY: I try, but I can't remember.

DR. PEPPER: Under from the? . . .

DOLLY: He won't let me have down pillows in the house. They crush, he says. We're into total foam rubber. I hate foam rubber.

DR. PEPPER: I'm allergic to it.

DOLLY: I'm up to my ass in it. Doctor, this is a man who goes around straightening license plates in a public parking lot.

DR. PEPPER: Now honestly, Mrs. Scupp . . .

DOLLY: If they're dirty, he wipes them!

DR. PEPPER: What about in bed?

DOLLY: In bed?

DR. PEPPER: I mean, what's he like in bed?

DOLLY: I don't remember.

DR. PEPPER: Surely, Mrs. Scupp . . .

DOLLY: I never noticed.

DR. PEPPER: Never?

DOLLY: Our wedding night was terrific. From then on, it's been downhill all the way. His hobby is tropical fish. I hate tropical fish, Doctor.

DR. PEPPER: You hate tropical fish?

DOLLY: Not all tropical fish. Harry's tropical fish. There's something about them. Maybe it's the fact he talks to them. Or the names he gives them. Eric, Tony, Pinky. There's one round, mean-looking once he calls Dolly. When they die he buries them in the backyard. We're the only house in Larchmont with a tropical fish cemetery in the backyard. I know this sounds crazy, Doctor, but I hate those fish. I resent them in my living room and I resent them under my lawn. I'm a mature, sensible and, I think, rather intelligent woman and I hate those fish. How do you hate a tropical fish? (*She stands.*) You know something else I hate? Stereo equipment. Harry's got woofers, weefers, tweeters, baffles, pre-amps. He puts gloves on when he plays those records. White gloves like your friend. (*She indicates Otto.*) Don't get me started, Doctor. There's so many things about Harry I hate. I hate his black Volvo station wagon with the snow tires on in August. He worries about early winters. He worries about everything. We're the only people in Larchmont with drought insurance. (*She is pacing.*) I know it's none of my business, but I hate the way he dresses. I hate his big, baggy boxer shorts. The only shoes he'll wear are those big clumpy cordovans. Even on the beach. But my favorite outfit is his "Genius At Work" barbecue apron he wears over the pink Bermuda shorts and black, knee-high Supp-Hose. Oh, I'm married to a snappy dresser, Doctor! And try taking a trip with him. He reads road signs. Every road sigh. Out loud. "Soft shoulder, Dolly." "Slippery when wet, Dolly." "Deer crossing, Dolly." "Kiwanis Club meeting at noon, Wednesday, Dolly" Who gives a good goddamn? He's not even a member of the Kiwanis Club! Who'd want him? A man who puts on an apron after a bridge party and vacuums up isn't exactly a load of laughs. Neither is a man who takes you to Arizona for your anniversary. You know what's in Arizona? The London Bridge! Don't get me wrong, Doctor. I love my husband. I just can't stand him. So don't make too much out of that incident with the lawnmower. That was just the straw that broke the camel's back!

DR. PEPPER: And a very attractive camel she is, too.

DOLLY: Thank you.

OTTO: (*Looking up from his magazine.*) Rubdown, Frau Scupp?

DR. PEPPER: *Nichts!* (*Turning to Dolly, as Otto resumes reading.*) Listen to me, Mrs. Scupp. I'm not famous for saving marriages. I'm not even certain I believe in them. I'm famous for successful marriages for people who want to be married. I think I can help you but you have to want me to help you. (*Harry is heard calling, "Otto! Otto!" offstage.*) Harry's coming. I've done all I can for him. It's up to you now.

DOLLY: I'm frightened.

DR. PEPPER: Given your track record, I think Harry is the one with cause for alarm. (*Harry enters. He, too, is dressed for swimming. He carries a small cardboard box.*)

HARRY: Otto! Otto! Good morning, Jason.

DOLLY: Hello, Harry.

HARRY: (*Embracing Dolly.*) Dolly . . . Doll. Doll! Doll, baby! Hey, this is terrific!

DOLLY: Harry, you're crushing me!

HARRY: I could eat you alive! You didn't tell me she was coming up.

DR. PEPPER: I didn't know.

HARRY: What a great surprise!

DOLLY: I'm beginning to wonder.

HARRY: What're you talking about? I've been up here so long even Fric and Frac down at the lake were starting to look good to me. So was Martin Borman over there. Good morning, Otto.

OTTO: *Gut morgen, Herr Scupp.* Ze usual?

HARRY: What time is it? It's early. I better stick with the Bloody Marys. Hot, Otto. Very, very hot. Lots of Tabasco and lots of the white stuff.

OTTO: *Jawohl, Herr Scupp.*

DOLLY: Harry!

HARRY: Otto makes a fantastic Bloody Mary. Takes the roof of your head off and leaves it there.

DR. PEPPER: Last call, Mrs. Scupp. (*Dolly shakes her head.*) *Bitte*, Otto . . . (*He holds up his martini glass. Otto nods and goes.*)

HARRY: You look wonderful. Doesn't she look wonderful, Jason?

DR. PEPPER: That's what I've been telling her.

DOLLY: I've lost a little weight.

HARRY: I can see that.

DOLLY: You haven't.

HARRY: It's that high-cholesterol diet they've got me on. You know, I never thought I'd get sick of Eggs Benedict and chocolate mousse!

DOLLY: You're meant to be on low-cholesterol.

HARRY: Talk to my doctor!

DR. PEPPER: Harry likes high-cholesterol. You'll excuse me for a few minutes, won't you? (*Dr. Pepper rolls offstage. Dolly composes herself.*)

HARRY: How are the kids?

DOLLY: Oh, Harry, they're just fine.

HARRY: Yeah?

DOLLY: Yeah . . . fine.

HARRY: That's great . . . that's just great.

DOLLY: I've got your *Hi-Fi Stereo Review*'s and *Popular Aquarium*'s in the car.

HARRY: Thank you.

DOLLY: And the summer pajamas you wrote for.

HARRY: The blue cottons?

DOLLY: I thought you meant the yellow drip-drys.

HARRY: That's okay.

DOLLY: I'm sorry.

HARRY: Really, it doesn't matter.

DOLLY: It's a pleasant drive up here.

HARRY: I hope you saw those warning signs on the bypass outside of Inglenook.

DOLLY: Oh, I did. I thought of you when I read them.

HARRY: An average of thirteen and a half people get killed there every year.

DOLLY: I'll be extra careful on the way back.

HARRY: When are you leaving?

DOLLY: I don't know. It depends. What's in the box?

HARRY: Oh . . . Henry.

DOLLY: Henry?

HARRY: My angel fish.

DOLLY: What happened?

HARRY: Evelyn killed him.

DOLLY: Who's Evelyn?

HARRY: My blue beta.

DOLLY: That's awful.

HARRY: It's just a fish. (*He throws the box over the wall of foliage.*)

DOLLY: You always used to give them such nice burials.

HARRY: I guess I'm getting cynical in my old age. So what's new?

DOLLY: Nothing much.

HARRY: I guess you sold the lawnmower.

DOLLY: No. It's in the garage waiting for you.

HARRY: Thanks.

DOLLY: It's broken, of course.

HARRY: I wasn't really trying to get you with it.

DOLLY: Yes, you were, Harry. Why?

HARRY: (*Exploding.*) There were a million reasons! It was hot. The refrigerator needed defrosting. The car keys were upstairs when they should have been downstairs. The house was still a mess from your bridge party. You forgot to renew my subscription to *High Fidelity* and they'd sent you three warnings already.

DOLLY: *Hi-Fi Stereo Review!*

HARRY: You knew how much I was looking forward to that compara-
tive analysis of Dolby-ized cassette decks with ferric oxide heads!
There was a new water ring on the telephone stand. Things like
that.

DOLLY: Did I have the toilet paper on right?

HARRY: As a matter of fact, you did. What happened?

DOLLY: I don't know. I lost my head!

HARRY: Only someone had been playing my stereo. There were fingerprints on my Christmas album.

DOLLY: Who would be playing a Christmas album in June?

HARRY: I didn't say *when* they were put there, I just said I found them.

DOLLY: What were *you* doing playing a Christmas album in June?

HARRY: I wasn't. I just happened to be doing my six-month record
cleaning that day. They weren't your fingerprints.

DOLLY: Thank you.

HARRY: They weren't the kids', either.

DOLLY: Well, at least I had the toilet paper on right.

HARRY: I conceded that point.

DOLLY: Well?

HARRY: It was blue!

DOLLY: That's all they had!

HARRY: It was blue! Our bathroom is red! Everything is red! The sink,
the tub, the tile, the towels, the shower curtain! You know I don't
like a clash. I like everything to match!

DOLLY: That's all they had!

HARRY: You asked me why. I'm telling you why. There were permanent press sheets on the bed.

DOLLY: Cotton's scarce.

HARRY: I can't sleep on permanent press. They're too hot. They're like
flame sheets. Things like that. Like I said, it was hot. There were
a million reasons. Then, when I saw you staked out on the lawn
in your bathing suit, I just kind of lost control with the mower.
What was it with me?

DOLLY: The coasters.

HARRY: Even that time in Acapulco?

DOLLY: It was always the coasters.

HARRY: I wasn't going to mention it, but . . . (*He motions to Dolly's glass. She picks it up from the table.*)

DOLLY: I'm sorry.

HARRY: It's okay! (*He takes the glass from her and puts it on the table without a coaster.*)

DOLLY: Dr. Pepper seems to think you're ready to go home.

HARRY: (*He takes out a cigarette.*) He's done wonders for me, Doll.

DOLLY: When did you take that up?

HARRY: A couple of months ago. You want one?

DOLLY: No, thank you.

HARRY: They're fertilized with chicken shit, honey.

DOLLY: I know. (*Otto has returned with the Bloody Mary.*)

HARRY: Thanks, Otto.

OTTO: Rubdown, Herr Scupp?

HARRY: Not just now, Otto. Maybe later, hunh?

OTTO: *Jawohl.* (*Otto exits.*)

DOLLY: You look terrible, Harry.

HARRY: I'm a little hungover.

DOLLY: From what?

HARRY: Margaritas. They're vicious, Dolly. Stay away from them.

DOLLY: What were you doing drinking margaritas?

HARRY: The Plungs.

DOLLY: What are the Plungs?

HARRY: Jeanine and Billy Plung. This young couple from Roanoke I got friendly with while they were up here. We had a little farewell party for them last night. Jeanine had me dancing the rhumba with her until nearly three.

DOLLY: You can't rhumba, Harry. You can't even foxtrot.

HARRY: Jeanine says I'm a natural.

DOLLY: I thought they were taking care of you up here.

HARRY: They are. I never felt better in my life.

DOLLY: Why would you start smoking at your age?

HARRY: I like to smoke.

DOLLY: That's not a good enough reason.

HARRY: I can't think of a better one.

DOLLY: Margaritas! And the rhumba, Harry! How old was this woman?

HARRY: Twenty-two, twenty-three.

DOLLY: Harry, what's gotten into you?

HARRY: I'm my old self again! It's me, Harry Scupp with the DeSoto roadster with the rumble seat and the good hooch and let's have a good time and "Beat Port Chester, Larchmont!" and Glen Island Casino and Dolly Veasey is my number one date. It's gonna be like the old times again, Doll.

DOLLY: We never had old times like that.

HARRY: It's never too late.

DOLLY: And what do you mean, "your old self?"

HARRY: I love you. I don't want to kill you anymore.

DOLLY: You never had a DeSoto roadster. We took the bus.

HARRY: I'm talking about life, Dolly. *Joie de vivre.* You want to see what I've been doing since I've been up here? Close your eyes! (*Dolly won't.*) I'm not going to hit you. Go over there and close your eyes. (*Dolly won't.*) I want to show you something. It's a surprise. (*She is still doubtful.*) Well, close your eyes! (*Dolly closes here eyes, and immediately extends her hand in front of her as a feeler. Harry takes something off the towel cart.*) It's incredible you should be here today. I just finished this last night. Okay, Doll, open.

DOLLY: What is it?

HARRY: An ashtray.

DOLLY: An ashtray?

HARRY: Isn't it pretty? I mean, did you know I had a sensitivity like that all bottled up inside of me? I didn't.

DOLLY: You're sure it's an ashtray?

HARRY: It's a nude study of Jeanine.

DOLLY: Jeanine Plung?

HARRY: Isn't that pretty?

DOLLY: She's naked!

HARRY: Well, how else do you sculpt a nude? I did one of Billy Plung I'm thinking of turning into a lamp.

DOLLY: What you're suggesting, Harry, is that you were somewhat more than just friendly with these people.

HARRY: Oh, I was! You'd go crazy over them and vice-versa.

DOLLY: I wouldn't count on it.

HARRY: Now wait right there. There's something else I want to show you. Don't move. (*He runs off.*)

DOLLY: Doctor!

DR. PEPPER: (*Emerging, with Otto following.*) What do you think of the change?

DOLLY: What have you done to him?

DR. PEPPER: He's called you "honey" several times at least.

DOLLY: "They're loaded with chicken shit, honey," is what he said. You mean Harry and these Plung people . . . ?

DR. PEPPER: Just Mrs. Plung.

DOLLY: Where was Mr. Plung while all this was going on?

DR. PEPPER: Rumor has it with Otto.

DOLLY: I wouldn't be surprised. And you just allowed all this to happen?

DR. PEPPER: There are no rules at Ravenswood, Mrs. Scupp.

DOLLY: Which means that you let my husband go off into the woods with that horrid Plung woman!

DR. PEPPER: How did you know she was horrid? That's one secret I thought I'd kept to myself. She's a dreadful woman. I don't know what your husband ever saw in her. He would've been better off with Otto.

DOLLY: I'm beginning to think you made my husband do all these horrible things.

DR. PEPPER: I've never made anyone do anything, Mrs. Scupp. That's the secret of my success here, such as it is. I allow everyone to do exactly as he pleases.

DOLLY: At your prices I'd hardly call that a bargain.

DR. PEPPER: You'd be surprised how few people know what it is they want.

DOLLY: I know what I want.

DR. PEPPER: Do you, Mrs. Scupp?

DOLLY: I thought I did until I saw Harry like this.

HARRY: (*From offstage.*) I'll bet you didn't know I was a frustrated song-and-dance man, did you, Doll? (*Harry rushes back in. He has a ukulele and a tap board.*) Now you're really gonna get a kick out of this. You know how I always overdo things? That's because of my masculine insecurity coming out. I didn't even know I had masculine insecurity until Jason here got his hands on me. It turns out I've got a singing voice. And feet, too. Dolly, I got rhythm! Sit down. I want you to see this. (*Harry hands Dr. Pepper the uke. Otto produces a small foot-pedal drum and a set of cymbals from behind the towel cart. They launch into a lively,*

twenties-type popular song. It's obvious Harry's been practicing.
He's still pretty terrible, but he's having fun. He tap dances, too,
and ends with a big finish.)

DOLLY: Stop it! I can't stand seeing you like this.

HARRY: You can't stand seeing me like what?

DOLLY: Singing, dancing, smoking, drinking! Making ashtrays!

HARRY: I told you it was a new me. Wait'll they see this down at the
country club! (*He launches back into the song. This time, his big
finish is even bigger than before. Finally Dolly hurls the ashtray
across the stage, smashing it.*) You broke my ashtray.

DOLLY: I'm taking you home.

HARRY: You broke my ashtray.

DOLLY: I thought you came here to get better.

HARRY: You broke my ashtray! (*He is advancing on her. Dolly is trying
to get something out of her purse.*)

DR. PEPPER: Harry!

DOLLY: (*Producing an aerosol can and pointing it at Harry.*) Harry!
(*Hiram and Francis are heard calling to Harry from the lakeside.
"Harry! Harry!"*)

HARRY: I promised Hiram and Francis I'd race them out to the raft.
They're like kids that way . . . they'll keep it up all morning until
I do. (*He runs down the aisle. Dolly's trembling.*)

DR. PEPPER: What is that?

DOLLY: Mace!

DR. PEPPER: It's too bad my wife didn't carry one of those. Too bad for
me, that is.

DOLLY: You said he was better!

DR. PEPPER: You still don't see the change?

DOLLY: Not the change I wanted!

DR. PEPPER: Harry loved that piece of sculpture.

DOLLY: What have you done to him?

DR. PEPPER: No, Harry's done it to himself. Maybe it's your turn now.

DOLLY: Maybe it isn't!

DR. PEPPER: Know what you want, Mrs. Scupp. That's the first step.

DOLLY: I want a good marriage.

DR. PEPPER: Then give me three months.

DOLLY: And I want to be happy.

DR. PEPPER: Make it three and a half.

DOLLY: That's not much, is it?

DR. PEPPER: Sometimes it's everything. Now: it's a beautiful summer's day, God's in his heaven and all's right with the world. Harry will be waiting for you down by the lake. I'd go to him if I were you.

DOLLY: I'm still a little frightened to be with him. With my foot like this, I can't go swimming. Maybe I could ask him to take me boating.

DR. PEPPER: I wouldn't push my luck. Try skimming stones, Mrs. Scupp.

DOLLY: It's Dolly. Please. Call me Dolly?

DR. PEPPER: Okay, Dolly.

DOLLY: It always happens.

DR. PEPPER: I know what you're going to say.

DOLLY: I always get a crush on doctors! (*Dolly exits down the aisle. Dr. Pepper sits sipping his martini and smoking. Otto starts his tape machine. We hear* "Wein Du Stadt Meiner Traume." *Otto picks up Harry's tap board, takes it to the towel table, and begins clearing the breakfast things.*)

DR. PEPPER: That's not at all what I thought she was going to say.

OTTO: Crush? *Was ist* crush?

DR. PEPPER: Mrs. Scupp thinks she likes me.

OTTO: Everyone likes Herr Doktor.

DR. PEPPER: That's because everyone thinks Herr Doktor likes them. You're playing your favorite song again, Otto.

OTTO: *Ja.* My mother used to sing this song.

DR. PEPPER: It's a beauty.

OTTO: My mother was a pig. Herr Doktor would like something?

DR. PEPPER: Herr Doktor just wants everyone to be happy. (*Just then a tennis ball bounces on stage. Roy and April Pitt, dressed for tennis and carrying their racquets, appear briefly down the aisle.*)

ROY: Hey, Mac, you want to send that back?

APRIL: What's the matter with you? Throw the ball back, you creep!`

DR. PEPPER: Otto. (*He points to the ball. Otto returns the ball to Roy.*)

APRIL: Thanks a lot.

ROY: Yeah, thanks loads. (*They disappear up the aisle.*)

DR. PEPPER: *Das ist* ze newlyweds Pitt?

OTTO: *Ja.*

DR. PEPPER: (*Holding out his empty glass.*) Bitte, Otto. (*Hiram and*

Francis are returning down the aisle. We hear Francis yelling, "We beat you!") Better make that three. Make that *drei* cocktails, Otto.

OTTO: *Jawohl.* (*He goes.*)

DR. PEPPER: Who won?

FRANCIS: (*Singing, skipping almost.*) Harry and me! Harry and me! Harry and me!

HIRAM: They ganged up on me as usual.

FRANCIS: We beat you! We beat you! Da da da we beat you!

HIRAM: Well, Harry beat you.

FRANCIS: And we both beat you!

HIRAM: I was worried about that turtle.

FRANCIS: Even with these on, I beat him. (*Indeed, water is sloshing out of his rubber bathing slippers.*) I beat you! I beat you!

HIRAM: I am going to beat you black and blue if you keep that up, Francis!

DR. PEPPER: Boys, boys!

FRANCIS: I'm still not speaking to you!

HIRAM: That's a blessing!

FRANCIS: But . . . (*Very softly.*) I beat you! I beat you!

DR. PEPPER: Hiram, did you tell Francis he looked like an embryo?

HIRAM: If I'd seen him in that bathing cap, I'd've said he looked like a prophylactic.

FRANCIS: Hiram is a poor sport! Hiram is a poor sport!

HIRAM: If there's anything more vulgar than swimming, it's a swimming race.

FRANCIS: It was his idea.

HIRAM: Does that sound like me, Jason?

FRANCIS: It was, too!

HIRAM: You see what I have to put up with?

FRANCIS: Last night after dinner you said, "Let's challenge Harry Scupp to a swimming race tomorrow."

HIRAM: Are you sure you can't do anything for him, Doctor?

FRANCIS: You did, you did!

HIRAM: I'd suggest a lobotomy but obviously he's already had one.

FRANCIS: I cross my heart, he did!

HIRAM: Several, from the look of it!

FRANCIS: (*Getting quite hysterical.*) He lies, Doctor, he lies! He did suggest a swimming race after dinner with Harry Scupp last night! He did! He did!

DR. PEPPER: Don't hold it back, Francis.

FRANCIS: (*A real tantrum now: feet and fists pounding the ground.*) Tell him! Tell him it was your idea, Hiram! Tell him, tell him, tell him, tell him, tell him, tell him, tell him, tell him! (*He is exhausting himself as Hiram interrupts.*)

HIRAM: All right! So it *was* my idea. I don't like to lose. It's the Spane in me. A Baltimore Tear wouldn't understand that. (*Genuinely.*) Oh I'm sorry, Francis. (*Francis sulks.*) Now get up. You know I can't stand to see you grovel like that.

FRANCIS: I'm not grovelling, Hiram. I'm letting it all out for once. Right, Doctor?

DR. PEPPER: Just keep going, I think we might be getting somewhere.

FRANCIS: He always wants to compete with me. I can't help it if I always win. I don't even want to win. I just do. Backgammon, bridge, whist, Chinese checkers, Mah-jongg . . .

HIRAM: You never beat me at Mah-jongg.

FRANCIS: Yes, I did. That time in Morocco.

HIRAM: I don't count that.

FRANCIS: Why not?

HIRAM: I had dysentery.

FRANCIS: So did I!

HIRAM: I said I was sorry!

FRANCIS: I always win! At anything! Anagrams, Parcheesi, Scrabble, tennis . . .

HIRAM: That's table tennis, Francis!

FRANCIS: Well I win, don't I? Like I always do? I can't lose to him at anything! And he hates me for it! Oh he just hates me to death!

HIRAM: While you're down there crowing, Francis, why don't you tell the doctor the *real* story?

FRANCIS: What real story?

HIRAM: What real story!

FRANCIS: I don't know what you're talking about!

HIRAM: Why don't you tell him about Celine? (*A short pause.*) I didn't think so.

DR. PEPPER: Who is Celine?

HIRAM: A Welsh Corgi we had when we lived on 69th Street.

DR. PEPPER: It's a lovely little dog.

HIRAM: Francis killed her.

FRANCIS: It was an accident.

HIRAM: He threw her out of the window.

FRANCIS: I didn't throw her out the window. She jumped.

HIRAM: Of course she did!

FRANCIS: You weren't there. She jumped out!

HIRAM: Celine hadn't jumped *anywhere* since Mummy's car backed over her in New Hope three years before! You threw that dog!

FRANCIS: She'd been trying catch this big fly in her mouth when suddenly she just sailed out the window right after it.

HIRAM: Do you really expect Dr. Pepper to believe that cock and bull story?

FRANCIS: It's true. It's true!

DR. PEPPER: What floor were you on?

FRANCIS: The fourteenth.

HIRAM: The fatal fourteenth.

FRANCIS: I didn't throw her.

HIRAM: Well who left that window open?

FRANCIS: You couldn't breathe that night.

HIRAM: And you were thinking of yourself first, as usual!

DR. PEPPER: No air-conditioning?

FRANCIS: This was years ago.

HIRAM: When dog-killers could still get away with something as simple as an open window. God knows what he'd come up with today.

DR. PEPPER: What a ghastly story.

HIRAM: Most crimes of passion are. Francis was jealous of her. Celine adored me, couldn't stand him. She used to pee in his closet out of spite. So he killed her.

FRANCIS: If you say that again I'm going to smack your face for you.

HIRAM: Say what? You dog murderer! (*Francis flies at him.*)

FRANCIS: I am not a dog murderer! You take that back!

DR. PEPPER: Don't hold it back. (*They struggle. They do minor violence to each other.*)

FRANCIS: Take it back! Take it back, take it back, take it back, take it back, take it back . . . (*Dr. Pepper, watching from the sidelines, offers encouragement during the encounter.*)

DR. PEPPER: That's right, boys, let it out. Let it out. No holding back, now. That's right, that's right. Just let everything out now. (*During the struggle Otto returns with the drinks. He looks to Dr. Pepper, who motions him to let the combatants be. Otto shrugs, sits down with his magazine. Finally, Hiram overwhelms Francis and, pinning him down, lightly slaps his face and arm.*)

HIRAM: Have you lost your mind? Don't you ever lift a hand to me again as long as you live, do you hear me! Ever! Ever, ever, ever, ever, ever. (*One last little slap.*) Ever. (*Hiram and Francis collapse with exhaustion.*)

DR. PEPPER: All right now?

FRANCIS: I don't think Ravenswood is working out for us.

HIRAM: Of course Ravenswood isn't working out for us! Why should it?

DR. PEPPER: Did you ever think of getting another dog?

HIRAM: No more dogs. Celine was a terrible shedder.

FRANCIS: Another one would probably just pee in my closet, too.

HIRAM: Or maybe mine next time.

FRANCIS: No more dogs, Hiram? Promise?

HIRAM: The only reason we stay together is because no one else in the world would put up with us.

DR. PEPPER: If you can leave here having realized that much, I'll be satisfied.

HIRAM: *You'll* be satisfied?

DR. PEPPER: And so should you.

HIRAM: We are, I suppose. We are.

FRANCIS: You're the only real friend I've ever had, Hiram.

HIRAM: And I'm sure Dr. Pepper can see why. Help me up, will you? I think I twisted something. (*Francis struggles to his feet, then helps Hiram up.*)

FRANCIS: Are we dressing for lunch?

HIRAM: I don't know about the end of the Baltimore Tear line but the last remaining Newport Spane is. Otto, where's my Bullshot? (*As they move toward the drinks, another tennis ball bounds across the stage. Roy and April are heard yelling from the back of the house.*)

ROY: (*Offstage.*) Ball!

APRIL: (*Offstage.*) Ball!

ROY: *Ball!*

APRIL: *Ball!*

HIRAM: Who are those dreadful people?

DR. PEPPER: The Pitts.

FRANCIS: Pitts? What kind of name is Pitts?

HIRAM: Appropriate! (*He gulps his Bullshot.*)

APRIL: Hey, you, Mac, you wanna throw that ball back for Christ's sake?

HIRAM: (*Speaking straight out in the direction of April's voice.*) My name is not Mac, I'm not your ball boy, and why don't you try fucking yourself, madam! Come on, Francis. (*They exit. Dr. Pepper is alone with the tennis ball.*)

ROY: (*Running down the aisle.*) Hey, you can't talk to my wife like that! (*To April, who is following him.*) Will you please go back there? We'll lose our place on the court.

APRIL: I'll get the court back! I want to see you handle something for once!

ROY: (*Leaping on stage.*) I told you: I'm gonna flatten that S.O.B.! Keep the court! (*April and Roy, still carrying their racquets, search around the stage.*) Where'd he go?

DR. PEPPER: Good morning.

ROY: We saw you talking to him!! Now where is he?

DR. PEPPER: Who?

ROY: The guy who insulted my wife!

DR. PEPPER: Your wife?

APRIL: What do I look like? His dog?

DR. PEPPER: You must be Mr. and Mrs. Pitt.

ROY: Yeah, as a matter of face, we *are.*

APRIL: And they got some nice class of people up at this place!

ROY: (*Cautioning her.*) Honey! I think we've been recognized.

DR. PEPPER: I'm afraid so.

ROY: Celebrity time!

APRIL: Oh, Christ!

ROY: (*Taking off his sunglasses and shaking Dr. Pepper's hand.*) Hi, Roy Pitt. Nice to see you. We were hoping to be a little incognito up here! It's just as well. I think actors who wear big sunglasses are big phonies. This is my wife, April James.

APRIL: Hi, April James. Nice to see you.

DR. PEPPER: April James?

APRIL: It's my professional name.

ROY: You see that, honey? Even with these things on he recognized us.

DR. PEPPER: And what do *you* do, Mrs. Pitt?

APRIL: What do you mean, "What do I do?" I'm an actress. Thanks a lot, buddy.

ROY: She's an actress.

APRIL: I don't even know you but I really needed that little ego boost.

ROY: Honey, of course he recognized me. My movie was on the Late Show last night. *Cold Fingers.* He probably caught it.

APRIL: God knows you did.

ROY: It's the power of the medium! You know that kind of exposure.

APRIL: *Cold Fingers* should have *opened* on the Late Show.

ROY: Now don't start with me.

APRIL: Boy, I really needed that little zap.

ROY: He's a dummy.

APRIL: You must have seen me in something. How about *Journey Through Hell* for Christ's sake! You didn't see me in *Journey Through Hell?*

DR. PEPPER: Were you in that?

ROY: That was my beautiful April all right!

APRIL: You bet your sweet ass it was!

DR. PEPPER: That was a wonderful movie, Mrs. Pitt.

APRIL: You see that? Another zap?

ROY: April wasn't in the movie. She created the role off-Broadway . . . didn't get the film version!

APRIL: Boy, this is really my day!

ROY: She was brilliant in that part!

APRIL: I know. Too bad the play didn't support me.

DR. PEPPER: I enjoyed the film, too.

APRIL: I bet you did.

ROY: Hey. Try to cool it with here, will you?

APRIL: Try *Random Thoughts and Vaguer Notions*, why don't you?

ROY: That one was on broadway. April was one of the stars.

DR. PEPPER: I wasn't able to catch it.

APRIL: It ran nearly eighty performances. You didn't exactly have to be a jackrabbit.

ROY: April!

APRIL: Before you zap me again, I didn't do the movie of that one, either.

ROY: You never read notices like she got for that one. Show 'em to him, honey.

APRIL: They're in the car. I break my balls trying to make that piece of garbage work and they sign some WASP starlet for the movie version thinking she's going to appeal to that goddamn Middle American drive-in audience.

ROY: I don't really think you can call Googie Gomez a WASP starlet.

APRIL: White bread! That's all she is, white bread!

ROY: (*Calling down the aisle.*) Hey, that court's taken, Buddy. We got it reserved.

APRIL: You heard him!

DR. PEPPER: I think that's the ground keeper.

ROY: That's okay, Mac! Sorry! Hang in there!

APRIL: Hi! April James! Nice to see you!

ROY: Hi! Roy Pitt! Nice to see you! Ssh! Sssh!

APRIL: What is it?

ROY: I thought I heard our phone.

APRIL: Way out here? What are you? The big ear?

ROY: You sure you told the service where I'd be?

APRIL: Of course I did. I might be getting a call, too, you know.

ROY: I'm expecting an important call from the coast. I'm not usually this tense.

APRIL: Hah!

ROY: This could be the big one, April.

APRIL: Almost anything would be bigger than *Cold Fingers.* (*Otto has appeared.*)

ROY: (*Starting to do push-ups.*) You got one hell of a thirsty star out here, waiter.

APRIL: Two thirsty stars.

OTTO: I am not a waiter. My name is Otto.

ROY: Hi, Otto. Roy Pitt, nice to see you.

APRIL: Hi, Otto. April James, nice to see you.

ROY: (*Now he is doing sit-ups.*) What are you having, honey?

APRIL: A screwdriver.

ROY: I'll have some Dom Perignon. The champagne.

APRIL: Roy!

ROY: It's included.

APRIL: Eighty-six the screwdriver. I'll have the same.

OTTO: The Fraulein would like a nice rubdown, maybe?

APRIL: From you?

ROY: Just bring the Dom Perignon, will you?

DR. PEPPER: Oh, and Otto! (*He holds up his glass.*)

OTTO: *Jawohl*. (*He goes.*)

APRIL: (*Sits, and looks at Dr. Pepper's wheelchair for the first time.*) I want to apologize for earlier when we yelled at you for the ball. We didn't realize you were . . . like that.

DR. PEPPER: Half the time I don't realize it myself.

APRIL: We do lots of benefits, you know.

ROY: April's been asked to do the Mental Health and Highway Safety Telethons two years straight.

APRIL: Easter Seals wanted me last month but they weren't paying expenses.

ROY: Nobody's blaming you, honey.

APRIL: I mean there's charity and then there's charity. I mean you gotta draw the line somewhere, right? What am I? Chopped liver?

ROY: Easter Seals wouldn't even send a limousine for her! Our agent told them they could take their telethon and shove it. (*Roy is opening up a sun reflector.*)

APRIL: What are you doing?

ROY: You don't mind if we don't play tennis for a while? I want to get some of the benefits.

APRIL: There's not enough sun for a tan.

ROY: That's what you think. It's a day like this you can really bake yourself. Just because the sky's grey doesn't mean those rays aren't coming through. Make love to me, *soleil*, make love to me.

APRIL: (*She is sitting near Dr. Pepper. Roy is sprawled out with his reflector under his chin. He just loves lying in the sun like this.*) What are you in for?

DR. PEPPER: The usual.

APRIL: A bad marriage, huh? That's too bad. You're probably wondering what we're doing here. I know on the surface it must look like we got a model marriage. But believe me, we got our little problems, too. Don't look so surprised. Roy's got an ego on him you could drive a Mack truck with. Show biz marriages ain't nothing to write home about. Half our friends are divorced and the other half are miserable. Naturally, they don't think we're going to make it. Think. They *hope*. But we're going to show them. Right, honey?

ROY: Right.

APRIL: Have you had a session with Dr. Pepper yet?

DR. PEPPER: Many. (*He picks up the book he took from Dolly and opens it.*)

APRIL: Is he all he's cracked up to be?

DR. PEPPER: I think so, but of course I'm prejudiced. (*He smiles at April and begins to read.*)

APRIL: He's gonna have his hands full with that one.

DR. PEPPER: (*Looking up.*) I'm sorry . . .

APRIL: Skip it. (*Dr. Pepper returns to his book. April silently mouths an obscenity at him and turns her attention to Roy.*)

ROY: Honey! You're blocking my sun.

APRIL: You're just gonna lie there like that?

ROY: Unh-hunh.

APRIL: So where's my reflector?

ROY: I told you to pack it if you wanted it.

APRIL: I want it.

ROY: You said you didn't want to get any darker.

APRIL: I'm starting to fade.

ROY: No, you're not.

APRIL: It's practically all gone. Look at you. You're twice as dark!

ROY: It's not a contest, honey.

APRIL: I mean what's the point of getting a tan if you don't maintain it? Roy!

ROY: (*For Dr. Pepper's benefit, but without lookin up from the reflector.*) Do you believe this? I was with my agents all day and I'm supposed to be worried about a goddamn reflector!

APRIL: Just give me a couple of minutes with it.

ROY: It's the best sun time now.

APRIL: You know I've got that audition Wednesday.

ROY: No. N. O. (*April gives up, gets the tin of cocoa butter off the cart and begins applying it.*) April's up for another new musical. They were interested in us both, actually, but I've got these film commitments.

APRIL: Tentative film commitments.

ROY: You're getting hostile, honey.

APRIL: What's hostile is you not packing my reflector.

ROY: I was busy with my agents. *You* are getting hostile.

APRIL: I've got a career too, you know.

ROY: (*Sitting up, he drops the reflector and motions for quiet.*) Ssshh!

APRIL: (*Grabbing the reflector.*) Hello? Yes, we're checking on the availability of Roy Pitt for an Alpo commercial!

ROY: Shut up, April. (*He listens, disappointed.*) Shit. (*Then he sees April.*) Hold it. Stop it! (*He grabs the reflector and lies back.*)

APRIL: Roy!

ROY: After that? You've gotta be kidding! I wouldn't give you this reflector if you whistled "Swanee River" out of your ass.

APRIL: I can, too.

ROY: I know. I've heard you.

APRIL: Just lie there and turn into leather.

ROY: I will.

APRIL: There are other things in the world more important than your suntan, you know.

ROY: Like yours?

APRIL: For openers.

ROY: Like your career?

APRIL: Yes, as a matter of fact.

ROY: Will you stop competing with me, April? That's one of the reasons we came here. I can't help it if I'm hotter than you right now.

APRIL: That could change, Roy. Remember *Star is Born.*

ROY: Well, until it does, love me for what I am: Roy Pitt, the man. But don't resent me for my career.

APRIL: I know, Roy.

ROY: I love you for what you are: April James, the best little actress in New York City.

APRIL: What do you mean, "best little actress?"

ROY: I'm trying to make a point, honey!

APRIL: As opposed to what? A dwarf?

ROY: If we're going to have a good marriage and, April, I want that more than anything . . .

APRIL: More than you wanted the lead in *Lenny?*

ROY: I didn't want *Lenny.*

APRIL: He would've crawled through broken glass for that part!

ROY: I didn't want *Lenny.* Now goddamit, shut up!

APRIL: I can't talk to you when you get like that.

ROY: Get like what? You haven't laid off me since we got in the car.

APRIL: You know I'm upset.

ROY: We've all been fired from shows.

APRIL: Before they went into rehearsal? I'm thinking of slitting the *two* wrists this time, Roy!

ROY: Actually, Heather MacNamara isn't a bad choice for that part.

APRIL: She's the pits!

ROY: We're the Pitts! (*Breaking himself up, then . . .*) We liked her in *The Sea Gull.*

APRIL: You liked her in *The Sea Gull.* I'd like her in her coffin.

ROY: Obviously they're going ethnic with it.

APRIL: She isn't even ethnic. She's white bread. I'm ethnic. I want a hit, Roy. I need a hit. I'm going crazy for a hit. I mean, when's it my turn?

ROY: Honey, you're making a shadow.

APRIL: I'm sorry.

ROY: That's okay. Just stick with me, kid. We're headed straight for the top.

APRIL: Roy?

ROY: What, angel?

APRIL: Your toupee is slipping. (*Roy clutches at his hair piece.*) Roy wears a piece.

ROY: It's no secret. I've never pretended. It's not like your nose job!

APRIL: Don't speak to me. Just lie there and turn into naugahyde like your mother!

ROY: Honey! I almost forgot. Your agent called! They're interviewing hostesses for Steak & Brew.

APRIL: Give him skin cancer, God, give him skin cancer, please!

DR. PEPPER: Excuse me, I know it's none of my business, but how long have you two been married?

APRIL: Three months.

ROY: And you were right the first time, it's none of your business.

APRIL: But we lived together a long time before we did.

ROY: Not long enough.

APRIL: Eight *centuries* it felt like!

ROY: Do you have to cry on the world's shoulder, April?

APRIL: I want us to work, Roy! I love you.

ROY: I know. I love you, too, April.

APRIL: You're the best.

ROY: *We're* the best.

APRIL: You really think this Pepper fellow can help us?

DR. PEPPER: I'm no miracle worker.

ROY: You?

DR. PEPPER: Hi, Jason Pepper. Nice to see you.

ROY: You're Dr. Pepper?

DR. PEPPER: Only to my worst enemies. Let's make it Jason, shall we?

APRIL: Oh Roy!

ROY: The least you could've done was told us!

APRIL: I'm so ashamed!

ROY: Talk about seeing people at their worst!

DR. PEPPER: I'm used to that.

ROY: Yeah, but you haven't heard the other side of the story.

DR. PEPPER: And I'm sure it's a good one, too.

APRIL: Roy, I could jut die. (*Hiram and Francis enter. They wear striped blazers, ascots, and white summer flannels. They cross to the table and will begin playing cards.*)

HIRAM: You know what they say about white flannels, don't you Jason? The devil's invention. Never out of the cleaners.

FRANCIS: I put mine on first, of course, and then he decided he was going to wear his!

HIRAM: Don't be ridiculous.

FRANCIS: We *look* ridiculous.

DR. PEPPER: I think you both look rather dashing.

HIRAM: Thank you, Jason.

FRANCIS: Monkey see, monkey do.

DR. PEPPER: This is Mr. and Mrs. Pitt.

ROY: And you owe my wife an apology.

HIRAM: I don't recall speaking to you, Mac.

ROY: Now, look, you . . .

APRIL: It doesn't matter.

ROY: To me it does. You're my wife!

APRIL: Not in front of . . . (*She motions toward Dr. Pepper.*) . . . please?

HIRAM: Hiram Spane of the Newport Spanes, Mrs. Pitt. I've got a foul temper and a vicious tongue. Someone yells "ball" at me and they start working overtime. And that's about as much of an apology as you're going to get out of me.

APRIL: Thank you.

HIRAM: This is Francis Tear of the Baltimore Tears.

APRIL: Hi. April James, nice to see you. This is my husband, Roy.

ROY: (*Pumping Francis's hand.*) Hi, Roy Pitt. Nice to see you.

FRANCIS: Do you like to swim?

HIRAM: Francis!

FRANCIS: I just asked!

ROY: (*Gesturing for silence.*) Ssshh! Sshh! Sshh!

HIRAM: I beg your pardon?

ROY: Shut up! (*He listens, hears something.*) There it is! (*He and April cross their fingers.*)

ROY and APRIL: (*In unison.*) Baby, baby, baby! (*Roy runs off.*)

HIRAM: Is your husband mentally deranged, Mrs. Pitt?

APRIL: He's been expecting that call.

HIRAM: That wasn't my question.

APRIL: He's an actor. It might be a job. Normal people wouldn't understand. (*She sits.*) How long have you two been married?

FRANCIS: We're not married, Mrs. Pitt.

APRIL: Oh!

HIRAM: Oh!

APRIL: How nice.

FRANCIS: That's what you think.

APRIL: We have lots of friends like that in the city.

HIRAM: Like what?

APRIL: Like you two. We're both in show business. We have to, practically.

HIRAM: Well, we're not in show business, Mrs. Pitt, and we certainly don't have to have friends like you.

APRIL: Did I say something wrong?

HIRAM: And I'm sure you're just getting started. Excuse me. (*He turns back to his card game.*)

APRIL: I was just trying to make small talk. I got better things to do than yak it up with a couple of aunties, you know!

HIRAM: I don't think normal therapy is going to work with that woman, Jason. Why don't you try euthanasia?

APRIL: Look, mouth!

DR. PEPPER: Children, children! (*Harry appears down the aisle.*)

HARRY: Otto! Otto, pack my bags and put them in the car. Just leave something out for me to change into. It's the black Volvo station wagon, the one with snow tires. You can't miss it. And then how about a round for everyone?

OTTO: *Jawohl, Herr Scupp.* (*He goes.*)

HARRY: I'm leaving, Jason.

FRANCIS: Harry's leaving, Hiram!

HIRAM: I can see that, Francis.

DR. PEPPER: I haven't officially released you, Harry.

HARRY: I'll save you the trouble. I'm officially releasing myself. What were you planning on, Jason? Keeping me here 'til Doomsday?

DR. PEPPER: Where's Dolly?

HARRY: She's decided to stay. Try to help her, Jason.

DOLLY: (*Entering from the aisle.*) Harry! Harry!

DR. PEPPER: What happened down by the lake?

HARRY: What didn't happen, you mean.

DOLLY: It was like our honeymoon.

HARRY: Don't make it sound too dramatic, Dolly. We just decided that our marriage was better than no marriage at all. I do what I want and she does what she wants. It's called compromise, honey, and it's the secret of a good marriage. If I want to fool around with someone you're going to let me because that's what I want to do and you want what I want. And if you want to fool around you won't because I don't want you to and you don't want what I don't want.

DOLLY: That's called compromise?

HARRY: That's called marriage.

DR. PEPPER: That's called *your* marriage.

DOLLY: That's called divorce.

DR. PEPPER: Take it or leave it. Mrs. Scupp.

DOLLY: There's a choice? I think I'm doing the right thing, Jason.

HARRY: I think we're doing the right thing, Jason.

DOLLY: I hope so, Harry.

DR. PEPPER: Just so long as it makes you both happy. (*Dolly reaches for Harry's cigarette and takes a deep, satisfying drag.*) How is it?

DOLLY: Like honey. It's like someone just poured ten years of honey down my throat.

DR. PEPPER: This is Mrs. Pitt. She and her husband have just arrived. (*Roy, returning, steps right in.*)

ROY: Hi, Roy Pitt. Nice to see you. Hi, Roy Pitt. Nice to see you.

APRIL: Hi, April James. Nice to see you. (*To Roy.*) Did you get it?

ROY: It looks good but nothing definite.

APRIL: When would you leave?

ROY: We'll talk about it later. (*To Francis.*) Hi, Roy Pitt. Nice to see you.

DOLLY: Wait a minute! Wait a minute! The Retarded Children Telethon, right? That's her honey! The girl we were so crazy about. You sang . . . "Do, do, do."

APRIL: That was for Leukemia, actually, the Leukemia Telethon.

DOLLY: Oh, we think you're just terrific. You're headed straight for the top. I hope your line of work keeps you busy, Mr. Pitt. You're in for a lot of lonely days and nights.

APRIL: Roy's an actor, too.

DOLLY: Are you, dear? (*She turns to Harry.*) You know something: I don't think we would've had so many problems if we'd had more in common.

APRIL: Dr. Pepper's really helped you, then?

DOLLY: Helped him. We'll see about me. (*Harry lets out a sudden, urgent scream.*)

DR. PEPPER: How was it?

HARRY: Fantastic.

DOLLY: Is he going to be doing that often?

DR. PEPPER: That depends on you.

DOLLY: If he pulls that in the middle of a board meeting he's going to be looking for a new job.

DR. PEPPER: You might try it yourself sometime.

DOLLY: Me? I'm as cool as a cucumber.

DR. PEPPER: What brought that one on, Harry?

HARRY: The truth?

DR. PEPPER: You're still at Ravenswood.

HARRY: I want to shtup Mrs. Pitt.

ROY: Hey!

HARRY: You see how her tennis outfit's all slit up the side? There's no tan line. You know how women who are tan all over drive me crazy, Jason.

ROY: What did you say?

APRIL: It's okay, Roy. He just said he *wanted* to shtup me. He didn't do it. (*Dolly lets out a sudden, urgent scream.*)

DR. PEPPER: How do you feel?

DOLLY: Hoarse.

HARRY: You'll get used to it. (*Otto has returned with a tray of champagne. He passes it around. Everyone takes one as Harry turns to Hiram and Francis.*) I'm really gonna miss you two guys, you know. Take good care of her for me, will you?

HIRAM: When you come back for her, God knows we'll still be here. I think we're probably permanent.

FRANCIS: We're just lucky Hiram's mother can afford it.

HIRAM: You're just lucky Hiram's mother can afford it.

FRANCIS: Goodbye, Harry. I'll miss you.

DOLLY: No! No farewell toasts. I propose a welcome toast to the new arrivals.

HARRY: You can't drink to yourself.

DOLLY: All right! Here's to new marriage and the Pitts.

HARRY: Here's to our old one, honey.

HIRAM: Here's to friendship.

FRANCIS: Here's to Hiram.

HIRAM: Why thank you, Francis.

ROY: Here's to April James.

FRANCIS: April who, Hiram?

HIRAM: Some little RKO starlet, obviously.

APRIL: Here's to Hollywood and Mr. and Mrs. Roy Pitt.

DOLLY: Doctor?

DR. PEPPER: Here's to . . . all of you.

OTTO: Here's to Ravenswood. (*They drink. Then Harry starts to sing "Auld Lang Syne" and they all join in. Much applauding, hugging, and laughing.*) Lunch *ist* served. (*They break apart and start making their exits.*)

HARRY: Goodbye, Jason. And thank you. She's all yours now.

DOLLY: I'll walk you to the car.

HARRY: (*To Roy.*) Hey! Now I know where I've seen you! *Lenny!* You were in *Lenny!*

ROY: (*With a sudden, urgent scream.*) *LENNY!!*

HARRY: What did I say?

APRIL: Nothing. It's all right. Goodbye.

DOLLY: Come on, Harry.

HARRY: So long, Jason. (*Dolly and Harry are gone.*)

APRIL: He's a dummy. What does he know? You're Roy Pitt, the best actor in the business.

ROY: What am I? Chopped liver? I'll probably get that movie but it doesn't go for three months. (*They start off down the aisle.*)

APRIL: Listen, I wasn't going to mention this, but since you brought it up: you think there's anything in it for me?

ROY: A terrific part. They want a name but I'll mention you for it first thing.

APRIL: I'll test, but first-class, Roy. They're gonna have to fly me out there first-class. (*They are gone. There is more and more thunder. Dr. Pepper looks up at the sky.*)

FRANCIS: Hiram? (*He exits down the aisle.*)

HIRAM: Will somebody just look at these flannels? Soiled already! This time I'm sending your mother the bill. Old Bingo Money, that's all she is . . . (*He follows Francis off.*)

FRANCIS: (*From the aisle.*) Do you think Mrs. Scupp would like to play badminton after lunch?

HIRAM: If she did, she wouldn't want to play with you. (*Dr. Pepper watches everyone exit as Otto returns to wheel him in for lunch.*)

DR. PEPPER: *Lasse!*

OTTO: Herr Doktor does not want lunch today? (*Dr. Pepper shakes his head.*) Herr Doktor would like a martini? (*Dr. Pepper shakes his head.*) A little rubdown, maybe?

DR. PEPPER: Herr Doktor just wants everyone to be happy.

OTTO: Happy?

DR. PEPPER: *Du bist* happy, Otto?

OTTO: *Was ist* happy?

DR. PEPPER: A good question, Otto. (*Otto goes. Dr. Pepper lifts his glass in a toast.*) So long, Harry. (*Thunder and lightning. Dr. Pepper feels his skull. The guests are heard singing in the distance. Dr. Pepper sings along with them to himself, very quietly and slowly. His voice trails off. The curtain falls.*)

DUNELAWN

The setting is outdoors. The stage is bare except for a high wall running the length of the cyclorama. Also, there is a small stone bench and scraggly tree. Nurse Benson strides on. Nurse Hedges follows, pushing a medical cart.

NURSE BENSON: Hello. Ruth Benson, R.N. here. At ease. Let's get one thing perfectly straight before we begin. I am your friend. No matter what happens, I am your friend. So is Nurse Hedges. (*Nurse Hedges smiles.*) But you know something? You are your own best friend. Think that one over. I'll say the bell tolls. It tolls for all of us. Welcome to Dunelawn. Shall we begin? (*She claps her hands.*) Bruno! (*Bruno wheels in Mr. Ponce in a wheelchair. Bruno is a horror, Mr. Ponce is a crabby old man.*) Good morning, Bruno. Put him over there. Facing the sun! That's right, Bruno. Thank you, Bruno. Now go and get Mr. Blum.

BRUNO: (*Looking/leering/lusting at Nurse Hedges.*) I'm supposed to mow the lawn.

BENSON: After you've brought everyone out here you can do that.

BRUNO: (*Still leering at Nurse Hedges.*) Dr. Toynbee says I'm supposed to mow.

BENSON: You can mow later, Bruno, mow all day.

BRUNO: (*Taking a swig of whiskey from his hip flask.*) Mow and trim the hedges. All the hedges need trimming, Dr. Toynbee says. (*Provocatively to Hedges.*) It's going to be a hot one. A real scorcher all right.

BENSON: Bruno!

BRUNO: I'm going, Benson, don't wet your pants. (*He turns to go, then turns back to Hedges.*) Hey! (*Nurse Hedges looks at him.*) Hubba hubba! (*He winks, leers, laughs, exits.*)

BENSON: Ugh! (*Then, clapping her hands.*) Well, Mr. Ponce! Good morning, Mr. Ponce! How are we feeling today?

MR. PONCE: What do you think?

BENSON: I think you're feeling one hundred percent better, that's what I think!

PONCE: Who asked you?

BENSON: Maybe you don't realize it, Mr. Ponce, but you are.

PONCE: I want a drink.

BENSON: I didn't hear that.

PONCE: I want a drink!

BENSON: (*At a sound from Nurse Hedges.*) What is it, Hedges? You'll have to speak up, dear.

NURSE HEDGES: Are we using serum?

BENSON: Yes, serum! Of course, serum! (*The two nurses busy themselves at the medical cart during the following.*)

PONCE: Liquor! Liquor! I want liquor!

BENSON: Honestly, Becky, I don't know what's gotten into you lately.

HEDGES: I'm sorry.

PONCE: I want a drink, somebody!

BENSON: You're sniveling again, Hedges.

HEDGES: I am?

PONCE: Will somebody please get me a good stiff drink?

BENSON: I'll cure you of that if it's the last thing I do.

HEDGES: I don't mean to snivel. I don't want to snivel. I just do it I guess.

PONCE: I need a drink. I must have a drink!

BENSON: Well we'll soon put a stop to that.

HEDGES: You're so good to me, Ruth!

BENSON: I know. Syringe, please.

PONCE: I don't want to stop! I like to drink! It's all a terrible mistake!

HEDGES: (*Admiringly, while Benson prepares to administer the injection.*) No, I mean it. You're really interested in my welfare. I'm so used to women being catty and bitchy to one another, I can't believe I've found a friend who's deeply and truly concerned about me.

PONCE: How much do you want, Benson? How much cold, hard cash?

BENSON: It's called love, Becky.

HEDGES: I guess it is.

PONCE: Look at me, Benson, I'm making a cash offer.

BENSON: Good old-fashioned l-o-v-e.

HEDGES: Well I appreciate it.

PONCE: Where's Toynbee? Get me Toynbee!

BENSON: You're turning into a wonderful, warm, desirable woman, Hedges.

HEDGES: Thanks to you.

BENSON: Oh pooh! (*Mr. Ponce sees that she is about to stick him with the needle. He begins to yell and babble. He begins to jump up and down in the wheelchair as if he were strapped to it. His blanket falls off. He is! Also, he's wearing a straitjacket.*)

PONCE: Goddamn it, I want a drink and I want it now! I want a drink! I won't calm down until I get a drink! (*He's making quite a racket and carrying on like a wild caged beast. Benson stays in control. Hedges panics.*)

BENSON: Mr. Ponce! I'm not going to give you this injection as long as you keep that up. You're just wasting your time.

HEDGES: Do you want me to get help?

BENSON: I didn't hear that, Hedges.

HEDGES: I'm sorry.

BENSON: And don't start sniveling again.

HEDGES: So good to me!

BENSON: I'll have to report this to Dr. Toynbee, Mr. Ponce. I'm sorry, but my hands are tied. (*Dr. Toynbee strolls on. He has sad, benign eyes and a smile to match. Mr. Ponce immediately quiets down at the sight of him and hangs his head in shame.*) Good morning, Dr. Toynbee.

HEDGES: (*Almost a little curtsy.*) Good morning, Dr. Toynbee. (*Dr. Toynbee smiles, nods and looks at Mr. Ponce.*)

BENSON: Doctor, I think Mr. Ponce wants to leave Dunelawn.

PONCE: No!

BENSON: I don't think he deserves to be here. I'd say he's abused that privilege. (*Benson unfastens the straps that hold Ponce to the wheelchair.*)

PONCE: I'm sorry. I don't know what came over me.

BENSON: Get up.

PONCE: It was a temporary relapse, Doctor. I'm so ashamed, believe me, it won't happen again.

BENSON: (*Letting him out of the straitjacket.*) There's a long line of decent, honorable people waiting to get in here, Mr. Ponce. A very long line. And I think you'd better step right to the end of it. Well go ahead, you're free to leave now.

PONCE: I can't look at you, Dr. Toynbee, I'm so ashamed.

BENSON: No one asked you to come here and no one's keeping you.

PONCE: Don't look at me like that, Dr. Toynbee!

BENSON: He said he wanted a drink. He demanded one, in fact. He even tried to bribe me, Doctor. (*Toynbee, his eyes never off Ponce, sadly shakes his head.*) Naturally I refused. So did Nurse Hedges.

HEDGES: (*Almost curtsying again.*) Yes, yes I did, Dr. Toynbee.

BENSON: Fortunately he revealed his true colors before I was able to administer the syringe. I'll have Bruno pack your things at once, Mr. Ponce. You'll find your statement in the checkout office. You won't be charged for today, of course. Now should they call your wife and family to come and get you or would you prefer the limousine service?

PONCE: Benson, wait, please!

BENSON: Dr. Toynbee is a very busy man, Mr. Ponce. Your wife and family or the limousine?

PONCE: I'm not leaving. I won't let you throw me out like this. You're sending me straight back to the gin mills if you kick me out of here. I'm not ready to leave yet. I'm not strong enough.

BENSON: Dr. Toynbee's heard all this, Mr. Ponce.

PONCE: (*Putting the straitjacket back on.*) Look, look, see how much I want to stay?

BENSON: Take that off, Mr. Ponce.

PONCE: (*To Hedges.*) Fasten me up, fasten me up!

HEDGES: Dr. Toynbee?

PONCE: The straps, the straps, just fasten the straps.

HEDGES: (*Moved.*) Poor Mr. Ponce.

BENSON: I wouldn't do that, Hedges.

HEDGES: Dr. Toynbee? (*Toynbee, slowly, sadly, benignly, nods his head. Hedges buckles Mr. Ponce up in the straitjacket.*)

PONCE: Thank you, Doctor, thank you! (*He would like to thank Dr. Toynbee, but now, of course there is no way to do it.*) I'll be good, I'll be better! You'll see, you'll see! This will never happen again. Come on, Benson, you heard the doctor!

BENSON: Surely, Doctor, you're not going to . . . ? (*Again Toynbee nods his head.*) That man is a saint.

PONCE: God bless him.

BENSON: Dr. Toynbee is a saint.

PONCE: I am so grateful and so happy.

BENSON: A saint!

PONCE: I could kiss his hand for this. (*He tries to, and can't.*)

BENSON: Should I proceed with the injection, Doctor? (*Dr. Toynbee smiles and nods.*) Hedges. (*Hedges helps her prepare another syringe as Dr. Toynbee moves to Mr. Ponce and stands directly behind him. He looks down at him, puts one hand on each shoulder and fixes him with a sad and solemn stare.*)

PONCE: I can't bear it when you look at me like that. You're so good, Doctor, so good! I know how rotten I am. But someday I'll be able to look you in the eye. I'll make you proud of me. I'll make me proud of me. I don't want to be me anymore. (*Dr. Toynbee smiles and bends down to Mr. Ponce's ear. When he does finally speak, it is totally unintelligible gibberish.*) You're so right, Doctor! Everything you say is so right! (*Toynbee turns to go.*) God bless you.

BENSON: Thank you, Dr. Toynbee!

HEDGES: Thank you, Dr. Toynbee!

HEDGES: Goodbye, Dr. Toynbee! (*Toynbee acknowledges them with a wave of the hand and strolls off.*) What a wonderful man he is.

BENSON: That man is a saint.

HEDGES:: And so good.

BENSON: Why can't we all be like him?

HEDGES:: How do you mean?

BENSON: Perfect.

PONCE: Please, Benson, hurry up.

HEDGES: I think you're perfect, Ruth.

BENSON: You're sweet.

HEDGES: You are.

BENSON: Not really. And certainly not like Dr. Toynbee.

PONCE: Come on, Benson, before I get another attack.

BENSON: Do you realize he has absolutely no faults? Absolutely none.

HEDGES: No wonder he seems so good.

BENSON: He's perfect, Becky. I don't see why I can't get you to understand that. He has no place left to go.

PONCE: My hands, Benson, they're starting to shake!

BENSON: Dr. Toynbee wasn't born perfect. He worked on it and there he is.

HEDGES: You make it sound so easy.

BENSON: Take it from me, Becky, it isn't.

HEDGES: You're telling me.

BENSON: You're making wonderful progress.

PONCE: Oh my God, I'm starting to hallucinate.

HEDGES: Any progress I'm making is entirely thanks to you, I hope you know.

PONCE: A jeroboam of Bombay Gin!

HEDGES: I don't want to be perfect, Ruth, I know I never could be. Not like you.

BENSON: Oh pooh, Becky, just pooh!

PONCE: I'm salivating, Benson. Have you no mercy?

BENSON: Hang on there, Mr. Ponce, just hang on there another second.

PONCE: I'm going fast. I . . . I . . . I want a drink. I want a drink! I want a drink!!! (*Benson sticks him with the needle.*) I . . . I . . .

BENSON: Now what did you just say you wanted, Mr. Ponce?

PONCE: (*A beatific smile spreading across his face.*) I don't want anything!

BENSON: Let's fix your chair now, so you get the sun.

PONCE: Yes, that would be nice, miss. Thank you, thank you.

BENSON: (*As she makes Ponce more comfortable.*) I pity your type, Mr. Ponce. Two martinis before dinner, wine with, a cordial after, and a couple of scotch on the rocks nightcaps. Social drinking, you call it. Rummies, I say, every last one of you.

PONCE: (*A long, contented sigh.*) Aaaaaaaaaaah!

BENSON: All right now?

PONCE: I don't want anything. Any bad thing.

BENSON: Good for you.

PONCE: I'm going to make it, Benson. I'm going to be all right. (*His head falls over.*)

BENSON: Of course you are. And if you want anything, I'll be right over . . . (*She takes his head and points it towards the medical cart.*) . . . there.

PONCE: No, miss, I don't want a thing. (*Benson tiptoes over to Hedges.*)

BENSON: Whew!

HEDGES: I admire you so much!

BENSON: Becky Hedges!

HEDGES: You can help me to get rid of my faults until you're blue in the face, but I'll never be the beauty you are.

BENSON: You're an adorable person, Becky.

HEDGES: I'm not talking about adorable. I'm talking about beauty. No one ever told Elizabeth Taylor she was adorable.

BENSON: Do I have to say it? Beauty is skin deep. Besides, Elizabeth has a lot of faults.

HEDGES: You're changing the subject. Ruth, look at me.

BENSON: Yes?

HEDGES: Now tell me this is a beautiful woman you see.

BENSON: What are you driving at, Becky?

HEDGES: Nothing. I just wish I were beautiful like you. And I don't want you to just *say* I am.

BENSON: I wouldn't do that to you.

HEDGES: Thank you.

BENSON: I said you were adorable.

HEDGES: And I said you were beautiful.

BENSON: It's out of my hands.

HEDGES: It's out of mine, too.

BENSON: You're sniveling again.

HEDGES: I know.

BENSON: (*She pulls Hedges over to the bench and sits her down.*) Becky, listen to me. You think I'm beautiful. Thank you. I can accept a compliment. I know I'm beautiful. I can't lie to myself anymore. But what good did it do me as far as Hugh Gumbs was concerned?

HEDGES: Such a beautiful name!

BENSON: There you go again, Becky.

HEDGES: I didn't snivel that time.

BENSON: You made a stupid, faltering, self-serving, Minnie Mouse remark, which is much worse. Hugh Gumbs is not a beautiful name and you know it.

HEDGES: I'm sorry. I'll be good. I'll be better. Finish your story.

BENSON: I don't even remember where I was.

HEDGES: You were talking about your beauty and how little good it did you as far as Hugh Gumbs was concerned.

BENSON: That man wouldn't even look at me. Looks had nothing to do with it. I know that now. Ask Hugh Gumbs! And I know I'm more beautiful than that hussy he abandoned me for. In my heart of hearts, I know that Mildred Canby is not a beautiful woman.

HEDGES: Mildred who?

BENSON: Mildred Canby.

HEDGES: What a horrible name, too.

BENSON: Attractive, yes. Beautiful, no. Now what Hugh Gumbs wanted in a woman, what every man wants in any woman, is something deeper than beauty. He wants character. He wants the traditional virtues. He wants womanly warmth.

HEDGES: You can say that again.

BENSON: Believe me, Hugh Gumbs is a very unhappy man right now. How could he not be? Mildred Canby had even less character and more faults than I did. And less beauty, too. I knew that marriage wouldn't last. (*She takes out her compact.*)

HEDGES: Don't cry, Ruth.

BENSON: Me? Cry? Why should I cry?

HEDGES: Because you lost Hugh?

BENSON: I'm grateful to him! He broke my heart, I don't deny it, but if it hadn't been for Hugh I would never have been forced into the soul-searching and self-reevaluation that ended up with the 118-pound, trim-figured woman you say is so beautiful standing in front of you. No, when I think back on Ruth Benson then and compare her to Ruth Benson now, I thank my lucky stars for Hugh.

HEDGES: (*As Benson continues to gaze at herself in the compact mirror.*) You're so wise, Ruth.

BENSON: Am I?

HEDGES: Wise about love.

BENSON: I wonder.

HEDGES: You are.

BENSON: We'll see.

HEDGES: I'm not.

BENSON: (*Still distracted.*) Hmmmmmmm?

HEDGES: Wise about love. I'm downright dumb about it. If I weren't, I'd be married to Tim Taylor right this very minute. What I wouldn't give for another chance at him!

BENSON: (*Regaining herself.*) Buck up, Hedges.

HEDGES: Oh I will, Ruth. I'm just feeling a little sorry for myself. I don't know why. If you want to know the truth, I haven't thought of Tim Taylor one way or the other for a long time.

BENSON: I should hope not. A man who smokes is a very bad emotional risk.

HEDGES: Tim didn't smoke.

BENSON: But he drank. It's the same thing. Rummies, every last one of them.

HEDGES: Did Hugh Gumbs drink?

BENSON: Among other things.

HEDGES: It must have been awful for you.

BENSON: It was heck. Sheer unadulterated heck.

HEDGES: That sounds funny.

BENSON: Believe me, it wasn't.

HEDGES: No, what you just said. About it being heck. I'm still used to people saying the other.

BENSON: It won't seem funny after a while. You'll see. (*Dr. Toynbee strolls across the stage, smiling benignly, reading a book.*) Good morning, Dr. Toynbee!

HEDGES: Good morning, Dr. Toynbee! (*To Benson.*) That man is so good, Ruth!

BENSON: I worship the ground he walks on.

HEDGES: Oh me, too, me, too! I'd give anything to be just like him.

BENSON: Goodbye, Dr. Toynbee! And thank you!

HEDGES: Goodbye, Dr. Toynbee! And thank you! (*Dr. Toynbee exits down the aisle, waving.*) Ruth?

BENSON: What?

HEDGES: I know it's none of my business, but I've seen that look in your eyes whenever Dr. Toynbee passes.

BENSON: What look?

HEDGES: You know.

BENSON: The only look, as you put it, in my eyes when Dr. Toynbee passes is one of sheer and utter respect. Certainly not the look you're so grossly alluding to. You're out of line, don't you think, Hedges? You're certainly in extremely bad taste.

HEDGES: You're not sweet on the good doctor?

BENSON: Dr. Toynbee is above that.

HEDGES: I know but are you? (*Benson slaps her.*) Is any woman? (*Benson slaps her again and they fall into each other's arms crying.*) I'm sorry, Ruth. I didn't mean to hurt you. You've been so good to me! I'm such a different person since I've been with you! I don't even know who I am anymore and I say these silly, dreadful, awful things! I don't recognize myself in the mirror in the morning. I've changed so much it scares me.

BENSON: You haven't changed. You've improved, refined, what was already there. I always had this figure, don't you see? Even when I weighed all that weight, I still had this figure.

HEDGES: Even when you were up to 230?

BENSON: I was never 230.

HEDGES: You told me you were . . .

BENSON: I was never 230! Now shut up and listen, will you?

HEDGES: I'm sorry, Ruth.

BENSON: I didn't change anything. Mr. Ponce over there isn't changing. He's only emerging, with our help and Dr. Toynbee's, into what he really and truly was in the first place: a nondrinker.

PONCE: A rum swizzle!

BENSON: People are born without any faults, they simply fall into bad habits along life's way. Nobody's trying to *change* anybody, Becky. It's the real them coming out, that's all.

HEDGES: The real them!

BENSON: Look, face it, you've got big thighs, that's the real you. Now I've got nice thighs, as it turns out, but I didn't always know that.

HEDGES: I don't think I can get any thinner.

BENSON: I'm not talking about diets. I'm talking about the real you and your G.D. big thighs!

HEDGES: That's exactly what Tim Taylor didn't like about me. And now that I'm getting thinner they look even bigger. I *know!* I'm sniveling again! I don't know what to do about them, Ruth! (*She is desperately hitting her thighs.*)

BENSON: Wear longer skirts!

HEDGES: Now you really are cross with me!

BENSON: You can be so dense sometimes. I mean really, Hedges, I'm talking about a whole other thing and you start sniveling about diets. You can diet all you want and you're still going to end up with big thighs. That's not the point.

HEDGES: What is it, then?

BENSON: Oh there's no point in talking to you about it!

HEDGES: I'm sorry.

BENSON: And stop that horrible sniveling!

HEDGES: I'm never going to get any better. I have just as many bad habits as when I came here. We just keep pretending I'm improving when the real truth is, I'm getting worse! (*She races to the medical cart and hysterically prepares one of the syringes.*)

BENSON: What are you doing?

HEDGES: Why shouldn't I? I'm no better than any one of them and I'm supposed to work here!

BENSON: Give me that! (*They struggle.*)

HEDGES: Let me do it, Ruth!

BENSON: Have you lost your mind?

HEDGES: I wish I was dead! (*Benson topples Hedges, who falls in a heap, and takes away the syringe. Almost without realizing, she reaches inside her blouse and takes a package of cigarettes out of her bosom, puts one in her mouth and strikes a match. Hedges raises her head at the sound.*) Ruth!

BENSON: (*Realizing what she has done.*) Oh my God! I wasn't thinking!

HEDGES: You of all people!

BENSON: I wasn't going to smoke one!

HEDGES: It's a full pack.

BENSON: It's a courtesy pack. In case I run into someone. They're not mine. I've given it up. I swear to God I have. You've got to believe me.

HEDGES: I don't know what to think.

BENSON: Becky, please!

HEDGES: If you say so, Ruth. (*Bruno enters pushing Mr. Blum in a wheelchair.*)

BENSON: It took you long enough!

BRUNO: I suppose it did. Where do you want her?

BENSON: (*Pointedly.*) Him. I want *him* over there. Facing the sun, next to Mr. Ponce. That's where I want *him,* Bruno. And then when you've put him there, I want you to bring out Mr. Yamadoro. And I want you to do it quickly this time.

BRUNO: I told you I was supposed to mow.

BENSON: We know, Bruno.

BRUNO: Mow and trim me some hedges. Hey! (*He gives Hedges his hubba hubba leer.*)

BENSON: You're a beast, Bruno.

BRUNO: (*To Hedges.*) You got a light, baby?

HEDGES: No!

BRUNO: You, dog-face?

BENSON: You know I don't. Matches and all other smoking parapher-
nalia are strictly forbidden here.

BRUNO: (*Taking out a hip flask.*) Yeah?

BENSON: So is alcohol.

BRUNO: No shit. (*Bruno downs a swig.*)

BENSON: The only reason Dr. Toynbee allows them to you is to set an
example to the guests here. A bad example. On a human self-im-
provement ten scale, you rate about a minus fifty. You're a walking, subhuman nightmare, Bruno.

BRUNO: (*For Hedge's benefit.*) Sure is a hot one coming on. A real
scorcher.

BENSON: Must you, Bruno?

BRUNO: Must I what?

BENSON: Stand there like that?

BRUNO: (*To Hedges.*) Now she don't like the way I stand.

BENSON: It's deliberately provocative.

BRUNO: What is that supposed to mean?

BENSON: Only you're about as provocative to a woman as a can full of
worms. Now either get Mr. Yamadoro out here or I'll report you
to Dr. Toynbee.

BRUNO: I'm going Benson. Hold your bowels. (*He doesn't move. He is
trying to think.*) What you said about a can full of worms . . . I
got desires. That's all I know, I got desires and I like to do 'em.
(*He goes. Hedges curiously starts to follow. Benson claps her
hands, and Hedges joins her.*)

BENSON: Good morning, Mr. Blum! How are we feeling today? Doesn't
that sun feel good on you? And that delicious breeze from the
ocean! And listen to those birds chirp! It's a day like this that
makes you wish summer lasted all year! (*As she chatters away,
she is preparing a syringe for Mr. Blum.*) When I was a little girl,
we spent our summers in Vermont and my brothers and I used to
go swimming in a little pond!

MR. BLUM: Your cap, Benson. (*It's a gently desperate plea.*)

BENSON: Hmmmmmmm?

BLUM: Please. Just let me wear your cap. I won't hurt it. I'll just sit
here and wear it. I won't say a word.

BENSON: Mr. Blum, I thought you were improving!

BLUM: I am, Benson, I swear to God I am! I just want to wear your cap for a little while. What's wrong with that? It doesn't mean anything. It's just a cap. I mean it's not like I asked to wear your skirt or your shoes or your stockings or anything! I'm all over that. A man could wear a cap like yours without it meaning anything.

BENSON: Does Dr. Toynbee know this?

BLUM: Are you crazy? Of course not!

BENSON: I'll have to tell him.

BLUM: It's not what you're thinking!

BENSON: We were all so proud of the progress you were making!

BLUM: As well you should be! I'm proud, too! Benson, I haven't been in full drag in six weeks! You know what I was like when Martha brought me here. You've seen how I've changed. You couldn't force me at gunpoint to put your shoes on.

BENSON: (*Immediately suspicious.*) My shoes?

BLUM: Yes, your shoes! Don't torment me like this! Your cap, Benson, it's all I'm asking for. Stop me before I want more.

BENSON: It's out of the question, Mr. Blum.

BLUM: I want that cap! I need that cap! I'm begging you for that cap!

BENSON: Forget the cap! The cap is out!

BLUM: Five minutes, Benson, have a heart!

BENSON: Five minutes with the cap and next it will be the shoes and then the skirt and you'll be right back where you started. I know your kind, Mr. Blum.

BLUM: (*Bitterly.*) Do you, Benson?

BENSON: Give them a cap and they want your panty hose!

BLUM: What of it?

BENSON: You're here to change, not get worse! Think of your wife!

BLUM: What of her? I can't wear a size eight!

BENSON: Then think of your daughters.

BLUM: They're goddamn pygmies, too! I'm surrounded by stunted women.

BENSON: Do you know what they call people like you?

BLUM: Fashionable!

BENSON: You're a man, Mr. Blum, you were meant to dress like one!

BLUM: You're not God, Benson, don't you tell me how to dress!

BENSON: (*Holding back the syringe from him.*) I don't have to take that from you, Blum!

BLUM: What do you know about it?

BENSON: If you persist in defying me . . . !

BLUM: What does any woman know about it?

BENSON: Not only will I withhold this syringe . . . !

BLUM: Garter belts, Benson.

BENSON: I will fill out a report . . .!

BLUM: Merry widows!

BENSON: And give it to Dr. Toynbee!

BLUM: Black net stockings! Red garters, strapless tops! Sequins!

BENSON: All right for you, Blum, all right for you! (*She starts out.*)

BLUM: Picture hats! That's right, Benson, you heard me, picture hats! (*Dr. Toynbee strolls on.*)

BENSON: Good morning, Dr. Toynbee! (*Dr. Toynbee smiles and nods.*)

BENSON: I want you to see something, Doctor.

BLUM: (*Head bowed, suddenly mortified.*) Please, Benson, don't. (*Benson begins to take off her cap. Blum watches in growing terror. Toynbee looks at Blum with such a great sadness.*) Benson, don't do this to me, not in front of him. Please. I beg of you. I'll change. I swear I'll change!

BENSON: He asked to wear my cap, Doctor. I think he should wear it. (*She puts the hat on his head. Blum writhes and twists in his straitjacket in the wheel chair as if he were on fire.*)

BLUM: No! No! Take it off! Take it off! (*As Blum writhes and screams, Toynbee takes out his handkerchief and dabs at his eyes. Even Hedges cries.*)

BENSON: You've made Dr. Toynbee cry, Mr. Blum. I just hope you're pleased with yourself.

HEDGES: I can't watch, Ruth.

BENSON: (*Shielding her.*) It's all right, Becky, it's going to be all right.

HEDGES: To see the poor doctor cry!

BENSON: Sshh, sshh! Dr. Toynbee's here now. Everything will be all right. (*Dr. Toynbee slowly dries his eyes, puts away the handkerchief, and goes to Blum.*) Look Becky! (*Toynbee takes the cap off Blum. At once, Blum is silent and hangs his head. Toynbee stands looking down at him.*) That man is a saint. (*Toynbee hands the cap back to Benson, then turns and talks to Blum. Again we can't understand his gibberish.*) Dr. Toynbee has that rare spiritual quality that when he just looks at you with those clear grey eyes of his you suddenly feel so ashamed of yourself you could just vomit.

HEDGES: Such a good man! (*Now Blum is the one who is crying. Toynbee asks for the syringe with a gesture. Benson gives it to him and he injects Blum. Benson wheels Blum next to Ponce, who is beginning to stir restlessly.*)

PONCE: (*Very slurred.*) Bartender! I'll have a perfect Rob Roy on the rocks. I want a little service here, bartender!

BENSON: Doctor . . .? (*Toynbee smiles benignly and nods his head. He motions to Hedges that she should administer the shot.*)

HEDGES: Me, Doctor . . . ? (*Toynbee smiles at her and nods his head. Hedges approaches Ponce with a syringe.*)

PONCE: Make it a double Dewar's on the rocks and hold the ice. (*Hedges looks to Toynbee for encouragement. He smiles and nods his head. She injects Ponce.*) Ouch!

BENSON: (*Sharply.*) Hedges!

PONCE: Goddamn mosquitoes!

HEDGES: He moved! (*Toynbee prevents Benson from helping Hedges out with a benign "Let her do it" gesture. Hedges administers the syringe with no little difficulty. Ponce smiles blissfully.*) I did it, Ruth!

BENSON: We saw you, Hedges.

HEDGES: I really did it, all by myself! Doctor? (*Toynbee smiles and nods and begins to stroll off.*)

BENSON: Thank you, Dr. Toynbee!

HEDGES: Thank you, Dr. Toynbee!

BENSON: Goodbye, Dr. Toynbee!

HEDGES: Goodbye, Dr. Toynbee! (*Spinning herself around.*) Oh, Ruth, Ruth, Ruth!

BENSON: Calm down, Hedges, it was only an injection.

HEDGES: (*Still spinning.*) He's so tremendously, terrifically and terribly good!

BENSON: You're not telling me anything about him I already didn't know. Now give a hand here, will you?

HEDGES: And you know something else? I'm a little sweet on the good doctor myself! (*She is still spinning and singing and dancing when Benson slaps her.*)

BENSON: Snap out of it, Hedges!

HEDGES: I'm sorry. You were right to do that. I'm not even worthy to mention his name. Who am I to think Dr. Toynbee even knows I'm alive? I'm dirt, Ruth. Next to him, I'm dirt.

BENSON: Well . . .

HEDGES: Don't deny it. I know what I am. I've got big thighs and I'm dirt.

BENSON: You're too rough on yourself, Hedges.

HEDGES: I have to be if I'm ever going to get rid of my faults and be like you!

BENSON: I won't say "Don't aim too high, Becky" . . . how could I? But I will say "Don't aim too high too soon."

HEDGES: (*Hugging her.*) Why are you so good to me? Everyone at Dunelawn is so good to me!

BENSON: Because we all love you and want to see you reach your full potential.

HEDGES: Zero defects.

BENSON: That's right, Becky, zero defects. No faults, no failings, no fantasy. It's a beautiful goal.

HEDGES: It sounds religious when you say it. With me it just sounds hopeless.

BENSON: Mark my words, Rebecca Hedges, R. N., the day you become perfect will be the most important day in your life.

HEDGES: It will?

BENSON: Mark my words. (*Bruno wheels in Mr. Yamadoro in a wheel-chair. He, too, is straitjacketed and fastened down.*)

BRUNO: Okay, Benson, that's the Webster Hall lot. Where do you want him?

BENSON: Over there, Bruno.

BRUNO: Hey! (*Hedges looks at him.*) Hubba hubba!

BENSON: Thank you, Bruno. You can go now.

BRUNO: Who says I was talking to you?

BENSON: Aren't you supposed to mow now?

BRUNO: Maybe.

HEDGES: Mow and trim some hedges.

BENSON: Don't talk to that man.

BRUNO: That's right, pussycat. Mow and trim me some hedges.

BENSON: Then do it, Bruno.

BRUNO: Don't burst your bladder, Benson, I'm going. And don't think I ain't forgot that can of worms, horse-face.

BENSON: Bruno!

BRUNO: Stick around, kid. (*Hedges looks at him. He winks, leers.*) Yes sir, a good hot day to trim me some hedges. (*He saunters off.*)

HEDGES: The way he keeps saying that gives me the creeps. You'd think he meant me. (*She shudders.*) Jeepers creepers!

BENSON: Good morning, Mr. Yamadoro.

HEDGES: Ruth!

BENSON: What?

HEDGES: (*Referring to her charts.*) That's not Mr. Yamadoro . . . ! (*Benson pushes her away from Mr. Yamadoro, furious.*) But it's not. It's Mr. Luparelli. Vincenzo Luparelli, Ithaca, New York. It says so right here.

BENSON: He likes to be called Mr. Yamadoro. That's the reason he's here.

HEDGES: I'm sorry. I forgot.

BENSON: You forget everything! (*She turns back to Mr. Yamadoro.*) Good morning, Mr. Yamadoro, how are we feeling today? Any improvement?

MR. YAMADORO: Much better, thank you, Nurse.

BENSON: What about your urges?

YAMADORO: You mean . . . ? (*He lowers his eyes, blushes.*) . . . I can't say it.

BENSON: Yes or no? (*Yamadoro shakes his head no.*) Isn't that wonderful! Did you hear that, Becky? Mr. Yamadoro feels he's improving!

HEDGES: (*In all innocence.*) That's what they all say.

BENSON: Watch your step, Hedges.

HEDGES: Well, how come none of them ever seems to get any better? (*Benson slaps her and takes her aside.*)

BENSON: Don't ever say that again!

HEDGES: But they don't. (*Benson slaps her again.*)

BENSON: Don't ever think it! (*She is shaking Hedges.*) Dr. Toynbee knows what he's doing. It's not his fault if his patients don't.

HEDGES: I'm sorry. I just never looked at it like that.

BENSON: Well maybe it's high time you did.

HEDGES: (*Still being shaken.*) Now you're really, really cross with me!

BENSON: A word against Dr. Toynbee and what he's trying to do here is a slap in my face!

YAMADORO: Slap. (*He giggles.*)

BENSON: Now look what you've done. You've excited him (*Indeed, Yamadoro has been vibrating with pleasure ever since this outbreak of violence of theirs. Benson goes to him, Hedges following.*) Now calm down, Mr. Yamadoro.

YAMADORO: You hit her. You hit her. Good for you, Benson, good for you!

BENSON: I didn't hit her, Mr. Yamadoro.

YAMADORO: You slap her then.

BENSON: No one slapped anyone.

YAMADORO: (*Calming down.*) They didn't?

BENSON: Did they, Nurse Hedges?

HEDGES: Oh no.

BENSON: What you saw may have looked like a slap but it wasn't.

HEDGES: Why would anyone want to slap me, Mr. Yamadoro?

BENSON: Sshh! You'll provoke him again!

YAMADORO: Impossible! It was nothing, nothing at all. A momentary relapse. My urges all are gone, my desires now like water.

BENSON: Pain, Mr. Yamadoro? You're not thinking about pain?

HEDGES: Now *you* are, Ruth!

BENSON: I have to find out!

YAMADORO: Pain? There is no such thing.

BENSON: But in your fantasies? Come on, you can tell Benson.

YAMADORO: I'm over all that.

BENSON: Are you? Imagine, imagine Mr. Yamadoro, a beautiful, voluptuous woman . . . blonde, why not? . . . and she is at your mercy.

HEDGES: Ruth!

BENSON: I know what I'm doing!

YAMADORO: So far nothing.

BENSON: She looks at you, the tears streaming down her cheeks, the drug you've given her has begun to wear off, she's your prisoner and she can't escape. She sees your glowing slit eyes fixed on her fingernails. You want to pull them off, don't you, Mr. Yamadoro? One by one! (*Aside to Hedges.*) The fingernails, that's what they go for, these Jap sadists.

YAMADORO: (*Nonplussed.*) Continue.

BENSON: (*More and more graphically.*) Aaaaaiiiiiieeeeeeee! She screams. Aaaaaiiiiiieeeeeeee! Again and again! But you are implacable. Your cruelty knows no bounds. Your lust is insatiable. (*Angry aside to Hedges.*) Don't just stand there, Hedges, help me out!

HEDGES: Aaaaaiiiiiieeeeeeee!

BENSON: But the room is soundproofed and her bonds hold fast. Every exquisite torment the Oriental mind has devised you visit upon her helpless, quivering, palpable flesh.

HEDGES: Aaaaaiiiiiieeeeeeee!

BENSON: There is no mercy, God is dead, and Satan reigns triumphant!

HEDGES: Aaaaaiiiiiieeeeeeee!

BENSON: (*Savagely.*) Well, Mr. Yamadoro?

YAMADORO: (*Quietly.*) I feel a strange calmness over me. All human desires and passions spent. I desire nothing of the flesh.

BENSON: (*Triumphantly.*) You see?

HEDGES: He really does seem better.

YAMADORO: I really am, missy.

BENSON: Of course he is. (*They start to prepare a syringe.*)

YAMADORO: Dr. Toynbee is a saint.

BENSON: Back to work, Hedges.

YAMADORO: (*To Ponce and Blum.*) Don't tell Benson, but I just had an orgasm. (*He giggles.*)

BENSON: Can you manage this one yourself, too?

HEDGES: I think so.

BENSON: Good girl.

HEDGES: Thanks to you. (*Hedges moves in close to inject Yamadoro. He tries to bit her. She screams.*) Mr. Yamadoro, I thought we were over all that!

YAMADORO: It's never over! (*He is violent in the chair.*)

BENSON: Give me that. (*She takes the syringe, grabs him in an armlock, and injects him.*) This'll hold him.

YAMADORO: (*A long moan.*) Mamma Mia! (*Benson and Hedges begin readjusting the wheelchairs. All three patients smile out at us seraphically.*)

BENSON: Look at them. Like babies now. It's a beautiful sight.

HEDGES: Everyone should take Dr. Toynbee's serum. Then the whole world would be perfect. No wars, no greed, no sex. No nothing. (*Bruno enters with a letter from the office.*)

BENSON: Mr. Ponce, Mr. Blum and Mr. Yamadoro are going to be all right, Becky. It's only the Brunos of this world that are hopeless.

BRUNO: Hey, you in the white dress with the bird's legs!

HEDGES: I feel good just looking at them like this.

BRUNO: You want this, tight ass? (*He shows the letter.*)

BENSON: You're looking at the future, Becky.

HEDGES: In our lifetime?

BENSON: (*Sadly shaking her head.*) I'm afraid we're just the pioneers.

BRUNO: Hey, ugly-puss, I'm supposed to give you this.

HEDGES: A perfect world with perfect people.

BENSON: Someone has to do it.

BRUNO: There's a new patient, dog-face!

BENSON: Well, why didn't you just say so?

BRUNO: I did! (*Benson takes the papers from him, starts reading them over. Bruno exits, but not before a little "Hey!" and a few silent leers towards Hedges.*)

BENSON: Becky!

HEDGES: What is it, Ruth?

BENSON: I've been given another chance. Read this. I'm the luckiest woman alive. He's here. He's at Dunelawn. I've got him where I want him at last! Oh God!

HEDGES: Is it the same Hugh Gumbs?

BENSON: Do you know how many years I've waited for this moment? Hugh Gumbs wants to be a new person and I'll be the one helping him to mold his new self.

HEDGES: If I were you, I mean if this was Tim Taylor being admitted to Dunelawn, I wouldn't be standing here talking about it. I'd fly to him.

BENSON: But . . . (*Indicating the patients.*)

HEDGES: Go on. I can take care of everything.

BENSON: You're a doll.

HEDGES: Now it's my turn: oh pooh!

BENSON: What am I waiting for? Wish me luck!

BENSON: Luck! (*They kiss. Benson dashes off. Ponce, Blum and Yamadoro are smiling. Hedges goes to the cart, gets a book and crosses to the bench. Reading:*) A Critique of Pure Reason by Immanuel Kant. (*Bruno sticks his head up over the wall and whistles softly.*) "To Becky, with all my love, Ruth Benson, R.N." So good to me! (*Bruno whistles again. Hedges finally sees him.*) Please, Bruno, I'm trying to concentrate. It's difficult material.

BRUNO: I thought we'd never ditch horse-face.

HEDGES: We?

BRUNO: It's just you and me now, Hedges.

HEDGES: I don't know what you're talking about.

BRUNO: I seen you.

HEDGES: Seen me what?

BRUNO: Looking at me.

HEDGES: I never looked at you.

BRUNO: I'm provocative. You heard Benson.

HEDGES: Provocative as a can full of worms is what she said.

BRUNO: (*Climbing down from the wall and approaching her.*) Only it ain't what she meant, is it now?

HEDGES: I'm not speaking to you, Bruno.

BRUNO: Benson looks at me, too.

HEDGES: Don't be ridiculous.

BRUNO: I seen her.

HEDGES: Ruth Benson wouldn't look at you if you were the last man on earth.

BRUNO: Around this place, that's exactly what I am. What do you say, Hedges?

HEDGES: You mean . . . ?

BRUNO: I got a waterbed.

HEDGES: I don't care what you got. You're supposed to be mowing!

BRUNO: I'm done mowing.

HEDGES: Then trim some hedges! No, I didn't mean that. Stay back, Bruno. Don't Come near me. I'll call Dr. Toynbee.

BRUNO: Toynbee looks at me, too.

HEDGES: Mr. Ponce! Mr. Ponce!

BRUNO: They all look at me.

HEDGES: (*Freeing Mr. Ponce from his chair and jacket.*) You've got to help me, Mr. Ponce. He won't leave me alone. Im frightened. I'll get you a case of liquor if you help me!

BRUNO: (*Exposing himself.*) Hubba, hubba, Hedges. (*Hedges screams and frees Mr. Blum.*)

HEDGES: Mr. Blum, I'll let you wear my cap or anything you want of mine if you'll just listen to me a minute. You don't understand.

BRUNO: (*Exposing himself again.*) Twenty-three skidoo. (*Hedges screams again, turns to Yamadoro and releases him, too.*)

HEDGES: Mr. Yamadoro, you've got to help me! You're the only one left. I'll let you hit me, if you'll just get up now.

YAMADORO: A strange inner peace has subdued the fires of my soul.

HEDGES: Oh shut up, you dumb Jap!

BRUNO: Your place or mine, toots? Let's go, sugar!

HEDGES: Help! Help! Help! (*She runs off. Bruno goes after her.*)

PONCE: We're free.

BLUM: I know.

YAMADORO: Yes, yes, yes, yes, yes.

PONCE: I don't want to leave, though.

BLUM: (*Draping the sleeve of his straitjacket around him like a boa.*) Neither do I.

YAMADORO: Celestial harmonies ring in my ears.

BLUM: What does that mean?

YAMADORO: I don't know.

PONCE: I once drank twelve extra-dry Gordon's gin martinis in the Monkey Bar at the Hotel Elysee.

BLUM: You should have seen me at the Beaux Arts Ball that time I took first prize. I went as Anouk Aimée.

YAMADORO: Exquisite woman.

BLUM: Yes, yes.

PONCE: Never heard of her.

YAMADORO: Wonderful fingernails. (*Hedges runs across pursued by Bruno.*)

HEDGES: Bruno the gardener is going to rape me and the three of you just sit there! Doesn't anybody care?

BRUNO: Hubba, hubba, Hedges! (*They are gone.*)

PONCE: I was so rotten when I was out there and over the wall.

BLUM: I could never find a pair of white heels that fit.

YAMADORO: Did I ever tell you gentlemen about Monique?

PONCE: I used to love to drink on Saturday. There's something about a Saturday.

BLUM: Do either of you realize what a really good dresser Nina Foch was?

YAMADORO: Monique was from Trenton. A lovely girl. (*Hedges enters and tiptoes down to the house. Bruno suddenly appears from be-*

hind the hedge.)

BRUNO: Hubba, hubba, Hedges! (*Hedges screams as they run out down the aisle. From the back of the house, we hear a "Help!," then the ripping of cloth.*)

PONCE: It's nice here.

BLUM: Peaceful.

YAMADORO: I desire nothing now.

PONCE: Dr. Toynbee's serum.

BLUM: That man is a saint.

YAMADORO: Dunelawn is heaven on earth.

PONCE: I am so happy right now.

BLUM: We all are, Mr. Ponce.

YAMADORO: Life is beautiful.

PONCE: I can't stop smiling.

BLUM: And the sun smiles on us.

YAMADORO: And we smile back at it. (*He starts to sing, very softly—a World War I type campaign song is suggested, e.g. "Pack up Your Troubles." Blum joins him. It becomes a duet in close harmony. Ponce just looks at them. When they finish, he speaks.*)

PONCE: I hate that song. (*Hedges appears.*)

HEDGES: What is it exactly that you want from me, Bruno? (*Bruno, appearing, responds.*)

BRUNO: Hubba hubba, Hedges!

HEDGES: You'll regret this, Bruno, believe me, you won't be happy! (*Hedges screams, and they both disappear.*)

PONCE: We really could leave now, you know.

BLUM: We'd just go back to what we were.

PONCE: You think so?

BLUM: I know.

YAMADORO: Oh, Monique! (*The three of them are really smiling now.*)

PONCE: A gin fizz with real New Orleans sloe gin. Disgusting.

BLUM: Fredericks of Hollywood. Revolting.

YAMADORO: Nina Foch spread-eagled. Hideous. (*This time it is Ponce who starts singing the song. The others join him for a short reprise as they each try to banish their private demon. They are just finishing when Benson wheels in Hugh Gumbs, still wearing his bedraggled street clothes.*)

HUGH Gumbs: Aaaaaaaaaaaaaaaaaa!

BENSON: Mr. Gumbs, please!

HUGH: Aaaaa!

BENSON: You must try to control yourself.

HUGH: Aaaaaaaaaaaa!

Benson: You're disturbing the others!

Hugh: Aaaaaaaaaaa!

BENSON: It's obvious you're in great distress, Mr. Gumbs, but surely . . .

HUGH: I'm desperate, Nurse. You name it and I've got it, done it or used it.

BENSON: As soon as I've gone over your forms . . .

HUGH: Couldn't I just have my injection first?

BENSON: In a moment, Mr. Gumbs.

HUGH: I don't know if I can hold out.

BENSON: (*Keeping her head down, looking at her charts.*) Smoking. Three packs a day.

HUGH: That's right, Nurse.

BENSON: That's a lot, Mr. Gumbs.

HUGH: I'm not even being honest with you. It's closer to five.

BENSON: Five packs?

HUGH: Six, seven, I don't know! Some nights I set my alarm and wake up at fifteen-minute intervals and have a cigarette.

BENSON: Why?

HUGH: Why? Because that's how much I like to smoke! What kind of a question is that? Why? Why do people do anything? Because they like it! They like it!

BENSON: Even when it's bad for them?

HUGH: Yes! That's exactly why I'm here! I'm a liar. I'm a kleptomaniac. I chase women. I bite my nails. You've got to help me!

BENSON: Thank God, Hugh, thank God!

HUGH: What?

BENSON: (*Back to the forms.*) A terrible drinking problem.

HUGH: The worst.

BENSON: How much exactly?

HUGH: Bloody Marys at breakfast, martinis before lunch . . .

BENSON: How many?

HUGH: Two, and three before dinner.

BENSON: Wine with your meals?

HUGH: No.

BENSON: Well that's something.

HUGH: Aquavit. And three or four cherry herrings after dinner and hot saki nightcaps; that's in the winter.

BENSON: In the summer?

HUGH: Cold saki.

BENSON: It sounds like you still have your drinking problem all right.

HUGH: Still?

BENSON: I mean in the summer, too. (*Aside.*) Oh, Hugh, Hugh, you're breaking my heart!

HUGH: Aaaaaaaaaaaaa!

BENSON: I want to help you, Mr. Gumbs!

HUGH: Then do it! Can't we do all this after the injection?

BENSON: I'm afraid not.

HUGH: (*Indicating the others.*) Look at them! How cured they seem!

BENSON: You will be, too, Hugh. Excuse me, I meant Mr. Gumbs.

HUGH: That's the first thing I'd like to change about me. My name. How could any woman love a Hugh Gumbs?

BENSON: You mustn't torment yourself like that!

HUGH: I can't help it. I meet a woman and it's fine about the drinking, fine about the smoking, it's even fine about the . . . never mind . . . but when I tell her my name, it's all over. Ask yourself, nurse, would you want to go through life as Mrs. Hugh Gumbs?

BENSON: Surely there was one woman, somewhere in your life, who didn't mind your name?

HUGH: One, just one.

BENSON: You see?

HUGH: My mother, for Christ's sake! Please, can't I have my first injection?

BENSON: We're nearly done. A moment ago you said when you met a woman it was "even fine about the . . ." What's your "about the," Mr. Gumbs?

HUGH: I can't tell you.

BENSON: I must have it.

HUGH: Believe me, you don't want it.

BENSON: Your worst habit, Mr. Gumbs, I've got to have it.

HUGH: What are you going to do with it? (*Toynbee enters, smiling as usual.*)

BENSON: This is Hugh Gumbs, Dr. Toynbee, a new patient. He won't tell me what his worst habit is. (*Dr. Toynbee goes to Hugh and stands, looking down at him with his hands on his shoulders, then bends and mumbles his unintelligible gibberish. Hugh bows his head, deeply ashamed, then motions Dr. Toynbee to lean forward while he whispers his worst habit into his ear, with much pantomiming. Dr. Toynbee straightens up, clearly appalled at what he has just heard, and leaves without even looking at Benson.*) In addition to all that, what really brings you to Dunelawn?

HUGH: I've told you.

BENSON: I thought perhaps there might be a somewhat more personal reason. I only meant perhaps someone else is responsible for your coming here.

HUGH: Like who?

BENSON: A woman.

HUGH: You're telling me! Say, and you're going to think I'm crazy, did you ever work for an answering service?

BENSON: No.

HUGH: Your voice sounds so familiar.

BENSON: I know.

HUGH: There was this real battle-axe on my service about five years ago. For a minute, you sounded just like her. Where was I?

BENSON: A woman.

HUGH: Oh yeah, a woman. Yes, there is one.

BENSON: Tell me about her.

HUGH: (*With a sigh.*) She was very beautiful, very feminine, very desirable. Everything a man could want. Intelligent, decisive, yet strangely yielding.

BENSON: (*Almost a murmur.*) Yet strangely yielding!

HUGH: She's probably the finest woman alive on the face of this earth.

BENSON: Her name, Mr. Gumbs?

HUGH: Char-Burger! Did you ever work part-time in Char-Burger on East 63rd Street!

BENSON: I'm afraid not.

HUGH: You sound so familiar and I never forget a voice. Eleven o'clock news weather girl, maybe?

BENSON: No. Her name, Mr. Gumbs?

HUGH: (*A tormented memory.*) Mildred Canby! Can I have my injection now?

BENSON: What about Ruth Benson?

HUGH: Ruth Benson?

BENSON: I believe that's the name on your biography here.

HUGH: I don't remember telling anyone anything about Ruth Benson.

BENSON: You were delirious when they brought you in.

HUGH: I was?

BENSON: You were raving about a Ruth Benson. That's all you said. Ruth Benson, Ruth Benson. Over and over again.

HUGH: What do you know?

BENSON: She must have been very important to you.

HUGH: Not particularly.

BENSON: I'll be the judge of that. Tell me about her.

HUGH: The main thing I could tell you about Ruth Benson is that she was fat. About 280, I'd say.

BENSON: I'm sure she was never 280, Mr. Gumbs.

HUGH: You never saw Ruth Benson.

BENSON: 230 maybe, but not 280!

HUGH: The point is she was fat, right? I mean she was circus fat.

BENSON: I know the type. Go on, Mr. Gumbs.

HUGH: What else about her? I think Ruth Benson is the only person, man, woman or child, I ever asked to take a bath. She used to smoke six packs a day, minimum. Cigarillos. Nicotine stains right up to her elbow! I don't guess she ever drew a sober breath. My main image of her is passed out on the floor like a big rancid mountain. And talk about being a slob! She had dustballs under her bed the size of watermelons. She didn't just have roaches in her kitchen. She raised them. It was like a goddamn stud farm in there. You'd light the oven and there'd be a flash-fire from all the grease.

BENSON: It sounds like Ruth Benson was a woman with a lot of bad habits.

HUGH: She was an out and out pig.

BENSON: I can't help noticing a special glow that comes into your voice every time you mention her name.

HUGH: We had a lot in common, Ruthie and I. I'll never forget the night we each caught the other precisely the same instant picking their nose. God, she was gross.

BENSON: There's that glow again.

HUGH: Just thinking of her with all those fingers up there and I have to smile. You're bringing back a lot of bad memories, Nurse. I haven't though of Ruth Benson and her soiled sheets in a long time. Your voice sounds so familiar. (*Benson is making a big show of raising her skirt to fix a stocking.*) You have beautiful legs, Nurse.

BENSON: Familiar voice, unfamiliar legs.

HUGH: The legs look like some movie star, the voice still sounds like that answering voice.

BENSON: (*Straightening up.*) Don't you know who I am yet, Hugh? No, don't say anything until I've finished. I'm not going to turn around until you tell me that you want me to turn around. I'm glad you don't recognize me. There's no reason that you should. I did it all for you, Hugh. Hugh Gumbs. Like your name, it wasn't easy. But I didn't mind the suffering, the self-humiliation, the incredible self-discipline. I wanted to torture myself into becoming someone a man like you could love and I have. Let me finish! I'm brutally honest with myself. That's not enough, I know, but it's a beginning. When I look in a mirror now I can say yes, yes, I like that person. I'm not smug, Hugh, I just know my own worth. For five years I've made myself thoroughly miserable so that today I could make you happy and I did it all for love. (*A pause.*) Now yes or no, Hugh, do you want me to turn around? (*A pause.*)

HUGH: Who are you?

BENSON: (*Turning to him, ecstatic.*) It's me. Ruth.

HUGH: Ruth?

BENSON: Ruth Benson.

HUGH: Fat Ruth Benson?

BENSON: Yes, yes!

HUGH: You don't look like Ruth.

BENSON: (*She is so happy.*) I know, I know!

HUGH: You don't sound like her, either.

BENSON: Voice lessons, darling.

HUGH: You don't even smell like Ruth.

BENSON: Zest, Dial, Dove, Lava!

HUGH: You have such beautiful legs.

BENSON: I worked for them.

HUGH: Your teeth.

BENSON: All caps.

HUGH: And your . . . (*He indicates her breasts.*)

BENSON: Exercises.

HUGH: Your big hairy mole.

BENSON: Cosmetic surgery.

HUGH: It's really you?

BENSON: It's really me. The real me and it's all for you, Hugh, I did it all for you.

HUGH: You did?

BENSON: And now that I've found you again I'm not going to let you go this time.

HUGH: You didn't let me go the last time. I let you go.

BENSON: It doesn't matter. The point is you won't want to let me go this time. Oh Hugh, I'm going to make you very, very happy. You're the luckiest man alive.

HUGH: (*Shaking his head.*) No, Ruth, no.

BENSON: What's wrong?

HUGH: It would never work, Ruth.

BENSON: Of course it will work. It has to work.

HUGH: I couldn't do it to you.

BENSON: Yes, you can. You can do anything you want to me, don't you see?

HUGH: Ruth, I've committed myself to Dunelawn, I've gotten so bad.

BENSON: Do you love me?

HUGH: Love you?

BENSON: Be blunt with me, Hugh.

HUGH: I don't even recognize you, you're so terrific looking.

BENSON: Forget the way I look now and ask yourself: do you love me?

HUGH: You're so far above me now.

BENSON: From down there, do you love me?

HUGH: I didn't love you when you were fat and rotten. I can't love you now that you're beautiful and perfect and have such terrific legs.

BENSON: I'm not perfect.

HUGH: Well, nearly.

BENSON: Nearly's not enough. Nearly's never enough. I still have my faults, too, darling.

HUGH: Like what? Name one.

BENSON: I can't off the top of my head but I'm sure I do somewhere.

HUGH; You see, it's hopeless. You're the sky above and I'm the mud below. Maybe someday I'll be worthy of you but right now I want to forget all about you and try to improve myself, too, and maybe, just maybe, you'll still be up there in the stratosphere, all shiny like an angel, when I poke my head up through the clouds.

BENSON: That was poetic, Hugh.

HUGH: And what does someone like me do with an angel?

BENSON: Love her.

HUGH: From a very great distance.

BENSON: Where are you going?

HUGH: I don't know.

BENSON: I'm coming with you.

HUGH: Angels fly. I've got to crawl first.

BENSON: I'm not an angel. Forget the angel.

HUGH: You're an angel!

BENSON: I'm not an angel!

HUGH: You're an angel!

BENSON: I'm not an angel!

HUGH: No, you're an angel, Ruth!

BENSON: I'm not an angel! It's the goddamn white uniform!

HUGH: You're an angel. I can't even ask you for a cigarette.

BENSON: Yes. Yes you can. Take the whole pack. I'll light it for you. You want a drink, darling, I'll get you a drink. Bruno! Go ahead, bite your nails. Do anything you want. I love you. (*She puts her fingers in her nose.*) It can be just like old times together!

HUGH: Start that up again and I'll crack your jaw open! (*He pulls her hand away. Benson dissolves in tears.*) Oh, Ruthie, Ruthie! Don't you see how I'd drag you down? Trying to please me you'd only degrade yourself. Please, let's not talk about it anymore. Just give me the injection.

BENSON: Then you don't love me?

HUGH: I can't love you right now, you're just too darn good for me.

BENSON: (*Fixing him with a new glance, all heavy-lidded and seductive.*) You think? (*She starts coming for him. She kisses him. A very long kiss. Hugh hardly responds.*)

HUGH: Can I please have that injection now?

BENSON: (*Her last resort.*) All right, Hugh, and remember, you asked for it.

HUGH: (*Indicating the others.*) I just want to be like them.

BENSON: You will, Hugh, you will. (*Hedges and Bruno enter. Hedges's uniform is askew. She looks worn-out and dazed.*)

HEDGES: Ruth! Ruth! Ruth!

BENSON: Becky!

HEDGES: I'm turning in my cap, Ruth.

BENSON: Becky, what's wrong?

BRUNO: Hubba, hubba, Benson.

BENSON: What has he done to you?

HEDGES: Bruno and I are going to be married.

BENSON: What?

BRUNO: You heard her, mutt-face.

BENSON: What happened, Becky?

HEDGES: I'm in love, Ruth!

BENSON: What has that beast done to you?

HEDGES: Bruno's been saving up for a trailer. We're moving to Fort Lauderdale. Bruno's mommy has a pizza stand down there. This is goodbye, Ruth.

BENSON: (*Slaps her.*) Snap out of it, Hedges.

HEDGES: (*Finally, at long last and it's about time: snapping out of it and slapping her back.*) You snap out of it! That's all you do is slap people. (*She slaps her again.*) Only now you'll have to find someone else to slap!

YAMADORO: (*He is vaguely interested.*) Slap! (*Instead of doing anything, Hugh just sits there and pulls his coat over his head.*)

BENSON: All the time I've invested in you.

HEDGES: Are you ready, Bruno?

BENSON: You must be crazy.

HEDGES: I'm *happy!*

BENSON: I thought you cared about improving yourself.

HEDGES: Bruno likes me the way I am.

BENSON: He's a beast.

HEDGES: And I've got goddamn big thighs! Nobody's perfect!

BENSON: What about Dunelawn?

HEDGES: I won't miss it.

BENSON: What about Dr. Toynbee?

HEDGES: That man is a saint.

BENSON: Then why would you leave him?

HEDGES: He gives me the creeps.

BENSON: Zero defects, Becky?

HEDGES: (*Glowing.*) That's Bruno.

BRUNO: (*Triumphant.*) Hubba, hubba, Benson!

BENSON: Don't even speak to me!

BRUNO: Let's go, sugar.

HEDGES: (*She turns to Ponce, Blum and Yamadoro.*) If any of you had any sense, you'd come with us. There's enough room in Bruno's microbus for everyone. (*She fastens her cap on Mr. Blum's head, then turns to Hugh.*)

BENSON: Just go, you . . . you pizza waitress!

HEDGES: Are you Hugh Gumbs?

HUGH: Yes, yes I am.

HEDGES: Are you in for it!

BRUNO: Hubba, hubba, dog-face!

HEDGES: Hubba, hubba, Ruth! (*They are gone.*)

BENSON: You'll regret this, Hedges, you'll regret this for the rest of your life! (*She turns to Hugh.*) Oh, Hugh, you see how terrible other people are! Thank God for Dunelawn and Dr. Toynbee. I'll get your injection right away. (*Hugh gets out of his wheelchair.*) Where are you going?

HUGH: I can't stay here with you, Ruth. I'm not even worthy of Dunelawn. Maybe I'll come back to you one day, a better and worthier man. If not, I know you'll find someone good enough for you.

BENSON: It's a rotten world out there. It'll destroy you.

HUGH: It already has. (*He starts to go.*)

BENSON: (*Concealing the syringe.*) One last kiss. (*They kiss. Benson has the syringe in her hand, poised to inject him. Dr. Toynbee enters. Benson is mortified.*) Dr. Toynbee! I'm so ashamed. I . . . Mr. Gumbs was just leaving.

HUGH: That woman is perfect! (*He goes up the aisle.*)

BENSON: I don't know what happened, Dr. Toynbee. I left them with Nurse Hedges and she's gone off to Florida to open a pizza stand with Bruno and the love of my life is gone again and I'm having a nervous breakdown because I don't understand people anymore. It's so good here. You're so good. Why would anyone want to leave Dunelawn when all we're trying to do is help them to be perfect? (*Benson is shattered. She is holding onto Dr. Toynbee for support. He puts his arm around her and takes her to the wheelchair left empty by Hugh Gumbs.*) You're so good, Dr. Toynbee. It's the end of summer. (*Dr. Toynbee goes to the cart to get a syringe.*) I won't cry. I refuse to cry. It's you and Dunelawn I'm thinking of. Not myself. The world is filled with men like Hugh Gumbs. But someone somewhere is the man for me. Zero defects. No faults, no failings, no fantasies. Where is he, Dr. Toynbee? (*She looks up into Dr. Toynbee's eyes as he injects her. A wonderful smile lights up her face.*) Oh yes! (*Dr. Toynbee gets a straitjacket hidden behind the wheelchair and carefully puts Benson's arms through it. Meanwhile, Blum begins to sing again, very softly, the same World War I campaign son. Ponce, Yamadoro, and even Benson join him. They are all smiling blissfully. In the distance, we hear even more voices beginning to sing. Dr. Toynbee smiles benignly at his three male patients. Then down at Nurse Benson. Then up at us. He takes a step forward and starts to address us in his unintelligible gibberish. A few leaves fall from the scraggly tree. The lights fade.*)

The Ritz

for Adela Holzer

THE RITZ was originally performed at the Yale Repertory Theatre: It opened January 20, 1975, at the Longacre Theatre in New York City. It was produced by Adela Holzer. It was directed by Robert Drivas. Scenery and costumes designed by Michael H. Yeargan and Lawrence King. Lighting designed by Martin Aronstein. The production state manager was Larry Forde. The assistants to the director were Tony DeSantis and Gary Keeper. The cast was as follows:

ABE	George Dzundza
CLAUDE PERKINS	Paul B. Price
GAETANO PROCLO	Jack Weston
CHRIS	F. Murray Abraham
GOOGIE GOMEZ	Rita Moerno
MAURINE	Hortensia Colorado
MICHAEL BRICK	Stephen Collins
TIGER	John Everson
DUFF	Christopher J. Brown
CARMINE VESPUCCI	Jerry Stiller
VIVIAN PROCLO	Ruth Jaroslow

Patrons

PIANIST	Ron Abel
POLICEMAN	Bruce Bauer
CRISCO	Richard Boccelli
SHELDON FARENTHOLD	Tony DeSantis
PATRON IN CHAPS	John Remme
PATRON FROM SHERIDAN SQUARE	Steve Scott

Characters

GAETANO PROCLO: He is in his early 40's, balding and stout.
CHRIS: He is in his early 30's with a big, open face and features.
MICHAEL BRICK: He is in his mid-20's, very rugged and very handsome.
CARMINE VESPUCCI: He is in his 40's, balding and stout.
CLAUDE PERKINS: He is in his 40's and quite lean.
TIGER: He is in his early 20's, wiry and has lots of curly hair.
DUFFY: He too is in his early 20's, wiry and has lots of curly hair. In fact, he looks a lot like Tiger.
ABE: He is in his 50's and stocky.
THE PATRONS: They come in all sizes, shapes and ages.
GOOGIE GOMEZ: She is in her 30's and has a sensational figure.
VIVIAN PROCLO: She is in her early 40's and stout.
MAURINE: She's in her mid-40's, and very thin.

Setting

The time of the play is now.
The place of the play is men's bathhouse in New York City.

The Ritz

ACT 1

The house curtain is in, the house lights are on and the overture from "Tancredi" is playing as the audience comes in. The house goes to black. In the darkness we hear the sounds of the Rosary being recited. Occasionally a stifled sob overrides the steady incantation of the prayers.

PRIESTS AND RELATIVES: Hail Mary, full of grace, the Lord is with thee. Blessed art thou amongst women and blessed is the fruit of the womb, Jesus. Holy Mary, Mother of God, pray for us sinners now and at the hour of our death. Amen. (*Underneath all this the funeral march from "Nabucco" is heard. The lights have revealed Old Man Vespucci's death bed. Relatives and family are grouped around him, all in silhouette. Kneeling to his right is Carmine. Kneeling to his left is Vivian. They are weeping profusely.*)

CARMINE: Poppa . . .

VIVIAN: Poppa . . . (*The death rattles are beginning. Old Man Vespucci feebly summons the others to draw close for his final words.*)

AUNT VERA: *Aspetta! Aspetta!*

COUSIN HORTENSIA: Sshh! Speak to us, Poppa!

AUNT VERA: Give us your blessing, Poppa!

COUSIN HORTENSIA: One final word, Poppa!

AUNT VERA: *Un poccita parole*, Poppa!

VIVIAN: Give us your blessing, Poppa!

OLD MAN VESPUCCI: Vivian.

VIVIAN: Yes, Poppa?

OLD MAN VESPUCCI: *Vieni qua.*

VIVIAN: Yes, Poppa.

OLD MAN VESPUCCI: Get Proclo.

VIVIAN: Get Proclo, Poppa? Yes, Poppa. He's coming. The plane was late from Cleveland. He'll be here for your blessing. (*Old Man*

Vespucci dismisses his daughter with a hand gesture.)

OLD MAN VESPUCCI: Carmine, my son.

CARMINE: Yes, Poppa. I'm here, Poppa.

OLD MAN VESPUCCI: Get Proclo.

CARMINE: Get Proclo, Poppa?

OLD MAN VESPUCCI: Get Proclo. *Qui brute. Qui boce. Tha botania!* Kill him! Kill him! Kill him! Kill the son of a bitch!

VIVIAN: Proclo is my husband, Poppa!

OLD MAN VESPUCCI: (*Finally mustering all the strength he can, he raises himself up.*) GET PROCLO!!! (*He falls back dead.*)

RELATIVES: (Simultaneously.) Aaaaaiiiieeeee!

AUNT VERA: *Poppa è morto!*

PRIEST: *In nomine partis et filii et spiritu sancti requiescat in . . .* (*The lights fade on the death bed. At the same time, the sound of a pounding drum is heard. It is the opening of "One of a Kind." The lights come up, revealing activity inside The Ritz behind scrims. The main thing we see are doors. Doors and doors and doors. Each door has a number. Outside all these doors are corridors. Lots and lots of corridors. Filling these corridors are men. Lots and lots of men. They are prowling the corridors. One of the most important aspects of the production is this sense of men endlessly prowling the corridors outside the numbered doors. The same people will pass up and down the same corridors and stairways over and over again. After a while, you'll start to think some of them are on a treadmill. Most of them are dressed exactly alike; i.e., they are wearing bathrobes. A few men wear towels around their waists. Every so often we see someone in bikini underwear or an additional accouterment, such as boots or a vests. The number of men, referred to from now on as the patrons, can vary, but each actor must be encouraged to develop a specific characterization. Even though they seldom speak, these various patrons must become specific, integral members of the cast. We also see Tiger and Duff, two attendants. They are sweeping up and making beds. Over the music, we hear announcements.*)

ABE: (*Over the loudspeaker.*) 217 coming up, Duff! . . . Tiger, they're out of soap in the showers! On the double! And check the linens and robes on the third floor . . . Just a reminder that every Monday and Thursday is Buddy Night at the Ritz. So bring a friend.

Two entrances for the price of one. (*The lights dim, and the entrance area is flown in. The inner door and Abe's booth are moved on from left and right. The center scrim flies as the lights come up bright, and we are in the admissions area of The Ritz. The various patrons will pay, check their valuables, receive a room key and then be buzzed through the inner door adjacent to the booth. One patron has just finished checking in. As he is buzzed through the door, we see Abe announce his room number over a loudspeaker.*) 274! That's 274 coming up, Duff! (*The patron disappears. The phone on Abe's desk rings, and he answers.*) Hello. The Ritz. No, we don't take reservations! (*He hangs up, as another patron enters.*)

PATRON: Good evening.

ABE: Yeah?

PATRON: Nasty night.

ABE: Is it?

PATRON: I'm one big puddle.

ABE: Well watch where you're dripping. I just had that floor mopped.

PATRON: I'd like a room, please.

ABE: That's ten bucks. Sign the registration book and check in your valuables. (*The patron begins the check-in procedure. Claude Perkins has entered from the outside. He is wearing a raincoat over rather ordinary clothes. He carries a bag from Zabar's Delicatessen and has a Valet Pack slung over one shoulder. He gets in line behind the patron.*)

PATRON: You're dripping.

CLAUDE: What?

PATRON: I said, you're dripping.

CLAUDE: Of course I'm dripping. It's pouring out there.

PATRON: Well try not to. They don't like you dripping here. (*He starts for the door.*) See you. (*He is buzzed through.*)

CLAUDE: I hope not.

ABE: (*Over the loudspeaker.*) 376! That's room 376! Coming up, Duff!

CLAUDE: That's a good floor for that one. Nobody goes up there.

ABE: Well look who's back. Hello, stranger.

CLAUDE: Hello, Abe.

ABE: I thought you'd sworn off this place.

CLAUDE: I thought I had, too.

ABE: You got homesick for us, right?

CLAUDE: I didn't have much choice. I don't speak Spanish, so the Continental is out. The Club Baths are just too far downtown, I'm boycotting the Beacon, Man's Country's had it and I've been barred from the Everard.

ABE: You've been barred from the Everard?

CLAUDE: They'll regret it.

ABE: Nobody gets barred from the Everard. How'd you manage that?

CLAUDE: There was this man there.

ABE: A fat man, right?

CLAUDE: Fat? He was the magic mountain. He drove me into one of my frenzies. I went berserk and I kicked his door in. So they threw me out and told me never to come back. I was willing to pay for it. I just wanted to talk to him.

ABE: Pick on somebody your own size, why don't you, Claude?

CLAUDE: I wouldn't like that. How much do you weigh?

ABE: Forget it!

CLAUDE: Are you up to 200 yet?

ABE: Forget it!

CLAUDE: When you get up to 200 come and knock on my door.

ABE: Forget it!

CLAUDE: Couldn't we just install a weigh-in station here?

ABE: I said forget it! You want to check that?

CLAUDE: It's my costume for the talent show. (*He is heading for the door, still carrying the Valet Pack and Zabar's shopping bag.*) It's good to be back, Abe. I'm feeling strangely optimistic this evening.

ABE: Just don't kick any doors in.

CLAUDE: I hope I don't have to. (*Claude is buzzed through the door.*)

ABE: 205! Coming up! That's 205! (*Gaetano Proclo comes dashing in. He is carrying a suitcase and a big box of Panettone, the Italian bakery specialty. He is wearing a wet raincoat, a cheap wig, a big bushy moustache and dark glasses. He goes directly to Abe.*)

PROCLO: Can you cash a check for me? It's on Ohio State National.

ABE: What do I look like? A teller in a bank?

PROCLO: You don't understand. I've got a cab waiting. I'll be right back. That's why I got into the cab in the first place, to go somewhere, and it's here I've come. (*Sounds of a horn blowing.*) You hear that? That's him!

ABE: You got a traveler's check?

PROCLO: No.

ABE: Travelers are supposed to have traveler's checks.

PROCLO: Well this traveler doesn't. We left Cleveland in a hurry. Traveler's checks are for people who plan! (*More honking.*) There he goes again!

ABE: I'm sorry.

PROCLO: Look, I've got all the identification in the world. Driver's license, Social Security, Blue Cross, voter registration, Rotary Club . . . What about my business card? "Proclo Sanitation Services, Gaetano Proclo, President." That's me.

ABE: You got a credit card?

PROCLO: I don't want credit, I want cash!

ABE: N-o, buddy.

PROCLO: Oh come on! Do I look like someone who would try to pass a bad check? (*A realization.*) Why of course I do! (*He takes off his dark glasses.*) There! Now can you see me? (*More honking.*) Oh all right! (*He removes his moustache.*) Now are you satisfied?

ABE: I don't make the rules here.

PROCLO: Wait! Wait! (*He takes off his wig.*) Everything else is real.

ABE: I'd like to help you out, mac, but—

PROCLO: The only thing that's gonna calm me down is you cashing my check. My brother-in-law is a maniac and he's going to kill me tonight. If you don't let me in there I'm going to be a dead person. Please, mister, you are making a grown man cry. I'm begging you. It's a matter of life and death! (*More honking.*)

ABE: I shouldn't really be doing this but . . .

PROCLO: You are a good man . . .

ABE: Abe.

PROCLO: Abe. I'm gonna have a novena said for you when I get back to Cleveland. What's your last name? Abe what?

ABE: Lefkowitz.

PROCLO: I'm still gonna have that novena said for you! (*More honking. Chris has entered from the outside. He wears jeans, a blue nylon windbreaker, and a bright purple shirt. He carries an overnight bag. Also, he is wearing a policeman's whistle and a "popper" holder around his neck.*)

CHRIS: Does anybody have a cab waiting?

PROCLO: What?

CHRIS: Is that your cab out there?

PROCLO: Oh yes, yes it is!

CHRIS: Well you've also got one very pissed off driver.

PROCLO: (*To Abe.*) Can you cash this for me now? (*To Chris.*) How pissed off is he?

CHRIS: On a ten scale? Ten. (*More honking.*)

PROCLO: Christ! (*Proclo is fumbling with the money and heading for the door.*) Keep an eye on those for me, would you?

CHRIS: Sure thing. (*Proclo hurries out. Chris looks at the suitcase and the Panettone.*) Planning a big night of it, honey? (*To Abe.*) I had a friend who tried moving into the baths.

ABE: What happened?

CHRIS: He died from a lack of sunshine. He died happy and blind, but he still died.

ABE: We missed you last week.

CHRIS: How do you think your customers felt? I'm a legend in my own lifetime. (*Yelling into Abe's microphone.*) Try to hold out, men! Help is on the way!

ABE: Hold your horses, Chris.

CHRIS: That's all I've been holding all week.

ABE: You wanna sign in?

CHRIS: (*While he writes.*) How's that gorgeous son of yours?

ABE: You're too late. He's getting married.

CHRIS: That's terrific. Give him my love, will you?

ABE: Sure thing, Chris.

CHRIS: Does he need anyone to practice with?

ABE: He's been practicing too much. That's why he's getting married.

CHRIS: Compared to me, Abe she'd have to be an amateur. (*He returns the registration book.*)

ABE: Ronald Reagan! Aw, c'mon, Chris!

CHRIS: You know, he used to be lovers with John Wayne.

ABE: Sure he was.

CHRIS: Right after he broke up with Xavier Cugat.

ABE: People like you think the whole world's queer.

CHRIS: It's lucky for people like you it is. (*Proclo comes rushing back in.*)

PROCLO: He can't change a ten! Do you believe it? New York City, one of the great cities of the world, and this driver I have can't change a ten!

CHRIS: They still don't take anything over a five.

PROCLO: In Cleveland even a paper boy can change a ten!

CHRIS: Did I ever have you?

PROCLO: What?

CHRIS: I've got a rotten memory that way. You never used to live in Rego Park?

PROCLO: No!

CHRIS: 'Cause you look like someone I knew once who was from Rego Park.

PROCLO: I'm afraid not.

CHRIS: He was a large man like you and he was in ladies' shoes, I remember.

PROCLO: Well I'm from Cleveland and I'm in refuse.

CHRIS: I guess not then. Sorry.

PROCLO: That's perfectly all right. (*He hurries back out.*)

CHRIS: A gay garbage man!

ABE: You never can tell.

CHRIS: That's true. I mean, look at me. If you just saw me walking down the street, you'd think I was a queen. (*Chris blows his whistle as he is buzzed through the door.*) All right, men! Up against the wall. This is a raid!

ABE: 240! Two-four-oh. She's here, boys! (*A young man has entered from outside. His name is Michael Brick. He steps up to the admissions booth.*)

MICHAEL: I'd like a room, please. (*The first time we hear Michael's voice we are in for a shock. It is a high, boy sopranoish treble. A timbre totally incongruous with his rugged physique.*) One of your private rooms. How much is that?

ABE: You want what?

MICHAEL: A room, please. I was told you have private rooms.

ABE: Yeah, we got rooms.

MICHAEL: Then I'd like one, sir. How much is that?

ABE: How long?

MICHAEL: Is what, sir?

ABE: How long do you want it for?

MICHAEL: Three or four hours should be sufficient for my purposes.

ABE: I don't care what your purposes are: twelve's our minimum.

MICHAEL: All right, twelve then, sir.

ABE: That's ten bucks. Sign in and I'll take your valuables.

MICHAEL: Tell me something. Has a balding, middle-aged fat man come in here recently?

ABE: I don't believe what just came in here recently.

MICHAEL: Think hard. I'll repeat his description. A balding, middle-aged fat man.

ABE: We've got all kinds inside. Fat, thin, short, tall, young, old. I can't keep track.

MICHAEL: Well I guess I'll just have to go in and see for myself, sir.

ABE: I guess you will. You're not a cop, are you?

MICHAEL: I'm a detective, sir. Michael Brick. The Greybar Agency. Our client wants the goods on him and I'm just the man to get them. I've never failed a client yet. What do I do now?

ABE: Through there and up the stairs. Someone'll show you your room.

MICHAEL: Thank you, sir.

ABE: Let me give you a little tip, Brick. Stay out of the steam room.

MICHAEL: Why, sir?

ABE: It gets pretty wild in there.

MICHAEL: Oh, I can take it, sir. In my line of work I get to do a lot of wild things. This is my first seduction job. Wish me luck.

ABE: With that voice, you'll need it. (*Michael is buzzed through the door and is gone.*) 101 coming up! That's one-oh-one! Oh boy, oh boy, oh boy! (*Googie Gomez comes into the admissions area, protecting herself from the rain with a wet copy of* Variety. *She is carrying a wig box and wardrobe bag.*)

GOOGIE: No rain, he tells me! No rain, he says! No rain! That fucking Tex Antoine! That little *maricon*! I'd like to pull his little beard off! One spot on this dress and I'm finished! The biggest night of my life and it's pissing dogs and cats.

PROCLO: (*Who has entered behind Googie.*) That's cats and dogs. (*Googie has been so busy worrying about rain spots on her dress she really hasn't noticed Proclo yet. When she does, there is a marked change in her behavior and vocabulary.*)

GOOGIE: Joe Papp. Hello, Mr. Papp. It's a real pleasure to meet you. I seen all your shows. Uptown, downtown, in the park. They're all fabulous. *Fabulosa!* And I just know, in my heart of hearts, that after you see my show tonight you're going to want to give me a chance at one of your wonderful theatres. Uptown, downtown, in the park. I'll even work the mobile theatre. Thank you for coming, Mr. Papp. Excuse me, I got a little laryngitis. But the show must go on, *si?*

PROCLO: My name isn't Papp.

GOOGIE: You're not Joe Papp?

PROCLO: I'm sorry.

GOOGIE: But you are a producer?

PROCLO: No.

GOOGIE: Are you sure?

PROCLO: Yes.

GOOGIE: That's okay. I heard there was gonna be a big producer around tonight and I wasn't taking any chances. You never know. It's hard for me to speak English good like that. (*A new outburst.*) Aaaaiiieee! My God, not the hairs! *Cono!* (*Her hands are hovering in the vicinity of her head.*) Okay. Go ahead and say it. It's okay. I can take it. Tell me I look like shit.

PROCLO: Why would I want to say a thing like that to such an attractive young lady?

GOOGIE: You boys really know how to cheer a girl up when she's dumps in the down. (*She gives Proclo a kiss on the cheek.*) My boyfriend Hector see me do that: *ay! cuidado!* He hates you *maricones,* that Hector! He's a ballbreaker with me, too, mister. You know why you're not a producer? You're too nice to be a producer. But I'm gonna show them all, mister, and tonight's the night I'm gonna do it. (*Googie is moving toward the door.*) One day you gonna see the name Googie Gomez in lights and you gonna say to yourself "Was that *her?*" And you gonna answer yourself "That was her!" But you know something, mister? I was always her. Just nobody knows it. *Yo soy Googie Gomez, estrellita del futuro!* (*Googie is buzzed through the door and is gone.*)

PROCLO: Who the hell was that?

ABE: Googie.

PROCLO: I thought this was a bathhouse.

ABE: It is.

PROCLO: A *male* bathhouse!

ABE: It is.

PROCLO: Then what's she doing in there?

ABE: Googie sings in The Pits.

PROCLO: The pits? What pits?

ABE: The nightclub.

PROCLO: You've got a nightclub in there?

ABE: We've got a nightclub, movies, TV, swimming pool, steam room, sauna, massage table, discotheque, bridge, amateur night and free blood tests every Wednesday. . . (*Proclo turns at the sound of Maurine entering behind him from outside. She is wearing a duffel coat with the hood up, pants and tall rubber rain boots. No chic dresser, Maurine. She seems deep in concentration and takes no notice of Proclo as she moves toward the door.*) How'd it go today, Mo? (*Maurine just shrugs. She is buzzed through the door and is gone.*)

PROCLO: I don't even want to *think* what she does.

ABE: Mo's just our accountant.

PROCLO: I asked that cab driver to bring me to the last place in the world anybody would think of looking for me.

ABE: You found it.

PROCLO: Except everybody in the world is already in there. I need calm, privacy, safety tonight.

ABE: So stay in your room and keep your door locked.

PROCLO: Don't worry. I will. How much is that?

ABE: Ten dollars. (*Proclo looks at the registration book.*)

PROCLO: Ronald Reagan!

ABE: You can write John Doe for all I care. Just so long as we get some kind of a name down there.

PROCLO: Any name at all? Oh, Abe, I'm gonna speak to the Pope about getting you canonized! (*Reads what he's written.*) "Carmine Vespucci, Bensonhurst, Brooklyn."

ABE: Who's that?

PROCLO: My maniac brother-in-law who was going to kill me tonight!

ABE: What did you do to him?

PROCLO: I got born and I married his sister.

ABE: That's all?

PROCLO: Just my whole life. (*Proclo gathers his suitcase and Panettone, ready to enter now.*)

ABE: Do you mind if I ask you a personal question?

PROCLO: The man who just saved my life can ask me anything.

ABE: You ever been in a place like this?

PROCLO: Oh sure. We got a Jack LaLanne's in Cleveland. (*The door is buzzed and Proclo goes through.*)

ABE: 196! That's one-nine-six coming up, Duff. Oh boy, oh boy, oh boy! (*While Abe is speaking, the lights will fade on the admissions area and "Just Can't Get You Out of My Mind" comes up. The admissions area and the scrims are flown. Other lights are coming up and we are in the interior of The Ritz. On the lower level we see Tiger sweeping up. Chris enters behind him.*)

TIGER: Hey, Chris.

CHRIS: Hi, Tiger.

TIGER: What took you so long? They called your number ten minutes ago.

CHRIS: I was in the boutique.

TIGER: What'd you buy?

CHRIS: A red light bulb for my room and this month's *Viva*.

TIGER: You don't need a red light bulb.

CHRIS: And I hope I don't need this month's *Viva*. Much action tonight?

TIGER: With you here I'm sure there will be.

CHRIS: Slow, hunh?

TIGER: Real dead, so far.

CHRIS: Don't worry, honey, I'll shake this place up good.

TIGER: If anybody can it's you.

CHRIS: The thing that no one understands about me is that sex is just my way of saying hello.

TIGER: Yeah, but you want to say hello to everybody you meet.

CHRIS: Don't you?

TIGER: I work here!

CHRIS: I wish I did. (*They go. Claude Perkins has come up to the wandering and lost Proclo. The love theme from "Now, Voyager" plays.*)

CLAUDE: Hello, there.

PROCLO: Hello.

CLAUDE: What seems to be the problem?

PROCLO: I can't seem to find my room.

CLAUDE: Well you just come with me.

PROCLO: Why thank you. That's very kind of you. (*They leave together. On the upper level we see Duff. Chris comes up the stairs and pokes his head into the steam room.*)

CHRIS: Guess who!

DUFF: Hey, Chris.

CHRIS: Hi, Duffie.

DUFF: 240 again?

CHRIS: And it better be clean! Last time they were having a crab race on the sheets.

DUFF: I did it myself, first thing when I came on. (*He opens the door with Chris's key.*)

CHRIS: Home sweet home! If these walls could talk . . . !

DUFF: They don't have to.

CHRIS: I've spent some of the happiest hours of my life in this room.

DUFF: I know. We've all heard you.

CHRIS: When are we gonna get together, you cute little hump?

DUFF: I don't know. Ask Tiger.

CHRIS: That means "forget it." Out! Out! I've got a busy night ahead of me. I hope. (*Calling out loudly.*) There will be an orgy beginning in room 240 in exactly four minutes! That's an orgy in room 240 in exactly four minutes! (*He goes into his room and closes the door. We have been watching Claude lead Proclo to his—that is, Claude's—room. Claude has followed Proclo in and has closed the door.*)

PROCLO: Are you sure this is 196? I think this is someone else's room. Look, see the clothes?

CLAUDE: You'll never guess what I made for dinner tonight, so I'm just going to have to tell you.

PROCLO: I beg your pardon?

CLAUDE: A nice rich ground pork meat loaf with a mozzarella cheese center, gobs of mashed potatoes swimming in gravy, carrots floating in butter and for a salad, avocado chunks smothered in Roquefort dressing. Could you just die?

PROCLO: I could just . . . ! I don't know what I could just!

CLAUDE: And then: Dutch Chocolate layer cake with two big scoops of Baskin-Robbins mocha walnut ice cream and a fudge malted.

PROCLO: It sounds delicious.

CLAUDE: You could've been there.

PROCLO: I was in Brooklyn. Now if you'll excuse me, I'll—

CLAUDE: Wait! (*He is rummaging in his shopping bag.*) You want a bagel with lox and cream cheese?

PROCLO: No, thank you. I've eaten.

CLAUDE: An eclair? Some homemade brownies? I know! A corned beef on rye with a dill pickle!

PROCLO: Really, I'm not hungry. (*Claude is blocking his way.*)

CLAUDE: How much do you weigh?

PROCLO: What?

CLAUDE: Your weight! 210? 220?

PROCLO: 225. (*Claude has started to undulate, dance almost, and move towards Proclo.*)

CLAUDE: (*Singing in a low, sexy growl.*) "Jelly Roll Baby/You're my Jelly Roll Man . . ."

PROCLO: I think there is some confusion here.

CLAUDE: "Jelly Roll Cupcake/I'm your Jelly Roll fan. . ."

PROCLO: In fact, I *know* there is some confusion going on in here.

CLAUDE: "You got the roll/and I got the soul/that strictly adores/paying Jelly Roll toll . . ." (*Claude is still singing as he pulls Proclo toward him and they collapse heavily on the bed.*)

PROCLO: Stop it! Please! You're hurting me!

CLAUDE: I'm hurting you?

PROCLO: Help! Help! (*Tiger has been seen running along the corridor and uses his passkey now to come into the room. A small crowd of patrons starts forming in the corridor outside the room.*)

TIGER: (*Pulling Proclo off Claude.*) Okay, fat man! Leave the little guy alone! What are you trying to do? Pull his head off? (*He takes Proclo's key.*) Let me see your key. 195! Now get down there and don't cause any more trouble. What do you think this is? The YMCA? (*He puts Proclo's suitcase in the corridor and turns back to Claude.*) I'm sorry, sir. It won't happen again. (*Claude is moaning happily.*)

CLAUDE: I certainly hope not.

TIGER: Get down there, man! (He goes.)

PROCLO: He ought to be locked up! (*The crowd of patrons are all looking at Proclo.*) Hello. Whew! I just had quite a little experience in there. I think that guy's got a problem. People like that really shouldn't be allowed in a place like this. (*Stony silence from the patrons.*) What unusual pants. They look like cowboy chaps.

PATRON IN CHAPS: They are cowboy chaps.

PROCLO: I was thinking I thought they looked like cowboy chaps. Well gentlemen, if you'll excuse me, and let me get out of these clothes. Bye. Nice talking to you. (*Proclo beats an embarrassed retreat down the stairs. The group of patrons will slowly disband. Chris opens the door to his room, sticks his head out and yells.*)

CHRIS: Okay, boys, room 240! Soup's on, come and get it! (*He goes back into his room. Proclo hurries to his room. Michael Brick has appeared in the area of a pay telephone. He dials a number and waits.*)

MICHAEL: Hello, Bimbi's? Is this the bar across the street from The Ritz? There's a Mr. Carmine Vespucci there. I've got to speak to him. It's urgent.

ABE: (*Over the loudspeaker.*) Tiger! Duff! The linen people are here. On the double!

MICHAEL: Mr. Vespucci? My name is Michael Brick. I'm with the Greybar Detective Agency. You hired my partner to get something on a Mr. Gaetano Proclo, only my partner's sick so I'm taking over the case for him. I'm calling you from The Ritz. I just got here. Now let me see if I've got his description right. A balding, middle-aged fat man? That's not much to go on, but I'll do my best. (*Googie enters and signals to him.*) One of those transvestites is standing right next to me. Now you just stay by the phone in that bar across the street and I'll get back to you.

GOOGIE: *Ay, que cosa linda!*

MICHAEL: I can't talk now. I think he's surrounding me for unnatural things. (*Michael hangs up, gives Googie a horrified look and hurries off.*)

GOOGIE: Hey *chico*, I was just gonna talk to you! (*Tiger enters.*) Tiger, is he here yet?

TIGER: Who?

GOOGIE: Who? What do you mean who? There is only one who I am interested in you telling me about! Listen, you told me there was gonna be a big producer here tonight. I dress special. I do the hairs special. If you're lying to me, Tiger . . .

TIGER: Can't you take a little joke?

GOOGIE: My career is no joke. Nobody's career is never no joke.

TIGER: I was just trying to build you up.

GOOGIE: I tell you something and I mean this: You ever hear of instant laryngitis? No producer be out there tonight and that's what I got—instant laryngitis—and you and Duff are gonna do the show alone. Those are my words, they are from the heart and I am now officially sick!

TIGER: Googie! (*Googie rasps an answer and leaves, Tiger following her. Proclo comes wandering into view, still carrying his suitcase and still shaken from his experience with Claude.*)

PROCLO: This place is like a Chinese maze. (*Proclo is standing there when Duff comes out of one of the rooms.*)

DUFF: Are you 196?

PROCLO: Something like that.

DUFF: I meant your room.

PROCLO: So did I.

DUFF: Follow me. (*He leads Proclo to the room.*) 196. Here it is. (*Duff has opened the door for him. Proclo goes into the room. It is a shambles from the previous occupant. Duff calls out into the corridors.*) Hey, Tiger! Room 196! On the double!

PROCLO: You're kidding. Tell me you're kidding.

DUFF: What did you expect?

PROCLO: I don't know. A room maybe. A normal size room.

DUFF: You should see some of the rooms they could've put you in.

PROCLO: You're telling me they come even smaller?

DUFF: Half this size.

PROCLO: Does Mickey Rooney know about this place?

DUFF: You got far out taste, mister.

PROCLO: Vespucci. Carmine Vespucci. What's your name?

DUFF: Duff.

PROCLO: It's good to see you, Duff.

DUFF: How do you mean?

PROCLO: I was beginning to think this place was a little too esoteric for my tastes, if you know what I mean. Like that guy up there with all the food.

DUFF: I think it's something to do with the weather. Rainy nights always bring out the weirdos.

PROCLO: They shouldn't let people like that in here. It'll give this place a bad name.

DUFF: This place already has a bad name. (*Tiger has arrived with a mop and a change of linen. The room will be very crowded with the three of them and Proclo's luggage.*)

TIGER: We're both up shit creek again.

DUFF: Who with this time?

TIGER: I told Googie there'd be a producer out front tonight.

DUFF: Maybe there will be.

TIGER: I promised her. No producer, she's not going on. She's locked in her dressing room with laryngitis.

PROCLO: She told me she was feeling better.

TIGER: You know Googie?

PROCLO: I met her downstairs. She thought 1 was a producer. She's very colorful.

TIGER: Right now she's also very pissed off.

DUFF: Let me talk to her.

PROCLO: Not so fast, Duff. What about slippers?

DUFF: Slippers?

PROCLO: Slippers.

DUFF: Where do you think you are? Slippers! (*Duff leaves as Tiger continues to clean Proclo's room and make up his bed.*)

PROCLO: I always thought they gave you slippers in a bathhouse. I mean, you could catch athlete's foot in a place like this.

TIGER: You're lucky if that's all you catch. (*Trying to make up the bed.*) Excuse me.

PROCLO: I'm sorry. (*He stands.*) Looking at you two, I think I'm seeing double.

TIGER: He's Duff. I'm Tiger.

PROCLO: How are people supposed to tell you apart?

TIGER: They don't usually. Just try to stay out of 205 this time.

PROCLO: What's in 205?

TIGER: That room I had to pull you out of. You could hurt someone doing that.

PROCLO: Now just a minute! I thought that guy was taking me to *my* room! You don't think I went in there because I wanted to?

TIGER: (*Dawning on him.*) You trying to tell me he's a chubby chaser?

PROCLO: A chubby what?

TIGER: Someone who likes . . . (*He gestures, indicating great bulk.*)

PROCLO: You mean like me?

TIGER: You're right up his alley.

PROCLO: I knew someone like that once. I just never knew what to call him. "Get away from me, Claude!" is all I could come up with. A chubby chaser! That's kind of funny. Unless, of course, you happen to be the chubby they're chasing. Room 205. Thanks for the tip. I'll avoid it like the plague. (*Duff has returned and is knocking loudly on the door.*)

DUFF: Fifteen minutes!

PROCLO: Oh my God!

TIGER: Relax! (*He opens the door.*)

DUFF: Come on, Tiger. Show time!

TIGER: What happened?

DUFF: Googie's Mr. Big is here. He's going to be sitting ringside for the first show tonight.

TIGER: How'd you manage that?

DUFF: I didn't. But with a little help from our friend here . . . !

PROCLO: Hey, now just a minute!

DUFF: Aw, now come on, Mr. Vespucci! Give two down and out go-go boys with aspirations for higher things a break.

PROCLO: I don't want to get involved in anything.

DUFF: All you have to do is listen to her act.

PROCLO: I don't want to listen to her act.

DUFF: I don't blame you, but that's not the point.

PROCLO: I'm not a producer.

DUFF: Googie's not really a singer.

TIGER: Come on, what do you say?

PROCLO: What if she finds out?

DUFF: That's our problem.

TIGER: Leave everything to us.

PROCLO: I came here to lay low.

TIGER: Man, you can't lay any lower than Googie's nightclub act.

DUFF: Come on, we gotta change.

TIGER: You're a prince, Mr. . . . .

DUFF: Vespucci.

TIGER: An honest-to-God prince.

PROCLO: Thank you, Duff.

TIGER: He's Duff. I'm Tiger. (*They run off. Proclo closes the door and shakes his head.*)

PROCLO: Seclusion! Is that asking so very much, God? Simple seclusion? I must be crazy! Allowing them to tell her I'm a producer! (*Michael Brick is seen outside Claude's door, which is ajar. He sticks his head into the room.*)

MICHAEL: Excuse me.

CLAUDE: I'm resting.

MICHAEL: May I come in?

CLAUDE: I said I'm resting.

MICHAEL: I'm looking for someone.

CLAUDE: I told you I'm resting.

MICHAEL: That's okay. I just want to ask you—

CLAUDE: What do you need? A brick wall to fall on your head? "Resting!" It's a euphemism for "not interested"! Skinny! (*Claude slams the door in Michael's face. Michael knocks on another door.*)

MICHAEL: Excuse me. May I come in? (*Michael starts into the room, then comes rushing out.*) Oh, I beg your pardon. Excuse me, may I come in? Thank you very much. (*He goes into another room. This time he comes rushing out almost at one.*) Oh, my goodness! (*Michael's mother never told him there would be nights like this. He steels himself and enters the steam room. On the swing of the door, he is back out and gone. Proclo has nearly finished changing when there is a knock on his door. He quickly puts his wig back on.*)

PROCLO: Yes?

CLAUDE: Are you there?

PROCLO: Who is it?

CLAUDE: Room service.

PROCLO: Who? (*He opens the door a crack, sees Claude and slams it.*) Go away!

CLAUDE: I've got a box of Hershey bars. (*He begins throwing bars of candy through the transom.*)

PROCLO: I said go away!

CLAUDE: Peter Paul Mounds, Milky Ways . . .

PROCLO: I know what you are now!

CLAUDE: I can make you very happy!

PROCLO: You're a chubby chaser!

CLAUDE: I know.

PROCLO: Well stop it!

CLAUDE: How?

PROCLO: I don't know! (*Proclo waits, listens.*) Are you still there?

CLAUDE: I'm never leaving.

PROCLO: You can't stand out there all night. This is my room and that's my door to it. Now go away or I'll call Tiger and Duff.

CLAUDE: I'm not doing anything.

PROCLO: You're making me nervous.

CLAUDE: (*He thinks, then sings.*) "Love your magic spell is everywhere . . ." (*He thinks.*) "Can't help loving dat man of mine . . ." (*He thinks.*) "Then along came . . ." (*He stops singing.*) Who? Then along came who?

PROCLO: Vespucci.

CLAUDE: (*An inspiration.*) Vespucci!/I just met a boy named Vespucci!/And suddenly that name . . . (*Proclo stops moaning and comes up with a plan.*)

PROCLO: Okay, you win. What room are you in?

CLAUDE: 205.

PROCLO: All right, you go back to 205. I'll be right up.

CLAUDE: Promise?

PROCLO: On my mother's grave! (*He is crossing his fingers.*) Just get away from that door! 'Cause if you're still standing out there when I come out of this room, the deal is off.

CLAUDE: And if you're not up in my room in five minutes . . .

PROCLO: What?

CLAUDE: I'll find you.

PROCLO: And?

CLAUDE: You don't want to make me do anything rash, do you, Mr. Vespucci?

PROCLO: Oh no, oh no!

CLAUDE: Five minutes then. Room 205. If you're not up there, I'm gonna come down here and break your knees. Don't push your luck with Claude Perkins. (*He goes. His name seems to have struck a distant bell for Proclo.*)

PROCLO: Claude Perkins. It can't be the same one. Claude Perkins. That's all I need. He's dead. He has to be dead. Claude Perkins. (*Proclo opens the door and looks out. No sign of Claude. Without realizing it, he shuts the door behind him and locks himself out.)* On no! Come on, will you? Open up. Damn! (*Calling off.*) Boys! Boys! You with the keys! Yoo hoo! Yoo hoo! (*Proclo is suddenly aware of a patron who is just looking at him and smiling.*) Hello. Just clearing my throat. Ahoo! Ahoo! Too many cigarettes. Ahoo! Hello there. I hear the Knicks tied it up in the last quarter.

PATRON: Crisco.

PROCLO: What?

PATRON: Crisco oil party.

PROCLO: Crisco oil party?

PATRON: Room 419. Pass it on.

PROCLO: Pass what on?

PATRON: And bring Joey.

PROCLO: Who's Joey?

PATRON: You know Joey. But not Chuck. Got that?

PROCLO: Crisco oil party. Room 419. I can bring Joey but not Chuck.

PATRON: Check.

PROCLO: What's wrong with Chuck? (*Patron whispers something in Proclo's ear. Proclo's eyes grow wide. He can't wait to get out of there.*) Chuck's definitely out! If you'll excuse me now . . . ! (*He starts moving away. The Patron leaves. Proclo starts pacing in rapid circles.*) Now wait a minute. Wait a minute. Stay clam. Be rational. Don't get hysterical. All he did was invite you to a Crisco oil party, whatever the hell that is, and told you to bring Joey. Of course, I don't know Joey, and I don't think I want to, and not to bring Chuck because Chuck —. It can't be one of those places. I mean, one or two weird people do not a you-know-what make. People are just more normal in Cleveland.

CHRIS: (*Leaning out of his room.*) Telephone call for Joe Namath in room 240. Long distance for Mr. Joe Namath in room 240!

PROCLO: Well *there!* You see? I knew I wasn't a crazy person! (*Proclo is heading toward Chris's room.*) There's just no way. . . . (*On his way, he composes a speech to himself.*) Mr. Namath? Excuse me. I wonder if I might trouble you for an autograph. It's not me. It's for my 12-year-old, Gilda. Say, did you hear the Knicks tied it up in the last quarter? Mr. Namath?

CHRIS: (*From inside his room.*) No, don't . . . I can't . . . Oooo! . . . Aaaa! . . . Oh my God! . . . Do it, do it! . . . Yes! Yes! (*He puts down the magazine he was thumbing through.*) If that doesn't get those queens up here nothing will.

PROCLO: (*Knocking on Chris's door.*) Mr. Namath? (*Chris comes out of his room and sees Proclo.*) You're not Joe Namath.

CHRIS: Neither are you.

PROCLO: I thought you were Joe Namath.

CHRIS: It's the lighting.

PROCLO: I was praying you were Joe Namath.

CHRIS: I don't blame you.

PROCLO: I mean, you just had to be him!

CHRIS: Eating your heart out, honey?

PROCLO: I don't know what I'm doing.

CHRIS: Join the club. It's like some strange heterosexual gypsy curse has been put on this place tonight. How's the orgy room doing?

PROCLO: I haven't—

CHRIS: The steam room?

PROCLO: No.

CHRIS: The pool? The sauna? The dormitory?

PROCLO: Sorry.

CHRIS: Well no wonder you haven't made out.

PROCLO: I don't want to make out.

CHRIS: Who are you trying to kid? This is me, sweetheart, your Aunt Chris. (*He starts pounding on closed doors.*) Fire drill! Everybody out for fire drill! (*A door opens. A patron looks out.*) I'm sorry. I thought this was the powder room.

PATRON: We're busy.

CHRIS: (*To Proclo.*) You like this one?

PROCLO: No!

CHRIS: Neither do I!

PATRON: I said we're busy! (*He slams the door.*)

CHRIS: You've got my son in there. Tell him his mother wants to see him.

PATRON: (*From behind the door.*) Buzz off!

CHRIS: One mark on that boy's body, Wanda, and I'm calling the police! (*To Proclo.*) Well I tried.

PROCLO: Really. I don't want you to do anything for me.

CHRIS: You're not going to believe this line, but "You're new around here, aren't you?"

PROCLO: I'm afraid so.

CHRIS: I never forget a face and I've seen a lot of faces in this place. Some people think I'm a sex maniac. They're right. If I don't get laid at least twice a day I go home and beat my dog. Here's hoping for you, Jeanette! (*He offers a "popper" to Proclo, who shakes his head no.*) It's fantastic stuff. I got it from this queen I know who just got back from a hairdresser's convention in Tokyo. He does Barbra Streisand's hair, so they gave him the Gene Hersholt Humanitarian Award. (H*e laughs and backslaps Proclo.*) Come on, I'll show you around.

PROCLO: That's all right. I was just going back to my room.

CHRIS: Come *on!* I don't do this for everyone. I'm an expert guide. A lesser person would charge for this sort of tour.

PROCLO: There's something I better tell you.

CHRIS: Sweetheart, relax, you're not my type. I just want to help you find yours. (*To a snotty patron who is walking by.*) Hi. (*Snooty Patron turns his back.*) We said hello. (*Snooty Patron turns his back some more. Chris turns to Proclo, gives him an eye signal and starts talking to him in a very loud voice.*) Do I know her? Darling, she is what is known as a Famous Face. She's out cruising 24 hours a day. She must live in a pup tent on Sheridan Square. If I had a nickel for every pair of shoes she's gone through . . . ! (*Snooty patron finally turns around and glares at him.*) Margaret Dumont! I though you were dead!

SNOOTY PATRON: There's a reason some of us don't ride the subways and I'm looking right at him. (*He huffs off.*)

CHRIS: Is that supposed to mean me? (*After him.*) Screw you, honey! (*To Proclo.*) One thing I can't stand is a queen without a sense of humor. (*After him.*) You can die with your secret! (*To Proclo.*) Miserable piss-elegant fairy.

PROCLO: I have to tell you something. I'm afraid I'm not a . . .(*He will try to convey something with his hands.*)

CHRIS: You're not gay?

PROCLO: No.

CHRIS: Then what are you doing here?

PROCLO: That's what I'd like to know.

CHRIS: Baby, you're very much in the minority around here.

PROCLO: That's what I'm afraid of.

CHRIS: Or maybe you're not and that's why I'm having such rotten luck tonight. What are you? A social worker or something?

PROCLO You mean *everybody* here is . . . ?

CHRIS: Gay. It's not such a tough word. You might try using it some time.

PROCLO: Nobody is . . . the opposite?

CHRIS: I sure as hell hope not. I didn't pay ten bucks to walk around in a towel with a bunch of Shriners.

PROCLO: What about Tiger and Duff?

CHRIS: What about them?

PROCLO: I thought they were normal.

CHRIS: They are normal. They've also been lovers for three years.

PROCLO: I'm sorry. I didn't mean it like that.

CHRIS: Yes, you did.

PROCLO: Yes, I did.

CHRIS: I'll tell you something about straight people, and sometimes I think it's the only thing worth knowing about them. They don't like gays. They never have. They never will. Anything else they say is just talk.

PROCLO: That's not true.

CHRIS: Think about it.

PROCLO: I'm sorry. I didn't know what I was getting into when I came in here tonight. I'm in trouble, I'm scared and I'm confused. I'm sorry.

CHRIS: That's okay.

PROCLO: You're gonna think I'm crazy but somebody is planning to kill me tonight. My own brother-in-law.

CHRIS: Are you putting me on?

PROCLO: I wish I were. And if Carmine caught me in a place like this he'd have *double* grounds for murder.

CHRIS: What do you mean?

PROCLO: My brother-in-law. For twelve years I was the butt of every sissy joke played at Our Lady of Perpetual Sorrow. It was a good name for that place. And then, when I married his only sister . . .! They're very close, even for Italian brothers and sisters, and you know what they're like. (*He claps his hands together.*) Cement! Except for Vivian, Vivian's my wife, that whole family's always hated me. At our wedding, her own mother had a heart attack while we were exchanging vows. Vivian said "I do" to me and Mamma Vespucci keeled right over in the front pew.

CHRIS: It's kind of funny.

PROCLO: Not when it happens to you. Yesterday, at their own father's funeral even, Carmine had all the relatives giving me that look.

CHRIS: What look?

PROCLO: That look. (*He gives a look.*)

CHRIS: I would've laid him out.

PROCLO: That's you.

CHRIS: Why didn't you?

PROCLO: The truth? I'm scared to death of him. I guess I always have been.

CHRIS: Maybe that's why he always hated you.

PROCLO: "Get Proclo." Those were their father's dying words. Do you believe it? This far from his Maker and all he can say is "Get Proclo."

CHRIS: Get Proclo?

PROCLO: That's me. With their father dead now, there's a lot of money involved that Carmine would love to screw me out of. And I'm not so sure it's particularly clean money. Carmine can chase me all over town but this is one night he's not gonna "Get Proclo."

CHRIS: And you picked a gay baths to hide out in?

PROCLO: I didn't pick it exactly. I asked my cab driver to take me to the last place in the world anybody would think of looking for me.

CHRIS: Don't worry, you found it.

PROCLO: Only now I've got a chubby chaser and someone who thinks I'm a producer after me.

CHRIS: Listen, it beats someone like your brother-in-law trying to kill you. Why don't you just stay in your room and try to get some sleep?

PROCLO: Sleep!

CHRIS: Strange as it may seem, no one's gonna attack you.

PROCLO: Somebody already has.

CHRIS: Beginner's luck! Standing around out here like this, you're just asking for it. Go to your room.

PROCLO: I can't! I locked myself out!

CHRIS: Well try and find Tiger and Duff. They'll let you in. Now if you'll excuse me, darling, I want to try my luck in there. Us B-girls work better solo.

PROCLO: See you.

CHRIS: See you. (*He throws open the door to the steam room and blows the whistle.*) Hello, everybody, my name is June! What's yours? (*He is gone. Proclo is alone. He stands undecided for a moment but we can see that his curiosity is getting the better of him. He opens the door to the steam room and peers in. He goes in. The door closes. There is a long pause. The stage is empty. And at once, Proclo comes bursting out of the steam room. You have never seen anyone move as fast. He comes tearing down the stairs and runs into Duff.*)

PROCLO: The key to 196, quick!

DUFF: You're supposed to wear it.

PROCLO: I know!

DUFF: What's the matter?

PROCLO: Just let me in, please.

DUFF: Try to hang onto your key from here on out, okay?

PROCLO: Believe me, I'll make every effort. (*He is admitted.*) Thank you.

DUFF: The show's about to get started.

PROCLO: (*Puffing for breath.*) Fine, fine!

DUFF: You won't be late?

PROCLO: Of course not!

DUFF: Googie's all keyed up.

PROCLO: So am I, so am I!

DUFF: Thanks a million for helping us out like this, Mr. Vespucci.

PROCLO: Tell me something, you and Tiger are . . . lovers?

DUFF: Three years. I think that's pretty good, don't you?

PROCLO: It's terrific.

DUFF: I better get ready. See you downstairs! (*He goes, closing the door.*)

PROCLO: I wouldn't go down there and see *her* act for a—! Her act? Of course I knew there was something funny about that Gomez woman. She's not a woman! Female impersonators . . . chubby chasers . . . B-girls . . . Baby Junes! When I grow another head is when I'm gonna leave this room! (*He sits on the bed, exhausted. Where to go now? What to do? His eyes go to the Panettone. He looks a little more cheerful. Meanwhile, Michael has raced back to the area of the telephones and dialed a number.)*

MICHAEL: Bimbi's? Oh! Mr. Vespucci. Michael Brick. No one fits your description. It's pretty hard getting the goods on someone you've never see. And you didn't tell me about that steam room. (*We see Googie entering. She sees Michael. She stops. She eavesdrops.*) If you need me I'm at 929-9929. And I'm in room 101. 101!

GOOGIE: Room 101!

MICHAEL: He's here again. (*Michael hangs up and hurries off.*)

GOOGIE: I'll be there, *chico.* Googie's gonna straighten you out between shows. (*She turns to Proclo's room. Proclo is eating his Panettone when she knocks on the door. He jumps.*) Guess who, Mr. Vespucci? (*More knocking. Proclo tries to ignore it but it is very urgent. Finally he goes to the door and opens it a crack. A fatal mistake.*)

PROCLO: Now wait a minute! (*Googie barges in and closes the door.*)

GOOGIE: I know what you're going to say.

PROCLO: You couldn't possibly!

GOOGIE: I don't believe in bugging producers just before they catch your act, so I just want to tell you one thing. In my second number, "Shine On Harvest Moon," the orchestra and me sometimes get into different keys, but if you know that it won't matter. Other than that, the act is fabulous and I just know you're gonna love it.

PROCLO: I'm sure of it!

GOOGIE: You know what *guapo* means? Handsome.

PROCLO: Oh no, I'm ugly. I'm very, very ugly.

GOOGIE: With a face like that, you could've been an actor. You still could. It's never too late. Look at Caterina Valente or Charo or Vicki Carr.

PROCLO: Of course they're *real* women.

GOOGIE: Oh no!

PROCLO: They're not?

GOOGIE: Plastic Puerto Ricans. I am the real thing. You are the real thing and I knew you were in show business.

PROCLO: Me?

GOOGIE: I knew I'd seen you someplace.

PROCLO: I was in the Cleveland Little Theatre Masque and Mummer's spring production of "The Sound of Music," but I'd hardly call that show business.

GOOGIE: Oh yeah? What part?

PROCLO: It was really more of a walk-on.

GOOGIE: I was in that show.

PROCLO: You were in "The Sound of Music"?

GOOGIE: Oh sure.

PROCLO: Where was this?

GOOGIE: Broadway, the Main Stem, where else?

PROCLO: The original cast?

GOOGIE: I was more original than anyone else in it. They fired me the first day of rehearsal, those bastards. They said I wasn't right for the part.

PROCLO: What part was that?

GOOGIE: One of those fucking Trapp kids. But you know what the real reason was, mister?

PROCLO: They found out what you really were?

GOOGIE: Seymour Pippin!

PROCLO: Who?

GOOGIE: Seymour Pippin! If there's one man in this whole world I was born to kill with my own two hands it is Seymour Pippin. You want to hear something funny? If you didn't have all that hair you would look a lot like him and I would probably fly into a rage and tear all your eyes out! I never forget that face and I never forgive. He was the company manager and if there is one thing worse than a producer or a press agent, it is a company manager.

PROCLO: It *is* a family show.

GOOGIE: But I fix them. I picket that show till they was crazy. I picket, I picket, I picket. Every night! They couldn't stop me. I picket that show every night until I got a part in "Camelot."

PROCLO: You were in "Camelot," too?

GOOGIE: Oh sure.

PROCLO: That's a wonderful show.

GOOGIE: It's a piece of shit.

PROCLO Oh, they fired you from that one, too?

GOOGIE: Sure they fired me! What do you expect? Thanks to Seymour Pippin I get fired from everything.

PROCLO: I can't imagine why.

GOOGIE: You see this face? It's a curse! (*She is moving in for the kill.*

Proclo is backing off, horrified.)

PROCLO: Keep away!

GOOGIE: Don't fight it, *chico!*

PROCLO: Believe me, you won't be happy! I won't be happy! You're making a terrible mistake.

GOOGIE: I am suddenly all woman.

PROCLO: No you're not. You're someone with a lot of problems.

GOOGIE: Make me feel like a real woman, *chico.*

PROCLO: I can't help you out in that department! It's out of my hands.

GOOGIE: Kiss me! (*Sounds of an orchestra striking up.*) Oh shit! That's my music! (*She is dragging Proclo by the hand. She throws open the door.*) Come on my Mr. Big Producer. You're gonna love my show. I got you the best seats. I see you ringside. We save the hanky-panky for later. (*Googie hurries off.*)

PROCLO: Ringside! Hanky-panky! What am I doing here? (*Claude appears on the third level.*)

CLAUDE: Vespucci!

PROCLO: It *is* the same Claude Perkins. We were in the Army together. Compared to those two, Carmine wanting to kill me is sanity! (*He rushes off, followed by Claude.*)

CLAUDE: I warned you, Vespucci! You promised, I waited, and you didn't come! Hey, where are you? (*The music is building as the lights dim and the nightclub, complete with twinkle lights and mylar, flies in.*)

ABE: (*Over the loudspeaker.*) And now, on the great Ritz stage, direct from her record-breaking bus and truck tour with "Fiddler on the Roof," the sensational Googie Gomez! With Duff and Tiger, those amazing now you see it, now you don't golden go-go boys! (*There is a roll of drums.*) Here's Duff. (*Duff runs on. Another roll of drums.*) Here's Tiger. (*Tiger makes a great entrance. Another roll of drums.*) And here's Googie! (*Googie bursts on and launches into her first number. She is very bad but very funny. It's the kind of number you watch in disbelief. Sincerity is what saves her. Such a lack of talent is appalling, yes, but it does come straight from the heart. Tiger and Duff are doing their best, too. They dance well enough and they look pretty good up there. When the number ends, during the applause, we see Proclo run across pursued by Claude. Googie, followed by Tiger and Duff, goes after them.*) Hey, wait a minute! Where are you going? I was just gonna introduce you! (*They are gone. Suddenly the figure of a very wet, very angry balding middle aged fat man comes storming through the mylar into Googie's spotlight.*)

CARMINE: I'm Carmine Vespucci of the Bensonhurst Vespuccis. I want a room in this here whorehouse and I don't want any shit. (*There is a mighty roll of drums as Scarpia's Theme from "Tosca" is heard. A crack of cymbals. Curtain.*)

ACT 2

Carmine is seen coming along the corridor. He is still in street clothes. He looks all around and then knocks softly on the door of Michael Brick's room.

CARMINE: Brick? Are you in there, Brick? It's Vespucci. Don't open. I don't want anyone to see us. If you can hear me, knock once. If you can't, knock twice. Are you there, Brick? (*Michael knocks once.*) Good. Our signals are working. Now listen to me, have you seen that balding fat brother-in-law of mine yet? (*Michael knocks twice.*) What does that mean? No? (*Michael knocks once.*) Okay, I think I read you. Now I know he's in here somewhere. What I don't know is how you could miss him. He's a house. Listen, Brick, none of these fruits tried to pull anything with you, did they? (*Michael knocks twice.*) You can thank Our Blessed Lady for that. Meet me in 102 in fifteen minutes. Knock three times. Got that? (*Michael knocks three times.*) Not now, stupid, then. And you don't have to worry about him leaving this place. Leaving it in one piece I should say. I got all my men outside. Ain't that great, Brick? Hunh? (*Michael knocks once.*) I knew you'd like that. Keep looking. (*Carmine goes into his room, starts to undress. We will see him take out a revolver, a stiletto, and a pair of brass knuckles. From offstage, Claude calls.*)

CLAUDE: Vespucci! (*Proclo appears on the third level and races into a room. Claude runs past the room and sees a patron.*) Say, have you seen a Vespucci go by? (*Proclo leaves his hiding place and heads down to the second level. Claude yells as he follows him down the stairs and they disappear.*) Vespucci! Vespucci! (*Googie appears and pokes her head into Proclo's room.*)

GOOGIE: Where are you hiding, Mr. Vespucci? (*She disappears. Proclo appears and starts down the stairs to his own room on the first level. Midway he crosses paths with Tiger and Duff.*)

TIGER: There you are!

DUFF: Why did you run away? (*Proclo escapes and continues down to his room. Tiger and Duff disappear, looking for Googie. Meanwhile Googie appears in a corridor, now looking for Claude.*)

GOOGIE: Where is this person who ruin my act? Where is this skinny little man? I kill him! (*She disappears. Tiger and Duff appear and criss-cross again.*)

TIGER: Googie! Googie!

DUFF: Googie! Googie! (*They are gone. As soon as Proclo reaches his room, Claude comes down the corridor looking for him. He opens the door, but Proclo has hidden behind it.*)

CLAUDE: Vespucci! (*As he leaves, he shuts the door, revealing Proclo, who quickly makes the sign of the cross and starts gathering his things. Meanwhile Googie has appeared down the corridor. She sneaks up on Claude and tears his robe off.*)

GOOGIE: Ah hah! *Carbron!* (*Claude races off, pursued by Googie, who is in turn pursued by Tiger and Duff.*)

TIGER: Googie!

DUFF: Googie! (*They are all gone. Proclo is in a terrific hurry. We can hear him muttering to himself as he frantically packs his bag.*)

PROCLO: I'd rather spend the night in Central Park in the rain than spend another minute in this place! They're all mad! I thought *I* had problems! If I ever get my hands on that cab driver, he's finished! So long, room, I won't miss you. (*He comes out of the room carrying his clothes, his suitcase and the box of Panettone. He slams the door.*) Hello, Cleveland! (*He sees a patron walking by.*) Which is the way out of here?

PATRON: That way. (*Proclo goes up the stairs to the second level, looking for an exit. Claude appears on a side balcony.*)

CLAUDE: Vespucci! Vespucci! (*Proclo has made his decision: it's the steam room or else. He goes rushing in with his clothes, his suit-*

case and the Panettone. Claude leaps over the balcony in hot pursuit.)

CLAUDE: I hope you know what a cul-de-sac is, because you're in one. *(He goes into the steam room. Now Googie enters on the rampage. We see her tearing up and down the corridors, Tiger and Duff following, trying to clam her down.)*

GOOGIE: Where is this skinny little man who chase a producer out of my number? No one chases no producer out of Googie Gomez' number! *(She is pounding on doors. One of them is opened by the patron in chaps.)*

PATRON IN CHAPS: Howdy, pardner.

GOOGIE: Don't howdy me, you big leather sissy! *(She pushes him back into the room.)* You think I don't know what goes on around this place? All you men going hee-hee-hee, poo-poo-poo, hah-hah-hah! I get my boyfriend Hector in here with his hombres and he kill you all! *(She is heading for the steam room.)*

DUFF: You can't go in there!

TIGER: Googie, no! *(Googie storms into the steam room, Tiger and Duff following. The door closes behind them. A moment later, Googie lets out a muffled yell.)*

GOOGIE: *Pendego!* *(Patrons start streaming out. Googie goes right after them. She has Claude firmly in tow.)* There will be no more hee-hee-hee, poo-poo-poo, hah-hah-hah around this place tonight! *(She slings Claude across the hall.)*

CLAUDE: You're hurting me!

GOOGIE: I'm just getting started! *(Tiger and Duff attempt to subdue her.)*

CLAUDE: You could use a good psychiatrist, mister!

GOOGIE: What did you call me?

TIGER: He didn't mean it!

GOOGIE: What you call me?

TIGER: Tell her you're sorry!

CLAUDE: I haven't seen such tacky drag since the Princeton Varsity Show!

GOOGIE: Tacky drag?

CLAUDE: Thirty years ago, sonny! *(Googie has gotten herself into good street-fighting position by now. With a bloodcurdling yell she leaps for Claude and chases him off, Tiger and Duff close behind. The stage is bare for a moment. We hear Claude.*)

CLAUDE: Help! (*From the yell, it sounds as if Googie's got him. The steam room door opens and Chris comes out.*)

CHRIS: I'm going straight. (*Suddenly the steam room door slams open and Proclo, or what's left of him, staggers out. He is fully dressed, wearing the wig, dark glasses and moustache from his first entrance, and carrying his suitcase. He has visibly wilted. He doesn't seem to know where he is.*)

PROCLO: I don't believe this whole night.

CHRIS: Were you in there for all that? (*Proclo just nods.*) Where? (*Proclo just shrugs.*) You don't want to talk about it? (*Proclo just shakes his head.*) Why are you wearing your clothes?

PROCLO: I'm going to Central Park.

CHRIS: I thought you were going to stay in your room.

PROCLO: (*Blindly walking downstairs.*) I can't. I told Googie I was Carmine Vespucci. Claude thinks I'm Carmine Vespucci. Everybody thinks I'm Carmine Vespucci.

CHRIS: Well who are you?

PROCLO: Tonight I'm Carmine Vespucci.

CHRIS: I give up! (*Chris sees Michael Brick coming along a corridor.*) What have we here? Now this is a little more like it. Play it cool, Chris. (*He arranges himself attractively.*) If you don't mind, Mr. Vespucci, I'd like to try my luck with this one. Hey, Vespucci, I'm talking to you. Snap out of it!

MICHAEL: Are you Mr. Carmine Vespucci, sir?

CHRIS: You live around here, kid?

MICHAEL: No, I came in from Astoria. Are you Mr. Vespucci?

CHRIS: Say yes, say yes!

PROCLO: Yes!

MICHAEL: I'm Michael Brick. My room's right over here. (*He will start leading Proclo to his room.*)

CHRIS: Hi, I'm Chris. My room's right up there.

MICHAEL: Hi, Chris. (*Michael and Proclo have gone into Michael's room and closed the door.*) Am I glad to see you, Mr. Vespucci. (*Chris has been watching their encounter in envy and disbelief.*)

CHRIS: I don't date out-of-towners. (*He starts to exit, but is stopped by the ring of the pay phone. He answers it with an enormous scream of frustration. He hangs up and disappears. A somewhat still-*

dazed Proclo is sitting in Michael's room.)

MICHAEL: Now this is what I thought we'd do. Get under the bed.

PROCLO: (*Beginning to cry.*) Another one!

MICHAEL: All right, stay there. We'll pretend you're him and I'm me and the real you is under the bed.

PROCLO: (*Tears are really flowing.*) Only this one's the worst.

MICHAEL: Now get the picture. The lights are low, he's moving down the hallway and he sees me leaning against the door. I flex for him. Pecks and biceps are supposed to be a turn on. Don't ask me why. I catch his eye. I've got a cigarette dangling from my lips, I put one knee up, I wink, I kind of beckon with my head and finally I speak. "See something you like, buddy?" That's the tough guy approach.

PROCLO: Is that your own voice?

MICHAEL: Yes.

PROCLO: I mean, your real voice?

MICHAEL: Yes.

PROCLO: Your natural speaking one?

MICHAEL: Yes.

PROCLO: Thank you.

MICHAEL: Why? Does it bother you?

PROCLO: Oh no, no, no!

MICHAEL: Some people find it very irritating.

PROCLO: I can't see why.

MICHAEL: Me either. But of course I'm used to it. I've had it ever since I was a kid. I mean, I grew up and matured, only my voice didn't. Where was I?

PROCLO: The tough guy approach.

MICHAEL: Oh! And *then* . . . and this is where you're going to have to jump out—

PROCLO: I am having a nightmare.

MICHAEL: Very, very, very casually . . .

PROCLO: I can hardly wait.

MICHAEL: I thought I'd let my hand just kind of graze against my . . . (*He hesitates, then whispers in Proclo's ear.*)

PROCLO: I'm getting out of here!

MICHAEL: (*Pulling him down.*) But you're going to have to help me catch your brother-in-law, Mr. Vespucci.

PROCLO: My brother-in-law?

MICHAEL: I haven't seen anyone who fits Mr. Proclo's description.

PROCLO: Proclo? My brother-in-law?

MICHAEL: The balding middle-aged fat man you hired me to catch.

PROCLO: Where do you know my brother-in-law from?

MICHAEL: I don't yet. That's why I called you at that bar across the street.

PROCLO: What bar?

MICHAEL: Where you and your men have this place surrounded so Mr. Proclo can't leave in one piece.

PROCLO: Who are you?

MICHAEL: Michael Brick, sir.

PROCLO: What are you?

MICHAEL: A detective. (*Michael is suddenly alerted by the alarm on his wristwatch.*) It's time!

PROCLO: For what?

MICHAEL: Get under the bed. He'll see you.

PROCLO: Who will?

MICHAEL: Your brother-in-law. He'll be here any second. Since I couldn't find Mr. Proclo I'm making him find me. I left a note by the coke machines saying "Any middle-aged balding fat man whose initials are G.P. interested in a good time should meet me in Room 101 at midnight sharp." When he gets here you're gonna have to help me. You see, I'm not queer.

PROCLO: (*Already climbing under the bed.*) You could've fooled me.

MICHAEL: I'm right on top of you.

PROCLO: I can't tell you how comforting that is. (*Chris is seen moving along the corridors, playing "The Lady or the Tiger." He knocks softly at different doors, and finally on Carmine's.*)

CARMINE: I said knock three times!

CHRIS: He's being masterful with me already, the brute. (*He knocks three times.*)

CARMINE: That's more like it.

CHRIS: I think I'm in love. (*Carmine opens the door and pulls Chris violently into the room slamming the door behind them.*)

CARMINE: Quick! Don't let anyone see you. Now let me get a look at you. (*He circles Chris appraisingly.*) I'm not a judge of fruit bait, but I guess you'll do.

CHRIS: Just cool it, sweetheart. This isn't the meat rack.

CARMINE: You can can the fag act with me, Brick. Now listen, I think I've come up with something. I know this sounds like the oldest stunt in the book, but I'm going to hide under your bed.

CHRIS: On the contrary, it's a first.

CARMINE: You never tried the old under-the-bed technique?

CHRIS: Not recently.

CARMINE: What kind of a detective are you?

CHRIS: That's a good question, honey.

CARMINE: Can it, Brick, just can it. One thing I don't like is a wise guy. The only thing I don't like more is a queer wise guy. I'm calling the shots now and I'm getting under your bed.

CHRIS: Where am I supposed to be?

CARMINE: On top of it, stupid!

CHRIS: It sounds fabulous. Then what?

CARMINE: You know, do what you have to do.

CHRIS: What's that?

CARMINE: How should I know? Wiggle your fanny, shake your towel in his face.

CHRIS: Whose face?

CARMINE: My brother-in-law's, you dummy! The guy I hired you to catch. And then I pop out, catching you both in the act of fragrant delicto and whammo! I got him.

CHRIS: Your brother-in-law?

CARMINE: Who else? Jesus, you're like talking to a yo-yo.

CHRIS: Dumb and dizzy, that's me, darling! (*In a very "butch" voice.*) Just a little more of that gay humor. Ho ho ho!

CARMINE: All right, now you go back to 101. (*Chris desperately starts to leave.*) Not yet! If the coast is clear, whistle like this . . . (*He whistles with two fingers.*) . . . and I'll high tail it to your room and slide right under and we're in business. Got that?

CHRIS: Check.

CARMINE: It's about time.

CHRIS: Only I can't whistle.

CARMINE: Goddamnit, you can't whistle either?

CHRIS: Tell you what, Mr. . . .

CARMINE: Vespucci, Carmine Vespucci. Only don't call me that! He might hear us. I need a code name.

CHRIS: Evelyn.

CARMINE: Naw, I don't like Evelyn. Sounds effeminate.

CHRIS: How about Bunny?

CARMINE: Okay, Bunny.

CHRIS: All right then, Bunny, you get under *this* bed. That way I won't have to whistle and you won't have to high tail it to 101.

CARMINE: Maybe you're not so dumb after all, Brick.

CHRIS: Just to refresh my memory, give me his name again.

CARMINE: It's Proclo, Gaetano Proclo.

CHRIS: What did he do?

CARMINE: He married my sister. I told her. I pleaded with her. I was on my knees to her. "Viv, honey, marry this Proclo character and you're marrying to stick a knife in me." She loves him, she tells me. Well I hate him, I tell her. I've always hated him. He's not of the family. He's not like us. He don't belong in Poppa's business. But she wouldn't listen to me. And so what happens? Twenty years she thinks she's happily married, my sister, but the truth is it's twenty years she's been a martyr, that woman. My sister is a saint and she don't even know it. I'll tell you one thing: with Poppa gone now . . . (*He breaks into uncontrollable sobs.*) . . . Poppa, God bless him . . . I ain't sharing Vespucci Sanitation Services and Enterprises, Inc., with no fairy!

CHRIS: Your brother-in-law is a fairy?

CARMINE: He's gonna be when I get through with him.

CHRIS: What are you going to do to him?

CARMINE: I'm gonna kill him!

CHRIS: Good!

CARMINE: You know what a *delitto di passione* is, Brick? 'Cause you're gonna see one tonight. A crime of passion. An enraged brother catching his dear sweet sister's balding fat slob husband in an unnatural act with one of these these fruitcakes around here! There's no court in the country that would convict me. Twenty years I waited for this night. You're looking at a man of great and terrible Italian passions, Brick.

CHRIS: I can see that, Bunny. (*He turns off the room lights.*)

CARMINE: What happened?

CHRIS: That's how they do it here. Now get under the bed. I'm leaving the door open so he can come in. Once he gets here, you take it from there. I'm right on top of you. Now don't say another word. (*Chris has tiptoed out of the room, leaving the door ajar and Carmine under the bed. He knocks on Michael's door.*)

MICHAEL: That must be your brother-in-law, Mr. Vespucci!

PROCLO (*Ready to meet his Maker.*) I'm sure it is.

MICHAEL: (*Unlocking the closed door.*) Hold, your horses, stud! (*He stretches out on the bed. We see Proclo's face looking out from the foot of the bed.*) It's open! (*Chris enters.*) See something you like, buddy?

CHRIS: You've got to be kidding.

MICHAEL: False alarm, Mr. Vespucci.

CHRIS: Where's your friend?

MICHAEL: He's under the bed.

CHRIS: Why not? Everybody else is. I always wondered what you straight guys did together. Now that I know, I'm glad I'm gay. If you didn't have all that hair, I'd ask you if your name was Guy something.

PROCLO: (*Crawling out from under the bed.*) It is.

CHRIS: And you really do have a garbage man brother-in-law who's out looking for you, don't you?

PROCLO: Unh-hunh!

CHRIS: Well, the maniac is right across the hall and he's got a gun. I just thought I'd mention it.

MICHAEL: Now he's after you, Mr. Vespucci! And you didn't mention anything about a gun. (*Googie appears in the corridor and knocks on the door.*) I'm scared! (*Chris dives under the bed.*)

PROCLO: You're scared? Move over!

CHRIS: There's not enough room.

PROCLO: I can fit.

CHRIS: I was here first.

PROCLO: It's my brother-in-law!

CHRIS: It's my ass! (*Michael has opened the door a crack and peeked out. Now he slams it shut and dives under the bed from the other side. Proclo still hasn't managed to get under.*)

PROCLO: Where do you think you're going?

MICHAEL: It's not him, Mr. Vespucci!

PROCLO: Well who is it then?

MICHAEL: It's that transvestite again!

PROCLO: What are you talking about? (*The knocking is getting louder.*) Who's there?

GOOGIE: I know you're in there, *chico!*

PROCLO: Oh, no! (*He goes to the door and opens it. Googie comes flying in, closing the door behind her and clapping one hand over Proclos mouth.*) Now, look—!

GOOGIE: Don't speak. Don't say nothing. Say one word and Googie's out on her ass. She's breaking every book in the rule doing this. (*She has pushed Proclo onto the bed and is lying on top of him.*) You know why you don't like women? Because you never tried it, that's all. Or maybe you did and that's why. She was a bad woman. Forget her. Believe me, *chico,* it don't hurt. It's nice. It's very nice. Just lie back and Googie's gonna show you how nice.

PROCLO: Look, I'd like to help you out—!

GOOGIE: Think of a tropical night! A beach.

PROCLO: What beach?

GOOGIE: The moon is shining on the sea and in the distance, over the waves, you hear music . . . (*She sings.*) "Besame, besame mucho!" (*Proclo is terrified. Almost involuntarily, under the bed, Michael and Chris join in singing. For several moments, there is almost a trio going between them, as Googie tries to take off Proclo's clothes.*)

GOOGIE, MICHAEL, and CHRIS: *Como si fuera esta noche/La ultima vez/ Besame, besame mucho/ Piensa que tal vez mañana/ Estare lejos muy lejos/ De ti.* (*Suddenly, Proclo comes back to his senses.*)

PROCLO: This isn't going to work out, Mr. Googie!

GOOGIE: Mister?

PROCLO: There's just no way!

GOOGIE: Mister? You thought I was a drag queen? No such luck, *chico!*

PROCLO: You really are a miss?

GOOGIE: This is all real. (*She has clasped his hands to her breasts. Proclo can't believe what he is feeling. His voice goes up at least an octave.*)

PROCLO: It feels real, it feels real!

GOOGIE: I just hope I'm gonna find me some *huevitos.*

PROCLO: What are *huevitos?*

GOOGIE: (*Finding them under his raincoat.*) Ay ay ay!

PROCLO: They're real, too!

GOOGIE: We're gonna make such a whoopee, *chico!*

PROCLO: Thank you.

GOOGIE: Thank you? You're gonna thank me.

PROCLO: The trouble is my bother-in-law is trying to kill me and there's someone under this bed.

GOOGIE: Oh no you don't! I'm not falling for that old hat and dance routine. You're not pulling no wool over my ears so easy.

PROCLO: I swear to God there is!

GOOGIE: Never try to shit an old pro, *chico.*

MICHAEL: He's not! There is someone under this bed.

CHRIS: Us! And if you two want to bounce around like that I'll gladly go back to my own room.

GOOGIE: (*Leaping off the bed.*) That's a rotten stunt, mister. I could lose my job for this. I told you: I threw wind in caution coming down here!

PROCLO: It's really very simple.

GOOGIE: I don't need no explaining. You rather make hee-hee-hee, poo-poo-poo, hah-hah-hah with that *maricon* you got hiding under the bed!

CHRIS: Two *maricons,* Googie!

GOOGIE: Who's that down there?

CHRIS: It's me, Chris.

GOOGIE: Hi, Chris. What are you doing down there?

CHRIS: I wish I knew.

MICHAEL: (*Poking his head out now.*) The reason we're under this bed—

GOOGIE: You!

MICHAEL: Now wait!

GOOGIE: Not only you got a fat boyfriend, you *maricon* hump—you got a mean one! (*She is hitting Michael with the pillow.*)

MICHAEL: I'm not his boyfriend!

PROCLO: He's not!

MICHAEL: And I'm not gay!

GOOGIE: With a voice like that you're no straight arrow either.

MICHAEL: I was born with this voice.

GOOGIE: So was Yma Sumac. I saw you talking on the telephone and I said, "Googie, that boy could make your blood go boil."

PROCLO: I thought you said that about me.

GOOGIE: I say that about everyone. (*Proclo is making an escape.*) Where are you going?

PROCLO: Look, I'm just someone who's in a lot of trouble, lady.

GOOGIE: You're not staying for my second show?

PROCLO: I'm not a producer. It was all your two friends' idea. Now if you'd just let me get out of here—

GOOGIE: Hey, now wait a minute!

PROCLO: Now what?

GOOGIE: Wait just one big fat minute! (*She grabs for Proclo's wig. It comes off.*)

PROCLO: Hey!

GOOGIE: I thought maybe it was you!

PROCLO: Who are you talking about?

GOOGIE: Seymour Pippin! You don't fire Googie Gomez from no show and get away with it. (*She is trying to kill Proclo.*) You think I forget a face like yours, you bastard? I'm gonna tear your eyes out! (*Chris and Michael will eventually subdue her.*)

CHRIS: It's not him, Googie.

MICHAEL: That's Mr. Vespucci.

GOOGIE: You promise?

PROCLO: I promise.

GOOGIE: I thought you was Seymour Pippin.

PROCLO: I wish I were.

GOOGIE: What do you know? I thought he was Seymour Pippin!

MICHAEL: Seymour Pippin! (*Carmine has come out of his room and knocks on the door.*)

PROCLO: Oh my God! (*They all start scrambling for a place under the bed.*)

GOOGIE: What about me?

CHRIS: That's my place!

MICHAEL: Hurry up!

GOOGIE: Suck your gut in!

PROCLO: I am!

GOOGIE: More!

PROCLO: Who is that?

CHRIS: Relax, mister. I told you: you're not my type.

PROCLO: Well just get your hand off my—.

GOOGIE: It's okay! It's my hand.

MICHAEL: If it's him, Mr. Vespucci, just give me the word. (*Proclo, Chris, and Googie have somehow all managed to squeeze under the bed. Michael opens the door. Carmine storms in.*)

CARMINE: What the hell happened to you? You said you'd be on top! I've been under that damn bed so long I can hardly walk! (*As he turns he sees Michael, who has gone into his flexing routine.*)

MICHAEL: See something you like, buddy?

CARMINE: What the—?

MICHAEL: You new around here, mac?

CARMINE: You're not Brick! Where's Brick? What have you done to him?

MICHAEL: Lie down.

CARMINE: Get your hands off me! (*Michael shoves Carmine onto the bed. Googie cries out.*)

GOOGIE: Ow! *Ay, cono!*

PROCLO: Sshh!

CARMINE: What the—?

MICHAEL: Relax.

CARMINE: Somebody's under there!

MICHAEL: Just stretch out on the bed, now.

CARMINE: What are you doing in here?

MICHAEL: Just relax: I'm trying to seduce you.

CARMINE: Get your hands off me, you goddamn Greek, or I'll lay your head open.

MICHAEL: (*Pinning Carmine down.*) Is it him, Mr. Vespucci?

PROCLO: Yes!

CARMINE: Vespucci? I'm Vespucci.

MICHAEL: Is it?

PROCLO: Yes, yes! It's him! It's him!

CARMINE: I know that voice! (*He leans over the bed just as Googie rolls out.*) What the hell is this? One of them goddamn transvestites, sure you are!

GOOGIE: Seymour Pippin! (*She is attacking Carmine, swatting him with a pillow.*)

CARMINE: Fight fair, you faggot! (*Michael knocks Carmine out with a karate blow.*)

MICHAEL: Hi-ya! (*Carmine falls onto the bed. Proclo groans.*)

GOOGIE: Aw, shit! Why you do that? I was gonna fix his wagon for him good!

MICHAEL: He's out cold, Mr. Vespucci!

PROCLO: Just get me out of here.

CHRIS: And we were just starting to have so much fun!

GOOGIE: You know something? This man is not Seymour Pippin either. He sure got a mean face though! I wonder who he is. (*Proclo and Chris are up from under the bed now.*)

PROCLO: It's my brother-in-law.

GOOGIE: Is he in show business?

PROCLO: He's in garbage.

GOOGIE: A gay garbage man?

MICHAEL: You're sure it's him?

PROCLO: I'm afraid so.

GOOGIE: What are you two talking about?

MICHAEL: I'm a detective. Mr. Vespucci here hired me to get something on his brother-in-law Mr. Proclo there so Mr. Proclo doesn't inherit one-half the family business.

PROCLO: So that's it. (*He tries to strangle Carmine. The others hold him back.*)

MICHAEL: Mr. Vespucci wanted to catch us together so he could commit a *delitto di passione*. What's a *delitto di passione*, Mr. Vespucci? (*Again Proclo goes for Carmine's throat.*)

PROCLO: You're about to see one!

CHRIS: Hey, now take it easy! You can't do that!

PROCLO: *He* was going to! (*Michael has been getting ready to photograph Carmine on the bed.*)

MICHAEL: Look out now. You'll be in the picture.

CHRIS: (*Primping his hair.*) Picture? What picture? (*Suddenly Googie grabs the camera.*)

GOOGIE: Oh no! I see what you do! If that man want to be here, let him be here. What you care? I don't stand still for no blackmail! I tell Tiger and Duff what you do and you're out on your ass, big boy! Come on, Chris! (*She goes with the camera.*)

CHRIS: Excuse me, but I promised Mark Spitz we'd do a quick ten laps around the pool. (*He goes.*)

MICHAEL: Mark Spitz comes here, Mr. Vespucci?

PROCLO: I don't care!

MICHAEL: What should I do with him?

PROCLO: Kill him.

MICHAEL: I'm a private detective, Mr. Vespucci. I'm not a hit man.

PROCLO: You got something to tie him down with?

MICHAEL: Cuffs.

PROCLO: Hurry.

MICHAEL: Give me a hand with him, will you?

PROCLO: Can't you hit him again?

MICHAEL: That wouldn't be ethical, Mr. Vespucci.

PROCLO: Ethical? Your line of work and you're telling me what's ethical? Come on, let's get out of here.

MICHAEL: If you don't need me anymore, I want to find that Googie and get my camera back.

PROCLO: Fine, fine. (*Michael goes. Proclo stands looking after him, then down at Carmine on the bed.*) You blew it, Carmine. By the time you get out of this place I'll be back in Cleveland with Vivian and the kids. (*He goes, leaving the door open. He passes into Carmine's room. We will see him gather up Carmine's clothes as he yells out.*) Fat man in 101! Come and get it. Fat man in 101! He's all yours. Fat man in 101! (*As Proclo comes out of Carmine's room, he sees Tiger in the corridor.*)

PROCLO: Duff.

TIGER: I'm Tiger.

PROCLO: Whatever! Burn these for me, will you?

TIGER: Burn 'em?

PROCLO: You heard me.

TIGER: (*Scooping up Carmine's clothes.*) You're sounding happy.

PROCLO: I'm close to feeling terrific!

TIGER: What happened?

PROCLO: I'm catching the next plane to Cleveland.

TIGER: Good luck.

PROCLO: You're too late. I've already got it! (*Tiger is gone. Proclo grabs his suitcase and starts to head off. The pay phone rings and Michael answers it.*)

MICHAEL: Hello? This is The Ritz. Michael Brick speaking. It's for you, Mr. Vespucci.

PROCLO: Who is it?

MICHAEL: Who is this? It's Mrs. Proclo, calling from that bar across the street.

PROCLO: Mrs. Proclo? My God, it's Vivian. Tell her I've left.

MICHAEL: I'm sorry but he just left, Mrs. Proclo. She doesn't believe me.

PROCLO: Tell her she has to believe you.

MICHAEL: He says you have to believe me. She says she's not staying there another minute. She's taking a man's hat and raincoat and coming right over here and nothing's going to stop her. Hello . . . hello? (*He hangs up.*) I didn't even get to tell her the good news.

PROCLO: What good news?

MICHAEL: That we got our man! (*Googie is coming along on her way to the nightclub.*) Miss Gomez?

GOOGIE: Don't Miss Gomez me now, *chico.* I got a show to do.

MICHAEL: I can explain about downstairs.

GOOGIE: I don't talk to no detectives.

MICHAEL: Then about my camera! (*They are gone.*)

PROCLO: He'll kill me. She'll divorce me. My children will grow up hating my memory. Oh my God! (*Tiger is passing.*)

TIGER: What happened?

PROCLO: I just ran out of luck! There's a woman trying to get in here. Keep her out.

TIGER: They don't let ladies in here.

PROCLO: It's my wife.

TIGER: Relax. She'll never get past Abe. (*He is gone.*)

PROCLO: I did! (*He runs into his room. We see Claude come in behind him. Proclo doesn't. Yet. He sits on the bed and pants.*)

CLAUDE: Your door was open.

PROCLO: What?

CLAUDE: I'm giving you one more chance. (*He starts to sing his song.*) "Jelly Roll Baby/ You're my Jelly Roll Man. . ."

PROCLO: Please, I'm too weak.

CLAUDE: "Jelly Roll cupcake/I'm your Jelly Roll fan. . ."

PROCLO: Look, this is a lot of fun, I can't tell you! I don't know about you, Claude, but I'm in terrible trouble.

CLAUDE: Claude!

PROCLO: I didn't say that.

CLAUDE: Wait a minute! Wait a minute! Guy! It's you, Guy!

PROCLO: Absolutely no!

CLAUDE: Gaetano Proclo, the fifth division, Special Services, the Philippines.

PROCLO: I was 4-F. I never served.

CLAUDE: It's me, Claude! Claude Perkins!

PROCLO: Get away from me, Claude!

CLAUDE: That's right! "Get away from me," Claude! We had an act together. A trio with Nelson Carpenter. We pantomimed Andrew Sisters records. "Rum and Coca Cola." Remember?

PROCLO: I don't know what you're talking about. I hate the Andrew Sisters.

CLAUDE: You hate the Andrew Sisters?

PROCLO: Look, I'm in desperate, desperate trouble, mister, and I wish you'd just go away.

CLAUDE: Just wait until I write Nelson Carpenter about this!

ABE: (*Over the loudspeaker.*) 253 coming up! That's two-five-three. You're not going to believe what's coming up, boys!

PROCLO: O my God, it is Vivian!

CLAUDE: There are other fat fish in the ocean, Gaetano Proclo, and 253 just may be one of them.

PROCLO: Just don't touch 253, Claude!

CLAUDE: We'll see about that. (*He sweeps out. Proclo returns to his room, kneels beside his bed, and quietly begins to pray. The patron in chaps walks in on the awakening Carmine in Brick's room.*)

PATRON IN CHAPS: Howdy, pardner. Handcuffs? Outta sight! (*He sinks to his haunches and just stares. Tiger, Duff, Googie and Michael are running by. The three entertainers are dressed to go on.*)

GOOGIE: If I don't hit that note, cover for me.

DUFF: How?

GOOGIE: Take your clothes off! Anything!

MICHAEL: Miss Gomez! (*They are gone. Carmine is starting to come around. The patron in chaps is still staring.*)

PATRON IN CHAPS: Far out! Far out! (*Chris pokes his head into the room.*)

CHRIS: Hi, girls!

CARMINE: Brick!

CHRIS: Don't believe a word she says. She thinks she's a detective or something.

CARMINE: Who she? What she?

CHRIS: You she. And who do you think you are? Dale Evans? (*He starts to go.)*

CARMINE: Let me out of here! I'll kill you!

CHRIS: I've got a date with 253. (*He is gone.*)

CARMINE: Gaetano! Gaetano! (*The patron in chaps runs off. On the second level we see Vivian. She is wearing a man's hat and raincoat over her black pants suit. She carries a shopping bag. Chris approaches her.*)

CHRIS: I had a hunch it would be bad, but nothing like this. (*To Vivian.*) Welcome to the city morgue. (*Vivian recoils and lets out one her giant sobs: an unearthly sound.*)

VIVIAN: Aaaaaaaeeeeee!

CHRIS: Forget it, mister, that's not my scene! (*Opening the door to the steam room.*) Avon calling! (*He goes in. Claude has approached Vivian in the corridor, and again the strains of the "Now Voyager" theme are heard.*)

CLAUDE: Looking for 253? (*Vivian nods, stifling her sobs.*) Right this way. (*He leads her to his own room, of course, carefully concealing the number as they enter. He slams the door and start to sing.*) "Jelly Roll Baby/ You're my Jelly Roll Man . . ." (*Vivian really lets out a big sob as he starts moving toward her.*)

VIVIAN: Aaaaiiiiieeeee! (*No sooner does she scream than Vivian faints dead away on Claude's bed. At that moment, Carmine manages to free himself from his handcuffs by banging the bed noisily on the ground. Proclo, in his room, Carmine's threats and Vivian's screams ringing in his ears, is literally quivering, as he softly calls out.*)

PROCLO: Help. Help. Help. (*Carmine is on the rampage. He shoots the lock off his own door. The door gives and he runs in.*)

CARMINE: My clothes! Somebody took my clothes! (*He runs out of the room, brandishing the revolver.*) Okay, Gaetano! I know you're in here! I'm gonna find you if it's the last thing I do! (*He disappears. Meanwhile, Claude is trying to revive Vivian.*)

CLAUDE: All right, lie there like a beached whale. (*No response from Vivian.*) Look, I'd love to stay here and play Sleeping Beauty with you but I've got to get ready for the Talent Contest. (*He starts getting his things together for his record pantomime act.*) What's in the bag? You bring your own lunch? (*He is looking in Vivian's shopping bag.*)

ABE: (*Over the loudspeaker.*) Just a reminder, boys and girls. It's amateur night at The Ritz.

CHRIS: (*Coming out of the steam room.*) You can say that again!

CLAUDE: You've got to be kidding. (*He takes a long mink coat out of Vivian's shopping bag. He can't resist putting it on.*) What becomes a legend most? (*Carmine comes storming up to Chris.*)

CHRIS: Hi, Bunny. How's tricks?

CARMINE: You! (*He points his gun.*)

CHRIS: Is that thing loaded?

CARMINE: And you're lucky I'm not using it on you. Now where is he?

CHRIS: Who?

CARMINE: My brother-in-law, you dumb dick!

CHRIS: He was just here.

CARMINE: And?

CHRIS: He went in there. (*He motions towards Claude's room.*)

CARMINE: Well why didn't you say so?

CHRIS: I just did. You're really planning to shoot him?

CARMINE: *You* if he's not in there! (*Carmine starts for Claude's room. Chris hurries off in another direction. Carmine starts banging on Claude's door.*)

CLAUDE: Who's that?

CARMINE: You know goddamn well who it is. (*Claude opens the door, takes one look at Carmine, and starts his song.*)

CLAUDE: "Jelly Roll Baby/ You're my Jelly Roll . . ."

CARMINE: What the —? (*He pulls his gun.*) Get out of here! (*Claude escapes, taking his clothes and Vivian's mink with him. Carmine turns at a moan from Vivian on the bed.*) Okay, Gaetano, the jig is up! (*Then realizing who it is.*) Viv! Vivian, baby. What have they done to you? (*He tries to revive her.*) Speak to me, Viv! Viv! (*Chris has come up to Proclo's door. Proclo is slumped. He is too tired, too defeated, to call for help anymore.*)

CHRIS: It's me, Chris! Open the door! (*Proclo does.*) That brother-in-law of yours means business.

PROCLO: Why can't he just find me and get it over with?

CHRIS: You're just going to sit there?

PROCLO: What's the use?

CHRIS: Hide somewhere.

PROCLO: I came here. He found me.

CHRIS: Wear a disguise.

PROCLO: I am! (*He tears off his wig and moustache.*) I thought you were mad at me.

CHRIS: I am but I prefer you alive to dead. I'm funny that way. (*Claude wearing the mink, comes along the corridor.*)

PROCLO: Claude!

CLAUDE: Oh sure. Now you know me.

PROCLO: You've got to help me.

CLAUDE: I've got to get ready for the talent contest tonight.

PROCLO: My brother-in-law's here with a gun.

CLAUDE: So that's who that maniac is! (*Proclo, Claude, and Chris go.*)

CARMINE: Viv! Viv! Sis!

VIVIAN: (*Reviving.*) Where am I? Carmine!

CARMINE: What are you doing here?

VIVIAN: I couldn't stand being in that bar anymore.

CARMINE: Do you know what kind of place this is?

VIVIAN: It was horrible, Carmine. He wanted me to roll on him.

CARMINE: Who?

VIVIAN: I don't know. Some little thin man.

CARMINE: I'll kill him. I'll kill 'em all.

VIVIAN: I was afraid something terrible had happened. I asked myself what Gilda would do.

CARMINE: Gilda? Gilda's twelve years old.

VIVIAN: Not my Gilda. The one in *Rigoletto.*

CARMINE: This isn't an opera, Viv.

VIVIAN: She disguised herself as a man for the man she loved and came to a place very similar to this one.

CARMINE: And then what happened?

VIVIAN: (*New sobs.*) She was stabbed to death!

CARMINE: You weren't stabbed. You were only rolled on.

VIVIAN: Take me home, Carmine, please.

CARMINE: Home? But he's here. I can prove it to you.

VIVIAN: I don't want proof. I just want to go back to Cleveland.

CARMINE: With a man like that?

VIVIAN: I don't care. He's my husband.

CARMINE: I'm gonna kill the son of a bitch when I find him.

VIVIAN: No killing, Carmine. I don't want killing.

CARMINE: All he's done to you.

VIVIAN: He hasn't done anything to me.

CARMINE: That's what you think. Now I want you to get out of here and take a cab back to Brooklyn. Leave that husband of yours to me.

VIVIAN: I'm not going!

CARMINE: Then stay in here and don't let anyone in.

VIVIAN: No!

CARMINE: This is between him and me, Viv!

VIVIAN: If you hurt him, I'll never speak to you again!

CARMINE: It's Poppa's honor that's at stake!

VIVIAN: Poppa's dead! (*This statement causes them both to collapse into sobs.*)

CARMINE: Poppa! He's stained the Vespucci honor!

VIVIAN: Carmine, please!

CARMINE: It's like he peed on Poppa's grave!

VIVIAN: Aaaaaiiiieee!

CARMINE: I'm thinking about Poppa, Viv. Believe me, it's not for me.

VIVIAN: What about me?

CARMINE: You, too. He peed on you, too. You've been dishonored, too, sister.

VIVIAN: Give me the gun.

CARMINE: What?

VIVIAN: Give me the gun. I'm going to kill myself.

CARMINE: Are you crazy?

VIVIAN: I want to die, Carmine. You've made me so crazy I want to kill myself.

CARMINE: It's him I'm going to kill. (*By this time, Vivian will have the gun. Suddenly, she becomes aware that her mink is missing.*)

VIVIAN: Carmine! No, no!

CARMINE: What is it?

VIVIAN: No! . . . No! . . . No! . . .

CARMINE: What is it?

VIVIAN: My mink!

CARMINE: Your mink?

VIVIAN: It's gone. They've taken it. It was in here.

CARMINE: Why weren't you wearing it?

VIVIAN: I didn't want to get it wet. It cost 900 dollars.

CARMINE: I'll get your mink back, too.

VIVIAN: He gave it to me for our anniversary. Now I really want to kill myself.

CARMINE; I'll get your goddamn mink. Now let go of me.

VIVIAN: I'm coming with you.

CARMINE: You're staying here.

VIVIAN: I don't want him dead, Carmine.

CARMINE: It's not up to you. This is for Poppa! (*He starts off.*) Gaetano! Gaetano!

VIVIAN: Carmine! (*But he is gone. Vivian runs out of the room and sees the snooty patron.*) Stop him.

SNOOTY PATRON: Who?

VIVIAN: My brother. He'll kill him. You heard him. He's a violent man.

SNOOTY PATRON: Kill who?

VIVIAN: My husband. And my mink! They took my mink! (*Vivian and the snooty patron disappear up a corridor. Proclo, Claude, and Chris go running by on their way to the nightclub.*)

CHRIS: I don't know any Andrew Sisters numbers!

CLAUDE: Well fake it!

PROCLO: This will never work!

CLAUDE: He never really knew any either. Nelson and I carried you for years. (*Carmine enters and comes face to face with Chris and the others. Proclo hides behind the mink coat as Chris blows his whistle.*)

CHRIS: He went up to the steam room, boss.

CARMINE: Thanks. (*He heads upstairs. Claude, Proclo, and Chris turn on their heels and run in the opposite direction. Vivian appears on the first level.*)

VIVIAN: Carmine, wait!

CARMINE: I said stay in there! (*He continues toward the steam room. Vivian sees Proclo and his group just exiting.*)

VIVIAN: My mink! Stop, thief! (*They are gone, Vivian in pursuit. Carmine runs into the steam room. This time all the patrons come flying out. Carmine follows, brandishing his gun. They all run off. Music is heard. It is a bad baritone singing the end of an operatic aria.*)

BAD BARITONE: (*Singing over the loudspeaker.*) Il concetto vidisi/ Or ascoltate/ Comeglie svolto,/ Andiam./ Incominciate! (*This is the transition to the nightclub. The talent show is in progress. There is applause as Googie steps onto the stage.*)

GOOGIE: That was Tiny Naylor singing "The Prologue" from *Pagliacci*.
Bravo, Tiny, bravo. It's gonna be a close race tonight. (*She con-
sults a card.*) Our next contestant is Sheldon Farenthold, song
stylist. Take it away, Sheldon! (*Sheldon enters, encased in red balloons. He plays directly out front, thus making the audience in the
theatre the audience in The Pits. During the number he will pop
his balloons and do bumps and grinds.*)

SHELDON: (*Singing.*)

Why are we here? What are we doing?
It's time we all found out.
We're not here to stay,
We're on a short holiday,
'Cause . . .
Life is just a bowl of cherries,
Don't take it serious,
Life's too mysterious.
You work, you slave, you worry so,
But you can't take your dough when you go, go , go,
So keep repeating it's the berries,
The strongest oak must fall . . .
(*Suddenly, two groups of patrons, one chased by Carmine, the
other by Vivian, crisscross and disappear into the "backstage" area
of the nightclub. Sheldon shoots them a blinder but goes on per-
forming like the good little trouper that he is. Spoken.*)
Thanks a lot! (*Sung.*)
The sweet things in life,
To you were just loaned,
How can you lose what you've never owned.
Life is just a bowl of cherries,
So live and laugh at it all.
C'mon . . .
Live
And laugh at it all!
(*When the number ends, Sheldon takes his bows and goes. Googie
steps forward.*)

GOOGIE: Thank you. You know, it gives me a real pleasure to emcee
these amateur shows because I began as an amateur. (*Sounds of*

disbelief from the offstage band members.) It's true! I didn't get where I am over night. Oh no, *chicos!* It took a long, long time. A star is born, that's true, I mean, you have "it" in the cradle or you don't, but she doesn't twinkle over no one night. (*She laughs at her own joke, then regains herself.*) Okay. (*Suddenly a group of patrons, led by Sheldon and his balloons, races across, chased by Carmine. Googie chooses to continue unflustered.*) Our last contestant is Mr. Claude Perkins and partners recreating their famous Army act. Hit it, boys! (*Music is heard. It is a '40s sounding swing orchestra. A spotlight picks up Claude in his WAC uniform, Proclo in his wife's mink coat and a long blonde wig, and Chris in an elaborate makeshift gown made from sheets. The Andrew Sisters are heard singing one of their big hits, "The Three Caballeros." Claude, Chris and Proclo begin to pantomime to the record and jitterbug. At first, Proclo is all nerves and Claude does a Herculean job of covering for him. But as the number progresses, we see Proclo getting better and better as the act comes back to him. After a while, he's close to enjoying himself.*)

THE ANDREW SISTERS: (*Prerecorded.*)
We're three caballeros, three gay caballeros,
They say we are birds of a feather,
We're happy amigos,
No matter where he goes,
The one, two and three goes,
We're always together.
(*Suddenly all of the patrons, including poor Sheldon, balloons and all, with Tiger and Duff, are chased across the stage and into the house by Carmine and Vivian.*)
We're three happy chappies, with snappy serapes,
You'll find us beneath our sombreros;
We're brave and we'll stay so,
We're bright as a peso,
Who sez so, we say so,
The three caballeros.
(*Chris accidentally steps on Proclo's foot, but the number continues.*)
Oh, we have the starts to guide us,
Guitars here beside us,

To play as we go;
We sing and we samba;
We shout *"Ay Caramba."*
What means *Ay, Caramba?*
Oh yes, I don't know . . .
(*The number is really building no. Proclo is boogying away like crazy. Suddenly Carmine fires a shot in the air. There is total pandemonium as the group of patrons returns to the stage from the back of the house. They run into a big huddle. Proclo and Claude manage to lose themselves somewhere in the middle of the crowd.*)

CARMINE: Now everybody slow down! Nobody's going nowhere. And get some lights on. I want to see who I'm talking to. (*The followspot hits Carmine.*) Not on me! I want the room lights, you dumb fruit! (*All the lights come on.*) Okay, I want all the fairies in a line.

CHRIS: What about us butch types, boss?

CARMINE: Shut up, you.

CHRIS: It's me, Bunny, Brick.

CARMINE: You're fired. Get over there! (*He motions with his gun for Chris to form a line. He turns and sees Michael.*) I can't believe it. A good-looking, rugged boy like you.

MICHAEL: Believe what, sir?

CARMINE: I believe it. Get going.

GOOGIE: Wait a minute. All of this because some fat woman who lost her mink?

CARMINE: One more word out of you, you goddamn transvestite and—

GOOGIE: What you call me?

SHELDON: Careful, Googie.

GOOGIE: You make me see red, mister, and when I see red I tear you apart. Shit! You think I'm scared of a little gun? (*Carmine fires in the air again.*) That's okay, mister. You don't bother me, I don't bother you. (*She backs into the main group of patrons.*)

CARMINE: Okay, Cowboy. Your turn.

PATRON IN CHAPS: I don't know what your name is but you belong in Bellevue.

CARMINE: Who says?

PATRON IN CHAPS: A trained psychiatrist.

CARMINE: Get outta here! (*Duff and Tiger try to sneak up on Carmine.*) What are you two? The Cherry Sisters?

DUFF: Up yours, mister.

CARMINE: Get over there. All right. The rest of you! (*The group crosses the stage, revealing Claude and Proclo, whose face is turned. Claude approaches Carmine.*)

CLAUDE: You really know how to mess up an act, you know that, mister?

CARMINE: Christ, another one!

CLAUDE: I'm an entertainer. Pantomime acts are coming back, you'll see.

CARMINE: In the meantime, you're still a transvestite. Move! (*Only Proclo remains now. Carmine is savoring every moment of his humiliation.*) I guess that makes it you. Look at you. I could vomit. Jesus, Mary, and Joseph! Is that her mink? (*Proclo turns around. Not only is he wearing the mink and the Patty Andrews wig, he has added the dark glasses and the moustache. He nods.*) Give it back to her. (*Proclo shakes his head.*)

VIVIAN: I don't want it now. That's not Gaetano. I just want to go home.

CARMINE: Okay, Gaetano, the jig's up. Take the crap off. The wig, the glasses, the moustache, the mink. Everything. I'm giving you three. (*To the others.*) I want you all to meet my splendid brother-in-law, Gaetano Proclo.

MICHAEL: That's not Mr. Proclo! He is!

CARMINE: Who is?

MICHAEL: You are! (*Carmine spins around. Proclo bites his wrist and grabs the gun. The others subdue Carmine. For a few moments he is buried as they swirl about him. Vivian just sobs hysterically.*)

CARMINE: Get your hands off me! This time you've really done it, Gaetano!

PROCLO: Shut up, Carmine.

CARMINE: Sure, you got some balls now, you're holding a gun.

PROCLO: Don't worry about my balls, Carmine.

CARMINE: I'm gonna kill you!

PROCLO: Keep him quiet. Sit on him. I don't want to hear that voice. (*Tiger, Duff, and Chris hold Carmine down and muffle his mouth, though Carmine will try to get his two cents in during the conversation that follows. Proclo has approached Vivian.*)

PROCLO: Don't cry, Viv.

VIVIAN: Don't cry, he says. Look at him like that, telling me not to cry!

PROCLO: You want your coat back?

VIVIAN: I want to know what you're doing in it!

PROCLO: It was the only thing that fit.

VIVIAN: Aaaaiiiiieeee!

PROCLO: Carmine was going to kill me!

VIVIAN: AAAAIIIIEEEE!

PROCLO: Vivian, please!

VIVIAN: My husband, the man in the mink coat! I can't wait to go to Bingo with you like that next week but I won't be there if God is merciful because I'm going to have a heart attack right here.

CARMINE: This is grounds for an annulment, sis. I asked Father Catini.

VIVIAN: I don't want an annulment. I want to die. *Mi fa morire, Dio, mi fa morire!*

PROCLO: Is this what you wanted, Carmine?

CARMINE: You're finished, Gaetano.

PROCLO: I can understand you hating me as a brother-in-law but killing someone over a garbage company?

VIVIAN: *Un delitto di passione*, Carmine?

CARMINE: *Si! Un delitto di passione!*

VIVIAN: *Ma perchè?*

CARMINE: *Perchè* you're married to a flaming homo, that's *perchè!*

VIVIAN: Aaaaiiiiieeee!

CARMINE: He came here tonight, didn't he?

PROCLO: A cab driver brought me here.

CARMINE: Because you told him to.

PROCLO: I never heard of this place.

CARMINE: You see that Vivian? Even a cab driver knows what a *fata* he is!

VIVIAN: I just hope you're not going to insist on mentioning this in confession.

PROCLO: Mention what?

VIVIAN: He knows your voice, Guy.

PROCLO: Who knows my voice?

VIVIAN: Father Bonnelli. He knows everyone's voice. For my sake, Guy, for the children's don't tell him about this.

PROCLO: I wasn't planning to!

VIVIAN: You're going through a stage. Last year it was miniature golf.

CARMINE: This ain't like no miniature golf, Viv.

VIVIAN: I'll get over this. I get over everything. It's my greatest strength.

PROCLO: There's nothing to get over, then or now!

VIVIAN: Aaaaiiiieee!

PROCLO: Vivian, what do I have to do to convince you?

CARMINE: She is convinced! Cry your hear out, sis, it's all right. Carmine's here.

PROCLO: How the hell do you prove something like that to your wife? I give up. You win, Carmine. Let him go. (*Tiger, Duff, and Chris reluctantly release Carmine, look at Proclo, and then leave.*)

CARMINE: Come on, sis, let's get out of here.

PROCLO: Vivian, wait!

CARMINE: Don't you ever speak to my sister! (*Proclo stands there helpless. Maurine has appeared. She goes directly to Carmine and hands him a long sheet of figures.*)

MAURINE: Thirty seven thousand five hundred on the week. The rain killed us tonight. And next week we got the Jewish holidays coming up. Good night, boss. (*She goes.*)

VIVIAN: Who was that?

CARMINE: Just a person.

VIVIAN: She called you boss.

CARMINE: A lot of people call me boss. (*He starts to eat the sheet of figures.*)

VIVIAN: Give me that.

CARMINE: It's not what you're going to think, Vivian.

VIVIAN: "Vespucci Enterprises, Inc. Carmine Vespucci, President." This is a statement!

CARMINE: I was going to tell you about it.

VIVIAN: We own this place?

CARMINE: Poppa's done a lot of expanding while you were in Cleveland.

VIVIAN: We own this place, Guy!

CARMINE: He doesn't have to know the family business, Viv! Now come on, this isn't the place to talk about it.

VIVIAN: So you knew what kind of place this was.

CARMINE: So did he obviously. That's why he came here. I can't help it if we own it. It's just a coincidence.

VIVIAN: What kind of cab was it, Guy?

PROCLO: What?

VIVIAN: The one that brought you here.

PROCLO: I don't remember.

CARMINE: A fairy cab!

VIVIAN: Do you remember the name of the company?

CARMINE: The Fairy Cab Company! Fairy cabs for fairy passengers! Now come on, Vivian, let's get out of here. What do you care what kind of cab it was?

VIVIAN: Think hard, Guy. It's important.

PROCLO: It was an opera . . . Aida Cab!

VIVIAN: Aida Cab! We own that company!

PROCLO: We do?

VIVIAN: Carmine, did you tell that driver to bring Guy here?

CARMINE: Of course I didn't!

VIVIAN: What did the driver look like, Guy?

PROCLO: All I remember about him is his stutter.

VIVIAN: His stutter?

PROCLO: He stuttered and smoked pot.

VIVIAN: Cousin Tito! I should've guessed. It's going to be very hard to forgive you for this, Carmine.

CARMINE: What's to forgive? I don't want no forgiving!

VIVIAN: Now take the hit off him, Carmine.

CARMINE: Vivian!

VIVIAN: Take it off!

CARMINE: No!

VIVIAN: If you don't take if off, Carmine, I am gonna tell Frankie di Lucca about you muscling into the Bingo concessions at the Feast of St. Anthony and then Frankie di Lucca is gonna put a hit out on you and you are gonna end up wearing cement shoes at the bottom of the East River and then there will be even more grief and less peace in our fucking family than there already is!

PROCLO: I am married to an extraordinary woman!

CARMINE: You wouldn't do this to me, sis!

VIVIAN: You know me, Carmine.

CARMINE: Vivian!

VIVIAN: I swear it, Carmine. *Lo giuro.*

CARMINE: *Non giura,* sis!

VIVIAN: *Lo giuro*, Carmine. *Lo giuro*, the Bingo and the cement shoes.

CARMINE: "Get Proclo." You heard Poppa.

VIVIAN: I've got Proclo, Carmine, Not take the hit off!

CARMINE: I'll lose face.

VIVIAN: Not under the East River!

CARMINE: (*Writhing in defeat.*) Aaaaiiiieee!

VIVIAN: Now take the hit off him, Carmine! Is it off? (*He nods.*) On Poppa's grave? (*He shakes his head.*) I want it on Poppa's grave and I want it forever! (*He shakes his head.*) I'm calling Frankie di Lucca.

CARMINE: It's off on Poppa's grave!

VIVIAN: (*Finally breaking down.*) Poppa! All right, now I forgive you.

CARMINE: I told you: I don't want no forgiving.

VIVIAN: You already have it. And now I want to see you two forgive each other. *Il bacio del pace*, Carmine.

CARMINE: You gotta be kidding!

PROCLO: Over my dead body!

VIVIAN: I want you to kiss each other as brothers.

PROCLO: I wouldn't kiss him for a million dollars.

VIVIAN: That's exactly what it's worth, Guy.

PROCLO: I wouldn't kiss him period.

VIVIAN: I want you to make your peace with Carmine.

PROCLO: Vivian!

VIVIAN: For me, Guy, for me.

PROCLO: I forgive you, Carmine. With a little luck nobody's gonna die in your family for a long, long time and we won't have to see each other for another twenty years. Just be sure to send the checks. *Andiamo!* (*By this time, all the patrons will have gathered as an audience to the proceedings. Proclo opens his arms and moves towards Carmine for the kiss of peace.*) Hey!

CARMINE: Hey! (*They make a slow, ritual-like circle. Of course, both men do look rather ludicrous as they circle one another: Proclo in his wife's mink coat; Carmine in his bathrobe. Carmine hesitates.*)

VIVIAN: Frankie di Lucca! (*The circling resumes. Just as they are about to kiss, Carmine gives Proclo a good punch in the stomach. But as Proclo bends over in pain, he knees Carmine in the groin. Carmine goes down. The others give a mighty cheer and congratulate Proclo.*)

PROCLO: (*Amazed.*) I did it. I did it. (*Now jubilant.*) I won. I didn't fight fair but I won! (*To Carmine.*) You can go *va fangool* yourself, Carmine. People like you really do belong in garbage. People like me just marry into it. Get him out of here, men!

CHRIS: Bring her up to the steam room, girls! (*The others pounce on Carmine, who is protesting mightily, and drag him off.*)

CARMINE: I'm coming back here and I'm gonna kill every last one of you fairies!

CHRIS: Sure you are, Nancy! (*It is a gleeful, noisy massed exit. All the patrons sing* "La Marseillaise." *For several moments we can still hear Carmine yelling and the others cheering. Vivian has been following them in concern. Proclo stops her.*)

PROCLO: Vivian!

VIVIAN: Where are your clothes? I want to go home.

PROCLO: I'm not leaving.

VIVIAN: Don't make any more waves in the family now, Guy.

PROCLO: It's the perfect time. If I don't do it now I never will. Your family's run herd on me since the day I met you. I'm sick of it. I'm sick of Carmine and Connie and Tony and Tommy and Sonny and Pipo and Silva and Beppe and Gina and your Aunt Rosa and Cousin Tito! I'm sick of all of them. The living and the dead. What am I? Some curse on a family? "Get Proclo." Those were your father's dying words!

VIVIAN: He was my father. I was his only girl. You expected him to like you?

PROCLO: Yes! Yes, I expect people to like me. I want people to like me. It's called self-esteem, Vivian.

VIVIAN: I think we have a wonderful marriage.

PROCLO: I do, too. It's nothing personal, Viv.

VIVIAN: A beautiful home, all paid for.

PROCLO: I'm not talking about that. I'm talking about me. I'm talking about wanting things. And I do want things. I've always wanted things. I wanted so many things I didn't get I can't even remember them. I wanted to send Momma back to Italy before she died. I didn't have the money in those days.

VIVIAN: Not many eight-year-old boys do, Guy.

PROCLO: I want us to be terrific forever. I want to go on a diet. No, I want to *stay* on one. I want a boat. I want a brand new fleet of trucks. I want Proclo Sanitation services to be number *one* in Cleveland. I want people to stop calling me a garbageman. I want to be known as a sanitary engineer. I want to be honored as an ecologist! I want changes! I want changes! I want changes! (*He has exhausted himself.*)

VIVIAN: I want to go back to Cleveland.

PROCLO: You know something? So do I. (*She goes to him and kisses his cheek. Claude enters with three trophies.*)

CLAUDE: We won! We won! (*He hands one of the trophies to Proclo and heads upstairs.*) We won the talent contest! We won. God bless the Andrew Sisters! Chris! Chris, where are you?

CHRIS: In the steam room.

CLAUDE: We won!

CHRIS: We won? (*Claude meets Chris in the steam room with screams of joy.*)

PROCLO: You see that, Viv? I never won anything in my whole life. That was Claude Perkins. We were in Special Services together.

VIVIAN: He seems like a nice person.

PROCLO: I wouldn't go that far, Vivian. To him I look like Tyrone Power.

VIVIAN: So did I. Now where are your things? (*They return to Proclo's room, where he will dress and pack. Googie comes storming on, followed by Tiger and Duff. She is dressed in street clothes and carrying all her belongings.*)

TIGER: We're sorry Googie.

GOOGIE: You build someone up like that and it's all a lie. Ay, that's a low-down dirty trick to play.

TIGER: Look at it this way; one night there will be a Mr. Big out there and you'll be all keyed up for it.

GOOGIE: There ain't never gonna be no Mr. Big in this place. There ain't never gonna be me no more in this place neither. I quit.

DUFF: Come on, Googie, we adore you.

GOOGIE: You adore yourself. (*Michael appears.*) Would you believe it? They told me that Mr. Big was gonna be here tonight

MICHAEL: Who's Mr. Big

GOOGIE: Only the man you wait for all your life. Only the man who opens miracles. Only the man who can make you a star over one night. A producer, who else?

MICHAEL: My uncle is a producer, Miss Gomez.

GOOGIE: Oh yeah? What's he produce?

MICHAEL: Shows.

GOOGIE: Legitimate shows? I don't do no dirty stuff.

MICHAEL: Right now I think he's casting "Oklahoma" for a dinner theatre.

GOOGIE: "Oklahoma"? It's a stretch but I could do that part. You could get me an audition with him?

MICHAEL: Sure thing.

GOOGIE: You see? I had this hunch the whole evening. I got another show to do. I meet you in Bimbi's across the street. We run into my boy friend Hector and we tell him you're my agent. (*To Tiger and Duff.*) I see you two skunks later.

DUFF: I thought you quit.

GOOGIE: That's show business. (*She is gone.*)

TIGER: You got an uncle who's in show business?

MICHAEL: Seymour Pippin. He's a producer.

DUFF: Forget it, mister.

TIGER: Come on, Duff. (*Michael, Tiger, and Duff leave. Chris has entered.*)

PROCLO: (*To Vivian.*) Are you ready?

CHRIS: I suppose you're wondering what happened to Bunny. We entered her in the Zinka Milanov look-alike contest. First prize is a gay guide to Bloomingdale's. We're still awaiting the judge's decision.

VIVIAN: Who's he talking about?

PROCLO: Carmine.

VIVIAN: He said she.

CHRIS: We've called the 16th Precinct. They'll be right over for him.

VIVIAN: Oh, Guy, you've got to do something for him.

PROCLO: I will, Vivian. Thanks for the help back there.

CHRIS: Just let me know the next time you three are coming in. I want to be sure not to be here. I haven't had so much fun since the day they raided Riis Park.

PROCLO: If you're ever in Cleveland Vivian makes a great lasagna.

CHRIS: Well, that's the best offer I've had all night.

PROCLO: Goodnight, Chris

CHRIS: So long, boss. (*He heads back up to his room. We hear Googie offstage, singing a song from her third show, "Shine on Harvest Moon.")*

ABE: (*On the loudspeaker.*) 316 coming up! That's three-one-six, Duff!

PROCLO: Let's go!

VIVIAN: Guy, promise me you'll take good care of Carmine.

PROCLO: On Poppa's grave.

VIVIAN: (*A new outburst of grief.*) Poppa! (*She exits. Proclo calls off to her.*)

PROCLO: Not your Poppa's. Mine! (*As Proclo starts off, a policeman races on. Proclo stops to watch with a contented smile. Chris blows his whistle, and the policeman runs up to the steam room, where he finds Carmine, bound and gagged and dressed in a green brocade ball gown. Claude sees Carmine, too, and sings his "Jelly Roll" song as he plays tug-o-war with the policeman over Carmine. Patrons are filing the halls. Duff and Tiger start making fresh beds. And Proclo just smiles.*)

CHRIS: Orgy! Orgy! Orgy! In 240! (*The lights are fading. The play is over.*)

Prelude & Liebestod

PRELUDE AND LIEBESTOD was produced by Manhattan Class Company (Executive Directors: Robert LuPone and Bernard Telsay; Associate Director: W.D. Cantler), in New York City, on March 3, 1989. It was directed by Paul Benedict; set design was by Dan Conway & Gregory Mercurio; costumes by Dianne-Finn Chapman; lighting by John Hastings; sound by Lia Vollack; production supervisor, Laura Kravets-Gautier; casting by Bernie Telsey Casting and Laurel Smith; associate producer Maggie Lear. The stage manager was Dennis Cameron. The cast was as follows:

CONDUCTOR'S WIFE .... Leslie Denniston
MAN .... Simon Brooking
CONCERT MASTER .... Dominic Cuskern
CONDUCTOR .... Larry Bryggman

Characters:

CONDUCTOR: Mid-40's, handsome, magnetic, moves magnificently.

CONDUCTOR'S WIFE: Mid-to-late 30's, beautiful, perfectly groomed, elegant carriage and gestures.

MAN: Mid-to-late 20's, informally dressed, not as sure of himself as he'd like to be or thinks he is.

CONCERTMASTER: Mid-50's, rough looks, florid complexion, looks and acts as if he's seen it all. He has.

SOPRANO: Early 30's. Full-figured. Still very green on the concert platform but she doesn't know it.

Setting

The present. The stage of a concert hall.

Prelude & Liebestod

Lights come up on a conductor's podium, a small, square, raised platform about 15 inches high. There is a waist-high railing running the length of the upstage side of it. Sounds of a symphony orchestra tuning up at random.

Spot up on a beautiful woman in a box seat somewhat upstage of the podium. She is the Conductor's Wife. She is perfectly dressed. She looks at her program. She looks at her watch. She looks at the orchestra in the orchestra level below her. She looks up at the higher tiers and balcony above her.

Spot up on a Man in an orchestra level seat stage left, also somewhat upstage of the Conductor's podium. He is looking at the Conductor's Wife through a pair of opera glasses. She is not aware of this.

Spot up on the Concertmaster who is seated in a chair just a little downstage right of the podium. He raps with his bow on his violin stand and gives the note.

An unseen symphony orchestra tunes up to his note.

The Conductor's Wife opens her purse and takes out a small box of mints.

The Man continues to stare at her through the opera glasses. At the same time, he reaches in his breast pocket and takes out a roll of Lifesavers.

The house lights dim in the concert hall where the Conductor's Wife and Man are sitting.

At the same time, the lights will come up on the concert stage, i.e. the theatre itself.

A spotlight hits a door leading to the backstage area. After a longer time than necessary, it is opened by unseen hands and the Soprano enters to strong applause. She is in full regalia.

As Soprano moves towards podium, she smiles at the unseen orchestra. The Concertmaster taps his bow on his stand in approval.

Soprano turns her back to orchestra (And us, in doing so.)
and bows deeply to heavy applause.

Now Soprano makes a great deal of arranging the panels of
her dress and stole as she finally sits in a chair just left and a little
downstage of the podium. Her back will be to us but we will see
her in profile as she turns from time to time to take a sip of water
from a glass on a low table next to her chair or turns to the other
side to smile at the Concertmaster. Silence.

The spotlight has gone again to the door leading to the back-
stage area. It waits there. Again the door is opened by unseen
hands. No one appears.

Silence in the auditorium. Someone coughs. Someone else
shushes them. Door starts to swing shut, then is swiftly pulled wide
open as Conductor hurries through. Tumultuous applause.

Conductor moves swiftly to podium and bows deeply. The Man
has risen and is clapping wildly.

MAN: Bravo! Bravo! (*Conductor's Wife is applauding. Conductor leaps*
off podium and goes to Concertmaster and shakes his hand vigor-
ously. Ovation continues as Conductor crosses to Soprano and
kisses her hand, then cheek. Man continues to stand and ap-
plaud.)

MAN: Bravo! Bravo! (*Conductor's Wife has stopped applauding. Con-*
ductor has returned to podium for final bow to audience [which
means his back is to us] as applause begins to diminish. Man con-
tinues to stand and applaud. This time his voice is especially
prominent as the general ovation continues to subside.) Bravo!
Bravo! (*Conductor looks to Man. Eye contact is made. Conductor*
Wife's looks at Man. Conductor looks up at Wife and smiles, then
turns his back to concert hall audience and faces orchestra [us].
Conductor is delighted with his reception. He gives orchestra mem-
bers a self-deprecating grin and raised eyebrows. Silence. He gets
serious. He passes his hands over his face. He takes a deep breath.)

MAN: (*Shattering the silence.*) We love you! (*Conductor ignores this.*
Angry shushes from audience. Conductor reaches to music stand
in front of him and closes the score. Gasps and whispers from the
audience. He picks up baton. He raises both arms. He waits. He
throws the baton onto the music stand and raises both arms again
but this time gives the downbeat almost at once. Wagner's Prelude

to Tristan und Isolde *is off and running.*)

CONDUCTOR: (*After the fourth rest.*) I love these pauses . . . Come on you suckers, play for me. Play through me, music. Course through me. Surge. Fill me. I am you. This is it . . . God, that was good. Now we're off and running. I'm up here already. That was quick. I like it up here. The view is glorious. Fill, lungs. Heave, bosom. Burst, heart. (*At this point, the sound of the orchestra is considerably diminished and the Conductor will seem to be speaking from within his own private place. The music will be more of a "surround" than a presence.*)

CONDUCTOR: There were no empty seats. Clean as a whistle. There's no one better than me. Is there? No one even close. God, I love Wagner. That one in the fifth row. I've seen him. Where? In your dreams, asshole. We don't do that anymore. You wanna bet? Oh shut up! Hey, third cello, look at me! Yes, you! Where did they find you? Yes, you're too loud. You think I'd be looking at you like this if you weren't? Jesus, where was I? Sometimes I think I do this on automatic. There we are, right on target! Somebody up there likes me. Yeah, Wagner, asshole. The Big Kraut in das Himmel Himself. I feel his eyes burning right into my back. He's mentally undressing me. They all are. All 2,187 of them plus the 131 in standing room. Maybe I could steal a look. Are you crazy? She's right up there in a box. I'd like to see her in a box. It's her box I'm sick of. You don't mean that. I don't mean that. You love her. I love you. (*He looks over his shoulder to Wife who is reading something in her program.*) She's reading! The fucking bitch is reading and you're conducting your fucking ass off. Fuck that shit. Bitch. You wanted to be married. No, you wanted to have children. You have to be married to have children. No, you have to be married to have children if you want to be the principal conductor of a big symphony orchestra with a big stuffy endowment. You're pissed off because you've got the hots for some groupie in the fifth row and your goddamn wife is right up there watching every move you make. Eagle eyes. Bionic ears. She can see and hear through lead walls if I'm talking to another man. It's one thing to be straight; it's another to be in a straight jacket. (*Suddenly aware of the Concertmaster.*) What are you looking at, asshole? I swear to God, sometimes I think he's calling me an asshole under his breath through the whole concert.

CONCERTMASTER: Asshole.

CONDUCTOR: There! Right now! I'm positive he's doing it. I'd like to see him get up here and conduct, he thinks he's so great. They probably all think they can conduct better than me. Sorry to disillusion you, assholes! That's why I'm up here and you're down there. Whoever said it was right: it is lonely at the top. It's lonely anywhere.

MAN: Look at me. You know I'm here.

WIFE: (*Still looking at program.*) Now that is what I call a stunning outfit. Oscar De La Renta. I should have guessed.

CONCERTMASTER: Asshole!

SOPRANO: Fuck you, too!

CONCERTMASTER: I wasn't talking to you.

SOPRANO: What did I do to him? I'm sorry, but we can't all be Kirsten Fucking Flagstad.

MAN: Turn around. You know you want to.

CONDUCTOR: He's talking to you. Go ahead. This climax. It's a perfect place. Shit! I can't. You blew it, asshole.

MAN: You know what I'd do if I had you alone with me? I have it all planned. I'd undress you. With my teeth. I'd start with a button. This button. (*He touches his collar button.*) Pop!

WIFE: Oh God, I hope Ralph can get away for that weekend when he's conducting in London. I don't think I can stand another week without him. I wonder what he'd do if he knew. Kill me. Punish me through the children. Both.

CONDUCTOR: Turn, turn, turn. To everything there is a season. The Beatles? The Turtles. Ten minutes with someone like that. Less. It doesn't take long. I want you so bad, fifth row.

CONCERTMASTER: Bloody, bleeding, blooming asshole.

CONDUCTOR: If I had a face like yours I'd kill myself.

SOPRANO: It's nearly me. There's got to be better ways to earn a living.

CONDUCTOR: Why did you have to be out there tonight, fatal beauty, or why did you have to be up there, faithful adoring wife? Why couldn't tonight be next week in London? I'm doing the Mahler 9th. I'm always so drained after the Mahler 9th. Drained and horny.

MAN: Look at me. They say if you stare at someone's left earlobe long enough eventually it begins to burn a hole and they turn around.

CONDUCTOR: It's all in the music. The longing, the yearning. The impossibility. I am loved. I want to love. I've never found anyone as interesting as me. As lovable. As worthy of my undivided attention. Fifth row is one thing, her up there is another. I'm talking about a whole other kettle of fish. (*The Prelude is drawing to an end. The Soprano stands and makes ready to sing.*) Good God, it's her turn already. Come on, cow, sing it, swing it, shake it, bend it.

MAN: Maybe it's the right earlobe. (*Soprano begins to sing. At first the music will be at concert hall volume, then subside to the level of the Prelude. Although her back is to us throughout, it should be clear that the Soprano is deeply involved with singing and communicating with her audience out front.*)

CONCERTMASTER: You're flat. Get up there, get up there!

WIFE: Now that's a gorgeous voice.

MAN: Sharp as ever.

CONDUCTOR: You're singing through the wrong hole, honey. This is twat music. Listen to it. Listen to the words. God, if I had your instrument!

SOPRANO: Place the tone properly. Support it. Always legato. Thatta girl.

WIFE: If I could sing like that!

MAN: They like her! They actually like her!

CONCERTMASTER: That's more like it. (*Surtitles will appear throughout.*)

SURTITLE: "Mild und leise wie er lächelt,
    wie das Auge hold er öffnet,
    seht ihr's, Freunde? Seht ihr's nicht?
    Immer lichter, wie er leuchtet,
    stern-umstrahlet hoch sich hebt?
    Seht ihr's nicht?

CONDUCTOR: Do you know what the words mean? Sing it like you know what it meant. It's about love. It's about dying. It's about trans-fan-fucking-figuration. Sing it like you meant it.

SURTITLE: "Wie das Herz ihm mutig schwillt,
    voll und hehr im Busen ihm quillt?
    Wie den Lippen, wonnig mild,
    susser Atem sanft entweht,

Freunde! Seht! Fühlt und seht ihr's nicht?

CONDUCTOR: This is not enough. Conducting it is not enough. Singing it is not enough. Writing it is not enough. Experience it. Love-death. Love-death Liebestod.

CONCERTMASTER: What is he doing?

CONDUCTOR: You're behind, honey, catch up, catch up!

SOPRANO: This is not the tempo we agreed—!

WIFE: That man looks like Ralph.

MAN: He's losing you, lady.

CONDUCTOR: Who do you love the most? Who do you love the best?

SURTITLE: "Höre ich nur diese Weise
die so wundervoll und leise,
Wonne klagen, alles sagend,
mild versohnend aus ihm tönend,
in mich dringet, auf sich schwinget,
hold erhallend um mich klinget?
Heller schallend, mich umwallend,
sind es Wellen sanfter Lüfte?
Sind es Wogen wonniger Düfte?

CONDUCTOR: What is transfiguration but an orgasm coupled with a heart attack?

SURTITLE: "Wie sie schwellen, mich umrauschen,
soll ich atmen, soll ich lauschen?
Soll ich schlurfen, untertauchen?
Suss in Duften mich verhauchen?

CONDUCTOR: Wagner knew a lot about fucking. I bet that guy in the fifth row does, too. My wife knows nothing about fucking. I'd like to fuck the entire world. No, I'd like to fuck every attractive man, woman, and child in the world. Child over 11. No, 14. 15, 15. Fuck it.

SURTITLE: "In dem wogenden Schwall, in dem tönenden Schall,
in des Welt-Atems wehendem All
ertrinken, versinken—,
unbewusst, höchste Lust—.

CONDUCTOR: It's over already. Shit. I don't even remember it beginning. (*Long pause as music fades to silence.*)

WIFE: Oh shit, now the Bruckner 4th.

CONCERTMASTER: Oh shit, now the Bruckner 4th.

SOPRANO: Isn't anybody going to clap?

MAN: Now he's got to turn around. (*Ovation begins. A tremendous one. Conductor doesn't move. Instead, he remains with his back to concert hall audience. Soprano accepts ovation with great humility.*)

MAN: (*Above all others.*) We love you! (*Conductor picks up baton and raps with it.*)

CONDUCTOR: Again! From the top!

CONCERTMASTER: But—! (*Conductor gives downbeat. Soprano looks startled but takes her seat. Man sits. Wife remains standing in her box, looking concerned, but will eventually sit. The* Tristan *Prelude will seem very loud at first. It will finally settle at same level of volume as previous rendition of it.*)

CONDUCTOR: Give them profile. Feed it to them. They love your profile. Move the body. They come for body movement. Those fabulous, famous, far-reaching shoulders. Magnificent arms on a mighty torso. High flying adored. You and Evita! Wiggle your ass. Tight firm buttocks worthy of someone half your age. Make them think about your cock and balls. Are they large? Is he clipped? Is he good? I'm terrific, baby. Ask her. Ask him. Ask anyone who's had the pleasure of my acquaintance. It's them who don't measure up. It's them who fail me. They're fucking me. Taking. Drawing my strength. Where's my equal? My match? I'm so alone. Up here. Everywhere. I really love this pause. What is this music really about? What is anything really about? I don't think this is such a great theme. I've written better but he's Richard Wagner — big fucking deal — and I am Marie of Rumania — big fucking deal. This music always makes me think of certain kinds of sex. Hot late afternoon damp sheets sweaty grunting people outside blinds drawn dark dirty make it last as long as you can come crazy, scream, rip the sheets, howl like a Werewolf, hurt him, hurt her, ouchy kind of sex. This will be in all the papers tomorrow. For 24 hours I'll be the most famous person in the world. 48 maybe. 72. Then next week when the magazines come out there will be a new spurt of fame. Then a gradual subsiding until the first major memorial service. A plaque will go up somewhere. Probably outside the hall. God knows, no one ever, anywhere, ever again will listen to this music without thinking of me. (*He glances at Wife. Their eyes meet and hold.*) You had the most beautiful skin and breasts and throat and everything when we met. They weren't enough. Nothing has ever been enough. The children. They're not real. Real in themselves but not real to me. Not real enough. Nothing, no one is real enough. I am the only person in the world and I cannot bear the pain of being so alone. I'm only alive when I come — the way I want to be alive — ecstatic, half-conscious, eyes closed, brain flaring, words, thoughts inadequate. (*He glances at the Man.*) The only satisfying sexual experience I ever had was with a man.

MAN: Finally.

CONDUCTOR: The kind of sexual experience this music is about.

CONCERTMASTER: This is more like it.

WIFE: Go on.

SOPRANO: I hate it when they look at me.

CONDUCTOR: I was 22 years old, studying in Milan, already made my debut in Salzburg that summer, an instant sensation, the old fool got sick, I took over, the Bruckner 4th and the Pathetique . . . God, that would have been next on the program. I loathe Bruckner! Who couldn't conduct the Pathetique? The toast of Europe. God, I was handsome that year. I could spend hours in front of the mirror talking to myself. I'd make faces. Scowl, smile. Flirt with myself. I could even get myself hard. This bastard . . . what was his name? . . . he was a journalist, political . . . the apartment was near the Piazza della Republica. . . it was over a pharmacy. . . the steps were exhausting . . . deep, steep Renaissance steps . . . there was a terra cotta Madonna in the apartment . . . he said it was a Lucca della Robbia and I wanted to believe him . . . God, I was already so famous but I was still so easily impressed! . . . What the fuck was your name?

MAN: Giorgio, Piero, Giacomo, Giuseppe, Gaetano.

WIFE: Does it matter?

CONCERTMASTER: Asshole!

MAN: Carlo, Mario, Fausto, Arturo, Vittorio, Fred.

CONDUCTOR: Guglielmo! Guglielmo Tell. Kidding, kidding. No, I'm not. Guglielmo Bianchini. He knew who I was. He must have. Everyone did. My picture was everywhere that summer. I was so beautiful that year — I was perfect — I was all I wanted — all anyone could ever possibly want — and this cocksucker, this arrogant

Wop, this goddamn glorious Dago, he led me on and on and on. A touch, a glance, a brush of thigh but no more. I wasn't even sure he was queer. Weeks went on like this. Torture. No one knew why I was staying in Milan. I'm doing research. What research? You know everything. It's true. I did. About music. But the promise of this person kept me on.

WIFE: My poor darling.

MAN: After the concert, when I ask for your autograph, I will pass you a slip of paper with my telephone number on it. No name, just a number. You'll know what to do with it.

SOPRANO: I better be paid twice for this. And I'm certainly not singing the *Tannhauser* for an encore.

CONCERTMASTER: Asshole, asshole, asshole.

CONDUCTOR: Finally, there was a weekend when his father, a widower and some sort of famous judge or lawyer, would be out of town at their place in Como. I went to the apartment. The door was ajar. There was no sign of him. I wandered through the empty apartment. It has been a palazzo. Everything was huge — molded, sculpted, ornate. I went into a bedroom — it must have been the father's — yes, that is where the Lucca Della Robbia was and I stood looking at this enormous bed and then I felt — I feel! — I feel! — hands on me from behind. I didn't turn around. Don't want to. (*The Soprano stands and begins to sing the Liebestod again. Only this time the surtitles will be in English.*) Hands here, hands there. Hands over my eyes, hands over my mouth. Four hands. Someone else is there. I didn't struggle. My clothes are being taken off — were being taken off — I don't know what tense I'm in — what tense I want to be in — the past is too painful, the present too forlorn — and I am being stripped and stroked and I am blindfolded and I am led to the bed and my cock is so hard and I am put on the bed and I let myself be tied spread eagle to it — no one has ever done this to me and I do not resist — and when it is done I am left there for what seems like hours and my hard on will not subside and once even it threatens to explode and I pray to the unseen Della Robbia Madonna above me not to let me come and I know this is blasphemy and I know that she forgives and understands because she is a good mother — all mothers are good mothers — and oh, it is so unimaginably intense to be there like that with him.

SOPRANO: "How gently and quietly he smiles,
how fondly he opens his eyes!
See you, friends? Do you not see?
How he shines ever higher,
soaring on high, stars sparkling around him?
Do you not see?
How his heart proudly swells
and, brave and full, pulses in his breast?
How softly and gently from his lips
sweet breath flutters:—
see, friends! Do you not feel and see it?
Do I alone hear this melody
which, so wondrous and tender
in its blissful lament, all-revealing,
gently pardoning, sounding from him,
pierces me through, rises above,
blessedly echoing and ringing round me?

CONDUCTOR: And after awhile I am unblindfolded and see my cap-
tors—Guglielmo and a young woman who can only be his twin
sister; she is a feminine mirror image of him — and they are both
nude and more beautiful than anyone I have ever see — more
beautiful than even I was that summer —and she straddles me
and lowers herself on my cock very slowly just once and I almost
come but I pray and then he — Guglielmo —what an absurd
name!— put his mouth on my cock and moves it up and down
the length of it just once and again I almost come and have to
pray and then they both just looked at me and I said, "Please,
make me come." "*Prego, farmi morire*" is what I said. "Please
make me die." I didn't know the Italian for "come," you see.
"*Prego, farmi morire.*"

SOPRANO: "Resounding yet more clearly, wafting about me,
are they waves of refreshing breezes?
Are they clouds of heavenly fragrance?
As they swell and roar round me,
shall I breathe them, shall I listen to them?

CONDUCTOR: And they just smiled at each other. He kissed one of her
breasts. She touched his cock. I knew they weren't really twins. I

wondered if they were even brother and sister. She took her panties, pink, and ran them the length of my body, toe to head. Then she very slowly pushed them into my mouth, gagging me with them. I didn't resist. The whole time our eyes held. He blindfolded me again. I felt their hands on me, their mouths. Everywhere. And then I heard the door close. After a while I stopped thinking about the Madonna and pray to her and when I thought of Guglielmo and Francesca — I'd named her by then, you see; I have a great need to know the name of things — adoring me I couldn't hold back any longer. I didn't want to and I came with an intensity that amazes me to this day and that I have never since even remotely equaled. I could feel my own semen on my lips, on my eyes, in my hair. Guglielmo and Francesca.

MAN: What are your secrets?

WIFE: I only deceive him sexually.

CONCERTMASTER: This is beautiful. I'll grant him that.

SOPRANO: "Shall I sip them, plunge beneath them,
   to expire in sweet perfume?"

CONDUCTOR: Of course, after I came I lost all interest in the game and wanted to be free. More importantly, I lost all interest in them. I lay there feeling the flood of semen grow watery, then dry and caked on my stomach, chest, and face. Hours passed. I could not free myself. The blindfold, the gag held firm. Once, I relaxed enough to mentally relive the episode and I immediately got hard and came again, though not nearly so much this time. The next thing I knew I heard a strange woman's scream, a man's angry voice and pretty soon I'm unblindfolded and the room is filled with people, most of whom are police, and an irate, bewildered couple in their 60's who had returned to their apartment after an outdoor performance of *Nabucco* in the Pizza del Duomo and who was I, how did I get there, what was I doing? Translation: what had I done? I never saw Guglielmo or Francesca again. It wasn't their apartment, of course. Were they even real? The orgasm was.

SOPRANO: In the surging swell, in the ringing sound,
   in the fast wave of the word's breath —
   to drown, to sink
   unconscious — supreme bliss!

CONDUCTOR: Once I asked her to tie me to the bed and sit on me. She loved it.

WIFE: This is so beautiful.

CONDUCTOR: Once I tied her. She loved it.

CONCERTMASTER: I gotta hand it to you, asshole.

CONDUCTOR: Once I let a fan — someone like you, sweetheart — try it but I'd had too much to drink or he'd had too much to drink or he smelled funny or he said something I didn't like — like Nixon wasn't such a bad President — or he was too big or too little or one of the ten million other things that don't let you connect perfectly with another person. That afternoon in Milan when I was young and first famous and still thought the answer to a good life was in my work, in other people, in success seems so long ago. There is no other person. There is a woman in a box who is my wife and bore me two children. There is a man in the fifth row who entertains fantasies about someone he thinks is me. There is a concertmaster who detests me but not half as much as I detest myself. There is a cow guest soprano who sings music that has no meaning for her in a perfectly ravishing voice. And so it goes. There are a lot of people. Five billion of us I read just this morning and pretty soon there will be six billion and the only time I ever felt connected to any of them was when I was 22 years old and tied spread eagled to a retired Milanese optometrist's bed wanting to be made love to by two people I'm not even sure exist. (*The last measure of the* Liebestod *are sounding. Conductor takes a small Japanese seppuku blade from the music stand in front of him.*) I know why I'm doing this. Wagner knew. Tristan and Isolde knew. That's four of us. Fuck the rest. (*He plunges the blade into his abdomen. Blood spurts onto the music stand. Conductor's face is transfigured. Another standing ovation has begun. Soprano bows deeply to the audience in the concert hall. The Man is already on his feet.*)

MAN: Bravo! Bravo! We love you! (*Wife rises in her box, afraid. Conductor continues to stare straight ahead, blood spurting from him onto the music stand, the transfigured, ecstatic expression on his face. The ovation is mounting. The Concertmaster is busily gathering his music, ready to leave the stage.*)

CONCERTMASTER: Asshole. (*Lights fade to black.*)

Andre's Mother

ANDRE'S MOTHER was first performed Off-Broadway by the Manhattan Theatre Club (Lynn Meadow, artistic Director; Barry Grove, Managing Director), in New York City, on May 18, 1988. It formed part of an evening entitled Urban Blight which was directed by John Tillinger and Richard Maltby Jr. The cast was as follows:

CAL . . . . John Rubinstein
PENNY . . . . Faith Prince
CAL'S FATHER . . . . Rex Robbins
ANDRE'S MOTHER . . . . E. Katherine Kerr

Characters

CAL
ARTHUR
PENNY
ANDRE'S MOTHER

Andre's Mother

Four people enter. They are nicely dressed and carry white helium-filled balloons on a string. They are Cal, a young man; Arthur, his father; Penny, his sister; and Andre's mother.

CAL: You know what's really terrible? I can't think of anything terrific to say. Goodbye. I love you. I'll miss you. And I'm supposed to be so great with words!

PENNY: What's that over there?

ARTHUR: Ask your brother.

CAL: It's a theatre. An outdoor theatre. They do plays there in the summer. Shakespeare's plays. (*To Andre's Mother.*) God, how much he wanted to play Hamlet. It was his greatest dream. I think he would have sold his soul to play it. He would have gone to Timbuktu to have another go at that part. The summer he did it in Boston, he was so happy!

PENNY: Cal, I don't think she . . . ! It's not the time. Later.

ARTHUR: Your son was a . . . the Jews have a word for it . . .

PENNY: (*Quietly appalled.*) Oh my God!

ARTHUR: Mensch, I believe it is and I think I'm using it right. It means warm, solid, the real thing. Correct me if I'm wrong.

PENNY: Fine, dad, fine. Just quit while you're ahead.

ARTHUR: I won't say he was like a son to me. Even my son isn't always like a son to me. I mean . . . ! In my clumsy way, I'm trying to say how much I liked Andre. And how much he helped me to know my own boy. Cal was always two hands full but Andre and I could talk about anything under the sun. My wife was very fond of him, too.

PENNY: Cal, I don't understand about the balloons.

CAL: They represent the soul. When you let go, it means you're letting his soul ascend to Heaven. That you're willing to let go. Breaking the last earthly ties.

PENNY: Does the Pope know about this?

ARTHUR: Penny!

PENNY: Andre loved my sense of humor. Listen, you can hear him laughing. (*She lets go of her white balloon.*) So long, you glorious, wonderful, I-know-what-Cal-means-about-words. . . *man*! God forgive me for wishing you were straight every time I laid eyes on you. But if any man was going to have you, I'm glad it was my brother! Look how fast it went up. I bet that means something. Something terrific.

ARTHUR: (*Arthur lets his balloon go.*) Goodbye. God speed.

PENNY: Cal?

CAL: I'm not ready yet.

PENNY: Okay. We'll be over there. Come on, pop, you can buy your little girl a Good Humor.

ARTHUR: They still make Good Humor?

PENNY: Only now they're called Dove Bars and they cost 12 dollars. (*Penny takes Arthur off. Cal and Andre's mother stand with their balloons.*)

CAL: I wish I knew what you were thinking. I think it would help me. You know almost nothing about me and I only know what Andre told me about you. I'd always had it in my mind that one day we would be friends, you and me. But if you didn't know about Andre and me . . . If this hadn't happened, I wonder if he would have ever told you. When he was so sick, if I asked him once I asked him a thousand times, tell her. She's your mother. She won't mind. But he was so afraid of hurting you and of your disapproval. I don't know which was worse. (*No response. He sighs.*) God, how many of us live in this city because we don't want to hurt our mothers and live in mortal terror of their disapproval. We lose ourselves here. Our lives aren't furtive, just our feelings toward people like you are! A city of fugitives from our parent's scorn or heartbreak. Sometimes he'd seem a little down and I'd say, "What's the matter, babe?" and this funny sweet, sad smile would cross his face and he'd say, "Just a little homesick, Cal, just a little bit." I always accused him of being a country boy just playing at being a hot shot, sophisticated New Yorker. (*He sighs.*) It's bullshit. It's all bullshit. (*Still no response.*) Do you remember the comic strip Little Lulu? Her mother had no name, she was so remote, so formidable to all the children. She was just Lulu's mother. "Hello, Lulu's Mother," Lulu's friends would say. She was almost anonymous in her remoteness. You remind me of her. Andre's mother. Let me answer the questions you can't ask and then I'll leave you alone and you won't ever have to see me again. Andre died of AIDS. I don't know how he got it. I tested negative. He died bravely. You would have been proud of him. The only thing that frightened him was you. I'll have everything that was his sent to you. I'll pay for it. There isn't much. You should have come up the summer he played Hamlet. He was magnificent. Yes, I'm bitter. I'm bitter I've lost him. I'm bitter what's happening. I'm bitter even now, after all this, I can't reach you. I'm beginning to feel your disapproval and it's making me ill. (*He looks at his balloon.*) Sorry, old friend. I blew it. (*He lets go of the balloon.*) Good night, sweet prince, and flights of angels sing thee to thy rest! (*Beat.*) Goodbye, Andre's mother. (*He goes. Andre's Mother stands alone holding her white balloon. Her lip trembles. She looks on the verge of breaking down. She is about to let go of the balloon when she pulls it down to her. She looks at it a while before she gently kisses it. She lets go of the balloon. She follows it with her eyes as it rises and rises. The lights are beginning to fade. Andre's Mother's eyes are still on the balloon. Blackout.*)

The Wibbly, Wobbly, Wiggly Dance That Cleopatterer Did

THE WIBBLY, WOBBLY, WIGGLY DANCE THAT CLEOPATTERER DID was produced by Naked Angels in New York City on March 10, 1993. It was directed by Ray Cochran. The cast was as follows:

TIM . . . . Scott Cohen
TOM . . . . Michael Mastrototaro

Characters

TIM
TOM

The Wibbly, Wobbly, Wiggly Dance That Cleopatterer Did

Tim and Tom are in bed. They have just made love.

TIM: So, what do you think of women?

TOM: (*After a very long pause.*) I like Madonna. I mean, she's very interesting. Politically. You know, as a symbol. She's got a great body.

TIM: That wasn't quite my question.

TOM: You mean, do I like them? Is that what you're asking?

TIM: Yeah, I guess. You know, as people. As a sex.

TOM: Sure I do. I like a lot of them a lot. Not all of them, of course. I don't like all men either. One of my best friends is a woman. We're very close, I tell her everything. I love her. I told her, "I'd marry you if you had a dick." I didn't say it quite like that, I mean, I'm not that gross, but it's true, if she were a man I'd marry her. If more women had dicks, I think there would be a real decline in homosexuality.

TIM: You have a great chest. Really, really, really nice tits.

TOM: Thank you. So do you. Think about it. I'm right. Women are so much more emotionally available than men. I mean, they're just *there*. Most men are somewhere else. Too much attitude. Too much macho my-dick-is-bigger-than-your-dick posturing if you ask me.

TIM: My dick is bigger than your dick.

TOM: So? I know. That doesn't threaten me. Big deal.

TIM: It is, as a matter of fact.

TOM: That's just what I'm talking about. A woman would never make a remark like that.

TIM: Jesus, I would hope not!

TOM: I'm being serious. You asked me what I thought was a serious question and I'm trying to give you a serious answer.

TIM: I'm sorry, but what did you say your name was? Jim, right?

TOM: Tom. You're Tim, I'm Tom.

TIM: Tim-Tom. Cute. We sound like twins! Are you gonna want to cum again?

TOM: I don't know. We just did. Jesus! I know most men have a problem with intimacy but you seem to have a problem with transitions. Women, your big dick, child actors, do you want to cum again? — all in 30 seconds.

TIM: I cut to the chase. I asked you what you thought about women. You told me — not much. So then I asked you if you want to cum again. I assume you're saying no.

TOM: I said, I don't know. And I think a lot of women! I don't know where you got nothing from.

TIM: I didn't say nothing. I said not much. (*He gets out of bed.*)

TIM: I think, my friend, that what I shall do is this: I shall bid you a fond farewell.

TOM: I thought you were going to stay over. I mean, I thought we had discussed that. Settled it.

TIM: I have a big day tomorrow. I could use a good sleep. I don't usually sleep well in strange beds. And then there's the problem of sharing the bathroom with a stranger. You know, the smells. My mother used to tell me. "Light a match." There ain't enough matches on this planet for when I'm done in there. Believe me, you'll thank me for this in the morning. (*He starts dressing.*)

TOM: I'd like you to stay.

TIM: I better not. It's like I said: sleep, the bathroom, etc. etc. Besides, if we're not going to get it on again, what'd be the point? Oh, shit!

TOM: What's the matter?

TIM: Is tomorrow the 4th?

TOM: Yeah, I think so.

TIM: It's my girlfriend's birthday. I want to get her something really nice this year. Something from Tiffany's. You think Tiffany's has anything for under a hundred bucks?

TOM: Sure. Key rings, and . . . hmm. . . what else?

TIM: You can't give a woman a key ring for her birthday. That's like giving her a baseball bat or a football. Pam would take one look at a key ring and say "Thank you, Tim" but her heart would break in two. I respect her too much to give her a fucking key ring. Do they have something feminine for under a hundred bucks?

TOM: Those are my shorts.

TIM: Yeah?

TOM: They are if they're Calvin Klein.

TIM:" There's another brand??!! (*He comes over to Tom who pulls down the waistband and reads the label.*)

TIM: I think that Marky Mark is a queer. You telling me a straight man would pose for an ad like that? Pam thinks he's a queer, too. Women have an infallible instinct when it comes to that. They can spot one a mile away.

TOM: They're mine.

TIM: Sorry. (*He changes shorts.*) I want to get a ripped body like Marky Mark's. I know I've got a better voice but it's not enough anymore. They all want ripped bodies, too. That fucking gym. I've spent a fucking fortune there. You know, you should work out more. I mean, you've got a nice body, don't get me wrong, it's very nice, but it's not exactly ripped. Ripped is in. Men and women. Straight and gay. Look at Madonna, ripped to hell. Can you imagine the kid she and Marky Mark could produce?

TOM: I think those are my socks.

TIM: Sorry. I don't want you to think I'm ripping you off. I'm not into that. A lot of guys, they come over, they give the guy a hand job and then they're out of there. I'm not like that. I'm more tender–er. Is that a word?

TOM: Without the qualifying adjective, it is.

TIM: I'm more tender. Yeah, you're right. That sounds better. Anyway, I respect the feminine side of my nature. I recognize it, which is more than most men do. That's why I get repeats. Most guys in my line don't get repeats. There's no reason to be nice. To be tender. They're not gonna see the guy again and they both know it. Face it, most men, when they've cum, you're out of there. They're off on cloud 9 thinking about what they're gonna tell their wife.

TOM: I don't have a wife. I'm gay.

TIM: I said most men.

TOM: I'm really, really gay and I'd like you to stay. I'm lonely.

TIM: I'm sorry to hear that. (*He sits on the edge of the bed and puts his hand on Tom's face.*) You know what you need? A lover.

TOM: I had a lover.

TIM: Or a girlfriend.

TOM: I don't want a girlfriend.

TIM: How do you know?

TOM: I have a girlfriend.

TIM: They're better for some things, girls are. Women are.

TOM: Not what I want.

TIM: What's that?

TOM: I don't know.

TIM: Not this?

TOM: Of course not this.

TIM: Women are good for more than this.

TOM: People are good for more than this.

TIM: Some people.

TOM: What's so wrong with this, all of a sudden?

TIM: Nothing. I didn't say that.

TOM: I had a good time.

TIM: It was mutual.

TOM: So let's not analyze it.

TIM: It just wasn't enough.

TOM: I know that.

TIM: Do you fuck what's-her-name?

TOM: None of your business. No. Yes. Once.

TIM: Did you like it?

TOM: Obviously I liked it or I wouldn't have done it.

TIM: You'd be surprised how many straight men don't.

TOM: You'd be surprised how many gay men don't. But just as obviously I didn't like it enough or I would have done it again.

TIM: Does what's-her-name have big tits?

TOM: As a matter of fact, she does.

TIM: I love big-titted women. Pam has tiny tits, practically non-existent, but what the hell, she's got a big heart and she thinks the sun rises and sets out of my asshole, and you can't have everything, right? Did you go down on what's-her-name?

TOM: No! And I wish you'd stop calling her that. Her name is Janet.

TIM: Janet! That's a name you don't hear much anymore. I love eating out a woman. I hate it when guys call it "Hair Pie." It's such a gross expression for such a beautiful thing. Maybe the next time you fuck Janet, you'll try it.

TOM: Can we change the subject?

TIM: Okay, you don't want to talk about women? We won't talk about women.

TOM: We're not talking about women. I don't know what we're talking about but we're not talking about women.

TIM: You need someone to shoot the shit with. We all do. That and our space. We all need our space. Pam gave me a great T-shirt that said it all. "I want you to: Fuck me, beat me, shit on me, tell me you love me and then get the hell out of here." I loved that shirt. It got ruined in the laundromat. All the letters ran. When we get married, one of the first things I'm gonna buy us is our own washer-dryer. The ones in commercial laundromats are just too violent for nicer things, you know?

TOM: This conversation is making me so sad.

TIM: It's not me?

TOM: No. You asked me what I thought about women and now you're telling me what's wrong about men!

TIM: There's nothing wrong with men or women. They're just different. You're a nice man. I can tell that. (*He pulls the covers back. Tom is naked now.*)

TOM: Why did you do that?

TIM: I just wanted to look at you. You watched me while I got dressed. Fair's fair. You've got a great dick.

TOM: Thank you.

TIM: Men are so funny about really looking at each other's dicks. We're too shy with each other. Pam studies my dick for hours. She says she's got it memorized. Every vein, every contour. I hate my dick. I think it's ugly. Yours is much nicer. I'd trade in a flash. Goodbye, sweet dick, and choirs of angels sing thee to thy rest. (*He pulls the cover back up over Tom.*) One of these days, it's going to make the right person very, very happy.

TOM: What? You do fortune tellings on the side?

TIM: Go ahead, make light. I'm trying to tell you something serious.

TOM: You mean, Mr. Right, One Day My Prince Will Come, Keanu

Reeves?

TIM: Well, maybe not Keanu Reeves. He's a movie star. Get real.

TOM: You mean, lower my expectations?

TIM: You're just looking for love in all the wrong places. (*He gives him a kiss on the cheek and stands up.*) So. All good things must come to an end.

TOM: Oh, your . . . the money. It's . . . (*He takes the money from where he had hidden it.*) Now I'm really embarrassed. But listen, you could have been an axe murderer or a maniac. You never know what you're getting into when you meet someone. I had a friend who jumped out his window and broke both his knees, he got so frightened by someone he brought home with him. The guy took everything. The TV, the stereo, his computer. His father's ring even and his father had been dead only about six weeks. And Mark's lying four floors below at the bottom of an airshaft. This way you could have murdered me but you wouldn't have found the money.

TIM: I would never have murdered you. I would never murder anyone.

TOM: I know. Here. (*He gives Tim the money.*)

TIM: Thank you. (*He begins counting it.*) It's not that I don't trust you. It's just better this way. No misunderstanding. You know, I get to your elevator and the $100 has mysteriously shrunk to an 80. Then I get pissed off and start banging on your door and—not that I'm saying you're the sort who would deliberately do such a thing. But like I said, it's just better this way. One hundred dollars. Slam, bam, thank you ma'am. That was a bad joke, I'm sorry. I'm not a crude person. I wish you well in your pursuit of love. I wish us both well. This is always the hard part: saying goodbye. I'd like to give you the biggest kiss and hug anybody ever had but that would mean I cared for you and I don't and you don't care for me and the truth is we'll never see each other again! I lied to you. I don't have repeats. There are no repeats in this business. C'est la vie. C'est la guerre. C'est la everything. I hate the look your doorman is going to give me.

TOM: Why did you ask me what I thought about women?

TIM: It was a trick question: I was curious what you thought about men.

Tom: And I failed. "Not much" was your verdict.

Tim: I think we all fail one another a lot lately. Male, female; straight, gay.

Tom: A pretentious hustler, just my luck.

Tim: A lonely faggot, so what else is new?

Tom: I'm sorry. I didn't mean that.

Tim: Neither do I.

Tom: You're right, this is the worst part.

Tim: I'll let myself out. Call me sometime. I left my card on your table.

Tom: I will. For sure. I'd like that. (*They shake hands.*)

Tim: Me, too. Goodnight.

Tom: Goodbye. *Breakfast at Tiffany's!* You saw the movie, now live it.

Tim: Everytime I buy her sexy lingerie, I get excited and I rip it off. I don't think something from Tiffany's is going to turn me on. Ciao, bello. (*Tim goes. Tom looks at the card and begins to rip it up into a million little pieces.*)

Street Talk

STREET TALK was first performed Off-Broadway by the Manhattan Theatre Club (Lynn Meadow, Artistic Director; Barry Grove, Managing Director), in New York City, on May 18, 1988. It was part of an evening entitled Urban Blight which was directed by John Tillinger and Richard Maltby Jr. The cast was as follows:

EUBIE BLADES . . . . Laurence Fishburne
CHARITY JONES . . . . Nancy Giles

Characters

EUBIE BLADES
CHARITY JONES

Street Talk

A man enters. His name is Eubie Blades. He is whistling or singing to himself. Loudly. Like he owns the place. He turns upstage from us and begins to relieve himself. All the while he continues to whistle or sing. The tune is "Stormy Weather". *After a while, he turns and looks right at us.*

EUBIE: You're just lucky I'm not taking a dump! (*He turns away and resumes relieving himself and* "Stormy Weather.") "Is he really peeing, Harold?" "How should I know, Margaret?" "Well I'm sorry, but I hate this!" "We all do, Margaret. Thank goodness it's only a sketch." (*Eubie has used two distinct voices for Harold and Margaret. The whole time he has kept his back to us and continued to relieve himself. Next, he shakes himself off before buttoning his fly.*) "Harold!" "Close your eyes!" (*Eubie turns and walks to the stage apron.*) I want to talk to you about audience confrontation. Not you personally! I just happened to be looking at you when I said it. Asshole! I wish you could see the expression on this guy's face. Utter panic. He thought I meant him. Relax, buddy. You're safe in your seat. But you're not, lady. I've had my eyes on you since I came out here. What are you laughing at, mister? You're next. Does anybody have a comb I can borrow? I bet you have *something* in there madame. You're not even looking. Never mind! I found mine. That was a test. You failed. (*He takes out a comb.*) Where was I? Oh yeah, theatre of confrontation. This is a subject I can really get into. See, I cut my theatrical teeth on the 60's. I mean, you couldn't go to a play without some actor talking right to you or coming off the stage and sitting in your lap or trying to get you up on stage with him. No sir, if you were uptight about actor/audience confrontation, it wasn't safe to go to the theatre in the 60's. (*He sits on the stage apron. During the following he will remove his shoes and socks and clean his feet of toe jam.*) I know one poor SOB who loved the theatre but who didn't see a single show between *Hair* and *Agnes of God*. He was so terrified of some actor looking right at him and talking to him. He missed a lot of good shows, poor guy. I see him back there in the 7th row. I guess he figures it's 1988, the 60's were a long time ago, what the hell! I mean, this is a nice, cozy, not-for-profit theatre, they gave us *Claptrap* for Christ's sake! Am I right? Is he wrong! Just when you thought it was safe to go back into a theatre, along comes *Urban Blight!* I'm kidding, I'm kidding! (*A woman enters. Her name is Charity Jones.*) This is Charity Jones. I'll tell you three things about her. One, she lives in a welfare hotel that you pay for. She's very grateful. Two, she can't find a public school less than a borough away that's willing to take even one of her three children. It's your Board of Ed. Three, Charity has a lovely singing voice. A real high, crystal clear, makes-you-feel-good kind of voice. Only I don't think Charity feels like singing right now. (*Charity shakes her head and sits beside him on the stage apron. During the following she will look at the audience with unblinking eyes.*) I'm telling these nice people about confrontational theatre. The old days. When actors would roam the aisles. When you went to the theatre at your own peril. Anything could happen. A play could be about Viet Nam and they'd throw pig's blood at you! Or civil rights and somebody would try to sign you up to join a protest march or register voters down South! Or gay stuff and you'd see two men, buff naked, a-hugging and a-kissing like it was the most natural thing in the world. But then all of a sudden it stopped. The war ended, the audience decided they had had enough of civil rights and they didn't care who was kissing who as long as they stayed on the stage and kept their clothes on. Some people, cynics I guess you'd have to call them, will tell you that it wasn't the audience that changed but the people that wrote the plays. What are they called? Playwrights. Nice word. That these playwrights stopped believing that theatre could end a war or get people of different races to live like brothers or get anyone to be a whole lot less uptight about who is sleeping with who. That these playwrights decided somewhere along the line that plays ought to go back to being more playful. The audience was delighted at this turn in events: they'd had their guts in a knot everytime they took their seat in a theatre for the better part of a decade. The producers said great and raised the price of tickets. "We promise no one's ever gonna sit in your lap again and ask what you did to end a war but that'll be $37.50." So far it's working out fine. The audience is happy, the playwrights are sort of happy. This place looks pretty full. I've got my tickets for *Phantom of the Opera* sometime in '92. God's in his Heaven. All's right with the world. *Still! (He sighs. Charity takes his hand.)* Sometimes I think, what if I jumped off this stage and swiped that lady's purse and ran like hell? I bet there's more money in there than I'll see in a year. What if I followed you home, yeah, *you!* and stood outside your door until you looked at me, really looked at me, and did something about the way I live? What if I took this knife I carry and plunged it into your heart, so maybe then you would know how much hate I carry in mine? What if some playwright could put me up here, the real me, so you would have some idea of how diminished my possibilities are? What if some actor could portray what it feels like not to eat maybe more than once every three days and then only what you wouldn't feed your animals? But you know all this. Theatre can't do it, brother. Yes, it can. Yes, it can. It doesn't want to. It's stopped trying. Who's kidding who? I'll be right outside when you leave here. I'll be holding an empty paper coffee cup. I'll be grateful for anything you can put in. Come on, Charity. *(They get up.)* I just thought of one more "what if." What if Charity Jones felt like singing again? That would be one happy ending. *(They go. Black out.)*

Hidden Agendas

Characters

CHAIRMAN
SUBSCRIBER LEADER
THEATRE SUBSCRIBER
REPERTORY THEATRE DIRECTOR
DIRECTOR OF HEDDA GABLER
RESIDENT PLAYWRIGHT
THEATER SUBSCRIBER'S WIFE
OPERA HOUSE DIRECTOR
MRS. HARRIDAN
SYMPHONY SUBSCRIBER
SYMPHONY DIRECTOR
GENERAL SUBSCRIBER
LAST SUBSCRIBER

Setting

The board room of a performing arts complex in any city in America
big enough to afford one. There is a large Maplethorpe on the wall.
Its constituents, including one Afro-American, one Asian-American,
one Hispanic-American, no Native American, one homosexual
and it doesn't matter how many women.
The time is now.

Hidden Agendas

CHAIRMAN: Our theatres are full. The opera house, the symphony hall, the repertory theatre, the ballet, even the underground garage. I think we can pat ourselves on the back. (*The constituents pat themselves on the back.*) This meeting is adjourned. (*The board-room doors burst open. A band of dread Disgruntled Subscribers storm the boardroom.*)

SUBSCRIBER LEADER: We demand to be heard!

CHAIRMAN: Go right ahead. We exist to please our audiences. (*Aside.*) Attend Mrs. Pettiworth! (*One of the board members has fainted at the intrusion.*)

THEATRE SUBSCRIBER: We demand plays that illumine the human condition and elevate the soul but without resorting to frontal nudity or too many four-letter words.

REPERTORY THEATRE DIRECTOR: That's why we're doing *Hedda Gabler* again.

DIRECTOR OF HEDDA GABLER: (*Bristling.*) What's wrong with frontal nudity?

RESIDENT PLAYWRIGHT: Exactly how many four-letter words are too many?

THEATRE SUBSCRIBER: Eleven. We have no problem with ten or under. The same with frontal nudity. A little goes a long, long way. Especially male nudity. I mean, I was with my wife when that guy popped out.

THEATRE SUBSCRIBER'S WIFE: And we didn't care for that avant-garde ballet where the women had hairy legs and armpits. What was your point? The human body is divine. Hairy women are disgusting. Ask anyone. Stick to *Swan Lake.* People can never get enough *Swan Lake.*

OPERA HOUSE DIRECTOR: Our production of *La Boheme* was 3.8 million dollars over budget! That's right, 3.8 million! No one can accuse the opera of not giving the public what it wants.

MRS. HARRIDAN: I paid for it. I'm mad for Verdi.

OPERA HOUSE DIRECTOR: It's people like our own Mrs. Harridan who keep the arts alive and well in this country. Who needs the N.E.A.? Next season we're mounting a new production of *Aida.* We're calling it *Harridan* in your honor. Here's a preview. (*Curtains part to reveal Placido Domingo, Luciano Pavarotti, and Jose Carreras who sing* "Celeste Harridan.")

MRS. HARRIDAN: What can I say, boys? I'm touched. I'm truly touched. The ability of the arts to touch our lives will never cease to amaze me. And people wonder why I spend so much money on the arts! Here, take 2 billion dollars for a new *Rink Cycle.*

OPERA HOUSE DIRECTOR: *Ring* Cycle.

MRS. HARRIDAN: Whatever. Oops, I'm late for the Disabled Modern Dancers' Luncheon. (*She exits.*)

SYMPHONY DIRECTOR: I'm happy to announce that thanks to our subscriber marketing, no music written after the four Sea Interludes from *Peter Grimes* or before the last six Mozart symphonies will be played for the next five seasons.

SYMPHONY SUBSCRIBER: I love contemporary music.

SYMPHONY DIRECTOR: Get real. No one loves contemporary music. If you insist on it, there's a Tower Records kitty-corner to the concert hall.

SYMPHONY SUBSCRIBER: I like live music.

SYMPHONY DIRECTOR: It was live when they recorded it. Next crank question?

GENERAL SUBSCRIBER: We wants stars! You promised us Horowitz. He died. You teased us with Baryshnikov. He retired. Then Tom Cruise was rumored for the new Irene Fornes play. He did *Top Gun 2* for 10 million bucks. Where does that leave me, the poor ticket holder? I don't want to go to a concert or a ballet or a play with just people in it.

CHAIRMAN: Neither do we. Hear, hear. I move the board pass a unanimous resolution condemning Tom Cruise for his lack of commitment to live theatre.

ENTIRE BOARD: Moved and passed. (*Ovation. The board members pat themselves on the back.*)

LAST SUBSCRIBER: I want to talk about art.

CHAIRMAN: I don't think this is the time or place but thank you for sharing that. Meeting adjourned. (*The board members begin to leave.*)

LAST SUBSCRIBER: What brings us into your halls and theatres is the expectation that the miracle of communication will take place. That a piece of music will touch us. That a dancer's movement will create a meaning where there was only space. Than an aria will speak to even one of us out there in a darkened auditorium in a way that no else ever has. That a playwright's truth will be revealed to an entire audience by an actor—totally clothed or not—in four-letter words or twenty-letter ones—whatever that truth demands. Words, sounds, gestures, feelings, thoughts! The things that connect us and make us human. The hope for that connection! That's why we fill your theatres. (*Most of the board has exited the boardroom during this.*) I can't imagine my life without the arts. (*He is alone in the boardroom. He looks at the Maplethorpe.*) Thank you for listening to me.

Smith and Kraus *Books For Actors*

THE MONOLOGUE SERIES

The Best Men's/Women's Stage Monologues of 1993
The Best Men's/Women's Stage Monologues of 1992
The Best Men's/Women's Stage Monologues of 1991
The Best Men's/Women's Stage Monologues of 1990
One Hundred Men's/Women's Stage Monologues from the 1980's
2 Minutes and Under: Character Monologues for Actors
Street Talk: Character Monologues for Actors
Uptown: Character Monologues for Actors
Monologues from Contemporary Literature: Volume I
Monologues from Classic Plays 468 B.C. to 1960 A.D.

FESTIVAL MONOLOGUE SERIES

The Great Monologues from the Humana Festival
The Great Monologues from the EST Marathon
The Great Monologues from the Women's Project
The Great Monologues from the Mark Taper Forum

YOUNG ACTORS SERIES

Great Scenes and Monologues for Children
New Plays from A.C.T.'s Young Conservatory
Great Scenes for Young Actors from the Stage
Great Monologues for Young Actors
Multicultural Monologues for Young Actors
Multicultural Scenes for Young Actors

SCENE STUDY SERIES

Scenes From Classic Plays 468 B.C. to 1970 A.D.
The Best Stage Scenes of 1993
The Best Stage Scenes of 1992
The Best Stage Scenes for Women from the 1980's
The Best Stage Scenes for Men from the 1980's

CONTEMPORARY PLAYWRIGHTS

Romulus Linney: 17 Short Plays
Eric Overmyer: Collected Plays
Lanford Wilson: 21 Short Plays
William Mastrosimone: Collected Plays
Horton Foote: 4 New Plays
Israel Horovitz: 16 Short Plays
Women Playwrights: The Best Plays of 1993
Women Playwrights: The Best Plays of 1992
Humana Festival '93: The Complete Plays
Humana Festival '94: The Complete Plays

GREAT TRANSLATION FOR ACTORS SERIES

The Wood Demon: Anton Chekhov *translated by N. Saunders & F. Dwyer*
The Seagull: Anton Chekhov *translated by N. Saunders & F. Dwyer*

OTHER BOOKS IN OUR COLLECTION

The Actor's Chekhov
Kiss and Tell: Restoration Scenes, Monologues, & History
Cold Readings: Some Do's and Don'ts for Actors at Auditions

If you require pre-publication information about upcoming Smith and Kraus monologues collections, scene collections, play anthologies, advanced acting books, and books for young actors, you may receive our semi-annual catalogue, free of charge, by sending your name and address to *Smith and Kraus Catalogue, One Main Street, PO Box 127 Lyme, NH 03768. Telephone 603.795.4331 Fax 603.795.4427.*